MEN AND COAL

McALISTER COLEMAN

McAlister Coleman was born in New York City on July 3, 1888. After graduating from Columbia University in 1909 he became a reporter on the old New York *Sun*. Except for an interval during the last war when he served with the Corps of Engineers, he has been reporting ever since.

He became vitally interested in the American labor movement very early in his career. After a period of publicity work for various trade unions with their headquarters in New York City, in 1921 he went out to the coal fields of Western Pennsylvania and West Virginia as a representative of the American Civil Liberties Union and the New York *World*. During the stirring decade of the twenties Coleman was never far from the world of the coal miner, covering strikes and trials, investigating conditions, editing miners' papers, sometimes getting arrested for his reportorial zeal in those closed areas which were presumed to be of no concern to the outside world.

Of his experience Coleman writes: "Though I've been hanging around coal mines most of my active life and though I have lived in coal camps from Pennsylvania to Southern Illinois, you could get all the coal I have ever mined under my fingernails. While up to yesterday there were always too many miners for the coal that was to be dug, there were too few men and women who could tell the miners' story to the topside world and I took that to be my job. I advise youngsters with a yen for writing who are not too fussy about eating regularly to take up with our coal miners, the salt of the American earth, find out what they are all about and then tell the world what they have found."

BOOKS BY McALISTER COLEMAN

Don't Tread On Me: A Study of Aggressive
  Legal Tactics for Labor
(with Clement Wood and A. G. Hays)

Pioneers of Freedom

Eugene V. Debs: A Man Unafraid

Red Neck
(with H. S. Raushenbush)

MEN AND COAL

BY

McALISTER COLEMAN

Foreword by John Chamberlain

NEW YORK

FARRAR & RINEHART, INC.

TORONTO

TO

Oscar Ameringer
Stalwart Fighter for
"The Men from the Picks"

TABLE OF CONTENTS

FOREWORD

TO JUDGE FROM THE SOLDIERS' letters printed last spring in *The Stars and Stripes,* the chief topic of conversation in the foxholes of Tunisia was John L. Lewis. The man who dared to call—or to permit—three strikes in a basic industry in the middle of war was plastered with just about every epithet in the army lexicon. And if a Gallup poll had been taken on the home front in May or June, Lewis might have received a popular rating only a notch or two above that of Benedict Arnold.

The pressure of hatred had no visible effect on the President of the United Mine Workers of America, even though it may have troubled him considerably in the privacy of his home and office. Regardless of his inner feelings, Lewis is used to maintaining an imperturbable mien, and it is never quite so imperturbable as when the storm is howling about his union and his own shaggy head. From long experience the miners' chief knows that it is durability, not short-term intensity, of public opinion that counts. And Lewis has his own way of sampling the probable quality of both intensity and durability. Just when people were most vehemently calling him a scoundrel and a traitor, Lewis, his face gone putty-gray from the strain of two months of ticklish negotiation, took a walk through Washington's Union Station. A draftee, a big, tall, gangling boy, recognized the soldiers' arch-devil. "Mr. Lewis," he said, "I had a good one-hundred-and-ninety-dollar-a-month job which I've had to give up to go into the army for fifty dollars a month. Do you think it's right for your miners to strike for more money when I'm giving up that much?"

Lewis, who can be a surprisingly gentle man when it suits his mood, nursed the colloquy along. And curious idlers in the Union Station were treated to the following Socratic stage play:

"Well, son—" the Lewis drawl was deliberate—"let's talk about this. One hundred and ninety dollars is a lot of money. What did you do with it?"

"I used it to support my family. A mother, father, and sisters."

"Who has your job now?"

"Well, I guess we're pretty lucky. My brother's got the job, so he's taking over in my place. But he has a lot of obligations and it's pretty hard to make ends meet."

"Should your brother get less money?"

"Certainly not. He ought to get more, because the family needs it."

"I think," said John L. Lewis with finality, "that you've answered your own question."

In telling the anecdote, Lewis insists the draftee came over to his side, carrying with him three or four of his buddies. But it is noteworthy that the conversation did not touch upon the ethics of using the strike weapon in the midst of a coal-consuming war, which was the main point at issue. Lewis's own attitude toward using the strike, however, is based on a reasoned, even if fallaciously reasoned, conception of "parities" in equity. When the U.M.W. still maintained its membership in the C.I.O., Lewis "went along" with the general A.F. of L.-C.I.O. no-strike agreement. But he argues now that he and his union ceased to be committed the moment the War Labor Board imposed the "rigid" and "arbitrary" Little Steel formula for holding down all wages regardless of the "equity" of the original base-line in individual industries. Besides, Lewis is convinced that the dynamite trains of inflation, which wage control is supposed to prevent, are being laid in a hundred subtle ways: in "cost-plus" patronage to industrialists, in the easy depreciation of new plants, in large "tax loss" advertising sums which flow into "institutional" advertising at the expense of the U. S. Treasury, and in a bond-financed rather than a pay-as-you-go-financed war. Inasmuch as he is convinced that everyone else is "getting theirs," Lewis doesn't see why anybody should object to a raise for the miners. He also regards the ordinary cost-of-living indices as highly fallacious: they do not take into account the progressive deterioration in the quality of goods, and they do not reckon with the fact that there is no food value in OPA-priced cuts of meat when such meat has disappeared from the butcher shops in mining towns. With price inflation an actuality in his opinion, Lewis thinks the Roosevelt administration has failed to live up to its part of the bargain in the no-strike agreement.

It may be argued that no one has a right to quibble and cavil over the question of justice to individuals and groups in the midst of total war. Certainly John L. Lewis would not have struck the mines if he had been a more magnanimous man. But Lewis's great strength derives from his inordinate pride. That pride has made him a great leader in the cause of a special interest. To ask Lewis to exercise magnanimity, to ask him to be humble, is just about as futile as trying to get gold from pyrites or blood from a turnip. The character of the man was set years ago, and he won't change until he dies. Knowing this, the government did the worst possible thing last spring when it tossed the miners' case around between Secretary Ickes on the one hand, and the members of the War Labor Board on the other. By baiting Lewis, by giving him hot-and-cold flash treatments, the government practically invited the strikes.

The "menace" of Lewis will never be gotten under control by a government that fails to understand him. And the first lesson in understanding is to go deep into the mining communities of the Appalachians and the "Egypt" region of Southern Illinois. It is probably decades since John L. Lewis has himself hefted a pick. Lewis's enemies insist that living in Alexandria, Virginia, and circulating in Washington "society," have altered John L.'s character. But Lewis's enemies are wrong. The man is still a miner in his psychology, still a "man from the picks."

Lewis is a man who believes in the strength of his own right arm, which was big enough to knock "Big Bill" Hutcheson of the carpenters back on his heels at the Atlantic City convention that started the schismatic movement of the C.I.O. Believing only in himself, Lewis naturally veers toward a personal and political isolationism when events aren't going his way. A psychiatrist might explain Lewis in terms of his frustrations, or his early life in Iowa, where his miner father was blacklisted for union activity. A believer in "racial" characteristics will insist that he is incalculable because he is Welsh. But the fact is that every single characteristic of Lewis is also a characteristic of the average coal-town community.

If you visit a mine-patch or go down into a mine, the correspondences that exist between Lewis and the psychology of his rank-and-file will strike you as uncanny. Despite the arguments of sentimentalists, miners like to mine coal. The work is dangerous, sometimes as dangerous as fighting in Africa and Sicily. But the rhythm of the work is such that it produces pride, not apathy. The temperature of the miner's oak-supported "room" averages from 65 to 70 degrees Fahrenheit winter and summer. And the pace of extracting the coal is set by the individual, who is not geared to a moving belt. Even where the mines are mechanized the effect on human beings is not mechanical. For the rhythm of Joy and Goodman loaders is set by the preliminary men who drill the holes for explosive "cardox" (carbon dioxide gas) or powder, and by the follow-up crews who move in after the coal extraction to clean away the loose slate from overhead and to cut and insert the oak props along the seam. Only in the open-pit "strip" mines of southern Illinois and Indiana do the machines dominate the movements of the men.

Mining, then, is no dull routine. It produces a human being who is tough, durable, proud, and as highly volatile as coking coal—in short, a human being very much like John L. Lewis. But the proud miner lives in an isolated community. He is up against rock and coal for eight hours of the day underground, and when he emerges into the sunshine he comes home to see his family and the families of other miners. That elusive thing called "public opinion," which Mr. Gallup chases so assiduously, means absolutely nothing to a miner, for he never comes into contact with it except by way of the radio, which can be turned on and off at will. Since the compulsions of middle-class America do not beat in upon him, the miner has his own notions of patriotism. He is willing to fight, he is willing to see his son drafted for fighting in the Solomons or in Italy. And he is willing to buy bonds. But he doesn't see why he shouldn't be paid as much for the job as John L. Lewis can get out of the operators. The more abstract aspects of inflation mean little in the mining coves, for these aspects are only understood by people on the lecture circuit.

Out of his pride and his isolation, the miner develops an inferiority complex. He feels that no one cares very much about him, and that coal is something which everyone takes for granted. The sense of inferiority acts as a cohesive which binds each and every miner to his group in a way that most Americans have difficulty in understanding. When miners strike, they strike as a body. They obey John L. Lewis without question, for John L. Lewis is the union. And the strike weapon is the only weapon they understand. The A.F. of L. and the United Automobile Workers know how to bring pressure on Congress and the President to keep OPA on the job. But miners are skeptical about such pressure, for they don't really believe in public opinion. They believe only in the strength of united action on the industrial front. "No contract, no work," is their slogan.

Since Lewis is a miner, and since he is *en rapport* with 600,000 other miners, it is useless to try to beat him down by raising public opinion against him. To cite angry letters from *The Stars and Stripes* is like threatening Lewis with a hippogriff, or at least a bogy-man. Lewis knows more about public opinion than does the average mine worker, for he comes into contact with it every day in Washington. But as his adventure in the Union Station with the soldiers goes to prove, he isn't too impressed with its long-term workings. And he cannot believe that public opinion ever really decides a coal-mine issue. The fight, as he conceives it, is—or ought to be—between himself and the operators. If it be argued that increased coal wages can only be paid for out of increased prices, Lewis will answer that "equity" demands a control in the coal industry that will keep the miner's body and soul together. The notion of a "consumer" with his own rights is, to Lewis, something alien, part of that "public opinion" that means nothing in a coal-patch.

It is not part of my intention in this foreword to justify Lewis. No one should strike in wartime except in a case of injustice that is completely raw. But it is a fact that coking coal goes into steel for tanks, planes and guns, and we won't have a certain supply of that coal if the miners are manhandled by a government that fails to understand their ways and the way of their leader.

This brings us to the subject of McAlister Coleman's book, *Men and Coal*. It is a pro-Lewis, pro-United Mine Workers book. Since Mr. Coleman once labored as a spokesman for the miners, it could hardly be different. Coleman is the voice of coal.

Pro-Lewis or not, *Men and Coal* is the only book with real human juices that has ever been written about the mine workers and their union history. Reading it, you come to understand the "men from the picks." When you have finished it, you may still want to condemn John L. Lewis for striking in war time. You may still say—and say legitimately—that Lewis can menace the war effort. But you will never condemn the mineworkers as a body, and you will understand the peculiar psychology of John L. Lewis as you have not understood it before. With the coal crisis promising to intensify once again this autumn, it is a duty to know its implications. "Men and Coal" not only provides the background for such understanding, but it offers a thrilling adventure—a really readable book about labor.

JOHN CHAMBERLAIN

September, 1943

AT THE PORTAL

AT THE TURN OF THIS CENTURY there appeared in the old *Life* magazine a drawing of a ballroom scene. The dancers, pompadoured Gibson girls, on the arms of incredibly elegant young men, were pictured drawing back in horror from something that had come crashing up through the polished floor. That something was the clenched and blackened fist of a coal miner.

Now, with the century nearly half gone, the fist thrusts up again. Since we became a world power, in every crisis in our national life, sooner or later, it seems, we have to reckon with coal and the men who mine it. Forgotten in fair economic weather, these coal miners become a major concern when the winds change. And in this weather of war theirs is an all-important part in our economy, as we have recently and painfully learned.

Around the coal miner there is always for the world above the pits an air of melodrama—the recurrent threat of the clenched fist, the terrifying picture of the concentrated power of half a million men, the realization that the workers in the lower depths, far removed from the main-traveled routes of American industry, may, if they so elect, put a sudden and calamitous stop to all our traffic.

If men turn emotionally, as they have of late, against this American proletariat—the coal miner—whose "proles" swarm across the cinder patches of the coal camps and whose most precious possession is still his ancient skill, come down to him through generations of diggers, it is partly because there is an uneasy awareness of the potentialities of this entombed power. Power for good or for evil such as the members of no other group of our working population can exercise.

Yet to picture the miner, as some leftist sentimentalists do, as forever surging from the pit to shake his fist in the face of all society is the crudest of distortions. The young machine tender who went into the mine following his graduation from high school is as amused at this popular conception as is his father who was driving a mule at the age of fourteen.

True, that in its fifty-three years of stormy existence the miners' union has been involved in more than fifteen major strikes. But it is also true that during that half century, year in and year out, from two hundred to five hundred million tons of soft coal and hard have been annually wrested from the earth by millions of American miners. The annals of these labors are necessarily "short and simple." They make no headlines, are meager meat for the historian, yet in every account of the American coal miner one must bear in mind that he produces more of the black stuff than any other miner in the world, both as regards total annual tonnage and as an individual worker. He is proud of his skill, the mine worker, whether he is at the controls of one of the new, ponderous mining machines that is changing over the nature of the industry or throwing a pick into the face after the manner of his coal-digging forefathers back there in Wales. And again, contrary to popular impression, he talks more frequently of the day's loading than of the chances of a strike in the spring. He is more often than not a religious man—familiarity with the contours of danger's "bright face" makes one contemplative of the ways of God—almost certainly a family man—of all our industrial workers miners have the largest families, somewhere above five members in the latest calculation. He probably belongs to one of the two major political parties and may belong to the Moose, the fraternal organization most favored by the workers. If you told him he was the last of the American proletariat, as indeed he is, he would sheer off from you suspiciously. As an individual he is a sober, God-fearing, patriotic, hard-working citizen, though he swears allegiance to the most militant, most hated, and most feared of all American trade-unions, the United Mine Workers of America. He walks out with his fellow unionists against the express orders of the President of the United States and the universal condemnation of the nation's opinion,

—and then goes home to tend his Victory Garden or stand in line at the local post office to buy War Savings stamps out of his meager earnings. He has learned the bitter lesson that in times of crisis, diligence, thrift, good citizenship and the rest of the conventional virtues are not enough. It is only in combination with his fellows that he achieves status. And so for him, as for few other workers, his union assumes a central place in his day-to-day scheme of things. He and his fathers before him have fought for the building and rebuilding of the union, for its sheer survival and its amazing expansion. They have so identified themselves with the organization that the history of the United Mine Workers of America and its pioneer predecessors comprehends the life stories of its members, individually and in the mass. One might, for example, write the story of the steel workers and not until near the end bring in mention of unionism. But with the miners, whether or not they belonged to the U.M.W. of A., the influence of that organization upon the life and fortune of every mine worker has been so preponderant as to make its story the bulk of any adequate chronicle of American coal mining.

This story starts in the spring of 1942 when though war was abroad, there was peace throughout the fields, when production was at a history-making peak and there was a chance to observe, without the distractions of industrial conflict, the workways of the mines. Since then a spate of angry waters has rushed over the dam, so that by the end of the following spring more labor history was made in a few crowded months than in many prewar decades. And made for the most part by the United Mine Workers of America and its leaders.

Here, however, is an American mining community at work, together with other communities clustered around the 6,000 mines of the nation. At work on the largest order ever placed in the history of coal mining, no less than the close to 600,000,000 tons needed for war industry and civilian use in 1942.

McA. C.

MEN AND COAL

I. MACHINES UNDER EGYPT

WINTER NIGHTS THAT CLOSE DOWN on the flatlands of America's "Egypt" are black as the coal beneath the prairies. Winds from a hundred desolate miles whirl round the huddled homes of the little mining towns. From November until March, fierce rains fall. On such rare days as the sun appears, its light is dimmed by the pall of coal dust drifting above this delta that is Southern Illinois.

Then, one day early in April, there is a quick march of green loveliness down the maple-lined streets, and over the hedges and yards on one side of the town square. There stand the substantial frame houses of the mine superintendents, and the doctors, dentists, lawyers, small shopkeepers—the middle people whose fortunes are as inextricably bound up with the mines beyond the town as are the fortunes of the men who dig the coal.

On the other side of the square, the miners putter in gardens back of their bungalows. Sometimes after nightfall, you see men who have worked on the day shift digging again by the light of pit lamps in their caps. Their barelegged children range the swollen creeks in search of catfish. Their women bend to the everlasting washing, care for the chickens, or tether the young goats, leaping stiff-legged across the cinder patches.

Now the old heads come out to revel in the soft sun that warms the ledges around the base of the courthouse. They swap tobacco, tell tall tales of "battles long ago," look with puzzled eyes at the young men going out to work in "them newfangled hard hats." The miners in their trim helmets swing down the street as men march to a battlefront. Their talk is of the new, underground machines, of duckbills and loaders and mother conveyers and caterpillars. Talk unintelligible to the veteran handicraftsmen on the courthouse ledges.

When the window curtains in the larger houses on Maple Avenue keep their laundry white too long, things are not good in Egypt. For uniquely, in these Southern Illinois towns, coal is everything. And the curtains have hung, unspotted with soot, overlong. Now, however, the nation's vociferous clamor for bituminous coal puts new hope in the hearts of men who have somehow lived stubbornly on through fifteen terrible depression years that have made these fields our counterparts to the "blighted areas" of England. Today men tell you that Egypt will once more take its proud place as an important producer of the black stuff that will energize our war industries and heat the homes and cook the meals of millions of Americans to boot. Ironically, war, that is already taking its toll of the youth of these coal camps, is giving new life to those who have stayed behind. With this national demand for 600 million tons of soft coal annually, an all-time production figure, it is in the books that Southern Illinois will be well up on the production front.

The coal is there in abundance. As has been the case since slaves first quarried coal outside of Richmond in 1750, mine capacity far outruns production. There is a wealth of bituminous 300 to 600 feet below Franklin County, where even in these last bad years the largest mine in the world has been yielding up 5,000 tons every working day. Coal is under Saline County with its '39 and '40 output of over 3½ million tons each year. And it is under the cornfields of Williamson, "Bloody Williamson," once a battlefield where union miners and strikebreakers, Klansmen and Knights of the Flaming Circle, and rival bootleg gangs from the North fought it out with machine guns and airplanes and other paraphernalia of modern warfare. Today this is an internally peaceful community, eager to take its parts in the winning of an official war.

In fact, in these flatlands that run down from Centralia to Cairo there is almost literally nothing but coal worth the taking. Farming is a matter of scratching at a little corn. One wonders how that story, told by old "swamp angels," as the pioneers in these parts are still called, that Egypt was named because in a time of drought in the rest of the state the southern delta saved the day with its farm products, could ever have been inspired. More likely it was the shape of the bottom end of the state from Centralia to Cairo that gave rise to the name. Agriculture in this sorry soil could hardly have supported the handful who attempted it. Since 1900, when the first drills of prospectors seeking coal for the Chicago market went through the clay to rich seams of soft coal beneath, no other important industry has come into Egypt to challenge coal's supremacy. For two generations in these intensely specialized coal counties, 150,000 Americans have moved through cycles of boom and bust, of tragically long unemployment, of bitter struggles for union, and of dizzying spells of perilous labor with all hands making good money. Today Egypt is a microcosm of coal's far-flung domain from the Appalachians to Colorado.

Within easy jalopy ride from a southern Illinois coal camp you can go to three mines, operating in the same territory but, as far as workways go, industrial ages apart.

Here is a strip mine, descendant of the first pre-Revolutionary coal quarries, where 1,000-ton electrically driven shovels with 30-cubic-yard dippers swoop down upon the earth above the black floor of coal. Or as an advertising copy writer for *Coal Age,* the trade paper of the industry, puts it: "This big stripping dragline waddles through the coal-fields on two abrasive-resistant steel feet . . . squats down on a steel base and gobbles overburden." The stripping cycle of dig, swing and dump is the simplest of all mining operations, thanks to the fact that a seam of coal, some fifty inches thick, has cropped up beneath nine feet of limestone, clay and shale. Before the shovels thrust their manganese lips into the soil, bulldozers, scrapers and rooters have been at work. Soon a pit some 65 to 100 feet in width has been dug out of Southern Illinois. Drilling machines, mounted on caterpillars, come along to make holes for the shots that will loosen the coal. Again the titan shovels swing and dip and dump. Hand shovelers work alongside the giants. Into trucks or, in some cases, conveyers the coal is loaded to be taken to the preparation plant in the pit where it is washed, crushed and sized. Then up the ramp to trucks and trailers or mine cars on a siding, bound for local or national markets.

Within the past few years more and more coalmasters have been turning to strip mining, always of course within the limitations of

geology and the large-scale financing of the costly machinery needed
for such operations. In 1937, 32 million tons of soft coal and 5½
million tons of hard were taken out of the strips of the nation. In
1941, approximately 47,300,000 tons of bituminous and 7½ million
of anthracite were mined by this process. Finding competition within
their own industry from the oncoming strippers, many deep-shaft
operators have included stripping in their enterprises.

The obvious advantages of stripping are freedom from the underground vexations of ventilation, drainage, the nice adaptation of
machinery to the dark wanderings of the seams, and most important,
the displacement of human shovelers with the big dippers. In 1940,
five strip mines in Southern Illinois produced two million tons of
coal with a maximum labor force of 400 men for all five strips. It
would have taken 1,200 men in deep-shaft mines to have got out
such a tonnage.

Stripping leaves great scars not only on the countryside but on
the total life of a mine community whose men are trained in underground work. There is no dancing on the streets when a new Bucyrus
or Marion shovel is set up in the fields. The key men on and about
the decks of the shovels are more electricians and hoisters than they
are miners. While there is still some handwork around the draglines
and trucks and cars, and good maintenance men are always in demand,
the opening of a strip mine means little in the way of new employment.

Down the road, a good bit from the strip, a tipple looms above
the corn. Smoke from the powerhouse stack signals good news. The
Black Beauty or Old Betsy or Saline Sal deep-shaft mine is working
again. This is a small, long-worked mine into which the latest products of Jeffery or Joy or Goodman, manufacturers of modern mining
machines, have not penetrated. Here an old head would find himself
very much at home. Today things in and around this mine are much
the same as when he worked there in World War I.

The diggers in their work clothes and carrying their lunch
buckets are waiting for the cage to take them down the shaft. There
is some quiet joshing going on, for these men, older than the youngsters who swung down the street on their way to a mechanized mine,
are feeling good. There is work today and there will be work tomorrow, and the day man will be making his $7 and, with any luck,

the skilled men, working directly at the face of the coal, can dig and load their eight to ten to twelve tons at a piecework rate varying from 90 cents to $1 a ton according to the terms of the Illinois District union contract.

The cage goes down two hundred, three hundred feet, past walls dripping with black water, to let the men off into a darkness that is comparable to nothing one would call dark on the surface. It is as though you could reach out and touch this darkness as one fingers black velvet. To be sure, the main haul is lighted, with bulbs strung far down the tracks, and there is light from the electric lamps in the diggers' caps. But the darkness is all around, in the deep shadows thrown by the naked bulbs, at the bend where the tracks curve, over your shoulder, as you turn to talk to your guide.

One time a traveling showman, advertising himself as "Daredevil Darnton," came down to these fields to put on a breath-taking motorcycle act. Round a saucer track he sped his machine with the greatest of ease until he was whizzing horizontally to the vast admiration of his miner audience. There was a man for you! By cripes, he didn't give a damn. Mr. Darnton accepted an invitation to go down to the mine with the superintendent and a union pit committeeman after the performance.

"Well, Bud," said the pit committeeman afterward, "when this Mr. Daredevil stepped on the platform of the cage I seen he was looking kind of peakéd, but I paid no attention. I was talking to the super on the way down and we was just stepping off at the bottom when all of a sudden this big brave bird slumped down like a fainting old woman! 'The dark! The dark!' he yells, 'take me out of here!' What do you know? This feller, that was riding his hell-fire motorcycle like nobody's business, he's afraid of the dark!"

The committeeman, who thinks no more of the plunge down the shaft and the darkness at the end than one thinks of an elevator ride to his unlighted office, was overcome by his discovery that courage is relative. This truism had been brought home to me when I once escorted a group of hard-boiled, big-city reporters through the pits. Many of them had come down filled with hostility toward all miners, who, they were told, were "ignorant, vicious men who had assaulted innocent nonunion workers in cowardly fashion." When they were on top again the newsmen, who had been around tight places, were visibly shaken. They got out their typewriters, some of them, and wrote about "the nonchalance with which our diggers daily face death itself."

Miners, in spite of the sentimental ballads describing their routine heroism, do seem to be casual about the ever-haunting perils of underground work. They often boast of their skill, no small part of which is devoted to safeguarding their workplaces, but they are always a little puzzled at the attitude of outsiders who look on them as endowed with exceptional courage. Most miners are acquainted with the grim statistics of deaths and injuries in our recurrent mine disasters. Figures show that in 1940 the death toll through accidents, most of them preventable, was 1,400 and in the same year more than 60,000 miners were injured, some of them so badly as to be permanently laid up. Eight out of every hundred miners may expect to be injured or killed. Our diggers scan these figures with the impersonal eyes of soldiers reading casualty lists, and then stand in line before employment windows at mines with long reputations for being gassy.

"It's just getting used to things," said a miner friend who visited us in New York on his first and only flight out of Egypt. He was describing his rush-hour ride in the subway from Grand Central to Fourteenth Street. "My God," he exclaimed, his eyes widening in awe, "what a man-trip that was! I wouldn't take it again for a hundred bucks and yet you folks do it every day."

Down the main haul from the portal, the men go in pairs to their workplaces, their "rooms." They may climb into empty coal cars drawn by an electric locomotive, or, in rare cases nowadays, mules, and be ridden on "a man-trip" the one or two miles to the face of the coal. Or they may walk down the tracks, squeezing themselves against the sides as the cars come by. On the way, they pass huge bays cut into the walls—mule stables and blacksmith shops in the older mines; railway, repair and maintenance shops in the more modern. From the main haul track, spurs run off to the various rooms.

Arrived in their room, the tonnage men, a pick miner and his buddy, technically the only workers called "miners," find themselves in an opening joined to the main line by a narrow-gauge track at the end of which is the face of the coal. The room may be some twenty-five feet wide. Its height is the height of the coal seam at the end. There are crosscuts in the side, or "ribs," for ventilation. The roof is supported with pillars of solid coal on either side of the room, and with props of timber as well. In this mine a shot-firer, a specialist in the handling of explosives, has drilled a hole into the face and touched off the dynamite that brings down the coal while the men are out of the mine. In most other states, the tonnage men do their own drilling and firing. A cutting machine has been down the track to loosen up the coal for the shots. These machines, with sharp, steel teeth running over the cutting bar, tear into the coal as no pick miner could, but their noisy presence in the mine does not mean that this is a "mechanized" mine. That magic word "mechanization" implies a lot more than the substitution of a power-driven machine for a hand tool. Back in the seventies, miners were gingerly handling Horace Brown's "Monitor Coal Cutters" whose teeth were driven into the face of the coal by steam. In 1877, mechanical picks took the place of hand picks in a few progressive operations. By the time we entered the last war, 18,000 cutting machines were working on 56 per cent of our tonnage and today, with nearly 90 per cent of the coal machine-cut, the saturation point for the cutters has about been reached.

Nowadays it is the cycle of mobile mechanical cutting and loading under strict supervision that denotes a "mechanized mine." In the operation we are considering, the definition of Carter Goodrich in his book, *The Miner's Freedom,* published in 1925, still holds good: "The miner is an isolated piece worker on a rough sort of craft work, who sees his boss less often than once a day."

It is this lack of supervision and the method of payment which give the miner in the old pits his independence or, if you prefer, "indiscipline." It is up to the two men in their room to get out the tonnage, after their own manner. The "bug dust"—piles of powdered coal left by the cutting machine—must be loaded onto cars and pushed up the track to the heading before the heavier coal is tackled. There is a deal of pick work, despite the cutting done by the machine. As a general rule the older man swings the pick and his buddy (often in Illinois an apprentice who will not receive his miner's certificate until he has worked two years at the face under the supervision of a full-fledged miner) is at "the stormy end of the shovel."

In a rough way, in the picking and shoveling, slate and dirt are separated from the good coal and thrown onto the "gob pile." As the miners advance into the face, they lay new tracks for the little cars that are brought up from the main haul to be loaded. There is the unloading and setting of props, the pushing of cars to the face and away from it, the constant scrutiny of the roof; but most of the miner's time is spent in picking and loading. Shoveling the heavy stuff into the cars is a job that takes not only a strong back but a hard-earned skill in rhythmic co-ordination of tool and muscle. It's a sweet sight to see an experienced miner handle a shovel. Mr. Goodrich tells of the admiration of the members of the 1920 Coal Commission for the way in which a miner "threw shovel after shovel of coal against the roof from which it caroms into the car."

Under the 1941 union contract, the miners labor in their rooms for seven hours in one day, thirty-five hours in any one week, with time and one-half overtime pay.[1] This is exclusive of the lunch period, which in the old mines still takes on the nature of a ritual. Miners come from their workplaces to gather on a gob pile with their lunch buckets, when some matter of general concern is up. Many a union leader has started his career as a "gob-pile orator." Then, too, the miners waiting for their turn of cars—and a great deal of time is spent in this manner—wander into other rooms whose occupants also are waiting. Isolation thus becomes a relative term. Men working a mile apart know pretty well what is going on in the other rooms.

When on occasion, in a room and pillar operation, a foreman comes into a workplace from the main haul, his is more a visit among equals than the visitation of a boss. A foreman may yell at the day or "company" men who constitute the service of supply for the front line workers at the face. These are inside men, greasers, trappers (opening and closing doors where there is no automatic ventilating system), flaggers and switch throwers, trackmen and timbermen helpers, or top men, car pushers and cleaners, sand dryers, slate pickers and other laborers. Old tonnage men will tell you, however, that they will have "no boss blowing down our necks." Foremen do not yell at the tonnage men, not if they know what is healthy. When they do, they are likely to confront irate members of the local pit committee, miners elected by their fellows to handle grievances, with any important complaint likely to go up the line to the international executive

---

[1] Since this was written, the mines have gone on a 6-day-week basis with overtime pay for the sixth day.

board of the United Mine Workers of America sitting with the representatives of the management.

To go from an old mine to one of the big, mechanized pits in this region is to pass within an hour's time from the "cottage" industry days, as the editor of *Coal Age* once named small-operation mining, to the era of mass production. In the new, "Fordized" mine-factory, the top men are members of a unit of six, eight or ten, tending the machine that cuts the coal and loads it onto conveyers, often with the mother conveyers taking it away to the tipple where it is shaken down into the mine cars on the siding outside.

These machines work along a much wider front than the old-fashioned room and pillar mining attacked. The bars dig into faces often a hundred feet long cut in V-shaped manner, with the coal coming onto the conveyer at the face and then emptied into cross-conveyers that in turn take the stuff to a mother conveyer on the main haul. A cutting or mining machine, a mechanical loader, conveyers, power drills, electric locomotives—these make a mobile unit in continuous operation in the new mines, moving through its own territory to as many as four or five workplaces.

"The heavy loading machine and the mining machine run on the mine track," writes Edward A. Wieck, in his book, *Preventing Fatal Explosions in Coal Mines,* "although some are tractor-mounted under their own power. The cycle of operations of a unit begins with undercutting by the mining machine, followed by drilling and blasting and then the loading by machine on cars which the locomotive takes to the sidetrack. The trackmen lay the track in the working places, extending it as the work advances. Timbermen place props and bars to support the roof, usually in accordance with a planned system of timbering. The whole unit is auxiliary to the loading machine, upon which production depends. Time lost by the loading machine because of failure of the mining machine to cut coal, or of the drillers and blasters to make it ready for loading, is an irretrievable loss, which is certain to draw frowns and demands for explanation from the unit foreman. He, in turn, will be asked to explain the delay when his daily report is reviewed by his superiors. Time studies of mechanized operations center on the process of loading, and on time taken to move a machine from one working place to another."

Now coal and electric power join hands. There is a heavy power load to be maintained and a steady demand for technicians to maintain it. Everyone in this mine uses electric lamp caps and often the operations are floodlighted. Electrically propelled shuttle cars with rubber tires scuttle around. The wise old, wicked old mine mules have been kicked upstairs by electrically driven locomotives, and the old-time trapper boy has been happily displaced by electricity that automatically opens and closes the doors on the haulways. Sometimes block signals on the main line are used to supplement dispatcher control.

The proper planning of ventilation, strategic in any deep-shaft mine, is complicated by the fact that the machines raise ten times as much dust as did the old hand picks. Flow of air through the mine is maintained by elaborate fan systems and measured by anemometers. In spacious underground workshops and warerooms, repairs are made and spare parts and props are stored. Props are often made of steel, wooden props are chemically treated.

On top in the big preparation plant, washing, screening, drying and mixing machinery separates the coal into various sizes of lump, egg, nut, stoker, etc. Rock is taken away on refuse conveyers to be thrown on the huge heaps of culm that lie like tawny mountains across this landscape. The flow sheet of a preparation plant with belt conveyers, air-pulsated washing units, vibrating screens, picking tables and crushers is an impressive document for any layman who thinks that coal is just a matter of digging.

Lest this sound too brisk and bouncing and incorrigibly efficient, let it be said that the grand strategy of the long-delayed technological revolution underground is dictated by the terms of the geological revolution which some twenty million years ago laid down beneath the United States the one and one-half millions of millions of tons of bituminous, to say nothing of subbituminous, lignite and anthracite. It is no easy task to standardize the coal seams or the men who mine them. By the nature of things underground, every mine presents its peculiar problem, which in many instances the most cleverly devised machine has difficulty in solving.

In a factory, machines properly powered and lubricated will go on fabricating raw materials (so long as there are men to guide them) to the point of complete breakdown. Not so in a mine. There the operator may have to attack a thinning seam whose sharp curves make the bulky conveyers impracticable. Cutting may be difficult even for the hardened steel alloy bits which must be adjusted just so. When the deafening racket of the machine suddenly stops, the dust-laden air is filled with the anguished shouts of the straw boss and foremen who will have to explain to a skeptical super what caused this unexpected stoppage of the entire production cycle. In a deep-shaft mine, when things go wrong they do so on a magnificent scale. At its best, the mining of coal is a dirty, dusty, noisy, back-breaking business. Nowhere in sight for mining is that pushing of buttons and throwing of levers that was the stuff of the technocrats' dream of yesterday.

What is in plain view, however, is the extension of mechanization to much of the remaining two-thirds of soft coal. Machinery salesmen, cost accountants, efficiency men, modern-minded technicians had paid little attention to the bulk of our mines up to the early twenties. Then there was a large-scale invasion, the tempo of which was slowed by the depression years. True, in those years the bigger companies, to cut labor costs, installed the new loaders and mining machines and conveyers; but it was not until the demands of the defense program became insistent that the mechanization figures took a sudden spurt. In 1940, 148,800,000 tons of bituminous were mechanically loaded; in 1941, approximately 183,500,000. Sales of loaders, the chief agents of the underground revolution, are steadily mounting. In 1941, 368 mobile loaders and 2,130 conveyers went into the mines for the first time, a percentage increase of 58 for the loaders over 1940 and 21 for the conveyers. Largely because of mechanization of the larger mines and more businesslike methods in the smaller operations, production per man-day for all the workers in and about the mines is now 4.9 tons, whereas in the last war it was 3.9 tons.

Even if this war lasts as long as some of our leaders tell us it will, while transportation clicks with coal production, and labor relations are comparatively peaceful there is no danger of a dearth of coal for industrial use. As has been said, in coal, capacity is far beyond production. Our major problem—unlike that of the Axis, already faced with a coal deficit of some 20 per cent despite all Hitler's conquered mines and, very literally, captive miners—is getting the coal out of the fields. Whatever happens, coal can no longer be thought of merely in terms of crisis. It is taking its place today with other large-scale mass production industries where the technician assumes an increasingly important role and rule-of-thumb, hit-or-miss workways go on the dump heaps. What the march of the machines is doing to the miners of our generation will be discussed in later chapters. Here it is enough to note that the "onward sweep" which Carter Goodrich and others were predicting in the twenties is in momentum today. In coal fields throughout the country there is repetition of the revolutionary rumblings under Southern Illinois.

II. MINERS AS ECONOMISTS

After a while they begin to talk about *Alice in Wonderland,* or use lines from Gilbert and Sullivan operas to illustrate their points—the economists who wander into our coal fields. Accustomed to dealing with commodities with fairly predictable functionings, when they come to coal they find themselves writing in terms of confused struggle.

"War," remarked Randolph Bourne in a grim moment, "is the health of the State." It was a mineral economist, with coal very much in mind, who wrote:

"In our present industrial civilization war is merely a normal and in many cases a necessary phase of our so-called peaceful competition; it is an unpleasant phase it is true; and its technique is not particularly efficient or economic. But it is a serious error to regard it as an abnormal feature of the machine civilization of the western world; it is on the contrary the most purely normal result of the industrial development in which all nations are now engaged, and there is no reason to expect war to disappear as long as the spirit of business enterprise survives."

This was written by Edwin C. Eckel in a symposium on mineral economics published in the spring of 1931, just as the Manchurian episode developed into Japan's invasion of China. Mr. Eckel was using coal and iron as the chief indices of national power. He was expressing, in other words, what a disgusted coal operator once shouted at this writer: "Sonny, the only way a feller can make money in this coal business is when folks is fixing to fight each other."

The operator was thinking not only of national wars but also of internecine wars between coal labor and management, with the consumers as the innocent victims. He was thinking of that feverish rush to pile up reserves just before a threatened strike—reserves with constantly increasing value throughout the duration—and the same feverish rush at the strike's conclusion to fill the empty bins.

In their devastatingly ironic book on coal—*The Case of Bituminous Coal*—published just as the mechanization march got under way in 1926, Walton H. Hamilton and Helen R. Wright put on the page usually reserved for a dedication: "Here's a pretty mess." At the conclusion of their last chapter, titled "The Great Confusion," they wrote: "In a jumble of mines which the natives love to call the bituminous coal industry it is proper for each individual to do good that evil may come of it."

The ways of coal are often still primordial, and at their best distressingly cantankerous. The mere magnitude of our coal reserves with our trillion tons of bituminous alone, enough to last us, with any luck, some thousand years, acts as a deterrent to scientific, long-view planning, a spur to the gambling instinct. On the other hand, the increasing exhaustibility of the individual mine, with no chance, as in a factory, for conversion into anything else, surrounds the working of every coal seam with unique problems. It is the history of coal that neither under the competitive system nor, as in the case of anthracite, under semimonopolistic control, is peace in the fields of any long duration. Yet here is the mineral upon which industrial civilization, East and West, ultimately rests. It is not likely that when the next international peace is made, a war-weary people will accept the ominous verdict that war is the health of coal.

As the mineral economists, rare birds in any gathering, point out, their study is in the status of agricultural economy some years back. Yet in agricultural economy progress has been made not only as regards general concepts but also in defining specific causes. There is no apparent reason why the scientific approach should not be made to mining not only from the standpoint of the technician with his improved methods underground, but also from the standpoint of the economist concerned with integrating mining with other major industries.

Of these industries the other power fuels, oil, natural gas, hydroelectricity, the swiftly growing synthetic organic chemical industry and, of course, transportation are so closely related to the mining of coal as to make integration imperative, if there is to be any lasting peace. Heretofore both coal management and labor have looked with undisguised hostility upon the ever-growing encroachment of rival fuels. In the advanced sectors of the coal front alone has any great attention been paid to conservation and by-producting. And while the railroads have been the top consumers of coal, feuds over freight rates, financial arrangements and even intra-union controversies have all too often been the order of the day.

How are these economic problems the concern of a book such as this, which deals with mine labor? It is true that at the outset of the national organization of the miners, labor disclaimed all intention of encroaching upon the fields of management in which such matters would ordinarily lie. The 1941 agreement between operators and miners specifically states: "The Mine Workers intend no intrusion upon the rights of management as heretofore practiced and understood." Nevertheless, during recurrent crises in coal, union representatives have urged measures ranging from price control to nationalization. Perhaps their most important contribution toward stabilization was the setting up of the Central Competitive Field with operator signatories to the union agreement competing on equal terms so far as all-important labor costs were concerned.

Like the proverbial Irish engaged in family warfare, both mine owners and mine workers have turned aside to fall upon the threatened invasion of other energy producers such as the cheap and abundant hydroelectric power promised with the development of the St. Lawrence Waterways, a development attacked with equal vehemence in the pages of the *United Mine Workers Journal* and *Coal Age,* the official organ of management. Legislation, however, looking to governmental control of the industry has been inspired at conferences between congressmen and union leaders. The miners have endorsed the setting up of sales agencies within the industry free from the restrictions of the antitrust laws. They have at times urged concentration in the sprawling bituminous industry despite the fact that such concentration might result in lessened union membership, and at the same time they have frowned upon the concentration of anthracite in the hands of the coal railroads.

It is, in fact, the lament of many an operator after a wage conference that his side is so poorly equipped with both knowledge of the industry as a whole and knowledge of its relationships to other industries, in comparison with the mine workers' leaders. Union leaders are daily tackling social, political and economic problems while the operators are playing golf. When John L. Lewis, who has been head of the United Mine Workers of America for the past twenty-two years, sits down at a table with the operators he has an intimate knowledge of the history of the industry, no small part of which he has made, and he knows the exact conditions of mining coal and the marketing of it as well. He can refute with facts and figures any false claim of an opponent as to costs of production. He knows freight rates and their importance in the price structure. At one session he will confront an operator of a gassy mine, where an explosion has killed a number of workers, with tragic carelessness in not using the latest preventive methods and at the next session he will engage in an intricate technical argument over the working of a new loading machine.

Up to yesterday, when the two men fell out over the war issue, Lewis could refer a disputed point to his quiet-spoken, right-hand man Philip Murray, vice-president of the United Mine Workers until Lewis threw him out. Mr. Murray would bring from his brief case a wealth of statistics on coal and allied industries which he would read in a rolling Scotch burr to the sullen but silenced operators. These last knew of Murray's long view of their industry. They knew that the gray-headed Scot had the advice of such shrewd and socially minded engineers as Morris Llewellyn Cooke with whom Murray collaborated on the thoughtful book, *Organized Labor and Production*. Or, if Murray wasn't at the conference there was, and still is, the bespectacled secretary of the U.M.W. of A., Thomas Kennedy, one-time Socialist, one-time lieutenant governor of Pennsylvania, from his days as breaker boy intimately connected with the problem of coal. The 55-year-old Kennedy, who went into the mines at the age of eleven, made some notable contributions to the literature of the industry in his reports to the U.S. Coal Commission of 1923, and what he has to say today is listened to with respect by any audience. Then there is K. C. Adams, acting editor of the *United Mine Workers Journal,* an authority on freight rates as well as coal prices, and Percy Tetlow, who learned his coal catechism in the hard way in war-torn

West Virginia, and James Mark, veteran of bitter struggles with the Mellon and other corporate coal interests in Western Pennsylvania.

Against such a formidable array, the average coal operator, more often than not an absentee owner who could not find his way around his own workings, can only present pleas of poverty when an increase in wages is suggested or pleas of ignorance when some larger issues are at stake. Once a year at the annual convention of the American Mining Congress at Cincinnati, he may grouse with his fellow operators in the hotel lobbies at the "interference" of government or the incorrigibility of labor. Or, if he is called upon to represent his people at a wage conference, he may attend a preliminary meeting or so at which last-ditch fights are agreed on. But by and large he is no match for the union men on the other side of the table.

So it has come about, as has been the case with the clothing unions, that the organized mine workers have approached their industry with a greater measure of social vision than have the operators, and have had more influence in bringing some degree of civilization to the mines than have the owners themselves. In the matter of mechanization, for example, whereas British miners fought the introduction of machinery into the pits in some instances in outright manner and in others by "ca'canny" indirections, it has been the policy of the United Mine Workers to go along with the technicians and the manufacturers of new machines. Alert-minded union leaders are not going to be classed with those who rioted against Watt's engines and Hargreaves's spinning jenny at the start of the Industrial Revolution. On the other hand, they are going to see to it that the benefits of mechanization are spread around in the shape of shorter work hours and higher wages. Murray and Cooke are agreed that "The triumphs of technology threaten to dwarf the importance of personality. But industry's master problem will always be human." [1] It is the union philosophy that the new machines shall not only yield more profit to the owner but a larger pay check to the worker and more leisure to spend it in.

Beyond the usual bargaining matters of wages and hours, organized labor in the mines has often been forced to police the industry for the sake of both safety and stabilization. The United Mine Workers have pioneered in industrial safety measures. The union long

[1] *Organized Labor and Production*, p. 213. New York, Harper & Brothers.

agitated for the setting up of the U.S. Bureau of Mines. Not until 1941 were the operators compelled by the Federal Coal Mine Inspection Act, sponsored by the union, to allow government inspectors in their mines. Now at long last the bureau, organized in 1910, can exercise some preventive authority. The legislation of the coal-mining states covering safety measures was written by union representatives.

The activities of the Bureau of Mines are not confined to safety measures, inspection and rescue work; they have also to do with fundamental research in that vast range of coal's by-products which runs from pitch tar to nylon stockings. Since the beginning of this war, army and navy men have been turning to the bureau as the basic laboratory for explosives. The more progressive of the miners' leaders have long been interested in the work of the coal chemists, partly because they see in the famous "Coal Tar Tree," pictured in our recent books on popularized science, a stable, year-round market for the black stuff their members mine. A convention of Illinois miners some years ago voted for the adoption of a "Giant Power" plan for the southern end of the state where the coal beds are near the Ohio and Mississippi rivers. Under this plan the bituminous coal would be by-producted and burned at the mine mouths. Electricity, generated by both steam and falling water, would be taken away to smoke-hung St. Louis and Chicago, as would the coal itself, rendered well-nigh smokeless by scientific treatment. This hopeful plan was forgotten by leaders absorbed in internal union rows, but the fact that the representatives of some 50,000 coal diggers voted for it, indicates fundamental thinking on the part of the rank and file.

That in the present race for synthetic rubber coal has been left at the starting mark is a matter for profane comment by many union leaders. Neoprene, which starts with acetylene made from coal, limestone and water, has bounce and flexibility that in the opinion of chemists would make it a good substance for tires. Again, as in the case of Friedrich Bergius, the German Nobel Prize winner who got gasoline, Diesel oil, fuel oil and coke from hydrogenating coal, powdered and mixed with heavy oil, under high temperatures and pressures, our native coal chemists have missed the bus. But it is significant that this same Illinois Miners Union attempted to enter into negotiations with Bergius when he was in this country between wars. Lack of funds prevented the setting up of a Bergius plant in Illinois under union auspices.

In the field of economics it can be safely said that every major attempt to bring order out of the coal chaos has been inaugurated by the workers, with a handful of enlightened operators applauding from the side lines and the majority in opposition. An outstanding exception to this was the case of a lone woman mine owner, Josephine Roche, whose agreement with the U.M.W. of A. we shall discuss later. On the whole, though, the opposition of the National Coal Association of operators to the first bill to provide for stabilization of the industry, written by counsel for the miners' union in 1928, is the best indication of owner sentiment in the industry. When the despairing members of a Senate investigating committee asked men with such large coal interests as the Mellons, the Rockefellers and Charles Schwab what solution they proposed for the current crisis in coal in '28, outside of the destruction of the union, the coalmasters had no proposal. President Lewis, Henry Warrum, of counsel for the U.M.W. of A., and K. C. Adams sat down with Senator Watson of Indiana and drew up a stabilization bill which was a mild combination of private business management and modified public control. Generally it followed the lines of regulation of electric light utilities before the New Deal. The exceptions were in the provision for licensing coal operators by a five-member commission appointed by the President and in the recognition of the collective bargaining rights for labor. In spite of the clause permitting the operators to combine without fear of the antitrust laws, the coalmasters fought the bill to death in Congress, though its philosophy was incorporated in the platforms of both old political parties in the campaign of 1928.

In 1932 the Davis-Kelly Bill, again sponsored by the U.M.W. of A., met a similar fate. This measure went a bit further than its ill-fated predecessor in that it provided for government action to "regulate interstate and foreign commerce in bituminous coal, provide for consolidations, mergers and co-operative marketing, require the licensing of corporations producing and shipping coal in interstate commerce and to create a Bituminous Coal Commission, and for other purposes."

The deepening depression led to the enactment of the National Industrial Recovery Act. In the famous section 7(a) of that act was incorporated labor's insistence on the right to organize in unions of the workers' own choosing, in practically the same language as the clause in the Watson Bill. When the Supreme Court killed the NIRA together with the Bituminous Coal Code, which incorporated many of the provisions of the old mine bills, there followed the Guffey Act, called "Coal's Little NRA." Again there popped up provisions for increasing governmental controls. Though the court wiped out the labor provisions of the original Guffey Act, the Bituminous Coal Division of the Department of the Interior, a relic of the act, carried on control over prices and practices in the industry. Failure of Congress to extend the act, in the spring of 1943, led to the abolition of the board.

The nature and extent of public controls will be discussed at greater length later on. Here it suffices to point out that we owe to the mine workers such control as we have had. As to Mr. Lewis, he has been on both sides of the control question. Up to the introduction of the Watson Bill, John L. Lewis was as firm in his opposition to any "outside" interference as the most individualistic operator. Whereas liberals in his union welcomed help from economists, researchers and other sympathizers with the union cause who were not necessarily coal experts, Mr. Lewis adhered closely to the no-philosophy philosophy of the American Federation of Labor of which he was once a vice-president. He wrote a book, which his intimates say he would as soon forget, the purpose of which seemed to be to prove that the U.M.W. of A., could get along without any help, governmental or otherwise. It was when he saw the operators ruthlessly destroy the 1923 Jacksonville Agreement with the miners, which was supposed to bring peace to the industry, when he saw outside forces far from the mine fields working to bring the entire industry into a subservient position, and when he saw at length that neither uncontrolled competition nor uncontrolled monopoly would provide fair profits for the operators with a living wage for the miners, that Lewis finally turned to public aid. He marched over to the side of those who had held with the Bituminous Coal Commission of 1923 that the coal problem could be solved "only by the Federal Government, in co-operation with the industry, working on a national scale and with a clearly defined national policy." Whereas in his book, *The Miners' Fight for American Standards,* he had placed full dependence upon the law of supply and demand for the cure of the industry's ills, he now sought other physicians, among them the formerly denounced economists and researchers. When Lewis is scolded by conservatives and joshed by liberals over his about-face on the matter of public regulation, his answer is that he has a better sense of timing than his critics. When he felt that unilateral efforts of the mine workers' union were unavailing, he plumped for outside controls to stabilize the industry and integrate it into the national economy. As, later on, he was to urge the mass organization of other large-scale industries than mining, when he was head of the C.I.O.

However it may have been with Mr. Lewis, the fact remains that there has always been an important body of liberal thought within the mine workers' union able to analyze the fundamental sickness of the industry and to propose common-sense cures. Though far removed from the main streams of American life, the majority of our mine workers realize that they are the all-important factor in an industry unusually sensitive to every economic repercussion. The "gob-pile orators" and their grimy audiences know the economic time of day. Though they are militantly jealous of their rights, won after bitter years of struggle, they are not in love with struggle for the struggle's sake. They hold today, as so many of their spokesmen have proclaimed, "that it is their policy to substitute amicable arrangements with management for dragging, costly and sanguinary strikes, to institute co-operation in the place of economic violence, to protect the public interest, and with mutual aid to mitigate the war of each against all."

Small wonder that industrial statesmen bypass the operators, owners and financial powers in coal to go straight to the miners' union. They know that among the workers they will find sympathetic hearing for any long-range program based on the realities of the situation. Builders of the industrial democracy of tomorrow can spend profitable time in the remote mining camps. There they will find men and women with a long democratic tradition who know how to value democracy because they and their forebears have had to fight for every bit of it that they have.

III. THE DARK BEGINNINGS

A COAL DIGGER, BORN IN A SMALL central European country, tells of his amazement on arriving in New York in the eighties to discover on the streets of the city something, in his eyes, more precious than the gold of the immigrant's dream. Walking up from the Battery, he and his buddy saw a pile of rubbish in front of a building that was being erected. From the pile the miner dragged a two-by-four plank. "Look," he cried, "it is wood! Wood that is being thrown out. How rich this land must be!"

Coming from a wood-starved Europe whose forests had been taken over by large landowners or by the government, the immigrant miner was in much the same state of mind as our American pioneers who looked across the long green seas of virgin timber to the far horizons. As had once been the case in Europe and England, a squirrel could leap from bough to bough for miles on end without once coming to cleared ground. What use for other fuel, when the pioneer with his ax could find all that was needed within a short distance from his clearing? Today in the fields above Pennsylvania's anthracite, you can see the rings of bright green grass made rich by potash deposits where the settlers burned charcoal for smelting ore.

In early England too, this profusion of wood held back the mining of coal. Cornishmen might mine tin, as did the Roman invaders before them, but the black, smelly stuff was for the wretched beachcombers who called the outcroppings "sea cole" and burned it in their hovels on cold winter nights. Burned it often to the point of suffocation of themselves and their neighbors, since they had no chimneys. In 1257, Queen Eleanor fled from her castle in Nottingham holding

24

her royal nose against the fumes that rose from the peasants' huts in the village below her. Some years before this, Henry III had granted a charter to the freemen of Newcastle to "dig for cole" but this was a mere stripping operation. In histories of the early part of the fourteenth century we read of "bell pits," small shafts that were enlarged at the bottom and whence the coal was taken up in baskets by windlasses. When one pit was robbed another near by would be opened, and it was not until a gallery was introduced at a working at Tyne that the industry which was to make Britain the mistress of the world's fuel got fairly under way. Soon miners were working in what old-time British miners call "bord and pillar" (our room and pillar) operations. Smoke and smells still made coal inacceptable in settled regions. There were royal edicts against burning coal within the limits of London. Its use was confined to dyers, brewers and blacksmiths, and the very poor outside the cities who had no access to wood. By Queen Elizabeth's time, however, nobility and the church simultaneously discovered that there might be money for both classes in this filthy "cole." Architects began planning chimneys for city and country houses alike, an innovation, by the way, which changed the entire trend of the profession. Mining became a perquisite of the church and the other large landowners; the state profited by imposing an export duty on coal.

Still the ax sounded in the forests and still charcoal was king. Coal was a perplexing problem at both ends. The poor wretches who mined it hewed away with clumsy tools in terrible darkness. The women of the miners, naked from the waists up, crawled along passageways dripping with water to pull out little carts of coal to which both women and children were harnessed. At the bottom of the mine shaft the coal was either loaded into the buckets brought to the surface by a windlass operated by horses or mules or hauled up by hand. In comparison with the lot of these driven workers, the life of the dwellers in the meanest of London's unspeakable slums was utopian. Technically, miners were not slaves. They were bondsmen, bound over by official documents, signed at the beginning of each April, to work for pitiful wages for the pitiless mine owners. They lived as they worked, like savages. Now and then they would indulge in sporadic revolts, only to be driven back by hunger into "the damnation of the mines." Shakespeare might have taken his Caliban from a Welsh or Scotch coal hewer of his times. As Louis Untermeyer suggests in his poem on a latter-day miner, "Caliban in the Coal Mines" whose last stanza is:

> Nothing but blackness above
> And nothing that moves but the cars. . . .
> God, if you wish for our love,
> Fling us a handful of stars!

Not that all prospered with the absentee owners of the pits. In *The Case of Bituminous Coal,* Hamilton and Wright quote with gusto this passage from a history of coal mining in Great Britain:

"Master Beamont, a gentleman of great ingenuity and rare parts, adventured into our mines with his thirty thousand pounds. . . . Within a few years he consumed all his money and rode home on his light horse."

This was in 1649. Hamilton and Wright suggest: "Since his time an order of the Knights of Master Beamont could have been founded. And the order would have been large and flourishing although the names of most of the members are unknown to fame. For almost as little account is taken of losses in the coal industry as of losses at the gambling tables."

At the other end, the consumer's clumsily constructed drafts in the new chimneys made the home burning of coal a problem in the prevention of asphyxiation. Learned men of the Sorbonne joined with British medicos in denouncing the fuel as a detriment to the health of the nation. There is a record, not without its irony, of the entire family of a large mine owner being done to death by coal gas. There were, however, better-contriving folk who somehow managed to heat the Englishman's chilly home with something more satisfactory than the blazing logs in the huge fireplace. More and more pits were opened in Wales and Scotland and Durham and the other English seams, and more and more people of good will were insisting that for sheer decency's sake, if for nothing else, something be done about the slavish state of the British miner. Besides, the sound of the ax was being muted.

No social reformers but rather the matter of fact Thomas Savery, Thomas Newcomen and James Watt lifted some of the burden from the back of the British miner. The first steam engine, called "The

Miner's Friend," was used not for transportation but for pumping water from the mines and for hoisting coal from the pits. In many workings, long ladders were still in the shafts, ladders up which men, women and children crawled with baskets of coal on their backs. Now the new, coughing little engines did this work.

So thoroughly had the timbermen done their job that there was a genuine wood famine in England toward the end of the eighteenth century and the demand for coal, despite the difficulties in mining and burning the mineral, constantly increased. By the time the engines arrived in the fields there was the by no means inconsiderable production of more than 6 million tons in 1770. The greater part of this went into household use, for the oncoming race of ironmasters who were to make England "the forge of the world" kept their works near the rapidly thinning forests. The sulphur in the coal used for smelting made the iron brittle. After 1770, however, the iron men began to move to the coal fields. The pioneer Wilkinson furnaces in Burslem and in South Wales utilized smelting coke for building iron barges and for the precision job of boring cylinders for Watt's steam engine so that the device became a practical success. Then the first puddling furnace and rolling mill was set up under the direction of Henry Cort in 1784, with the coal and the pig iron in separate compartments joined by the flames from the burning coal over a fire wall.

Coal and iron, with the new textile machines, gave the fog-hung "tight, little island" her enormous head start over the rest of the Western world in the race for industrial supremacy. It was not until 1900, when coal production in the United States equaled that of Britain that our nation became a serious competitor for world trade. George Stephenson, inventor of the locomotive, was a bit of an economic seer when he said:

"The strength of England lies in her iron and coal beds; and the locomotive is destined above all agencies to bring it forth. The Lord Chancellor now sits upon a bag of wool, but wool has long since ceased to be emblematical of the staple commodity of England; he ought to sit upon a bag of coals."

The industrial revolutionists early discovered how inextricably the transportation problem is interwoven with coal. Ironmasters, moving their works near the pits, found the old roads that took the cars away from the mines inadequate and began laying iron rails from

the pit mouths. At the same time canals were dug to move the growing bulk of coal, Manchester getting her power by the Duke of
Bridgewater's canal from his colliery at Worsley as early as 1760. The
various "turnpike trusts" began to reconstruct their roads with the
use of metals and everywhere the improved steam engines were
whistling for more and more coal.

"Engineering, iron-founding, textile machinery and industrial
chemistry all hinged ultimately on coal. . . . Coal in the form of
coke was needed by the blast furnaces to smelt the iron ore into the
cohesive form known as pig-iron; coal was needed to re-smelt the
pig-iron and cast it into the form in which it was required by the
engineers; it was needed for the new motive power—steam. Coal could
not, however, have been obtained from the pits in sufficient quantities had not the engineers devised and made a steam-engine which
pumped the water out of the mines. Each of these series of inventions
depended in turn on the others and the reason for their spread in
the Nineteenth Century lies in the fact that they all reached a point
in the Eighteenth where they could be utilized together so that they
reacted on and stimulated each other." [1]

It is the grim history of the beginnings of the Industrial Revolution that, with the exception of some isolated instances, all this
sudden flowering of inventive genius and large-scale co-ordination
worsened the conditions of the workers. The plight of workers of both
sexes and of all ages brought cries of protest from such divergent
characters as Charles Dickens, Karl Marx and Elizabeth Barrett
Browning. Though in more progressive Northumberland and Durham, women did not go down into the mines after 1780, elsewhere
they worked alongside their men at backbreaking tasks underground.
A wild Amazonian race roamed the English and Scotch coal fields.
The mining women were valued for their muscle more than for their
feminine charm. "She is like the collier's daughter, better than she is
bonny." As for the children, at work as trappers opening and shutting doors or tugging with their mothers at the straps of the cars, their
working hell was even darker than that of the youngsters in the
Manchester factories.

Aside from sudden fierce uprisings, with the breaking of heads
and mine machinery, what could these "untouchables" of the mine

[1] L. C. A. Knowles, *The Industrial and Commercial Revolutions*, p. 21.

fields do to improve their lot? They had no votes, labor unions were illegal in England until the repeal of the Combination Laws in 1825, and such reform movements as those led by Robert Owen and the Chartists centered around urban workers far from the mine fields. Now and then Parliamentary commissions would venture out to the mines to incorporate the horrors they had seen there in reports destined for pigeonholes. For the coal- and ironmasters were also masters of the state, dictating the laws from the sacred book of laissez faire.

Yet from the middle of the nineteenth century on, through organization, inspired by a broad-visioned philosophy and led by men of intellect and courage, the miners of England achieved such status that their spokesman, William Straker, representing 800,000 members of the Miners Federation, the strongest labor union in the world, could rise in the King's Robing Room of the British House of Lords and demand of the Coal Commission assembled there that the entire mining industry be transferred from the hands of the coalmasters to those of the state and the workers. This was in 1919. Though the bold bid for nationalization was turned down by the government, it was only yesterday in the midst of the greatest international crisis in her history that England was again compelled to give ear to the voices from the pits. This time to concede a compromised form of nationalization in conjunction with a wage raise. It is a long cry from the days of the grimy, illiterate hewer working with his wife and children in the dripping darkness to the British miner of today talking of industrial democracy and workers' control of industry.

Strikingly, the early history of coal in America parallels that of the development of the industry in the mother country. Here, too, the mineral was long looked on as an unsatisfactory fuel, better for use in a blacksmith's forge than in the fireplace of a gentleman. With a wood lot on every farm and with virgin forests within easy range of the cities and towns along the eastern seaboard, why bother about coal? Then the clearing of the land, together with the demands of our infant industries, sent out prospectors, promoters, exploiters, all sorts of enterprising men to discover how much greater was our natural coal wealth than that of any other nation.

Beneath the rhododendrons and laurel and pine of the southern hills, on through the mountains and valleys of Pennsylvania, under

the prairie lands of the Midwest were hidden away the black poten-
tials of our national power, a third of all the world's available coal.
As in England, the taking of it involved at the beginning the practical
enslavement of the labor force. Generations of American miners were
to become despairing hostages to the tragic waste of men and materials which the mining of our coal entailed. They were to know
nothing of the ordinary amenities of American life. Set apart from
other workers by the nature of the stuff on which they worked, these
mudsill men had to find in themselves the qualities of courage, integrity and intelligence that would make them free. They could look
for no outside aid from the overlords of America. Like their English
fellow workers they had to hew out their own philosophy. And like
the English miners they emerged at length with a militant, compact
organization that has been in the vanguard of labor's army since the
turn of the twentieth century.

The first American miners were Negroes, slaves working in what
we now would call a strip mine in the bituminous fields near Richmond, Virginia, in 1750. To be sure, Joliet and Marquette and, later,
Father Louis Hennepin had reported the presence of what seemed to
be "cole mines" in the Mississippi Valley and along the Illinois River
in the previous century, and it is possible that the Indians had done
some casual digging. But the Richmond "coal quarries" were the first
to be put into continuous operation and by the outbreak of the
Revolutionary War the bituminous coal was being used by blacksmiths and other metal workers throughout this region. Coal was
employed in making cannon balls for the Continental artillery, and
after the war small amounts were shipped to Philadelphia and New
York smithies.

Farther north, Connecticut Yankees moving into Pennsylvania
took over large reservations in the Wyoming Valley beneath which
were rich beds of anthracite—"the last word in coal, the super-product
of all the mysterious processes of coal formation—gleaming, hard,
smokeless practically odorless, slow-burning, high heating," as John
Kimberley Mumford describes the hard coal in his book *Anthracite*.
William Penn's agents bought the reservations back from the Connecticut company, but it was Obadiah Gore, a Connecticut blacksmith,
who, settling near Wilkes-Barre in 1770, taught the Pennsylvanians
how to put their anthracite to use. He burned the "stone coals" in his

own and other shops throughout the region, but only by vigorous manipulation of the bellows.

The bulk of the earliest annals of American coal has to do with anthracite lying under Pennsylvania's soil in a region only 120 miles long with its greatest width 50 miles. Under those hills and mountains, slashed with swift-running rivers, nature took a million years of pressing down rock upon the titan trees and ferns of the Carboniferous era—an era estimated by geologists to have passed some twenty million years ago—before anthracite was ready to be burned. Theophrastus, the pupil of Aristotle, first used the Greek word "anthrakes" to describe the coal in 320 B.C. Marco Polo seems to have had anthracite in mind when he wrote home about the "black stones" in China in the thirteenth century. The Welsh were the first moderns to mine the stuff in workmanlike fashion, and England's coal-laden freighters spread the might of empire over all the seven seas. In America it was the iron and coal along the Monongahela, the Allegheny, the hard coal from the Lehigh and Wyoming and Schuylkill basins that built Wilkes-Barre and Scranton, Pottsville and Tamaqua and Shenandoah, and blackened the skies over Pittsburgh, and glowed in the grates of New England. Today anthracite has lost its proud position as "the householder's fuel," though the demands of war may give it a space of renewed life. Oil has shouldered anthracite aside and it is bituminous that men mean when they speak of our strategic fuel. Before Pearl Harbor they were calling the anthracite regions our "blighted areas." Yet for crowded years in the history of industry and labor, these areas were the scenes of fabulous triumphs and disasters that shook the Republic to its foundations.

At the outset it was no great trick to discover and dig up the anthracite; the problem came in its transportation and getting it to burn when it reached its destination. Hunters and trappers such as Philip Ginter, whose name is written high on the list of Founding Fathers of the industry, would come upon the shiny black stones cropping out from the hillsides or, like Nicholas Allen, would light campfires on beds of anthracite and awake to find the whole mountainside ablaze. One of the rich fields was stumbled on by John Charles who was hunting a woodchuck whose hole was in an anthracite outcropping.

Ginter took his black stones to Colonel Jacob Weiss at Fort Allen near Weissport and the colonel, together with Charles Cist, John Nicholson and Michael Hillegar, organized America's first coal company, the Lehigh Coal Mine Company. Down the boulder-strewn Lehigh River through perilous, rapids-torn waters, the new company succeeded finally in shipping two boatloads of anthracite to Philadelphia in 1803. Purchasers of the strange new fuel were derided and the scoffers were in high fettle when they saw the pioneer buyers dumping out the apparently unburnable stuff to be used as gravel for their front walks. There was, however, a grain of comfort for the promoters in a letter from Oliver Evans, the famed Philadelphia inventor.

"I have experienced the use of them [the Lehigh coals] in a close stove," wrote Evans in February, 1803, "and also in a fireplace that may be closed and opened at pleasure, so constructed as to cause a brisk current of air to pass up through a small contracted grate on which they were laid. I find them more difficult to be kindled than the Virginia coal, yet a small quantity of dry wood laid on the grate under them is sufficient to ignite them, which being done they continue to burn while a sufficient amount be added to keep up the combustion, occasionally stirring them to keep down the ashes. They produce no smoke, contain no sulphur and when well ignited exhibit a vivid, bright appearance, all of which render them suitable for warming rooms."

Then came Judge Jesse Fell of Wilkes-Barre announcing his success in burning anthracite in open fireplaces, and the venturesome folk of the region, anxious to encourage home industry, set up stoves and grates for the burning of hard coal.

Philadelphia was the richest market, however, and great "arks" were built to take the anthracite there. These early barges were 90 feet long by 16 feet wide. They were propelled through the dangerous river waters by crews of four men bending to huge oars and keeping the clumsy craft away from the rocks. It took seven days to bring sixty tons of anthracite down to tidewater on the Susquehanna and the cargo was sold at from $10 to $12 a ton. By now users of the coal were discovering that the best way to get anthracite to burn is to let it alone after it is ignited. Consumers, giving up attempts to poke or blow the coal into steady flame, would slam furnace doors in disgust, only to return later and find a good fire going.

Salesmen for the Lehigh Company and for John and Abijah Smith of Derby, Connecticut, who were the first large shippers, distributed handbills on the crooked little streets of Philadelphia, set up grates in public places, delivered sales talks all over town, and little by little sales resistance was overcome. After Philadelphia accepted the new fuel, the New York market was invaded, and in 1812, with the war blocking the importation of British coal, two hundred tons of anthracite were bought by wealthy New Yorkers and the firm of Price and Waterbury set up shop to retail anthracite for $25 a ton. Over in Jersey, anthracite was used for ore smelting.

As soon as there seemed to be a stable market for the hard coal, the companies began to blast the boulders out of the rivers. The Lehigh was transformed into a slack-water canal by a series of dams, so that whole flotillas of coal arks could be floated safely down its yellow waters. By 1829, four canals had been completed—the Schuylkill, the Pennsylvania, the Morris and the Delaware and Hudson—to cause such a boom in anthracite that production jumped from 77,000 tons to 112,000.

The first mining was done by farmers, who stripped off the overburden from the outcroppings or tunneled into the banks by use of drifts. There was a famous gravity railroad from Summit to Mauch Chunk down which the coal cars coasted; then with the coming of the steamboat and locomotive there was formed the powerful alliance between hard coal and rails that was to set the economic pattern of anthracite until well into the twentieth century.

IV. THE FOUNDING FATHERS

By THE MIDDLE OF THE NINE-teenth century, English immigrant miners, predominantly Welsh and Scotch, began arriving in the coal fields of America, fields hitherto largely worked by native-born farmers and their sons. These new-comers made two contributions to the young industry: the first, in introducing improved working techniques; the second, in giving to the heterogeneous working force a "sense of kind" that was to lead to national organization.

"They are a race apart, these English miners," says a recent book,[1] which might as well have been describing the British hewers of a century ago. "The London clubman may never see them. But go to the annual picnic of the Durham miners and you will see 110,000 men and their families—a distinctive race, all with the same dress, of curiously the same height, and even much the same cast of coun-tenance. 'They look so much alike!' exclaimed a keen American ob-server. 'Yes' said John Burns, 'and no wonder. They have been min-ing coal in Durham for 800 years. A man seldom marries outside the county. I could take you to good-sized villages where there are only five family names.'"

The bearded, burly men who settled in Northern Illinois, the coal camps in the Hocking Valley and around the collieries in Pennsyl-vania were proud of their skills with the picks and drill, a little amazed at the headlong manner with which our miners tore at the coal. Already the shafts in the mother country were going deep and would go deeper soon. The cream of the outcroppings overseas had

[1] Tryon and Others, *Mineral Economics.*

34

been taken, and as the shafts went down the working skills went up. Sir Humphry Davy's safety lamp had taken the place of candles thrust into crevices in the mine walls. Hoisting and pumping machinery had been steadily improved, and safer and more ingenious ways of robbing the coal were devised by British engineers and miners alike.

No sooner had the oppressive Combination Acts been repealed in England than the miners there began to organize. At first locally, in what they called "associations" or "societies" beginning in 1825 at Durham, the miners met to discuss grievances and to work out some way of bargaining with the owners that would not involve such disorders as perennially made the fields a battleground at "binding time." They sent delegates to the first central labor body in Britain, the National Association of Labour, meeting in 1831. Then they set up their own national organization, the National Miners' Association of Great Britain and Ireland, in 1841. A strike at binding time called out 100,000 miners, led by the die-hards around Glasgow, but the miners were beaten by sheer starvation, and by 1847 there was little left of the organization. The leaders turned then, as has always been the case, to legislation and by 1850 Parliament had passed the Mines Regulation Act providing for regular inspection, the first of a series of mine regulation measures leading up to the present "nationalization."

It was these experiences on both the economic and the political field that gave the arriving Britishers the sense of need for solidarity which the American diggers lacked. The immigrant miners already had their songs, chief among them the following:

> Step by step the longest march can be won, can be won;
> Single stones will form an arch one by one, one by one.
> And by union what we will, can be all accomplished still.
> Drops of water turn a mill, singly none, singly none.

American owners, as well as American diggers, were quick to adopt the ways of British mining. The "truck system," whereby miners were forced to deal with company-owned stores and buy their own powder and tools as well as other necessities; the tradition of signing contracts in April, a time disadvantageous to the miners facing the long summer slack season; the piecework system of payment by the ton mined by the skilled workers, which led in turn to the contract system in vogue in anthracite, whereby the older and more experienced miners hired and paid their own helpers—these were mainly taken over from English mine practice. And these led to unrest among the fiercely individualistic pioneer miner-farmers in Pennsylvania. Like their British brothers they were notoriously "impatient of control," and they looked at the continued encroachment of the companies upon their community life with no little alarm.

The first attempt to organize the American miners was made in Pennsylvania in 1849 by an Englishman named John Bates who rallied the anthracite diggers against the high prices in the company stores and the low wages at the company pay windows. Bates flits tantalizingly across mining history, apparently a man of considerable ability since his organization was called "Bates' Union" and took in most of the men working on the 4 million tons of anthracite that was being mined at the time. But the stories go that, like so many of his successors, he was seduced by the operators in the course of a strike, leaving behind him a bitterly disillusioned rank and file who would hear no more talk of unionism in hard coal for years to come.

These were days of vague utopianism in the labor movement at large. Many leaders looked on trade-unionism as a "sunshine activity," as Selig Perlman points out in *A Theory of the Labor Movement*. The long-time bad-weather planning for the movement must be along the lines of producers' co-operation. William H. Sylvis, the outstanding labor figure of the period, had organized in 1859 a strong industrial union among the iron moulders in answer to the formation of an association of ironmasters. He emphasized the fact that local strikes were bound to fail in the face of the united front of the bosses and called for the unionization of all iron moulders in much the same language as was to be used by the organizers of the Committee for Industrial Organization seventy-five years later. "Year after year the capital of the country," cried Sylvis, "becomes more and more concentrated in the hands of a few, and, in proportion as the wealth of the country becomes centralized, its power increases and the laboring classes are impoverished."

Yet Sylvis felt that trade-unionism was but preliminary to the co-operative movement which would eventually solve the workers' problems.

"Of all the questions before us," he wrote in his union paper, *The Ironmoulders' International Journal,* "not one is of so great importance, or should command so large a portion of our consideration as coöperation. . . . Coöperation is the only true remedy for low wages, strikes, lock-outs, and a thousand other impositions and annoyances to which workmen are subjected." By 1869 members of Sylvis's union were running fourteen co-operative foundries, chiefly in New York and Pennsylvania.

The realities of the Civil War, with the increased demand for coal for the munitions works and the consequent temporary raise in wages, turned the miners back to unionism. In Illinois the operators in the Belleville district, which furnished bituminous coal to the St. Louis market, took advantage of the short-lived financial panic that followed Lincoln's election by announcing a wage reduction of one-half cent a bushel.[2] The diggers walked out on strike, not only resisting the cut but charging fraud on the part of the operators in the weighing of the coal at the tipple. Their cause was taken up by 1,400 of Belleville's "best citizens," alarmed at a possible coal shortage in the midst of what now seemed to be the "inevitable conflict." So impressed was the Illinois legislature by the arguments of the spokesmen for the diggers that a "fair weights measure" for the district was passed providing for the appointment of impartial "coal scalers," the checkweighmen of today.

The strike was won in short order, as the operators feared the loss of their market, with coal selling at $3.75 a ton at St. Louis. Short-lived as was the strike, it gave the Illinois miners (who at the time of the Civil War were producing more than 700,000 tons of bituminous and earning an annual average wage of around $700) two objectives: a concentration on unionism rather than any sort of labor utopianism, and the agitation for specific legislation for the improvement of working conditions. The development of organization among miners has pretty closely followed these two lines first laid down in 1861.

In the course of the strike a remarkable "address" signed by Daniel Weaver had appeared in the friendly columns of the Belleville *Democrat.*

[2] Twenty-five bushels to a ton of 2,000 pounds.

Weaver was born in 1824 in Staffordshire, England, worked in the mines there, and then came to St. Clair County, of which Belleville is the seat, filled with the high idealism and the practical organizing sense derived from the leadership of Alexander Macdonald, head of the British miners. In his letter to the *Democrat,* addressed "To the Miners of The United States," he said:

The necessity of an association of miners, and of those branches of industry immediately connected with mining operations, having for its objects the physical, mental and social elevation of the miner, has long been felt by the thinking portion of the miners generally.

Union is the great fundamental principle by which every object of importance is to be accomplished. Man is a social being and if left to himself, in an isolated condition, would be one of the weakest creatures; but associated with his kind he works wonders. Men can do jointly what they cannot do singly; and the *union* of minds and hands, the concentration of their power becomes almost omnipotent. Nor is this all; men not only accumulate power by union, but gain warmth and earnestness. There is an electric sympathy kindled, and the attractive forces inherent in human nature are called into action, and a stream of generous emotion, of a friendly regard for each other, binds together and animates the whole.

If men would spread one set of opinions, or crush another, they make a society. Would they improve the sanitary condition of our towns, light our streets with gas, or supply our dwellings with water, they form societies. From the organization of our armies, our railroad and banking companies, down through every minute ramification of society to trade associations and sick societies, men have learned the power and efficiency of coöperation, and are, therefore determined to stand by each other. How long, then, will miners remain isolated—antagonistic to each other? Does it not behoove us as miners to use every means to elevate our position in society by a reformation of character, by obliterating all personal animosities and frivolous nationalities, abandoning our pernicious habits and degrading pursuits, and striving for the attainment of pure and high principles and generous motives, which will fit us to bear a manly, useful and honorable part in the world? Our unity is essential to the attainment of our own rights and the amelioration of our present condition: and our voices must be heard in the legislative halls of our land. There it is that our complaints must be made and our rights defined. The insatiable maw of Capital would devour every vestige of Labor's rights; but we must demand legislative protection; and to accomplish this we must organize. Our remedy, our safety, our protection, our dearest interests, and the social well-being of our families, present and future, depend on our unity, our duty, and our regard for each other.

In laying before you, therefore, the objects of this association, we desire it to be understood that our objects are not merely pecuniary, but to mutually instruct and improve each other in knowledge which is power; to study the laws of life, the relation of Labor to Capital; politics, municipal affairs, literature, science or any other subject relating to the general welfare of our class. . . . There must be an organization of Labor. One of America's immortals said, "To me there is no East, no West, no North, no South," and I would say, let there be no English, no Irish, Germans, Scotch or Welsh. This is our country, and

"All men are brethren—how the watchwords run!
And when men act as such is justice won."

Come then and rally around the standard of union—the union of States and the unity of miners—and with honesty of purpose, zeal and watchfulness—the pledge of success—unite for the emancipation of our labor and the regeneration and elevation, physically, mentally, and morally of our species.

It is all there in Weaver's Address, the wistful longing of men, set apart from the common run, for a place in society, for the "electric" warmth of friendship and brotherhood, the longing for "a sense of kind" which comes from organization and with organization the improvement of status through self-discipline and self-education. For the immediate future no more revolutionary program than the pressing for protective legislation, and at the end the appeal to patriotism.

Weaver knew his people. They came out of the pits to meet in convention at West Belleville on January 28, 1861. There the first national miners' union in this country was organized with its president, Thomas Lloyd, born in Staffordshire the same year as Weaver and coming to this country at the same time. Weaver was elected secretary and his hand was evident in the writing of the Constitution of the Miners' Association (later the American Miners' Association), which began with the words of the old song:

Step by step the longest march can be won, can be won . . .

To these two eloquent Staffordshire hewers was joined John Hinchcliffe, a Yorkshireman by birth, who had been by turns a tailor, a lawyer and a journalist. Hinchcliffe edited the first miners' journal, the *Weekly Miner,* the official organ of the association, and was to go on to the state legislature where he fathered many protective measures for the miners of Illinois.

In the spirit of Weaver's Address, Hinchcliffe announced that his paper would be "devoted to Family Literature, Agriculture, Social Science, General Knowledge and the current news of the day" as well as to union affairs. The *Weekly Miner* rated high among the 120 daily, weekly and monthly labor journals published at that time. Though it avoided propaganda for the "antimonopoly" issue and producers' co-ops, which occupied much of the space in the papers under Sylvis's influence, and though it looked upon the Machinists' and Blacksmiths' International Union as composed of "idealists and theorists," it maintained a high (often painfully high) moral tone, urging the personal as well as the social redemption of its readers.

Association organizers won converts in Missouri, Ohio, and in the hard-coal regions of Pennsylvania. The return of miner soldiers from the war, however, the general economic upset of "reconstruction," and in particular, the loss of a large-scale strike in the Blossburg fields of Pennsylvania, worked together to destroy the association by 1868.

In that year there came from the mines to lead what Weaver in a polysyllabic mood called, "this heterogeneous concatenation of genus homo—the organized miners," a brilliant, courageous and, at the end, tragic figure. This was John Siney over whose career another great miners' leader was to brood darkly.

Siney had organized a number of local unions into the Workingmen's Benevolent Association of Schuylkill County, Pennsylvania, and his spirited letters to the papers in defense of the aims of his organization showed a flair for propaganda and a grasp of the peculiar economic situation faced by his miners that was worthy of Weaver himself. The railroads were moving fast into the hard-coal fields now. Delaware, Lackawanna and Western, Central of New Jersey, Philadelphia and Reading, and the Lehigh and Susquehanna were taking over great tracts of anthracite-bearing lands, herding the miners into company towns, inaccessible to union organizers, and presenting the diggers with the first of the "yellow-dog contracts" whereby the miner agreed not to join a union. Siney sent his followers out to insist that operators share a 75 per cent rise in the price of coal with the men who dug it. The committees came trailing back with a 17 per cent raise in wages. Whereupon Siney called a successful strike in the spring of '69 and forced a sliding scale for the Schuylkill and Lehigh regions which tied wages to the prices of anthracite at tidewater. A year later he sat down with the representatives of the Anthracite Board of Trade in a joint conference with the Benevolent Association, continuing the sliding scale which had worked out well for his men—the first joint agreement in the industry.

The new leader could see clearly enough the part that was being assigned to coal in the swift-paced industrial revolution that followed the war. The fuel, strategic to the entire westward thrust of the railways was to be mined cheaply, swiftly, wastefully if you like, but always kept in a role secondary to that of the rails. "He who owns the rails owns all," the reformers had it, and coal, while it was essential to keeping the giddy expansionist race going, was in the ownership setup, so far as anthracite went, something for absentee speculation. Agents for the railroad companies bought up farm land in Luzerne and Schuylkill and the other anthracite counties at prices ranging from $75 to $200 an acre, or leased the unmined coal at the rate of 10 cents a ton. In 1871 the Philadelphia and Reading bought 100,000 acres of coal land in the Schuylkill region for $40 million. With such large-scale investments there was not time for anything but taking off the cream of the mine and getting it into the boilers of the onrushing iron horses and the furnaces of the new steel plants along the Monongahela and Susquehanna. Anything went. Forty per cent of the possible take of coal from an opening was a fair enough average. The rest was left underground never to be recovered. "What has posterity done for me?" was the question of the enterprising men in Pittsburgh, Philadelphia, New York. There was plenty of coal where that came from. The big money was in railroad stocks and in speculation in the free lands, larger by far than all New England, which a grateful government had presented to the rail owners in the West.

Where did the miners come in? That was the question asked by Siney and the capable George Archibald from the Pittsburgh district, Andrew Roy, who was writing for the miners' papers under the name of "Jock Pittbreeks," and other alert-minded men from the pits. "Can it be possible," asked Siney, "that men supposed to know the transactions of corporations would for a moment believe

that the corporations have the least sympathy for their workmen or
the general public? Contrast the individual operator of Schuylkill
with a railroad, monopolizing and extorting whenever the least opportunity offers, with no redress from their charges whatever they may
be. The rise of coal is very little advantage to our operators, for as
fast as it rises, the Reading Railroad takes the lion's share. Then come
the middlemen with their haul and nothing less than doubling the
usual charge is demanded by them. . . . The miner and laborer may
well wish to be united, to withstand such odds—combined corporations."

Siney took his followers to an industrial congress of all colds,
workers held in Cleveland in 1873 and after the usual rays actions
were passed denouncing monopoly and calling for co-operation, the
hard-coal men met with the delegates from the bituminous field, chief
among them John James of Braidwood, Illinois, to discuss the peculiar
problems of the diggers. The result was a call to a convention to be
held in Youngstown, Ohio, on October 13, 1873, for the purpose of
forming another national miners' union. "Come and reason together,"
urged Siney, "form an organization in which brother will be pledged
to brother, an organization which will form a bulwark alike in the
day of prosperity and adversity. Will you do so, or do you prefer to
occupy your present unenviable position? The answer and the issue
are in your hands." The miners answered by going to Youngstown
to form their second national union, the Miners' National Association
of the United States (generally called the National Union) with Siney
as president and John James as secretary.

Though the delegates at Youngstown had read in their papers
of the panic closing of the New York Stock Exchange the month
before the convention, the repercussions of Wall Street's distress had
not yet hit the hinterlands. It was not long, however, before the men
were back in the fields when the full force of the '73 depression fell
upon them. As Siney said in his address to the second convention of
the National Union:

"When the last convention adjourned none among us, and few
in the country, dreamed of the terrible blight that had set in upon
our industries generally, and none upon which it fell heavier than
our own coal and iron department. The panic, a national misfortune,
had just rolled in before the chariot of the world's progress. Its storms

were howling in the East and in this state before the association had its birth. The iron markets were failing at a rate never before experienced. Factories of every kind were closing down and coal became a drug in the market and we began to think the very foundation had fallen out of our business fabric. . . . Our men were to be seen lying around our mining towns and villages having no work to do, yet willing to work."

Siney told of the piling up of grievances during the past year, of the insistence of the operators in requiring the signatures on yellow-dog contracts before the little work there was could be had. He had advised his men, under the circumstances, to sign the contracts anyhow, "on the same grounds Galileo took before the inquisition, exclaiming, 'But it does move after all!'" And he had urged against the calling of strikes in such unpropitious times.

The despairing rank and file, however, going into a second black year of steadily reduced wages for the few days the mines worked, looked on the advice of Siney as a weakling's surrender. Wildcat strikes, soon broken by the operators, sent blacklisted strikers to Siney's offices begging for relief. Siney and Xingo Parks, a vigorous young organizer, went through the camps counseling against violence and further futile strike moves. Everywhere the two leaders went they were shadowed by operators' detectives. The pliant newspapers of Philadelphia and Pittsburgh pictured Siney and Parks as conspiring for revolt in the mine regions. The flour and corn meal furnished out of union funds to strikers, whom Siney supported against his better judgment, was no nourishment for prolonged militancy and when the men drifted back to work at reduced wages, lacking other scapegoats, they turned on their union leaders. Then the operators sprung the trap in the shape of an indictment of Siney and Parks for violation of the criminal conspiracy law of Pennsylvania. At the trial the prosecutor thundered: "By the testimony those men, John Siney and Xingo Parks, did assist, in this combination of miners, for the purpose of raising wages, and it is your bounden duty under the provision of the law to bring in a verdict of guilty." Siney was acquitted, Parks sentenced to a year in the penitentiary, a sentence commuted by Governor Hartranft. The miners, who had crowded into the courtroom at Clearfield, cheered Siney as he walked out into the free sunshine, but he knew in his heart the agonized road that he had to tread.

The depression deepened, and Siney moved in its shadows pleading with his followers to hold on, to cling to such organization as was still left, and above all not further to imperil their position by headless strikes. He made a last desperate attempt to salvage the union by negotiating for coal lands in Tennessee to be run on a co-operative basis by blacklisted diggers. But there was no money in the treasury when Siney came back from the South. All across the fields, men ousted from company-owned houses were cursing the name of Siney, tearing down the structure of unionism which their own hands had built. In the spring days of 1876, Siney went out of the national offices at Cleveland, a broken man. His last official act was to refuse permission to his faithful secretary to attempt to raise funds for the president's long overdue salary. Within a few years, just as the magic of his name was reviving, he died at his home in St. Clair.

Years later, John Mitchell, faced with the same terrible decisions as Siney had to make, cried out to his rank and file:

"You are not going to do with me as your fathers did with John Siney."

To the youngsters the allusion was meaningless, but the old-timers knew well enough what crucifixion John Mitchell had in mind.

V. "UNITY! UNITY!"

WITH THE NATIONAL UNION GONE, the Fabian tactics of its leaders repudiated, guerrilla warfare spread across the hard-coal fields. In the spring of 1877, the Pennsylvania and Baltimore and Ohio railroads announced reductions in wages. The railroaders struck and they were joined by the miners in the Pittsburgh region. Coming into the cities to stand with the railroaders, the diggers faced the guns of the militia in Pittsburgh, of a "Citizens' Corps" in Scranton. In Pittsburgh, twenty-six persons were killed, the militia barricaded in a roundhouse and $5 million of railroad property destroyed. In Scranton, the vigilantes, headed by the mayor, fired point-blank into a crowd of strikers, killing three. Before the strikes were broken and the workers had gone drifting back to switchyards and mines, the entire eastern press talked of "revolution."

Two secret organizations of labor operating in the railroad and mining centers of Pennsylvania had created panic in the hearts of the editors. One of these was the Molly Maguires, an offshoot of the Ancient Order of Hibernians, the Irish-American society devoted originally to sick benefits and charity work among newly arrived immigrants. The Mollies had their name from a group in the old country which, in the forties, had terrorized English landlords. Irish-born miners had always been impatient of the "gradualness" of their English fellow workers. The latter in turn had shown their contempt for the diggers from "John Bull's Other Island." In the Mollies young hotheads found an outlet for their resentment against the operators who were now constantly hacking away at wages. At first the Mollies contented themselves with running imported strikebreakers out of the

45

fields. They went on from there to the derailing of mine cars and the burning of breakers. Before long they were hiding in the hills, sniping at mine supers and unpopular foremen.

The operators called on Allan Pinkerton, the head of the detective agency, to furnish the first in a long succession of labor spies. Pinkerton's man, a young Irish Catholic named James McParland, soon ingratiated himself with the leaders of the Mollies. They took him into their inner circles and before long, after the manner of agents provocateur the world over, he was suggesting deeds of violence on a large scale. McParland had been chosen general secretary of the organization when his connections were discovered. Promptly he took the stand as chief witness against the Mollies in a series of murder cases that divided the anthracite counties into two hostile camps. Largely through his unsupported testimony, gallows went up at Mauch Chunk, Pottsville, Bloomsburg. In all, fourteen Mollies were hanged, the innocent along with the guilty, suffering from the bad odor into which the organization had come not only in the nostrils of the general public but of the conservative miners as well.

These last, more and more of them, were themselves joining another secret order. From time to time there appeared in the pages of the labor papers announcements signed with the mystifying five stars (*****). This was the symbol of the Order of the Knights of Labor of America and the World.

The Knights had been organized by Philadelphia garment cutters, under the idealistic leadership of Uriah S. Stephens in 1869. In everything save its extreme secrecy, a measure deemed necessary by the Philadelphians because of the fear of blacklisting, the organization was as far as the poles apart from the hell-for-leather Mollies. The pioneer Knights were sober-sided, God-fearing needle workers with the high hopes of organizing all save the actual owners of industry into a single union. This union was not to advocate strikes but rather ameliorative legislation, together with popular education, temperance, producers' co-operation, a Bureau of Labor Statistics—the amalgam of the aspirations of the workers for status at a time when all conventional labor organizations were going down before the massed strength of the combining owners.

In a few short years the Knights had gone far beyond the little halls in Philadelphia, where their first Assemblies were held. Now they welcomed into their order, with a complicated ritual and hair-raising pledges to secrecy, workers in every field, women as well as men, Negroes in the South, unskilled immigrant "greenhorns" in the North. While the Order's Constitution provided that three-fourths of every Assembly must be composed of wage earners, professional men and women, small businessmen and farmers were eligible. All classes in fact save: "Bankers, stockbrokers, professional gamblers, lawyers, and those who in any way derive their living from the manufacture or sale of intoxicating liquors." In the matter of teetotalism, the Knights were strict, serving only tea, coffee and light drinks at their affairs and penalizing any bibulous Knight who turned up tight. Over and over again in his huge history of the Knights, *Thirty Years of Labor,* the bespectacled, big-mustached Terence V. Powderly, one-time labor mayor of Scranton and for many years leader of the Order, stresses the need for strict temperance on the part of his followers. He devotes a chapter in his book to the subject, illustrating it with a steel engraving depicting the horrors of a drunkard's home life. And this was the man dubbed a revolutionist and free lover by the press of his time.

To the first Assemblies of garment workers "sojourners" from other trades were admitted who, after learning the principles of the society, went out and preached the gospel of the Knights to mechanics, carpenters, mill workers, railroaders, goldbeaters and miners. John M. Davis, energetic editor of the *National Labor Tribune,* an influential publication, was top organizer of the coal diggers in the Western Pennsylvania regions. In Ohio, Chris Evans, later to become official historian of the miners' union, was active in setting up Assemblies among the soft-coal miners.

The eastern press was filled with dark rumors of the power of the secret organization to cripple all American industry. Naturally the Mollies were used as a horrible example of what havoc a secret body of workers could cause. Philosophies of communism and anarchism were attributed to such mild reformers as Stephens, Powderly, Evans, and the other leaders. Now quite evidently the time had come to abandon the mumbo jumbo of passwords, grips, initiation rituals and to come out in the open with the aims of the Knights, before their enemies further confused the public. How tame in comparison to the reported conspiratorial aims were the fifteen points of the published Constitution! The spirit of the Knights was reflected in the wordy preamble denouncing the "recent alarming development and aggression of aggregated wealth." Democratic co-operative effort was the alternative. In Point One the chief objective was stated: "to bring within the folds of organization every department of productive industry, making knowledge a standpoint for action, and industrial and moral worth not wealth, the true standard of individual and national greatness." The establishment of Bureaus of Labor; the setting up of both producers' and distributers' co-ops; the reserving of public lands for genuine settlers—"not another acre for railroads or speculators"; the substitution of arbitration for strikes; an antichild-labor clause and a demand for equal pay for equal work for both sexes—these were the goals of men who had been identified in the public's mind with night-riding Mollies and bomb-throwing anarchists.

The delegate elected in Chicago to attend the convention at Reading, Pennsylvania, on January 1, 1878, was not able to be there because of lack of carfare. There was evidently no such wealth in the Order's treasury as its critics charged. The convention voted an annual salary of $200 to Grand Master Workman Stephens and a $50 a year salary to the grand treasurer, who at the time could find nothing in the treasury.

Adopting as their motto, "That is the most perfect government in which an injury to one is the concern of all," the Knights rode gallantly ahead, with coal diggers sitting alongside of doctors, small shopkeepers and schoolteachers at the mixed Assembly meetings, the miners a bit perplexed at this large utopian talk. The miners liked certain parts of the program, an organization to include all workers in an industry irrespective of skills or race or creed, they liked the antimonopoly clause especially as it applied to the railroads. But they could see no alternative to the use of their most trusted weapon, the strike, in the vague proposals for arbitration, and they were too hard pressed to take much interest in long-run reforms. The immediate concern of the miners was with such everyday matters as the election of a checkweighman, prices at the company-owned "pluck-me" stores, the fight against the constant menace of wage reductions. While leaders of the mine workers retained their membership in the Knights, a fast-growing organization now that its conspiratorial stigma was removed, and took an active part in the deliberations, they listened to the grievances of the men from the pits and were convinced that something more practical than the utopianism of the Knights was called for.

The grievances came to a head in the Hocking Valley of Ohio with the combination of a reduction in wages of 20 cents a ton from the 60 cents which the tonnage men were earning, the refusal to allow checkweighmen, elected by the miners, on the tipples, and the introduction of new mining machinery. There was a 20-cent differential between the tonnage men and the machine runners against the latter. The presence of the first Lechner mining machine in the Central Mine at Straitsville, Ohio, threatened the entire wage structure.

Led by the energetic, irrepressible John McBride, a devoted follower of Siney's, the Ohio miners called on their fellow workers in other states to help them in the common struggle. Another short-lived national union called the Amalgamated Association of Miners of the United States was hastily organized in 1883. No sooner had it been formed, than the Hocking men took their tools out of the mine and a long and bitter strike began with clashes between strikers and Pinkertons, company police and vigilantes. Neither the new national organization nor the Ohio miners' union could survive a struggle as prolonged as the Hocking Valley strike turned out to be. Reluctantly in the spring of 1885, McBride called on Chris Evans to order the men back to the mines.

McBride of Massillon, Evans of Straitsville, the bearded Daniel McLaughlin from Braidwood, Illinois, where in a near-by mine a youngster named John Mitchell was swinging a pick against a three-foot vein—these pioneers were tenacious men. With the rank and file of the miners in the soft-coal regions beaten down to an average yearly wage of $239, they nevertheless issued another call for another national union. This time thirty-five delegates from seven states showed up at Indianapolis and there on September 9, 1885, the National Federation of Miners and Mine Laborers was formed.

During the Hocking strike the miners had found an unexpected sympathizer in W. P. Rend, an Ohio operator who said out loud that he could make money paying the scale the union demanded, and urged his fellow operators "to stop this war upon their poor employees." Rend, together with Chris Evans, suggested to the Ohio operators that they arbitrate their differences with the diggers. Judge Allen G.

Thurman was appointed umpire and in December, 1885, he decided that the operators could pay 60 cents a ton and compete with other districts. Encouraged by this, union leaders and more progressive operators organized a joint conference in Columbus, Ohio, on February 24, 1886, at which the first interstate wage agreement covering Ohio, Pennsylvania, Indiana, Illinois, Iowa and West Virginia was signed. A joint board of arbitration was established and the blueprint for today's collective bargaining practices in coal was worked out. Wages ranged from 95 cents a ton in Illinois to 60 cents in the Hocking Valley.

Despite their official endorsement of arbitration and conciliation, the Knights were being drawn, against the protests of the distressed leaders, into the head-on conflicts which labor historians call the "Great Upheaval" of 1884-1887. A rush of unskilled, immigrant workers, the bulk of them of Southern European origin, had vastly swelled the membership of the Knights. During the eighties more than 5 million immigrants entered factories, mines and mills, two and one-half times the number coming to this country in the seventies. Depressed conditions brought on a wave of wage cuts in all industries with resultant strikes of the die-hard Hocking Valley sort. With a bettering of general business conditions in 1885, the more militant of the Knights' organizers led two stunningly successful strikes of workers on the railroads owned by Jay Gould, then generally thought of as the most arrogantly powerful of the rail owners. The Knights' prestige reached its peak in the year following those strikes. Now 700,000 men and women in 6,000 assemblies were proud to proclaim themselves Knights of Labor.

It was in this same year, however, that the Order's supremacy was challenged, and from an unlikely source. On the East Side of New York an English-born Jew named Samuel Gompers, squat, with pale, grayish complexion, his eyes hidden behind heavy spectacles, had been analyzing the triumphs and disasters of the "Great Upheaval" with cold precision. His solution to the labor problem of those days, which was to endure for the next fifty years of labor history, was to concentrate on the organization of skilled workers in craft unions. What of the unskilled and the utopian plans for their uplift through education, co-operation, legislation? All that could wait. Eventually a high wage scale for the craftsmen would have its effects on all payrolls. The standards of living of the men and women in the sheltered, strongly held "business" unions would seep through the whole mass of America's labor force—in the long run. It was a philosophy of compromise, opportunism, a philosophy of no-philosophy, if you like, but it worked. Worked so well that within an amazingly short time the loosely knit trade-unions were to drive the all-powerful Knights from the field.

In 1886 Gompers, with his fellow cigarmaker, the German-born Adolph Strasser, and P. J. McGuire, founder of the carpenters' union, formed the American Federation of Labor in open opposition to the Knights. And in that same year Gompers granted a charter in the Federation to the official miners' union, the National Federation, headed by John McBride as president and Chris Evans as secretary. Though the latter belonged to the Knights as did a large cross section of the National Union's membership, the leaders saw more hope for immediate lightening of the miners' lot through direct and businesslike trade-union tactics than in the long-range program of the old Order.

In the meantime the leaders of the Knights, alarmed at the rise of Gompers and anxious to keep the miners within the fold, had organized a special miners' Assembly, Number 135, duplicating the structure of the National.

With two miners' organizations in the field, there followed four years of disastrous internecine strife. The struggle for jurisdiction, the running sore of the labor movement, set brother against brother, kept the rank and file in anxious turmoil, vastly enheartened the more reactionary among the operators. Conferences between leaders of the rival groups broke up in bitter wrangling. Dirty union and Knights' linen was washed in the public press. The National accused the Knights of accepting wage cuts and derided them for their failure in the much-publicized co-operative mining venture at Cannelburg, Indiana, the first and last attempt of the Knights at co-operative mining.[1] Representatives of the Knights, who also belonged to the union, were refused hearings at conventions of the National.

From the side lines, Samuel Gompers watched this infighting with the keenest interest. He wanted the National to win out. True, the miners' union was not cut to the craft pattern of the Federation of Labor. The union accepted the rawest immigrant laborer as well

[1] The railroads refused to run a spur to the co-op mine.

as the skilled veterans wielding picks in both hard- and soft-coal fields. It took in all workers "in and around the mines," white and black, and it considered with equal concern the grievance of a trapper boy and that of a tonnage man. Further, it organized coke workers and made friendly gestures in the direction of the iron laborers. In its many preambles to its various Constitutions, the union echoed the rhetorical idealism of the Knights' "uplift" pronunciamentos. Altogether, not at all the sort of strictly business union Gompers had in mind when he organized the Federation.

Yet Gompers had eagerly signed the A.F. of L. charter for the miners' union, realizing what a strong weapon this gave him in his fight against the Knights. He realized also that the rank-and-file miner had other things on his mind than reformist regulation of the lusty infant monopolies. What hope had a spokesman for labor in influencing a legislature snugly in the pockets of the railroad corporations? What good was a Bureau of Labor Statistics to a coal miner earning less than $400 a year? As for the most immediate of the Knights' demands, that for an 8-hour day for all labor, Gompers had boldly appropriated this. He was in the forefront of the fight for shorter hours, a fight in which the miners actively participated until the movement was blown up for the time being by the explosion of the bomb in Chicago's Haymarket Square in May, 1886. So, though it was an industrial and no craft union which the shrewd little cigarmaker was chartering, he knew what prestige would accrue to his young Federation by having the National on his side. Soon he could boast of a membership in the Federation's unions of some half million workers.

By the end of 1888, it was plain to the cooler-headed among the leaders on both sides of this Knights-National controversy that its continuance would be disastrous for all labor. A get-together conference between a splinter group from Assembly 135 and the National union was held for the purpose of calling a general convention of both bodies for the formation of a single miners' organization. The name of the National Federation was changed to the National Progressive Union of Miners and Mine Laborers to give the impression of a fresh start, but the leadership of the new union remained in the capable hands of John McBride, Daniel McLaughlin, Chris Evans, soon to be elected secretary of the A.F. of L., and the other founders of the National. From New York, Gompers sent a telegram to this first joint convention: "Unite the miners and mine laborers of the whole country in one grand organization. Remember your present opportunities do not often occur; do not allow them to pass; the man who dares to stand as an obstacle, brush him aside."

Unity, however, was not easily to be won. Conferences behind closed doors dragged on through all the contentious year of '89.

Finally the two sides came together at a unity convention at the City Hall in Columbus, Ohio, on January 23, 1890. Master Workman John B. Rae of Pennsylvania, big-framed, heavily bearded, a somber man, spoke for the Knights. John McBride hammered out the proposals of his union. Rae was elected to preside over the tense convention. When the report of the steering committee was read, the Knights gagged at some of the qualifications for officers of the proposed amalgamated union. The persuasive McBride won them over. Delegates with ancient grudges were allowed to air them. And then John Nugent of Ohio, a Knight, rose to move the acceptance of the steering committee's proposal: "To unite the two organizations under one head, to govern and protect the interest of the miners and mine laborers. This union to be effected without sacrificing the essential features of either organization."

There was silence as the tellers counted the votes and then when Rae announced that the Knights had voted unanimously for the proposal and only ten die-hard unionists had voted against it, a sound such as full-lunged men can produce when deeply moved rattled the windows. Men banged one another on broad backs, wept unashamedly, climbed up on collapsing chairs and yelled "Unity! Unity!" "John Nugent and Alexander Johnson who led the rival organizations in the Hocking Valley, shook hands and swore allegiance to the miners' union, and to show his sincerity, Mr. Johnson kissed Mr. Nugent in the mouth." [2]

The United Mine Workers of America was born.

[2] From the Columbus (Ohio) *Evening Dispatch,* quoted by Chris Evans in *History of United Mine Workers of America.*

VI. "MILLIONAIRES AGAINST MINERS"

JOHN B. RAE, THE SPOKESMAN FOR the Knights at the unity gathering, had learned his mining in Scotland. He had been one of the organizers of the special miners' Assembly 135 and was Master Workman of that body when he came up to Columbus from Pennsylvania. A formidable figure with a high domed head, eyes that shone darkly under heavy brows, and whiskers that cascaded down his chest hiding the front of his stiff, white collar, he looked more like the minister of the gospel he had once been than the leader of the mudsill workers, when he thrust a hand into the bosom of his Prince Albert and exhorted his followers to stand fast.

Miners like their leaders distinguished in appearance, eloquent in address, so they elected Rae to be the first president of the United Mine Workers of America at a salary of $1,500 a year.

The first Constitution of the U.M.W. of A. is a dignified, rather touching document, worthy of a place in the archives of our democracy.

"There is no fact more generally known, nor more widely believed," it begins, "than that without coal there would not be any such grand achievements, privileges and blessings as those which characterize the nineteenth century civilization . . ."

Contrasted to the privileges and blessings is the lot of the nineteenth century miner as set forth in the objects of the U.M.W. of A. Among them are the demand for payment in "lawful money" rather than scrip, the prohibition of child labor below the age of fourteen, more adequate safety laws, and the use of arbitration and conciliation in industrial disputes. The miners from the start had laid special emphasis on their determination "to uncompromisingly demand that eight hours shall constitute a day's work, and that not more than eight hours shall be worked in any one day by any mine worker. The very nature of our employment, shut out from the sunlight and pure air, working by the aid of artificial light (in no instance to exceed one candle-power), would in itself, strongly indicate that, of all men, a coal miner has the most righteous claim to an eight-hour day."

The miners of the nation were divided into districts of the U.M.W. of A., twenty-one of them, with the anthracite workers in District 1. These districts had charge of local affairs under the loosely held supervision of the National Executive Board. Local unions paid monthly dues of 20 cents per member into the national treasury and initiation fees varied from 50 cents to $1 according to local conditions. Discrimination against any qualified union member because of race, creed or nationality was punishable by suspension from the union.

No sooner had Rae taken office, resolved to give as much autonomy to the districts as possible, than he was handed a legacy from the old union in the shape of a strike of the coke workers in the Connellsville region. As this walkout had for one of its chief objectives the 8-hour-day, and as it petered out within three months, after draining the new union's treasury, the whole 8-hour-day movement which the miners were supposed to lead was ignominiously checked. Rae had to withdraw his order for a general walkout of the nation's diggers, and at the convention of the union in 1892 he could report only the failure of four strikes and the fact that the miners were not ready for a mass drive for shorter hours. At this convention, Rae refused to run for re-election and the miners turned once more to John McBride for leadership.

The affable, quick-thinking new president took over an organization with less than 20,000 members, with but $10,000 in the treasury and a sorry record of continued defeats in the field. As though this was not enough, the devastating panic of '92 had caused the Populists to cry out: "Corruption dominates the ballot box, the legislatures, the Congress, and touches even the ermine of the bench. The people are demoralized . . . the newspapers are largely subsidized or muzzled, public opinion silenced; business prostrated; our homes covered with mortgages; labor impoverished; and the land concentrated in the hands of the capitalists." With angry eyes the miners read of the slaughter of their fellow steel workers by the Pinkertons at Homestead. Many out-of-work miners joined in the demonstrations against the railroads led by the insurgent farmers who were to cast a million votes for old General Weaver, the Populist candidate for president. They liked the slogan uttered by the fiery Mary Ellen Lease of Kansas: "Let's quit raising corn and begin raising hell." So many miners were turning to farming when the mines were down that a special "corn-huskers' resolution" was passed at the first convention of the U.M.W. of A. reminding members that they must keep up their dues in the miners' union.

There were no words of cheer from McBride to the delegates to the 1893 convention, and the next year's report was even gloomier. Eugene Victor Debs had thrown up his well-paid job as editor of the *Firemen's Magazine* and quit the conservative Railway Brotherhoods to organize a union of all rail workers, along the lines of the United Mine Workers. The first strike of the new industrial union, the American Railway Union, against the arrogant James J. Hill, head of the Great Northern, had resulted in an amazing rank-and-file victory. The underpaid rail laborers—the maintenance men—under Debs's inspiring leadership fought off a wage cut, obtained a raise in pay within less than a month.

On the heels of this victory, Debs was called on to lead a strike of the employees of the Pullman Company, making cars in a company town outside of Chicago. The strike spread swiftly through the railroads of the Midwest and assumed such proportions that the papers were calling it "The Debs Rebellion." Against the protest of the greathearted Governor of Illinois, John P. Altgeld, President Cleveland sent federal troops into Chicago. These, together with railroad police and special deputies, herded the strikers, while the courts moved against the A.R.U. officials. Debs and his fellow executives were sentenced to the Woodstock jail in Chicago for violating the stern terms of an injunction issued against them. Young Clarence Darrow left a lucrative law job with the railroads to defend Debs, but his skill and eloquence were unavailing.

The injunction against Debs was based on the Sherman Antitrust Act of 1890. Though workers' leaders had been enjoined in connection with the strikes of the Knights, this was the first outstanding example of the large-scale effectiveness of this legal and lethal weapon in the hands of determined men. With their leaders in jail, the railroaders were either forced back to work or blacklisted, and the promising A.R.U. was destroyed. What labor leaders called "a gatling gun on paper" was to be turned from that time on into the ranks of the miners' industrial union at critical times in the union's history. The United Mine Workers' leaders had every reason to look apprehensively at the fate of the A.R.U. Though labor had a new hero in the lanky person of Eugene Debs, the mine owners had a new and powerful ally in the injunction-writing judge.

The cautiously conservative attitude of Gompers had estranged progressives in the A.F. of L. In 1895 McBride left his leadership of the miners to become president of the Federation, the first and only time that Gompers was ever beaten in an election. Phil H. Penna, of Indiana, took McBride's place as head of the United Mine Workers. The '95 convention of the diggers, which cheered Penna's fiery oratory, severed all connections with the Knights which by this time had plainly lost out to the Federation.

These were dark days when the unemployed who had marched out of Massillon following "General" Jacob S. Coxey in the anticlimactic descent on Washington were drifting back across the continent, lending a sympathetic ear to the exhortations of Populists and Socialists; when Altgeld wrote: "Never has there been so much patriotic talk . . . and never were there so many influences at work strangling Republican institutions"; when injunctions "fluttered down like leaves" upon the heads of strike leaders and the miners were taking wage reductions and abandoning their union, which did not seem to know how to fight. In '96 the union had less than $600 in the treasury, and only about 10,000 members. Disheartened, Phil Penna turned over the presidency to big-boned, handsome-featured Michael Ratchford of Ohio. Now Ratchford must make a bold decision if he was to save the union. He made it when he called a national strike of the miners to begin on July 4, 1897.

Though the depression was still on, here and there its clouds were lightening. In some places the promise of "the full dinner pail" in the event of a Republican victory was being redeemed. In the White House, William McKinley was putting heart in the industrialists with tariffs and subsidies. In the wings, Mark Hanna, the most astute of politicians, who had fended off the Democratic threat of "free silver" by the free expenditure of Republican gold, was giving business go-ahead orders. Hanna, by the way, was one large coal operator who saw no profit in fighting his workers. So far as the miners' union was concerned, the Ohio Warwick was as liberal in his labor policies as he was reactionary in national politics. The country was in an "expansionist" mood, on the verge of our first large-scale imperialist adventure in '98 when we all were "remembering the Maine." Reviving industries were calling for coal.

This time the Federation of Labor backed an industrial union, its own affiliate, to the limit. Gompers, back in the saddle, sent men and money to help the miners. For twelve long weeks the miners stayed away from the pits. To be sure, the injunctions rained down again. Men were jailed for combining to restrain interstate commerce, as indeed they were. But the operators were offering only 61 cents a ton in the Pittsburgh district, which was taken as a base for nation-wide union pay, and there was no decent living at such a rate. Finally, with public opinion very much on its side, the union forced an agreement for 65 cents at Pittsburgh—a clean-cut, desperately needed victory for the U.M.W. of A.

Ratchford and his militant miners had finally put a halt to the long retreat of labor through the nineties. The public liked the fighting qualities, and the looks, of this 37-year-old Irishman. When he reported to the 1898 convention, he was being acclaimed as one of the great labor statesmen, even in the usually hostile press. He told his cheering rank and file that as a result of the victory there were now 33,000 members of the U.M.W. of A. and $11,000 in the treasury. A dark-eyed, swarthy youngster from Illinois was elected vice-president of the union at that convention. He was John Mitchell and his fame was soon to eclipse that of Ratchford, or Siney or any other of the pioneer leaders.

John Mitchell was born in Braidwood, Illinois, in 1870. His father was a coal miner who had fought in the Civil War. The elder Mitchell was an active unionist, a friend of John James, the miner-mayor of Braidwood. Another mayor of the little coal town had been Daniel McLaughlin, pioneer union leader. Unionism was in the Mitchell heritage and environment. At eleven the boy was working in a mine as a helper to his stepfather. He was brought up in a deeply religious atmosphere. When in later years he adopted the high collar and ministerial black of men in public life in those days, there were many who took the youth for a Presbyterian parson. John Mitchell's religion, however, was more the mystic philosophy of brotherhood of the Knights of Labor than the Calvinist teachings of his Scotch Presbyterian stepmother. He implemented his religion by his early activities in the Order, which he joined in 1885.

Near Mitchell's home, at Spring Valley in 1888, newly arrived Italians, Poles, Austrians and Hungarians repudiated the idea held by the British-born miners that they would work in the mines for "a kick in the pants and a crust of bread." They struck and struck again in what the wealthy liberal, Henry Demarest Lloyd called "The Strike of Millionaires Against Miners"—strikes, wrote Lloyd, "against slavery in yearly installments," referring to the contracts for a year's work forced on the immigrants by the coal companies. Lloyd sent down a carload of food to the strikers, paid for out of his own pocket; Mitchell at strikers' meetings tried to find words to voice "the welcome men reserve for audacity" as his biographer Elsie Glück puts it. The strikes were lost, but their lessons of careful planning and cautious consideration of every factor that might lead to success were not lost on the young digger from Braidwood. He would never be responsible for calling on men to quit their jobs, no matter how meager those jobs were, unless there was some chance of winning.

Mitchell rose through the union ranks in his home state and in 1897 Ratchford sent him as national organizer to two of the hottest spots on the United Mine Workers' front, West Virginia and Southern Illinois.

South of the Ohio River, Mother Jones (Mary F. Jones) was using the forthright language of suppertime in a miners' boarding-house, over one of which she had once presided in Colorado, to express her contempt for the mine owners and their deputies. Her philosophy was a simple one. All bosses were exploiters who were trompin' on her "boys"—the workers everywhere. What you did was to strike and then strike again and if the scabs came in and tried to take your place it would be just too bad for the scabs. Mother Jones was in jail, no novel situation for the tempestuous woman, when Mitchell arrived with John Walker, a leading Illinois organizer,

to find the union so weak in West Virginia that only 375 miners
there were carrying cards. When Mother Jones was freed she went
to agitating again, but the three organizers could make no headway
against the strongly held lines of the feudal-minded Southern operators.

In Southern Illinois a dark pattern of violence was being laid
down which was to hold in "Egypt" until yesterday. As soon as he
was elected vice-president of the union, Mitchell tackled the critical
condition in his state. Egypt's great coal rush had not yet started
in earnest but the companies already on the scene realized that they
were in potentially rich territory. They had every intention of keeping costs of production down and prices in Chicago and St. Louis
up. They began importing Negro strikebreakers into a country, pre-
dominately southern in its culture, classed as a no-man's-land during
much of the Civil War. Southern Illinois had been settled by mountaineers bringing their feuds and passionate prejudices over with them
from Kentucky. They farmed a little, fought a lot, and when the
first mines were opened they went down into them, caring little
about unionism, but intensely jealous of their independence. The
presence of the imported Negroes, poor wretches who had no idea
of the dangerous ground they were treading, infuriated the Egyptian
diggers. That was all that was needed to make them the most militant
of unionists. They took the union obligation and went home to get
down their shotguns.

A group of armed miners seized the president and superintendent
of a company that had been bringing in strikebreakers. "The boys,"
an old-timer will tell you, "was marching these two bastards down
the road, kicking 'em and proddin' 'em along with their guns. We
kids looked to see a lynching. But then of a sudden, there was Johnny
Mitchell, standing there in the road lookin' kind of tired and sad,
and he held up his hand and spoke to the men who had the two,
and the boys let 'em go, by God, free and clear. But they didn't
bring in any more strikebreakers after that."

Farther north in a local union headquarters there once hung a
full-length enlarged chromo of a huge man, dressed in a long Prince
Albert coat and striped pants. He was wearing at a rather rakish
angle a stovepipe hat and holding proudly in front of him an umbrella decked with red, white and blue ribbons. This was a portrait

of Alexander Bradley, "General" Bradley, who was driving a mule in an Illinois mine when he heard the call of the union. He had won a reputation among his buddies as a writer of verse, mournful and many-stanzaed, describing the grievances of the diggers. Soon he turned his talents to composing a stirring summons to join the union. In response to this, the miners in his pit chose him as their leader and started off on a march to organize all the other mines in the neighborhood.

Seated on a board thrown across a farm wagon drawn by mules, the "general," holding aloft his star-spangled umbrella, led his cheering followers through the adjacent coal fields. At first no more than a few hundred made up the army, but as mine after mine closed down at their coming, the workers fell into line and presently there were a thousand or more men singing union songs and calling on the nonunionists to join them. Sympathetic farmers along the line of march supplied food to the foragers in a commissary wagon. Soon reporters from St. Louis were coming across the river to interview the general at his nightly headquarters by a campfire in some vacant field. The alarmed officials of one strongly antiunion operation kept their workers behind a barricade, and sent out armed deputies to draw a deadline across the road leading into the mine. The deputies had instructions to shoot to kill anyone crossing that line. The general looked over the situation and gave out his orders. The army was to camp that night about a mile from the barricaded mine. The next morning they were to march behind their leader in an orderly column, until he gave the command to halt. There were to be no guns carried, no rough tactics of any sort. At dawn, as the first shift of nonunion men started to work behind the barricades, the general up in front held high his umbrella and the army started down the road. The nervous deputies brought their rifles to their shoulders. A few yards away from the deadline the general boomed out the command to halt. "About face, boys," he called, "we're going back to camp."

At the next sunup the tactics were repeated; the deadline reached, the general wheeled round and led his men away, leaving jangled nerves around the barricades. The second night the leader called in his subordinates and said: "I'm going in tomorrow, but I'm going to be first to cross that line. If anybody's going to get killed or whatever, it will be General Bradley. You understand, no guns on our side."

For the third successive morning the guards saw the union miners come swinging down the road. So did the nonunion men of the day shift peering through the barricades. But this time when the deadline was reached, the general roared out, "I'm coming in, get out of my way." The deputies hesitated for a moment, saw that the mule driver meant what he said, and then broke. As the general stepped over the deadline, the guards threw away their rifles and made an undignified rush for the barricades. The army roared its delight as one of the terrified deputies hanged himself up by the seat of his pants to a sharp-pointed paling. The nonunion men swarmed out to grasp the huge hands of their deliverer, standing smiling, on their side of the deadline.

Across the way from St. Louis, later on, the army was camping in a ball park, when they missed the general. The commissary was low, one or two mines had not come out, and there were ugly rumors from town that Bradley had been seen drinking with some St. Louis operators. A committee started out to find the lost leader when a wagon was seen approaching the camp with a high-hatted, frock-coated man on the seat waving a beribboned umbrella. It was General Bradley all right, but where had he got those fancy duds? The general would explain. When the army assembled, the general reared up in his full sartorial glory and told how he had been secretly sent for to meet with the St. Louis mine owners. He met them in a downtown saloon, and there, after many drinks, they gave him $200 as bribe money.

"I figured your general needed some clothes that was befitting your leader," said Bradley, "so I got me these duds, secondhand. But here is all the rest of the money," he went on, bringing from his back pocket a roll of dollar bills and flinging it out to the crowd with a free-handed gesture, "go get yourself eats, boys, the goddam operators is paying for it."

The army ate well that night and the next day they were off again with the general in front, organizing the union across all that territory.

Sterner business was under way farther north, at Virden, Illinois, where the Chicago-Virden Coal Company attempted to break a strike in the fall of 1898. Colored miners from Alabama were coming into the coal camp daily, despite the warnings of union officials that serious trouble was sure to follow. Trouble of the sort that had happened at near-by Pana when strikers and Negroes fought it out on the streets of the little town, with several strikebreakers dead at the end of the battle. Nevertheless, the mine manager insisted on bringing a trainload of colored laborers up a siding to a stockade erected in front of his mine. In the melee that ensued, with the guards firing from behind the stockade, seven union miners were killed and eight wounded, and five guards were fatally shot. Governor John Tanner, of Illinois, sent in troops and gave orders to the operators that no more strikebreakers be imported. Mitchell, on his arrival at Virden after the riot, was placed under arrest charged with inciting his men. The charge against the young union leader, whose whole philosophy was based on nonviolence, was never pressed.

In this war year of 1898, the new organizing strength of the United Mine Workers was revealed by the acceptance on the part of the operators in the Central Competitive Field—Illinois, Indiana, Ohio and Western Pennsylvania—of the long-demanded 8-hour day. Phil Penna, now representing the operators as an Indiana commissioner, had persuaded his new employers that it would be to their advantage to yield to the union's insistence on shorter work hours. There was the unusual spectacle of the union miners at a joint conference, rising to cheer an operator's spokesman when Penna came on the platform.

As the year closed, the young vice-president took over the duties of Ratchford, who had resigned to accept a position as a member of the United States Industrial Commission. At the 1899 convention John Mitchell was elected fifth president of the United Mine Workers of America at the age of twenty-nine. His salary was $1,200 a year. He reported that in the past year the union had participated in 260 strikes of which 160 were won, 29 compromised, 36 lost and 35 still pending. The new president was leading men who were feeling their united strength, tasting the first sweet fruits of victory after long years of defeats. Within the next few years this man, with his hair growing low on his high forehead, his dark, brooding eyes, and his sensitive mouth—the physiognomy of the poet or priest—was to take the miners, "the shock troops of American labor," to the acknowledged leadership of all the union world. His name was to be spoken with those of the great of the land and his people were to worship him as few leaders have ever been worshiped in our history.

THE YEAR JOHN MITCHELL TOOK UP the president's gavel, 270,000 miners were taking 193 million tons of bituminous coal out of the ground. There were 82,000 soft-coal diggers in the union. Over in the anthracite fields of Pennsylvania, however, where there was an annual production of more than 50 million tons, only some 9,000 miners were organized. These last sent a Macedonian call to the United Mine Workers headquarters in the Stevenson Building in Indianapolis. Such wage scales as the unionists could get were ranging from $2.66 a day for a fire boss to $2.23 for a company miner and less than a dollar a day for outside driver boys. Though the operators insisted that a skilled miner under his contract could earn $150 a month working full time in a good seam, when the miner-subcontractor had paid his laborer $2 a day and further paid for his powder, oil, fuses, etc., there wasn't much of this $150 left. And of course few miners worked full time on good seams.

Homer Greene, who was well acquainted with the conditions in the anthracite mines at the end of the nineteenth century, wrote:

The miner's appearance as he passes along the street or road on his way home from work is, to eyes unaccustomed to the sight, anything but favorable. He wears heavy hob-nailed boots, flannel shirt, coarse jacket and pantaloons, all of them black with coal dirt and saturated with oil. He has a habit when he comes from his work, of throwing his coat loosely about his shoulders, and wearing it as he goes to his home. He usually wears a cap on his head, sometimes a slouch hat, rarely the helmet or fireman's hat with which artists are accustomed to picture him. This latter is too heavy and clumsy for common use; he only puts it on when working in places where water comes down freely on his head. Hooked to the front of his cap is the little tin lamp. When he goes to or from his work in the dark he allows it to burn and light him on his way. His face and hands are black with coal dirt and powder smoke, and his features are hardly recognizable.[1]

Or as a poet of the miners, George Dresch, had it:

> Tired and hungry he comes from the mine,
> Limping along with a kink in his spine.
> He reaches his shack more dead than alive—
> He's been in the dungeon from seven to five.

It was not in the mine itself, however, but rather in the most important mechanical contribution America has made to the industry—the breaker—that a visitor to the hard-coal fields found the most shocking conditions.

Gideon Best, of Wolf Creek, Pennsylvania, designed and operated the first breaker at a colliery at Minersville where with circular screens and cast-iron rolls he broke and cleaned two hundred tons of coal a day. In 1870 at the Hill and Harris colliery at Mahonoy City the picking table was introduced into the huge, winged buildings, alongside the mine mouths, that are still at the heart of the industry. For anthracite requires careful preparation before it is ready for market. The hard coal must be broken into uniform sizes: it does not fall to pieces when burned as does bituminous, but burns from the inside out. When 150,000 men are at work in the hard coal only about 40,000 of them are actually digging the coal. The rest are at work outside the mine "servicing" the product of the picks.

With the introduction of the picking table, a very real slavery fell upon the small boys of the mining region. The lot of the trapper boys and the mule drivers was light compared with that of the breaker boy.

Greene wrote:

At seven o'clock in the morning he [the breaker boy] must have climbed the dark and dusty stairway to the screen room and taken his place on the little bench across the long chute. The whistle screams, the ponderous machinery is set in motion, the iron-teethed rollers begin to revolve heavily, crunching the big lumps of coal as they turn, the deafening noise breaks

[1] *Coal and the Coal Mines*, p. 228, Boston, Houghton Mifflin Co.

forth, and then the black, shallow streams of broken coal start on their journey down the iron-sheathed shutes to be screened and cleaned, picked and loaded.

At first glance it would not seem to be a difficult task to pick slate, but there are several things to be taken into consideration, before a judgment can properly be made up in this matter. To begin with, the work is confining and monotonous. The boy must sit on his bench all day, bending over constantly to look down on the coal that is passing beneath him. His tender hands must become toughened by long and constant contact with sharp pieces of slate and coal, and after many cuts and bruises have left marks and scars on them for a lifetime. He must breathe an atmosphere thick with the dust of coal, so thick that one can barely see across the screen room when the boys are sitting at their tasks.

It is no wonder that a person long subjected to the irritating presence of this dust in his bronchial tubes and on his lungs is liable to suffer from the disease known as "miner's consumption."

In the hot days of summer the screen room is a stifling place. The sun pours its rays upon the broad, sloping roof of the breaker just overhead: the dust-laden atmosphere is never cleared or freshened by so much as a breath of pure, sweet air and the very thought of green fields and blossoming flowers and the swaying branches of trees renders the task here to be performed more burdensome. Yet even this is not so bad as it is to work here in the cold days of winter. It is almost impossible to heat satisfactorily so rambling a structure as the coal-breaker necessarily is, and it is quite impossible to divide the portion devoted to screening and picking in closed rooms. The screen-rooms, therefore, are always cold. Stoves are often set up in them but they radiate heat through only a limited space, and cannot be said to make the room warm. Notwithstanding the presence of stoves, the boys on the benches shiver at their tasks, and picking slate with numb fingers, suffer from the extreme cold through many a winter day.

But science [Greene was writing in 1889] and the progress of ideas are coming to their aid. In some breakers, recently erected, steam-heating pipes have been introduced into the screen rooms with great success: the warmth and comfort given by them to the little workers is beyond measurement. Fans have been put into the breakers also, to collect and carry away the dust and keep the air of the picking room clean and fresh, and electric lights have been swung from the beams to be lighted in the early mornings and late afternoons, so that the young toilers may see to do their work. Indeed such improvements as these pass beyond the domain of science and progress into that of humanitarianism.

When night comes no laborer is more rejoiced at leaving his task than is the breaker boy. One can see his eyes shine and his white teeth gleam as he starts into the open air, while all else, hands, face, clothing, are thickly covered with coal dust, are blackened unrecognizably. But he is happy because his day's work is done and he is free, for a few hours at least, from the tyranny of the "cracker boss." For in the estimation of the picker boys, the cracker boss is indeed the most tyrannical of all masters. How else could they regard a man whose sole duty it is to be constantly in their midst, to keep them at their tasks, to urge them to greater zeal and care, to repress all boyish freaks, to rule over them almost literally with a rod of iron? But alas! the best commentary on the severity of his government is that it is necessary.

Mitchell, going out to the collieries, was impressed neither with the "humanitarianism" of fans and electric lights nor with the "necessity" for the tyranny of the cracker bosses. He watched the breaker boys trudging away to their blackened homes in company with the tired youngsters who had been driving mules or trapping doors in the far darkness of the mines—boys who in spite of state laws forbidding the employment of children under fourteen years of age within the mines and setting limits of twelve for outside boys, were in many cases much younger than the legal limit. He recalled his own darkened youth back in Braidwood and was resolved to end this hideous business.

Before Mitchell started to work on the most difficult problem of his crowded career, union organizers had been in hard coal setting up locals for the handling of grievances, from the prices of the "pluck-me stores" and the rents for the company shacks to false weights and the ordeals of the picking tables. These locals were, it is true, mainly skeletons of organizations, refused recognition by the anthracite railroads, their chief function being to give union organizers a clear picture of the job ahead of them.

Mitchell moved into battle with characteristic preparation. He had the realities of the workways of anthracite at his slim finger tips. He had documents galore, affidavits as to unfair weights, statements of conditions from the mouths of the boys at the tables and at the doors, pay slips and rent bills and the prices charged for powder and oil, together with the figures showing the great gap between the pay the miner got for a ton and what the consumer in Philadelphia, New York and Boston paid for that same ton in his bin.

He called on influential liberals in the Pennsylvania cities, on politicians and newspaper editors, on priests and parsons and the agnostic followers of Robert Ingersoll, on small-town Republican lawyers and lone-wolf Socialists next door. He had no publicity man and needed none. The factual-minded he won to his cause by showing them his printed proof of corporate cruelty. Others were disarmed by the quiet integrity of the man, in no way resembling the flannel-mouthed "walking delegate" of the cartoonist's imaginings.

By the middle of August, 1900, Mitchell was ready to start firing. He called a convention in Hazleton to present grievances and await the answer of the railroad mine owners to the union's demands for a 10 per cent advance in wages and recognition of the United Mine Workers. When no answer was forthcoming, Mitchell called a strike throughout the anthracite fields on September 17th. There were, as we have seen, but 9,000 dues-paying union members in the collieries. Could this handful of loyal unionists persuade their fellow workers to come out in response to Mitchell's call? Mitchell didn't have to wait long for his answer. Before the strike was a week old, 112,000 miners out of a total labor force of 145,000 in hard coal had grounded their tools.

With the approach of cold weather, the operators, discovering an unexpected weight of public opinion behind the strikers, offered a 10 per cent increase. But Mitchell insisted on recognition of the union as well and the powerful Philadelphia and Reading Railroad Company, soon to be followed by the others, posted notices at the collieries accepting the union's terms. Mitchell, in an unusually assertive mood, said that this was "the only great contest in which the workers came out entirely and absolutely victorious." To his next convention he was able to report the unionization of anthracite and the startingly increased membership of 232,289 in both hard and soft coal. October 29th, the day on which the anthracite strike of 1900 was ended, has been set apart by the miners of this country as "Mitchell Day" ever since.

For all the exultation of the miners and the lavish praise of Mitchell's industrial statesmanship in a formerly hostile press, the problem of anthracite organization arose once more in aggravated form a short two years after the first great strike. This time there were no immediate political complications as in 1900, when many high in Republican circles had put indirect pressure upon the mine owners to settle before the national election. Mitchell had watched with worried eyes the breaking out of unauthorized "wildcat" strikes, violations of the agreement on both sides, the erecting of stockades at the big collieries, spying and blacklisting—all the ominous preparations for a new war. He told his followers that a strike in 1902 might be a losing one and advised against it. Nevertheless, when the operators flatly rejected Mitchell's request for a wage conference for a renewal of the agreement in February, the young president knew what was coming.

On the 12th of May, 140,000 anthracite miners, with no contracts signed, walked out in what was officially called a "stoppage" but which meant that no coal would come down the breakers until the matter was settled.

Now Mitchell had need of all the public's good will he had won two years ago, all the faith in him of the men and women of the most remote camps. This was a faith he had enkindled when, taking a leaf from old Dan Weaver's book, he had said: "The coal you dig isn't Slavish or Polish or Irish coal—it's just coal." To the aloof American- and British-born diggers he spoke words of warning against talking about "Hunks and Dagoes." To the Hungarians and Italians, with Bishop Hoban of Scranton and Father Curran of Wilkes-Barre at his side, he told the story of the union's democratic origins and gave them the chance to dream again those dreams of freedom that had brought them so hopefully to the Pennsylvania hillsides. No wonder they thought he was a holy man of some strange New World sort, and put his picture alongside the pictures of their saints. Now they were saying "Johnny da Mitch will win."

Far beyond the anthracite counties. men took heed of the coming struggle. Mitchell, unlike so many labor leaders, welcomed the aid of the intellectuals. It was not his idea that a man could be of no help to the movement because he was better at a typewriter than a pick. He had strong allies in such men as Walter Weyl, his collaborator on his book, *Organized Labor,* John Commons, the great historian of the movement, John Graham Brooks, Henry Demarest Lloyd. In Chicago, Clarence Darrow was drawling: "If you put a gun to man's head and force him to give you ten cents to buy food, it's robbery. If the coal barons get all the coal in the world and let the people freeze, it's business." [2]

[2] Quoted by Irving Stone in his *Clarence Darrow for the Defense,* p. 127.

Mark Hanna and Ralph Easley, founding spirits of the National Civic Federation, an organization with the object of getting labor and capital at the same table—"an heterogeneous concatenation of genus homo" if there ever was one—tried in vain to persuade the operators led by the hard-boiled, highly religious George F. Baer, president of the mine-owning Philadelphia and Reading Railroad Company, to talk things over with the union. This time, however, the owners were in a fighting mood. They saw a strike of the West Virginia soft-coal diggers collapsing before the hard-riding state troopers and the coal and iron police, and another strike fold up in Alabama. They knew that Mitchell had only $100,000 in the national treasury and that he was being attacked by the radicals in his own ranks for not calling a general strike of the bituminous workers. If he had done so, there would have been little for the conduct of the hard-coal struggle. As it was, he fought down the opposition, and instead of calling out the soft-coal men, he assessed them a dollar a week per member for the support of the anthracite strike.

In July, the militia fired on a march of pickets outside Shenandoah and George Baer wrote a letter. It was to a stockholder of his railroad, who has gone down in labor history only as Mr. Clark, "a photographer." Mr. Clark was seemingly concerned about the way things were going. Wrote "George the First," as Darrow dubbed him:

My Dear Mr. Clark:

I have your letter of the 16th inst. I do not know who you are. I see that you are a religious man; but you are evidently biased in favor of the right of the workingman to control a business in which he has no other interest than to secure fair wages for the work he does.

I beg of you not to be discouraged. The rights and interests of the laboring man will be protected and cared for—not by the labor agitators, but by the Christian gentlemen to whom God has given control of the property rights of the country and upon the successful management of which so much depends. Do not be discouraged. Pray earnestly that the right may triumph, always remembering that the Lord God Omnipotent still reigns and that His reign is one of law and order, and not of violence and crime.

Very truly yours,
George Baer, President

Wounded miners who had been marching unarmed at Shenandoah when the guardsmen fired into them, Socialists enjoined, clubbed and jailed for exercising the rights of free speech at strike meetings, the more profane of the operators and in especial their horrified press agents, read the pious words of President Baer with mixed emotions. Here was another "gatling gun on paper," this time to be turned on the owners. Even the most rabid antiunion newspapers gagged at the arrogance of "Divine Right" Baer, and his "Christian gentlemen."

Through the long summer the ranks of the strikers held firm. From the soft-coal miners and members of other unions enough relief money was coming in to keep the pickets on their feet and to give heart to the womenfolk of the strikers who in the long run can win or lose any such struggle. ("The strike is decided over the cookstove.") And now in October, with every mail that reached the White House demanding action to stop the struggle, Theodore Roosevelt sent for Mitchell. With the heads of the three anthracite districts, T. D. Nicholls, Thomas Duffy and John Fahy, Mitchell presented his people's case to a President who had no reason to love Baer and the other anthracite owners. The two presidents hit it off at once. Roosevelt liked Mitchell's quiet tenacity, Mitchell enjoyed the outgoing robustiousness of the man who was even now becoming suspect of Wall Street. Years later, ex-President Roosevelt in the old *Outlook* office talking to a group of newspapermen, of which the author was a member, pounded the desk in his enthusiasm as he shouted: "John Mitchell! They didn't come any finer."

Roosevelt could check on what Mitchell told him of conditions in the hard coal from the measured reports brought back from the fields by his special investigator, Carroll D. Wright, commissioner of labor. T.R. looked sternly from behind his pince-nez when Mitchell and his lieutenants talked about the 20,000 boys in the mines, between the ages of ten to sixteen. This was human stuff that meant more to the impulsive man in the White House than all of Wright's carefully marshaled statistics. Then Roosevelt had in the operators, Baer, and President W. H. Truesdale of the D.,L. and W., and W. T. P. Fowler of New York, Ontario and Western, and David Wilcox of the Delaware and Hudson.

Baer had learned nothing from the reception of his now famous letter. He growled at Roosevelt:

"Government is a contemptible failure if it can only protect the lives and property and secure the comfort of the people by compromising with the violators of the law and the instigators of violence and crime."

Then T.R. spoke some emphatic words and the conference broke up. "There was only one man in that conference," said Roosevelt after it was over, "who behaved like a gentleman and that was not I." Mitchell, still the gentleman, courteously refused to go into another White House conference with the obdurate railroad owners. He had read an interview with Baer in which the magnate had scoffed at the idea that the miners were suffering:

"They don't suffer; why, they can't even speak English."

Then of a sudden there arrived at the White House, on October 13th, the head of the New York banking house whose word was last on the whole contentious matter. "The operators will arbitrate," said J. P. Morgan, and all that Baer and the rest had to say went out the window. Ten days later the miners went back to work to await the decision of the arbitration commission appointed by Roosevelt. The strike had lasted 163 days and had cost the railroads, the mine operators and the miners an estimated $100 million.

At the hearings before the commission presided over by Judge George Grey of Wilmington, Mitchell sat alongside the sprawling Darrow, his chief counsel, and the impeccably clad, aristocratic Lloyd. These three men, with backgrounds as different as only the American scene could provide, faced the twenty-three lawyers for the operators, the pick of the American bar. Toward the end of the two months' hearing, Darrow, according to Irving Stone, his biographer, said that the operators had all the advantages. "Their social advantages are better; they speak the English language better; they can hire expert accountants; they have got the advantage of us in almost every particular." And then Stone tells us: "Judge Grey, glancing over at the battery of twenty-three corporation counsels, murmured with a faint smile: 'Except the lawyers.'"

Before the hearings started, the commissioners and Darrow and Lloyd had surveyed every cross section of the anthracite scene at first hand. Darrow had seen the pictures of Mitchell among the devotional images on the walls of the miners' shacks, he had talked with the youngsters from the picking benches and the underground mule stables, and with the skilled Welsh and Irish pickmen, and with supers and cracker bosses and the company guards. The United Mine Workers set up headquarters in a house on Vine Street, Philadelphia, near where the final hearings were held in the Federal Courthouse, and there the "Big Three," as the papers called them, prepared a carefully documented, emotionally charged case for the American miner against the industrial civilization under which he labored. Never before and rarely since has the American public had such a close-up view of what men do and hope and fear when they go down to the pits—one out of every forty American wage earners who earns his living by mining. The miners' representatives asked to see the books of the operators.

"This move to force industry to bring its books into the court of public opinion was for the mass of American working people almost as great a revolution as the one that had taken place in 1776," wrote Stone in *Clarence Darrow for the Defense*.

"The newspaper accounts," went on Stone, "broadcast to every crevice of the nation soon showed the public that this man Darrow was raising startlingly basic questions that they had never heard of before, revolutionary questions, really, going far beyond the immediate question of whether the miners were entitled to a raise. Could the coal mines pay a living wage and still earn a sufficient profit to justify remaining in business? Which was of greater importance to maintain, a living wage for workers or a dividend for stockholders? When business fell off, which should be cut first, wages or dividends?"

For four long days Mitchell was on the stand cross-examined by Wayne MacVeagh and other lawyers for the operators. At the end of the ordeal, MacVeagh, one of the nation's outstanding cross-examiners, said:

"Mr. Mitchell, you are the best witness for yourself I have ever faced in my life."

To the witness stand came 240 human exhibits of the ways of mining coal in Pennsylvania; crippled and maimed and sick, a skilled veteran working in a "parlor vein" making $20 every two weeks after the company had checked off his debts, a breaker boy earning 62 cents a week, families evicted in the middle of the night for nonpayment of rent for the company houses.

When Baer faced Darrow, the latter asked the rail president

about the child workers. "The unions," said Baer, "are corrupting the children of America by letting them join their illegal organizations."

"If the children," thundered Darrow, "had not been at work in the mine they could not have joined the union."

Darrow, admonished by Mitchell not to make "a Socialist speech," concentrated in his summation on wages, hours and conditions, not however without this Darrowesque peroration:

"The laborer who asks for shorter hours, asks for a breath of life; he asks for a chance to develop the best that is in him. It is no answer to say, 'If you give him shorter hours he will not use them wisely.' Our country, our civilization, our race is based on the belief that for all his weaknesses there is still in man that divine spark that will make him reach upward for something higher and better than anything he has known."

A strange thing happened when Baer had finished his able defense of the role of the owner in industry. Mitchell went across the courtroom and shook hands with his chief adversary. To this day veteran diggers speak of that gesture with perplexment. It might have been, they figure, that Mitchell, wearied of incessant warfare, wanted peace with honor. At all events, from that time on, the course of the president of the U.M.W. of A. ran more and more to conciliation.

On March 21, 1903, the commission announced the results of its consideration of the ten thousand pages of evidence. Contract miners got a 10 per cent raise with a scale hitched to rising coal prices. Company men were on a 9-hour day. The miners were to elect their own checkweighmen. A six-man board of conciliation was to handle all disputes. On the board were to be members of the U.M.W. of A. There was no outright recognition of the union, aside from this. Here was no such clear-cut victory as in 1900; on the other hand, the union had fought off a mass attack and gone forward in counterattack. Debs and Socialists in the miners' union denounced the decision, as did Mother Jones with emphasis. The public as a whole looked on it as a triumph for Mitchell and the union.

When Mitchell took up the gavel at the 1903 convention of the U.M.W. of A., representatives of 175,000 miners cheered their youthful leader. Secretary W. B. Wilson, later to be secretary of labor, reported that there was a balance of $1,027,000 in the treasury.

VIII. A JOINER FROM COSHOCTON

JUDGE THOMAS MELLON, FATHER OF the "Greatest Secretary of the Treasury since Alexander Hamilton," made a neat profit when his coal barges turned up in the nick of time to fuel Admiral Farragut's fleet off New Orleans in 1862. In another war, Andrew W. Mellon, head of Pittsburgh's Union Trust Company, followed his father's lead and added to the Mellon millions by selling coal to the government in 1898. With Henry Clay Frick, young Mellon was owner of rich acres of coal fields along the Monongahela and Youghiogheny rivers. The two enterprising men were very much on the ground floor when the rush for the soft-coal fields outside of Pittsburgh broke in full fury at the turn of the century.

"The entire Monongahela Valley went coal mad," writes Harvey O'Connor in *Mellon's Millions*. "Farmers forsook their plows to drive sharp bargains with land hawks who bought only with an eye to quick resale. Hundreds of thousands of acres were sold and resold. It seemed for a time that the money was not so much in coal-mining as in juggling the black-seamed acres."

Mellon persuaded the government to deepen the Monongahela and abolish tolls on the waterway. He and Frick organized first the Monongahela River Consolidated Coal and Coke Company ("River Coal") and then the Pittsburgh Coal Company. The two then consolidated river and rail mines in a formidable merger which at one time owned 150 mines in the Pittsburgh region with 80,000 acres of coal lands, 5,000 coal cars, and a veritable river fleet of steamboats and barges doing business in Cincinnati, Louisville, Vicksburg, Baton

Rouge and New Orleans, and shipping 4 million tons a year to the Great Lakes.

On a smaller scale, in Southern Illinois, legitimate coal operators and wildcat promoters swarmed across Egypt snapping up vast acreage from the bewildered farmers. Near Herrin, John ("Bet-a-million") Gates took title to a great block of Williamson County coal. At the little town of Zeigler, a young Chicago millionaire named Joseph Leiter, whose wife was the Mrs. Malaprop of the Windy City (she told a society reporter that she was going to a masquerade ball in "the garbage of a nun"), bought a solid block of 7,000 acres and brought down purchasing agents for the roads and the United States Steel Company.

From the boom year of 1900 to the panic of 1907, there was a concentration of ownership in bituminous along the lines of the pattern long laid down by the railroads in anthracite. To do business with the real owners, union leaders had to go to Wall Street and La Salle Street or the chilly sanctum of the Union Trust in Pittsburgh. It began to look as though the time had come when, in the words of Thorstein Veblen, "In coal, iron and transportation the conversion of public necessities into private assets has already reached a passably settled and conclusive state, so that these means of production are now held securely in absentee ownership and managed on the sound business principle of charging what the traffic will bear."

In the case of soft coal, however, geology, aeons ago, had written a veto to any comprehensive monopolization by absentee ownership. The newcomers in the bituminous field soon stumbled over the harsh realities of soft coal's unexpected appearances under lands next door to the supposedly monopolized territories. George Otis Smith, a student of the industry, once said: "Nature enforces the antitrust statutes in the bituminous industry." Across the way from the corporation holdings, groups of farmers would sink "gopher holes," small operations, with the coal carried off in wagons. Soon these wagon mines, underselling the corporations with their heavier production costs, would expand and presently there would be another full-fledged coal company in the field. And the old competitive cycle would get under way to the grim sounds of collective throat cutting.

In view of the fact that wages constitute 60 to 70 per cent of the cost of production, the first thought of the hard-pressed manager was to cut his miners' pay. North of the Ohio River, where the miners carried U.M.W. cards, this could not be done short of war. But in Tennessee, Alabama, Kentucky and West Virginia, there was little organization, and to these southern fields there began in this period a slow drift of mining entrepreneurs.

The alternative to wage cutting seemed to the management to be the introduction of laborsaving machinery. Against the machines, Mitchell and his lieutenants, in the long tradition of the union, waged no war. But they insisted that the wages of the machine men be subject to collective bargaining. The problem was a serious and growing one. In 1900 there were 3,907 machines in our mines cutting 25 per cent of the total output. Seven years later 11,144 machines cut 36 per cent of all the coal mined. In 1902 there was a total electric horsepower of 493,148 at work in the mines. More than a million horsepower was used in 1909. Tonnage output per man per day in 1900 was 2.98, by 1907 it was 3.29. Still the number of bituminous miners continued to grow, from 304,000 in 1900 to 513,000 in 1907. Evidently neither the trend to concentration nor the increasing use of laborsaving machines was checking the opening of more and more soft-coal mines.

Political as well as economic problems confronted the leaders of the miners in the years of comparative business (and hence mining) prosperity from the end of the second great anthracite strike to 1907. The newly organized Socialist party of America, formed as the result of an alliance between Eugene V. Debs and Victor Berger in the Midwest and the radical needleworkers in the East, was making dramatic progress. The younger miners were won by the indigenous, non-Marxist socialism of the eloquently emotional Debs and their spokesmen looked skeptically upon the cautious policies of Mitchell. When the president of the miners accepted a 5 per cent wage cut for his soft-coal miners in lieu of a strike in 1904, he was raked fore and aft by militant Socialists, inside and outside the union. The next year a far more bitter critic of Mitchell's than was the essentially gentle Debs came up out of a copper mine in Idaho. This was William D. Haywood, boisterous leader of the industrial union of the metal miners, the Western Federation of Miners.

Many union coal miners were in the audience that cheered "Big Bill" Haywood when he opened the first convention of the Industrial

Workers of the World at Chicago on June 27, 1905, by proclaiming: "Fellow workers! This is the Continental Congress of the Working Class. We are here to confederate the workers of the country into a working class movement that shall have for its purpose the emancipation of the working class from the slave bondage of capitalism. There is no organization, or there seems to be no labor organization, that has for its purpose the same object as that for which you are called together today. The aims and objects of this organization shall be to put the working class in possession of the economic power, the means of life, in control of the machinery of production and distribution, without regard to capitalist masters."

On the platform behind Haywood sat Mother Jones, who had resigned as organizer for the United Mine Workers as protest against the compromising tactics of Mitchell in the course of a bitter strike of the Colorado coal miners in 1903. The vigorous woman used all her arsenal of vituperation to express her disgust at the spectacle of Mitchell and Gompers sitting down with August Belmont and other millionaires at banquets of the National Civic Federation. No handshaking with the enemy for the fiery founders of the "Wobblies," as the I.W.W. were promptly nicknamed. They were hell-bent for the One Big Union, the general strike, an anarchosyndicalist order of society with industrial unions running the show and political action definitely out. Miner delegates to that colorful convention went back to the fields resolved to move the slim figure of John Mitchell farther to the left. With the Socialists, who for the time being had given their official blessing to the I.W.W., they formed an able and aggressive opposition bloc. They echoed on the floors of local unions and national conventions the words of Debs: "There is certainly something wrong with that form of unionism which has its chief support in the press that represents capitalism; something wrong in that form of unionism that forms an alliance with such capitalist combinations as the Civic Federation whose sole purpose is to chloroform the working class while the capitalist class goes through their pockets."

Still Mitchell had behind him the prestige of the two great struggles in anthracite and he could still persuade his membership in 1906 that the best way to end what was politely called a "suspension" in both the hard- and soft-coal fields was to sign agreements in the separate districts rather than to hold out for a national contract. This arrangement, satisfactory to no one, except the most intransigent operators, discontinued for a time the Central Competitive Field agreements and made Mitchell a potent enemy in the person of his vice-president, Thomas L. Lewis, who moved into the opposition ranks, making common cause with the radicals.

When the opposition reached its crescendo at the 1907 convention, Mitchell finally turned to his own defense:

"I am trying as best I can to promote a feeling of friendly business relations between the employers and ourselves, but my desire and my efforts to promote friendly reciprocal business relations do not detract one iota from my impatient desire to see the mine workers of this country among the best paid, the most humanely employed of all the workers of this land."

The radicals would not hear of "friendly reciprocal business relations." They wanted to know what was going on in unorganized West Virginia. In 1897, they pointed out, an organizer could go freely around that state. But now in 1907, "about the time you leave Cincinnati, you would have a company bodyguard to attend you." There were ugly charges that the nonunion West Virginia operators were keeping a lobby at the U.M.W. of A. headquarters at Indianapolis; charges that when he was a delegate to a mining congress abroad Mitchell had "wined and dined" with wealthy employers; charges that the change from the soft black hat of his pioneer days to the derby he wore to National Civic Federation meetings was emblematic of the change in the wearer. Charges ranging all the way from outright collusion to personal ways of life. And all of them striking cruelly—the more unfounded the more painful—so that Mitchell, talking about Siney and what his rank and file had done to that leader, fell ill, and from his sickbed handed in his resignation.

At the convention in 1908, which was to receive Mitchell's last report, William Green of Coshocton, Ohio, president of the Ohio subdistrict, was temporary chairman. Green had joined with T. L. Lewis and the Socialists in attacking Mitchell's policies. But all was forgiven at this emotional farewell convention at which even "Big Bill" Haywood lumbered up to praise Mitchell.

Gifts were piled high at the table at which Mitchell stood to say good-bye to the delegates. There were loving cups of all sizes and there were the words of a delegate from a remote little mining camp:

"We can't give you a cup, John, but you have the love from our hearts." Turning over the money gifts to his wife, Mitchell made his last speech to men who looked up at him through tears. He talked of the children still working in the mines, not only in Pennsylvania but in other states as well, and urged the miners to fight for a law making a minimum age exemption throughout the nation sixteen years. He warned of the march of mining machinery and the day when the skilled worker would be in the minority. He spoke for better safety laws. And then he had finished, this man from the pits of Braidwood who had taken his people out of their silent despair to a place under the American sun where they could stand as free men. He had compromised, he had led some retreats as well as surging forward marches; but he had built a declining organization of 33,000 harassed workers into a mighty union of 263,000. "God bless you, John," they called after him as he went out of the hall. "God bless you, John."

With the passing of Mitchell, the scramble among the epigones resulted in the election of Mitchell's most articulate opponent within the union, T. L. Lewis of Ohio. This bald, heavy-browed digger of whom they said, "If a feller asked Tom to walk down the street and get a good dinner, and another feller invited him down an alley to have a fight, Tom would go down the alley," fought his own rank and file as vigorously as he fought the operators. Any convention presided over by T. L. Lewis promptly turned into a free-for-all. Lewis howled at the Socialists and the mildly protesting William Green. He bellowed at big Frank Farrington and John Walker, from the hard-hitting Illinois miners, at Alex Howat of Kansas, and at the dignified, handsome John P. White, head of the Iowa District. To Lewis is generally attributed the perfecting of the self-perpetuating political machine through the appointment of national organizers, part of whose duties are to build fences for the administration in power. At repeated conventions the efforts of the progressives to break this strange device by the general election of organizers have met with failure. Today it remains an ominous flaw in the democratic structure of the United Mine Workers.

The first job Lewis undertook was to restore the old Central Competitive Field. While Pennsylvania, Ohio and Indiana operators signed a joint agreement, the Illinois operators wouldn't come along as a body. This was the beginning of the "exceptionalism" which has ever since marked Illinois union activities. The miners of the state organized to a man, in the van of every progressive movement in the union, have played the lone-wolf role time and again, coming out of negotiations with wage scales higher than those in other parts of the country. For their part, the Illinois operators have frequently neglected the headquarters of the U.M.W. of A. at Indianapolis to go straight to the substantial office building owned by District 12 in the heart of Springfield.

"Seems like every time two moneybags down in Wall Street get to swinging at each other they miss, and hit us out here, in the stummick." Again miners in far-flung coal camps were victims of a financial panic—that of 1907. Again contracts were violated, the breaking of a long strike marked by violence lost Alabama to the union, though in West Virginia the Kanawha miners fought off a wage cut. The year ended with the nation shocked by the terrible mine fire at Monongah, West Virginia, where 361 diggers lost their lives.

The movement for consolidation among the large operators was not proceeding according to the promoters' promises. Pittsburgh Coal Company was passing dividends, though its mines worked the choicest parts of the Pittsburgh seam. Out in Colorado, where Rockefeller interests had bought the Colorado Fuel and Iron Company, a congeries of mines, coke and steel works started by Julian A. Kebler in 1892, there was a running warfare between the representatives of the absentee owners and the miners, often led by the I.W.W. In Illinois, the railroads, U.S. Steel and the oncoming electric utilities were buying up mines, and mine acreage. But nowhere was there any "Bituminous Coal Trust" for the excoriation of the muckrakers of the day.

In 1909 Pittsburgh Coal introduced new methods of blasting coal by black powder, methods which the miners said would cut their wages on run of mine. They struck, and while Lewis was able to settle the matter, he had gone over the heads of the district union officials and made a new batch of enemies in that important territory. Although at a special convention Lewis had been forced to call on John Mitchell, who was on the floor as a visitor, to take the gavel and restore order, Lewis had not forgotten his grudge against the former president. Mitchell was now in the employ of the National

Civic Federation with a roving commission to look into labor matters and a salary of $10,000 a year. Still a vice-president of the American Federation of Labor, he was appealing a sentence for contempt of court in connection with the Buck Stove and Range injunction. In this case the workers had boycotted the stove company's product— illegally, the courts held. Mitchell was in court when he received a telegram informing him that the miners' convention of 1911 had passed a resolution to the effect that Mitchell either give up his membership in the United Mine Workers or his job with the Civic Federation. He did the latter, writing to the convention that he regarded the action as a "cruel injustice." "Nevertheless," he went on, "I submit to your wishes although I shall live in the consciousness that the men and women for whom I worked for so many years, will not concur in your conclusions."

The rank and file, wearied with the din of internal warfare, elected John P. White to succeed Lewis. Under White, changes in the aims of the union as set forth in the Constitution were adopted. Among the objectives were the 6-hour workday, the prohibition of employment of boys under sixteen, old-age pensions, and workmen's compensation. Members of the National Civic Federation, together with leaders of the Boy Scout movement, were added to the list of those ineligible to membership. Miners were not trusting their children to what was then the antilabor influence of the scoutmasters. Similarly, I have known veteran diggers to refuse to allow their youngsters to enter a library bearing the name of Carnegie over its portals. The memory of Homestead lingers on in many miners' camps today.

Early during White's administration the question of the basic structure of American unionism was raised by the miners. While their own industry was not subject to complete monopolization, the leaders of the mine workers, who had to deal with such forces as were taking control in Pittsburgh banks and New York investment houses, realized that the tightly held sheltered unions affiliated with the A.F. of L. could not be able to withstand any concerted attack made upon the movement by the organized absentee owners. Already the Federation had its hierarchy of labor placemen, perfectly content with their comfortable position in the status quo, pushing the "friendly business reciprocal relations" of Mitchell to an extreme of which the author of that phrase had never dreamed. The radicals among the diggers proclaimed that the craft union policy of the A.F. of L. could not attain the goal of the labor movement, which they (the radicals) insisted was "the emancipation of the working class from economic servitude." The leftists presented a resolution at the 1912 national convention demanding that the United Mine Workers invite other unions affiliated with the Federation to form a new body having for its object the industrial organization of labor. A substitute for this resolution said that it was the idea of the miners that wherever possible the A.F. of L. adopt "a method of organization by industry."

Speaking in favor of this substitute was the state senator from Ohio, William Green, the union's statistician. Green, who had been born in a mining family in Coshocton in 1872, had gone to work in the mines at the age of sixteen. He dug coal from 1888 to 1908. He was a serious-minded youngster, sociable, a natural joiner. He joined the Elks and the Odd Fellows and other fraternal societies around the small Ohio town. He was a faithful churchgoer, and later emphasized the fact that he was leader of the largest Baptist Bible class in Coshocton. Miners and white-collar townspeople, who liked Bill Green's air of earnest responsibility, sent him to the state legislature in 1911. There he served four years, introducing the Ohio workmen's compensation law. In the union he was the president of the strategic Ohio District 6, a training ground for many national mine leaders. He had run against T. L. Lewis for the presidency of the miners and been soundly beaten, though his followers protested that the election was stolen by the Lewis organizers. He had had a longer schooling than most of his fellow unionists and his experience in the legislature had given him a certain authority so that when he rose to speak the miners listened, though Green, except for his long-windedness, was not in the tradition of the "gob-pile orator." His speeches were, and are, colorless, pompous, devoid of gusto or humor. He lacked the platform presence of such stalwarts as Tom Lewis, Frank Hefferly, the introducer of a resolution about "the emancipation of the working class," the redheaded Frank J. Hayes, brilliant leader of the leftists. Nevertheless, Green, in 1912, was all for industrial unionism and he shouted to the convention:

"One of the fundamental principles of our organization, or one of the principles for which it has contended lo, these many years, is for an industrial form of organization. In fact the United Mine Workers of America is an industrial organization. We forced the American Federation of Labor several years ago to concede the right of the United Mine Workers of America to exercise jurisdiction over every man employed in and around the coal mines of this country. I believe, brother delegates, that what we ought to have is not only an emphatic endorsement of the substitute, but if possible, a most emphatic endorsement by this convention, regardless of the fact as to whether or not our principles or our ideas are accepted by the American Federation of Labor next year or the year following, of the fact that we are serving notice upon all the affiliated unions who compose the American Federation of Labor, as well as the advocates of the craft union idea, that we propose to stay in the American Federation of Labor and continue the fight until we have established in this country a complete industrial system of organization."

A little out of breath, Green sat down, beaming behind his eyeglasses at the roar of approval from the delegates on the left of the hall.

IX. THE DELEGATE FROM LUCAS

IN 1912, THE SOCIALISTS, SOBERED BY the responsibility of electing more than a thousand of their members to public offices from Congress, where Victor Berger sat as the lone leftist, to the mayors of many mining communities, began to ease Big Bill Haywood out of the party. They were distrustful of the syndicalism of the Wobblies, with its implications of sabotage, though they recognized the appeal which the I.W.W.—"a vanguard of discontent," as Veblen had it—carried for the most sorely oppressed workers, from the textile mills of New England to the mines of Colorado. At this time the Socialists were claiming a party membership of more than a third of the miners. The doughty Duncan McDonald, black-haired, big-framed Adolph Germer, who was to be national secretary of the party during the turbulent war years, and many another leader were carrying red cards. While Haywood and the other I.W.W.'s saw in industrial unionism the prelude to a revolution, the Socialists held it to be the only practical instrument for organizing the mass industries. Their criticism of Gompers's "business unionism" was as severe as their denunciation of sabotage and they served to keep always in the forefront the strategy of vertical organization of all the workers in a given industry, which later the C.I.O., under the leadership of the miners was to employ so successfully.

All debate at miners' gatherings about strategy and tactics, the "class struggle," the ethics of "the conscientious withdrawal of efficiency," as the Wobblies like to call industrial sabotage, came to a sudden stop when word reached the eastern miners of the tragic emergence of the class struggle at Ludlow, Colorado, on April 20, 1914.

Officials of the Rockefeller-owned Colorado Fuel and Iron Company, adopting the tactics of terrorism used against the miners in West Virginia and in the metal mining fields at Calumet, Michigan, were attempting to force their diggers, who had been intermittently on strike for three bitter years, to accept the owners' terms. Union officials were enjoined and indicted, men, women and children were evicted in the dead of winter from company houses, a march of unarmed strikers was ridden into by mounted militamen under the command of Adjutant General John Chase, Baldwin-Felts detectives were riding through the countryside firing at strikers from an armored car called the "Death Special." Mother Jones, as usual, was jailed.

On the morning of the 20th, the women were cooking breakfast, the children were playing around the streets of the Ludlow tent colony where the evicted strikers were living. At the request of the adjutant, most of the men had long since surrendered their arms and there had been no violence of any sort save the spasmodic sniping from the company guards and detectives. Of a sudden the tents were raked by machine-gun fire. The militia, under Major Patrick Hamrock and Lieutenant E. K. Linderfelt, two names anathema to union men to this day, had crept up on the Ludlow colony and without warning of any sort had opened fire on the defenseless workers. The strikers, snatching up some small arms and shotguns that had not been surrendered, ran to a hill near by in order to draw off the fire from their women and children. The latter crouched in their bullet-ridden tents and pits that had been dug beneath them for shelter. For all that day the firing continued: ". . . then came the darkness of night —a kindly darkness. Famished women and children, huddled in the holes beneath their tents, saw an opportunity to escape from their hell. Moaning, sobbing or crying, they crawled on the blood-drenched ground to escape the unceasing gunfire. All but two women and eleven children reached the haven of a freight train that had pulled in. Like savages, the militia trooped into the colony, set fire to the tents and conducted a war dance around the flames of what had been the homes of one thousand people." [1]

[1] From David J. McDonald and Edward A. Lynch, *Coal and Unionism*.

In what was called the "Black Hole of Ludlow," Mrs. Patria Valdez and Mrs. Pedelina Costa and their eleven children, the youngest a baby of three months, were either shot or burned to death. Charles Costa, the father, a striker, was killed by an explosive bullet. In all, twenty persons were killed. Though the story of Ludlow—notably the account of the massacre written by George Creel—created universal indignation leading to a Congressional investigation, no militiamen, company guard or detective was punished. In the autumn of 1914, President Wilson wrote a letter to the union and company officials suggesting a three years' truce with the setting up of a grievance committee at every mine. The miners were ready to accept the plan, the company rejected it.

Stung by widespread denunciation of the brutality of Colorado Fuel officials and urged by his canny press agents to save what he could of his family's reputation, John D. Rockefeller, Jr., came forward with a plan of his own, known to the public as the "Rockefeller plan" and dubbed by the union officials as a company union in thin disguise. Under the plan, which ruled out all recognition of the union, an elaborate system of handling grievances, suggested by W. L. Mackenzie King, of Canada, was established through the election of miners' representatives. In 1919-1920 Ben M. Selekman and Mary Van Kleeck of the Russell Sage Foundation made an exhaustive study of the working of the plan. In their book *Employes' Representation in Coal Mines* they summarize their findings as follows:

"The experiment which Mr. King planned and which Mr. Rockefeller has so often and so effectively interpreted to the public is as yet incomplete. Its fruits so far have been better living conditions and better relationships between managerial officials and miners. An 'industrial constitution' for the company or for the industry, or a partnership for labor, it has not yet become."

Backed by potent Rockefeller propaganda, however, the plan did become the model for company unions in other industries. Under the somewhat delusive titles of "Industrial Democracy," "Employes' Representation," etc., company unions in railroads, steel and rubber staved off genuine organization of the workers by unions of their own choosing. While officials of the U.M.W. of A. damned the Rockefeller Plan, there was little they could do about it. The machine guns of Ludlow had effectively taken the heart out of the union in the state.

In other sections of the country things went better for the United Mine Workers. The Central Competitive Field had been re-established, giving a broader and more satisfactory base for bargaining. At long last the operators had accorded complete recognition of the union in the war-torn anthracite field and membership in what were now three districts there jumped from 18,440 to 104,560 in 1912. In soft coal too there was an increase in membership, bringing the total for the U.M.W. of A. to 377,682 in 1914. In Washington during Wilson's first term there was an exceptionally friendly attitude toward the workers. William B. Wilson, former miner and union official was sitting in the Cabinet as first secretary of labor. Business generally boomed, due to orders from the nations warring overseas. To be sure, there was West Virginia, the Achilles heel of the union, with its history of defeats in strikes, evictions, martial law, and brazen abrogations of civil liberties. And there was an internal scandal in the union growing out of charges that Alex Howat, the bellicose Kansas district president who had taken the offensive against the International officials, had accepted bribe money from the operators. But on the whole the miners, in the days of national hesitation on the verge of war, had justice in their claim of being "the strongest body of organized labor in the world."

The Howat affair was dragged through the courts, with the Kansan suing his detractors and forming around his chunky person a perpetual opposition to the administration of the union. The rank and file never questioned Howat's militancy. He was a hefty fist fighter, the victor in many street brawls from his native mining town of Pittsburg, Kansas, throughout the Southwest. Nor did the diggers feel that in his right mind Alex would consciously sell out the union. It was the quality of that mind of which they were dubious.

Howat's chief forte was in yelling down his opponents. I have heard many long-winded labor orators in my time but none of them could exceed the length and loudness of Alex Howat. Sweating profusely, he would go on for hours, his speeches largely autobiographical, extolling the devotion of Alex Howat (he always referred to himself in the third person) to the cause of suffering humanity. On one occasion I was the sole survivor at the press table over which from the platform Howat was howling at a handful of weary but faithful disciples. The other reporters had drifted out when the Kansan took to the superfluous loud-speaker. I had stuck because of my curiosity as to the extent of human endurance. At the end of two and a half hours of steady bellowing, Howat, mopping his brow with his third handerchief, stopped at the table to ask me how he did. "My God, Alex," I said, "that was a long speech." He looked at me with surprise in his blue, doll-like eyes. "Long, nothing!" he said indignantly. "Why, son, I made a speech in a tent at a farmers' picnic in Oklahoma last month. It was one hundred and ten in the shade. I spoke six hours. Two women fainted after the first two hours but, by God, the boys that drug them out come back to hear me finish. Long speech, nothing."

His naïveté was childlike and disarming. He was accused of flirting with the Communists. At an Illinois convention he answered the charge by saying, "Sure, Bill Foster [William Z. Foster, the Communist leader] did come to see me and ask me to go along with his outfit. But I didn't see nothing in that for Alex Howat, so I didn't join up." The delegates roared with laughter and dropped the matter. For many conventions after 1914 Howat and his grievances were to be storm centers.

Now new shafts were going down, old workings being reopened to meet the increasing demand for coal, occasioned by war orders from the Allies and our own preparedness efforts. The country, as is the case in the present war, was becoming conscious of the strategic place of the black mineral in our economy. Consumers had good reason to think about coal as prices were steadily rising and the government was looking anxiously into the large profits accruing to the operators. The union had no great difficulty, in view of the heavy sales, in obtaining wage raises and extending organization work in fields bordering the Central Competitive.

Now the nation, which had re-elected Woodrow Wilson, whose campaign slogan was "He kept us out of war," followed the former college president into the European holocaust. One of the first acts of the Administration was to set up a Federal Fuel Commission under the leadership of another college president, Henry A. Garfield of Williams. In retrospect, Dr. Garfield does not appear to have been the man for such a job. He was dictatorial, querulously so, when the situation called for tact. His classroom manner impressed neither the operators nor the miners, who laughed at the well-meaning academician behind his back. To be sure, he had at his side the able John White who had left the presidency of the United Mine Workers to serve as the professor's labor adviser. But few men with Dr. Garfield's background could have done any better.

Into an agreement made on April 1, 1918, between the operators and the union, Garfield had inserted a clause guaranteeing that the diggers would not strike during the duration. The contract was to extend two years and provided for a raise of 10 cents a day for the pick miners, $1.40 a day raise to company men. Though progressives in the union foresaw trouble about the "duration" and protested, the contract was put into effect and all hands turned to, to get out the coal.

In World War I, bituminous coal furnished 69.5 per cent of the total mechanical energy of the country, a mark never reached since. The aggregate net income of the soft-coal industry was set at $149 million. In that war, as in this, the industry fully met its production demands. Over the tipples went 579 million tons of bituminous in 1918, a new high in production. And still there was an estimated capacity for that year of more than 700 million tons, estimated, that is, on the assumption that mines and miners were working full time. Then, as now, irregular work, absenteeism on the part of the miners, and transportation difficulties made production lag far behind capacity. Absenteeism, a fancy word for laying off, was due to car shortage, according to the heavy-browed statistician for the union and the manager of the *United Mine Workers Journal,* John Llewellyn Lewis. At the miners' twenty-sixth convention in 1917, presided over by the new president, Frank Hayes, the successor to White, Lewis said that the diggers could have sent to the top 50 million additional tons had the railroads been able to handle them. When a miner reported for work and found no cars on the siding, he went home to tend his garden. More than 19,000 diggers had gone off to the wars to give a good account of themselves.

Those who stayed behind asked Herbert Hoover, food administrator, to look into the exorbitant prices charged by company stores, endorsed the Rochdale co-operative stores plan, and came out for government ownership of the mines, with the proviso that the union be granted full bargaining powers in its dealings with the government. The rank-and-filers were unhappy over the decision of the Supreme Court in the Hitchman case. The Hitchman Coal and Coke Company of West Virginia had obtained an injunction against the representatives of the U.M.W. of A. restraining them from soliciting for union membership those employed by the company which had a "yellow-dog" clause in its contract. In signing up to work for the company the miner promised not to join the U.M.W. of A. Many such contracts included the I.W.W. on the proscribed list. The diggers loved the story of the Negro who was asked why he had promised not to join the I.W.W. "Boss," he answered, "I reckoned it was one of those animal societies like the Elks or the Moose." At any rate, the decision of the "nine old men" upholding the Hitchman injunction ruled out the possibility of peaceful persuasion in West Virginia and was a standing irritant which led eventually to the civil war in that state.

While this mine war was at its height, long after the Armistice, I interviewed one of the Hitchmans, who repeated parrot-like his contention that he had prevented the rise of anarchism and "commoonism" in West Virginia. Three days later I interviewed on his hospital cot an organizer for the U.M.W. of A. whose head had been split open by the ineffable Don Chafin, sheriff of Logan County. The sheriff had come up behind the union man and clipped him with a revolver butt. Chafin told me that he too was stopping "commoonism" in West Virginia.

Hayes, the new president of the union, was a good talker, a good mixer; but he had no heart for the routine work connected with the job. More and more he handed over the conduct of the complicated affairs of the union to other officials, while he sat around in the back room with the boys. So it came about that it was on the broad shoulders of Vice-President John L. Lewis of Iowa that the bulk of the work around the Indianapolis headquarters fell.

John Llewellyn Lewis was born in the little mining town of Lucas, Iowa, on February 12, 1880. There were four strapping boys, John, Tom, Denny and Howard, and a girl, Hattie, in this family of Welsh extraction. John went to the public school in Lucas, and at the age of seventeen he worked with his father and Tom, driving mules in the mines for ten hours a day for which he received

$1.60. His father was a Knight of Labor who had been blacklisted in a strike in 1882 and had worked for a while as a policeman in Des Moines.

Though there are a host of stories about John L.'s youth, some of them obviously apocryphal since they are told about the early days of many other labor leaders, there seem to have been no indications that the broad-beamed youngster was to become one of the most contradictory, contentious and altogether compelling figures in the history of American labor. Except, perhaps, for the fact that in the mining town, the Lewis boys, headed by John, had the reputation of being a pugnacious lot, putting into action the Knights' philosophy that an "injury to one is an injury to all."

John drifted west to Colorado, working in the coal mines there and in the copper, silver and coal mines in the West. He came back to marry Myrta Edith Bell, an Iowa schoolteacher, a daughter of a doctor from Ohio, of old American stock. At twenty-six years of age he was a delegate from Lucas to his first convention of the U.M.W. of A. In 1909 he was working in a mine at Panama, Illinois, where he was a one-man pit committee. The following year he came out of the pits and worked as a state legislative agent for the union.

Sam Gompers liked the cut of the broad-shouldered, great-lunged young digger, and from 1911 to 1917 Lewis was a field representative for the A.F. of L. traveling all over the country, learning the ropes of both labor and national politics. Now, owing to the aberrations of Frank Hayes, he was heading a union of more than 400,000 coal diggers working to fuel the furnaces of war. Lewis would go from his union duties to meetings of the National Council of Defense and the Fuel Administration, of which he was a member. He would consult with Henry Warrum of Indiana, the miners' lawyer, about the proceedings in the Coronado case where the Coronado Coal Company had entered suit against the United Mine Workers for a cool $2 million damages under the Sherman Antitrust Law. The charge was conspiracy on the part of the union representatives to stop the shipment of the company's nonunion coal. Eventually in 1925, when Charles Evans Hughes had appeared for the miners for a large fee in the arguments in the Supreme Court, the union won; but the case was a source of harassment to the United Mine Workers' officials.

Then on November 11, 1918, the whistles blew in the mining

camps and the cages brought the diggers up to celebrate the signing of the Armistice. They had "loaded their turn," they were confident that a request for a wage raise for the soft-coal miners now resting on Woodrow Wilson's desk would be favorably received. A world to be rebuilt would have need of coal.

X. WAR IN WEST VIRGINIA

No SOONER HAD THE ARMISTICE been signed than there was a marked change in the National Administration's attitude toward labor. President Wilson rejected the miners' plea for increased wages, noting that, while the diggers' case might be just, the time was not "propitious" for increases.

American labor, with the exception of certain left wing groups—the Socialists and the I.W.W., had enthusiastically supported the war. At the outset the A.F. of L. called upon workers in the name of "Labor, Justice, Freedom and Humanity" to give full devotion to the war effort. And Samuel Gompers was rewarded by being invited to participate in political and industrial affairs of the nation as no labor man before him had thus been recognized. Though there was nothing on paper, Wilson's labor policy throughout the duration was quite evidently the recognition of the rights of labor to organization, collective bargaining, and a greater say in management.

While the miners, in view of their production record at home, their fighting record overseas, and the wholehearted participation of their leaders in the official conduct of the war, believed that unionism would play an increasingly important part in postwar reconstruction, powerful forces moving behind the scenes were at work to keep labor in a subordinate role. Large industrialists, thoroughly frightened by the repercussions in this country of the Russian Revolution, looked with dismay upon the forthright declaration of the secretary of the War Labor Board in 1919: "The right of workers to organize in trade unions and to bargain collectively through chosen representatives is recognized and affirmed. That right shall not be denied, abridged, or interfered with by the employers in any manner whatever." Many employers who had reaped large profits from the war were eager to divert the public's criticism to labor. The press first talked about the silk shirts and expensive cars of shipworkers, steel puddlers and coal diggers and then went on to ring the changes on the "Bolshevik menace." ("A menace to whom?" asked Veblen, with his tongue in his cheek.) In steel, on the roads, and in mining, nonunion forces were swinging into line to start the open-shop drive which reached its climax in 1920.

Apprehensions of the industrialists lest labor take a leftward turn were shared by Administration leaders. Postmaster General Burleson had suppressed or curtailed many newspapers critical of the war conduct and his rigid censorship extended into the immediate postwar days. Socialist and I.W.W. headquarters had been raided, leaders of both organizations jailed or indicted. In the penitentiary at Atlanta, Eugene V. Debs paced behind the bars of his cell, the most prominent of many political prisoners, and the most persistently pursued of all dissidents from Wilson's war policies. Returned soldiers, unable to find jobs that had been promised them, lashed out in sadistic attacks upon any suspected of "bolshevism." The American Legion was used to lead the shock troops of reaction. Under the Quaker Attorney General A. Mitchell Palmer, a reign of terror ensued which was summed up in a report of twelve leading lawyers, headed by Zachariah Chaffee. The report read:

Under the guise of a campaign for the suppression of radical activities, the office of the Attorney-General, acting by its local agents throughout the country, and giving express instructions from Washington, has committed illegal acts. Wholesale arrests both of aliens and citizens have been made without warrant or any process of law; men and women have been jailed and held incommunicado without access of friends or counsel; homes have been entered without search-warrant, and property seized and removed; other property has been wantonly destroyed; workingmen and workingwomen suspected of radical views have been shamefully abused and maltreated. Agents of the Department of Justice have been introduced into radical organizations for the purpose of informing upon their members or inciting them to activities; these agents have been instructed from Washington to arrange meetings upon certain dates for the express object of facilitating wholesale raids and arrests. In support of these illegal arrests and to create sentiment in its favor, the Department of Justice has also constituted itself a propaganda bureau, and has sent to newspapers and magazines of this country quantities of material designed to excite public opinion against radicals, all at the expense of the government and outside the scope of the Attorney-General's duties.

In 1918, William Z. Foster moved into steel, as secretary of a committee of twenty-four unions, the majority of them skeleton organizations, for the purpose of organizing the steel workers into an industrial union. Foster, born in Taunton, Massachusetts, in 1881, had gone to work at the age of ten as a sculptor's apprentice. At one time or another he was a type founder, factory worker, steam engineer, steam fitter, railroad brakeman, fireman, logger, salesman, streetcar motorman, longshoreman and farmer, according to his autobiographical sketch in *American Labor Who's Who*. He had been expelled from the Socialist party during a Right-Left family fight, and had joined the I.W.W. that year. Now, with the none-too-cordial blessings of Sam Gompers, he was back in the orthodox trade-union movement storming the strongest-held antiunion bastion in the country.

Foster was a first-class organizer with a wealth of grievances of the steel workers to exploit. In September, 1919, he went into action. The men came out in response to his call. At the height of the strike Foster claimed that 400,000 men had left the mills. In the Cabinet, in Congress, and on the front pages of the press there were fearful rumors of a revolution via Pittsburgh. Then the steel press agents dug up the early writings of Foster in praise of syndicalism. Company police and state troopers rode down the picket lines on which marched many sympathetic miners. With exceptional ferocity the steel workers were driven back to the mills. The breaking of the strike gave enormous impetus to the open-shop drive, increased the activities of the Department of Justice, and convinced many a rank-and-filer that the A.F. of L. was of no use to unskilled workers at a time of crisis. Foster, emerging from the strike as the outstanding leader of the extreme labor union leftists, went on to organize his Trade Union Educational League which was to plague the orthodox labor leaders, among them the officials of the United Mine Workers.

In the meantime the miners were becoming more and more restive. Their "silk shirt" days had been short-lived. A surplus of 100 million tons of coal after the Armistice had closed down many a mine, and the officials of the union and the operators were unsuccessful in their efforts to restore the export market. Despite unemployment, wage cutting, and the general unrest in the labor movement from Pittsburgh to Seattle, the union's twenty-seventh convention in 1919 was mild in tone. Voting in favor of the organization of a labor party, the nationalization of the mines, and the Plumb plan for the ownership of the railroads by tripartite boards, at the same time the delegates added members of the I.W.W. to the list of those ineligible to membership in the United Mine Workers.

Although the Fuel Administration was dissolved soon after the Armistice, the Lever Act, designed originally to end profiteering in foods and fuel, was still on the statute books. It was the contention of the Wilson administration that the promise of the mine union not to strike for the duration of the war still held, even though the guns had ceased firing. The delegates to the 1919 convention held differently. They instructed their officials to demand large increases of pay for both day laborers and tonnage men in the bituminous fields and in the event of the refusal of the operators to grant such raises, voted that all war contracts should terminate, so far as the union was concerned, on November 1, 1919.

A joint conference with the operators in Buffalo broke up without agreement and Acting President Lewis ordered the soft-coal miners to strike on November 1, 1919. Wilson immediately said that the strike was "not only unjustifiable but unlawful." He had the Lever Act in mind, as did Federal Judge Anderson, who in Indianapolis issued a temporary order for the union officials to withdraw the strike instructions. Lewis and his board complied with the order and then went into conference with the flurried Dr. Garfield, who had been called back into action, and Secretary of Labor Wilson. While both officials were agreed that the miners were entitled to a raise, neither side to the dispute would sign a contract and the miners stayed away from the pits in a "stoppage." Dr. Garfield tried to put a maximum price ceiling on coal prices, but bootleggers among the operators did a flourishing business while the country shivered through November. The A.F. of L. executive committee called Judge Anderson's injunction "so autocratic as to stagger the human mind." A union organizer said: "About all you can do under this injunction is to go by night to your room, lock the door and pray, in a whisper, that the miners will win."

On December 3rd, Judge Anderson cited eighty-four union officials for contempt. Lewis and the rest of the international officers were arrested in Indianapolis. Four days later, after a White House conference, John L. Lewis called off the work stoppage saying:

"I will not fight my government, the greatest government on earth."

The radicals in the union remembered this statement and attributed the decline of the organization's militancy to this "surrender" as they called it.

It was not, however, a complete surrender. Under the agreement made at the White House the workers were to return to the pits with an immediate raise of 14 per cent. A commission was set up to make more lasting arrangements. The final decision of this body was an increase of 34 per cent to tonnage men, 20 per cent to day men. The day men, some 30 per cent of the mine workers, went out on wildcat strikes. Finally, through district arrangements, the day men won a raise of $1.50 per diem, giving them $7.50 in organized districts with contracts running until April 1, 1922.

Depletion of the soft-coal stocks, together with an increased demand from industry overseas, started the great coal boom of 1920 to which some operators still look back with nostalgic eyes. It began in the South, where mine companies, running away from unionism, were working large holdings. Those were the fantastic days when again "anything went." "If it is black, load it." Fireproof contents of culm heaps were shoveled onto the cars along with the good coal from the tipples. The "snowbirds" came down to open up high-cost, tragically wasteful operations for the quick money that was in spot coal selling at $3.75 per ton, f.o.b. the mine—twice the normal price. Some coal sold at the seaboard for as high as $25 a ton. There was a $300 profit on the loading of some of the small gondolas. They still tell stories about diggers in the nonunion fields earning $50 a day, subcontractors making $2,000 a month. From the spring of 1920 to the autumn of that year the miners brought more than 550 million tons to the top with profits for 1,059 concerns, a third of the total number of coal companies reporting for income tax purposes, at the astronomical figure of 50 per cent or more, and 498 companies cleaning up 100 per cent or more.

Ten years before the boom, such a remote mine field as Harlan County, Kentucky, was a backwoods community populated by Scotch-Irish who rarely "went over the ridge" into an adjoining county. By 1917, the names of Mellon, Insull, U.S. Steel, Detroit Edison, International Harvester were well-known in the region under which lay the thick seams. Malcolm Ross, in his *Machine Age in the Hills,* figures that the Appalachian Mountains over the seams of Harlan were 50 million years old when the Rockies upthrust. In 1920 this long-hidden black wealth was being frantically torn from under the laurels and rhododendrons and pines in every ravine. And at the same time, over the way, in West Virginia a new war had broken out.

Frank Keeney was head of the West Virginia district of the United Mine Workers with his stronghold in the Panhandle region around Fairmont in the northern part of the state. All told, Keeney headed some 40,000 organized miners. The state's output in 1919 was 79 million tons.

Keeney was intent on organizing the rich Williamson field lying along the Tug River over which the Hatfields and McCoys had long waged their bloody feuds. As is the case with its namesake in Southern Illinois, Williamson, county seat of Mingo County, West Virginia is exclusively a mining territory, a rough, wild country which, together with the Logan field up the Tug, constituted at that time the chief nonunion fields in the state.

Sid Hatfield, of the feuding family, was chief of police of the little town of Matewan in this region. He was sympathetic to the union miners and had no love for the Baldwin-Felts operatives who were busy harassing all those suspected of membership in the United Mine Workers. In May, 1920, Albert and Lee Felts led a group of their men out to a mine near Matewan to evict from company houses miners and their families who had shown union leanings. Hatfield confronted the Felts crowd on their way back to take a train to Williamson. He said what he thought of such proceedings, and all hands reached for their guns. When the shooting ended, the Felts brothers and four of their men lay dead. The mayor of Matewan, a small boy, and a union miner also were killed. Hatfield and a number of union men were tried and acquitted. Later the detectives had their revenge. In response to a court order, Hatfield, unarmed and accompanied by his wife, had gone to the courthouse at Welch, the McDowell County seat. On the steps of the courthouse the couple were surrounded by Baldwin-Felts men. Sid was shot to death while his wife tried to shield him. The detective in charge of the ambushers was tried and acquitted on the grounds of "self-defence."

On both sides that summer men were shooting from the cover of laurel bushes and from behind mine buildings. Man-trips carrying nonunion diggers coming into the open were rained with bullets from the mountainside and automobiles loaded with deputies would drive past the tent colonies of evicted unionists with an exchange of shots between the cars and the tents. There was a constant call for the militia. In August federal troops marched into the fields. The tent colonies grew, affording a meager shelter to the mounting number of families evicted.

Spokesmen for the operators said: "These tent colonies were instituted at the beginning of the strike by the United Mine Workers' organization. They furnished shelter for the workers who had been induced to strike and in them that organization supported in idleness all those who preferred to stay on the spot rather than seek work elsewhere. The companies offered to pay the moving expenses to union fields of former employees, their families and household goods. The organization used these tent colonies as a means of securing public sympathy and as a reason for raising a national assessment. The tent colony has come to be recognized as primarily a weapon of offense of the United Mine Workers' organization and not as a relief institution." (Statement before U.S. Senate Commission on Interstate Commerce.)

Local church, charitable and relief agencies accepted this viewpoint of the operators without much question. A group of Charleston ministers told Sherwood Eddy of the Y.M.C.A., in the fields to investigate conditions in the tent colonies, that there was considerable "immorality" in the tents. The Red Cross refused relief to the strikers on the ground that no "Act of God" had caused their suffering and that they could obtain food, shelter and clothing if they went back to work at the operators' terms. The secretary of the Young Men's Christian Association at Charleston told me that his organization regarded strikes as a controversial issue into which the Y could not enter. He also told me that a local operator had made a handsome contribution toward the construction of a new left wing for the Y building. When I later printed this in the *Survey Graphic,* he journeyed to New York to have me fired, but did not deny the story. I was not fired.

Whatever use the United Mine Workers may have made of the tent colonies, their immediate use was for the sheltering of men, women and children thrown out of their homes with a brutality that to this author, at any rate, was unique in the recent history of industrial disputes. I have seen violence on both sides of picket lines, I had at first hand the sickening stories of the murders of the strikebreakers at Herrin, and in my native New York I have seen plenty of slugging and head-cracking even among the supposedly peaceful needleworkers, but these West Virginia evictions were planned in cold blood and carried out in sadistic manner, with the women and children of the miners as their innocent victims.

Sheriffs and their company-subsidized deputies, with an eye for melodrama, would generally choose the hour just before dawn for their eviction jobs, and if the weather was foul so much the better. Fortified by liberal potions of white mule and ostentatiously showing sawed-off shotguns, high-powered rifles and revolvers they would descend upon a sleeping town. Along the cinder streets in front of the company houses, each the drab counterpart of its neighbor, they would march, huddled together, until they came to the home of the miner on whom the order had been served. If the door didn't open at once to their pounding they would break it in and come piling through to pull the digger out of bed and stand him up against the wall at the points of their guns. Then they would herd the women and children out into the street and go to work on the mean furnishings of the place. Negroes were often employed to do the actual work of "setting out" beds, bureaus, cookstoves, pictures, etc. The deputies would not fail to point out to the white miner, backed against the wall with his hands on high, that he was being "set out" by "niggers."

I once drove up on a union truck loaded with tents and food to the outskirts of a town where an hour before sunup six families had been set out. Through slashing rains, our truck sloshed along a valley trail to the coal camp where we found the women in drenched house dresses trying to calm their frightened children. They had taken refuge under the shed back of a small church. The men were standing ankle-deep in the creek water that had overflowed its banks and was swirling past the doorsills of the company houses. In the sulphur-yellow water there was a confusion of broken bedsteads, cribs, chairs, tables, toys. Some of the crew of the truck lent a hand to the men in salvaging what they could, while the rest tackled the difficult job of erecting wet tents, once used by the Canadian Army in World War I. When finally the tents were up and a communal cookstove had been coaxed into action in the mess tent, the women went about the job of setting up housekeeping all over again, swapping jokes about the pleasures of camping out. There was no child psychologist around, but had there been he would have approved the effect of this serene behavior upon the jangled nerves of the youngsters. Once out of earshot of the children, however, these women expressed themselves in no uncertain terms. Their lives of "idleness," as the press agents for the operators had it, were shortened by active service on the picket lines that were thrown around the mine tipple (lines which strikebreakers hesitated to cross), by toting water to the tents from a mountain spring a mile distant, by scrubbing and cooking and trying as best they could to keep their children from "running wild."

A hundred such women stood fast on a picket line at a struck mine outside of Fairmont while state troopers and deputies took off their leaders to the lockup in the town. The women promptly slept through the long day on the floor of the bull pen where they were imprisoned. Toward ten in the evening they awoke refreshed to sing their union song:

> Just like a mule,
> A goddam fool
> Will scab until he dies.

Across the street from the jail was Fairmont's crack hotel. Soon the sheriff's telephone in the office in the jail was buzzing with the angry protests of the hotel's patrons. The sheriff went in to plead almost tearfully with the women. They sang another union song, more caustic if anything in its analysis of the ancestry of scabs.

Finally the sheriff was forced to turn the women loose. The next dawn they were out on the picket line again.

In one strike the union women were enjoined from holding "prayer meetings" on the public roads. At such meetings held by the pickets, a deep-breasted woman with evangelical training would stand in front of her kneeling companions and as the strikebreakers came down the road, she would pray in hog-calling tones that God A'mighty would spare the lives of these poor, misguided "un-union" men who were taking the bread out of the mouths of decent workers. She prayed that these strikebreakers would not throw their picks into a gassy pocket, that rocks would not fall on them, leaving them crushed and bleeding, and that they would not have their limbs severed by runaway mine cars. By the time a nonunion man had run that gantlet, he wasn't fit for much when he got to the coal.

Guerrilla warfare reached its climax at a meeting of the union miners at Marmet, a small mine camp up the Kanawha River ten miles from Charleston, on August 20, 1921. There it was decided to organize a march on Logan County, the feudal field dominated by gun-toting Sheriff Don Chafin. From Logan it was planned to march into Mingo County where martial law had been declared in the course of a strike.

The organization of the march of the union men was in charge of war veterans whose efficiency surprised veteran army officers sent down to head the marchers off. Patrols were flung out along the roads leading into Logan, a commissary was set up, and mess halls opened at various schoolhouses near the front. Trains and automobiles were commandeered for the "citizens' army" and the men, armed with all sorts of weapons, were accompanied by nurses in uniform, wearing instead of the Red Cross the letters "U.M.W. of A." on their caps. The union men wore blue overalls with red handkerchiefs around their necks. On August 24th the army marched from Marmet twelve miles to Racine on the Big Coal River and, finding little opposition, went on to camp at the ball park at Madison fifteen miles farther on. In the meantime Don Chafin was organizing some two thousand nonunion men, professional strikebreakers and deputies and, according to union witnesses, carefully sequestered himself in the loft of a barn far behind the firing line when the shooting came nearer. President Harding sent General Bandholtz of the United States Army into

Logan. The general asked Keeney and other union officials to urge
the men in the ball park, now numbering close to 6,000, to disperse
and go home. Though Keeney made the plea as directed, matters
had now gone too far for retreat on either side. The invaders took
up positions along a wide front and there was heavy firing on Blair
mountain, where some state troopers were trapped, and along the
Beech Creek. A witness who had been in the Philippine fighting
during the Spanish-American War said the shooting in West Virginia was heavier than any he had heard in the Orient. Prisoners
were taken by both sides, but in view of the heavy firing there were
remarkably few casualties.

By now dispatches sent back by war correspondents from the
eastern papers, among them Floyd Gibbons, indicated that civil war
on a large scale was raging in Logan. On August 27th in response
to urgent calls from General Bandholtz, detachments of the 19th In-
fantry of the Regular Army moved into Logan, accompanied by
machine guns and airplanes. The union army offered no resistance
to the federal troops, giving up their arms and going back home.

William Blizzard, head of a union subdistrict and leader of the
march, was later tried for treason and acquitted. Keeney and other
union officials were tried on murder charges, and also acquitted. Don
Chafin came down from his loft and once more swaggered through
the streets in search of union organizers. The backbone of unionism
south of the Ohio was broken. It was not until 1933, with the signing
of the National Industrial Recovery Act, that there was any large-
scale organization in West Virginia.

XI. THE OPPOSITION
ORGANIZES

ITH THE UNORGANIZED SOUTH "a pistol pointed at the heart of the union," the great coal boom of 1920 no more than the memory of a glorious bender, now that the mines overseas were once more in production, and with a steady laying-off of union miners, the fortunes of the United Mine Workers went into a decline that was to last from 1921 to 1933, twelve years of increasing misery.

For the first part of this period the only official weapon for its long rear-guard action which the union could seem to find was the strike. No strategy was formulated at headquarters during this time other than the oft-repeated phrase of John Lewis's "We will take no backward step." Taking advantage of what they termed the bull-headedness of the miners' leader, the opposition within the union rallied its forces. From the outset, however, it was evident that the bulk of Lewis's enemies had no more concrete proposals for the immediate solution of the problem of maintaining union standards in an industry half of whose production was nonunion than did the much excoriated U.M.W. of A. president. All the rank-and-filers could get out of Howat was a bellowing and empty bellicosity. In Illinois, Frank Farrington was a more dangerous adversary, but Farrington at that time had no answer other than to get his diggers better conditions than the rest of the organized miners and, some said, tacitly to encourage wildcat strikes for the embarrassment of the national office. Only in Pennsylvania in the soft coal where the alert-minded John Brophy was a district president was any serious attempt made to evaluate the situation in other than strike terms.

John Brophy, the son of a Lancashire miner, was born in St. Helens, England, in 1883, and started to work in the mines of Pennsylvania when he was twelve years old. He was a studious lad, a devout Catholic, though he early came to socialism of the Fabian variety. The rank and file respected him for his book-learning and shining integrity and elected him checkweighman for his mine for three successive years. In 1917 he was elected president of District 2 of the U.M.W. of A. with headquarters at Clearfield, Pennsylvania, and from Clearfield, it was evident, soon after Lewis took over the gavel from Hayes, the most formidable opposition to the administration's intransigent policy was to issue.

Brophy, like Mitchell, and very much unlike the Lewis of those days, welcomed the help of men and women, whether members of the union or not, who could contribute anything to ending the recurrent crises in coal. The United Mine Workers in their 1921 convention had created, with a rather casual air, a Nationalization Research Committee to study the whole matter of taking over the mines. This committee was headed by Brophy, with William Mitch of Indiana and C. J. Golden of Pennsylvania as its members. It was a routine matter for the miners to vote for nationalization, but this was the first time anyone had done anything about trying to find out what nationalization might mean to the miners. At all events, Brophy took his job seriously as he takes everything in life, and for help in the committee's researches, he invited in two men whose sagacious counsel and long social view did much to make Brophy and his committee a focal point for such genuine progressivism as there was in the United Mine Workers. These two "outsiders" were Robert Bruere and Heber Blankenhorn of the Bureau of Industrial Research and in their way they contributed as much to the miners' cause in their time as did Walter Weyl and Henry Demarest Lloyd in the Mitchell regime. Bruere was a self-effacing writer and researcher, a veteran of the Bull Moose campaign, Blankenhorn, a top-flight newspaperman whose work on the report of the Interchurch World Movement on the steel strike of 1919 raised a storm that eventually put the Movement out of business. But not before it had set church people everywhere to thinking about the problems of labor.

Under Brophy's aegis, several healthy co-operative stores were set up, his district paper broke long labor press precedents by being readable, his report on the subject of nationalization called "How to Run Coal," published in 1922, started discussions in circles far beyond the mine fields as to the social implications of mining. The report said:

The coal industry has been so disorganized and mismanaged that the situation in recent years has approached what big business men and stand-pat Senators describe as a "catastrophe." Intelligent men, with the welfare of the industry at heart, agree that the game is up—the old game of speculative profits, over-production, shortages, sky-high prices, unemployment, gunmen, spies, the murder of miners, a sullen, desperate public. Unless unification and order enter the industry, there will be a blow-up somewhere, followed by drastic, angry and frenzied legislation. The American Kingdom of Coal is today in as chaotic and explosive condition as the states of Europe. No single constructive suggestion has come from the operators. No large leading idea has come from the public. The public is feeling intensely, but is not yet thinking wisely.

The operators have a fresh explanation for the annual crisis as often as it rolls around. One year it is car shortage, another year, high wages, then the war, then government interference. Of thought-out plan and remedy they have offered none.

The only large-scale proposal has come from the United Mine Workers of America in their demand for nationalization. It is the only proposal that grapples with slack work for the miners, high prices and irregular supply for the consumer.

The Brophy plan, as it soon came to be called, followed the general outlines of the Plumb plan for the nationalization of the railroads and indeed there were economists who pointed out that for full performance of rails and mines, the two must be interwoven. The miners' proposal was the purchase by the government of the mines from the private owners at an estimated cost of $4½ billion, as of 1922. The mines would be run by a Federal Commission of Mines, with a secretary of mines in the Cabinet. The eyes of this commission would be a permanent fact-finding agency. The commission would be an eleven-man board with five members named by industrial, technical and engineering bodies and six appointed by the President. With this commission the United Mine Workers would bargain for a basic national wage. Regional councils, made up of technicians, consumers and miners, would have charge of actual administration of the mines, appointing mine managers. A labor party would press for nationalization. The rise of the British Labour party was being closely watched by progressives in the American movement.

Brophy was interested in the most ambitious project for workers' education then afoot. This was the Brookwood Labor College at Katonah, New York, a coeducational, residence college to which young workers could come for courses from six months to two years—courses in labor history, economics, journalism, dramatics, etc.

William Mann Fincke, the son of a coal operator, who had been a manager of a mine after his graduation from Yale's Sheffield Scientific School in 1901, had strayed from the conservative path of his fathers. A popular athlete in his undergraduate days, seemingly about to retell the family's success story, he had become more interested in the lot of the diggers at the mine than in the cost accounting sheets in the office. He turned to the ministry and in 1918 he was director of the Labor Temple, that Presbyterian contribution to free speech and workers' education, which makes Fourteenth Street and Second Avenue, New York, one of the most exciting places on the East Side. Young Fincke was arrested for exercising free speech during the great steel strike of 1919 and was jailed in Duquesne, Pennsylvania.

In 1921 he called in a number of labor leaders, Brophy, James Maurer, Socialist and steam fitter, head of the Pennsylvania State Federation of Labor, and a close friend of the mine union officials in his state, Fania Cohn of the educational department of the International Ladies' Garment Workers' Union, and others. To them Fincke outlined his plan for handing over to the labor movement the buildings and grounds of his family's estate at Katonah. With the tenuous blessings of the Old Guard in the A.F. of L. and the enthusiastic sponsoring of the needle trades and the progressives in the United Mine Workers, the old Fincke farmhouse high on a hill, overlooking a lovely countryside that ran to the banks of the Hudson, was opened to its first students, men and women picked by their local unions to go to college with the promise that in return for their union fellowships they would come back into the labor movement. Miners and garment workers and railroaders under the inspiring leadership of Abraham John ("A.J.") Muste struggled with the immediate problems of their industries as thrown against the larger backgrounds of the national economic setup and then went to the kitchen to wash dishes or down the road to lay the foundations for the new dormitories. Muste, a young minister who had come out of his church to stand on the picket lines at Lawrence, Massachusetts, and Paterson, New Jersey, in the textile strikes of 1919, was a born educator with a nonacademic attitude essential to this pioneering job. While he was head of Brookwood the college was the dynamic for genuine educational effort among the workers for more than a decade.

Lewis joined with Sam Gompers and Matthew Woll of the inner circle of the A.F. of L. in contemplating with suspicion all these deviations from pure and simple unionism. Lewis, to be sure, had been badly beaten when he ran against the Old Man for the presidency of the Federation in 1921. (Incidentally he was nominated by William Green in a "man who" speech which set some sort of record for adulatory heights.) Nevertheless, as vice-president of the Federation Lewis exerted an enormous influence upon the shaping of policy for the entire organized movement and his influence was invariably thrown, at that time, to the extreme right. In his own union Lewis was now being sniped at by guerrilla warfare carried on by the Communists under Foster with his newly organized Trade Union Educational League. Though the T.U.E.L. was generally recognized as a Communist propaganda instrument for "boring from within" the organized labor movement, it was no great trick for the embattled labor officials of the right to confuse the rank and file by putting the Communist label on anything educational. When Brophy ran against Lewis for the presidency of the United Mine Workers this label was liberally applied. Lewis was returned to office with a regularity which caused the followers of Brophy to charge that the Lewis-appointed organizers, the members of the union's legal department, and the tellers who counted the paper ballots cast at the various local union halls in the biennial elections were influenced, to put it mildly, by the source of their appointment.

A slim, dark-haired, handsome youngster, with a background somewhat similar to that of Fincke, aligned himself with Brophy in headlong opposition to the Old Guard at the Indianapolis headquarters of the U.M.W. of A. Powers Hapgood, son of a socially minded businessman in Indianapolis, had been educated at the exclusive Phillips Academy at Andover, Massachusetts, and was graduated from

Harvard in 1920. His father, William, and his uncle, Norman Hapgood, the brilliant journalist who was ambassador to Norway in later years, were both interested in the advancement of industrial democracy. William Hapgood was president of the Columbia Conserve Company of Indianapolis, which was to work out a labor-management arrangement that was hailed as a model by progressives. Norman Hapgood, when editor of *Hearst's Magazine,* printed a biographical sketch of John Brophy by Benjamin Stolberg, which gave the lithe, ascetic-looking progressive his first national prominence. Upon his graduation from Harvard and to the vast amazement of his classmates, Powers went down into the coal mines of Pennsylvania as a mine laborer and then as a skilled pickman. For a while he worked in nonunion fields, and the diary he kept of those days is a rich lode for any researcher interested in the actual work conditions of the unorganized in the days after the last war. When he joined the U.M.W. of A., District 2 acquired its most fearless and energetic organizer.

Pennsylvania had taken over from West Virginia its techniques of warfare upon the union, in the unorganized fields. In company towns, surrounded by coal and iron police, behind barbed-wire entanglements, the nonunion workers were supposedly immune to the wiles of any United Mine Workers spokesman. In these closed towns the miners were to all intents and purposes captives, inasmuch as they were paid in scrip issued by the company and good only in the company store in the immediate locality. All automobiles or wagons attempting to enter these strongholds were searched, their occupants cross-examined some distance from town by the police patrols mounted on horses trained for riot duty. These animals had the unpleasant habit of rearing up at the touch of a spur, pawing the air with their front legs and showing their teeth. To a man afoot or in an open car looking up at such an array of hoofs and gaping mouths, immediate retreat seemed the dictate of discretion. Not so with young Hapgood. He would saunter down the road past the guards, calling out to the nonunion men passing one another on shifts: "Don't scab, brothers. John the United Mine Workers of America. We are on strike. Don't take the bread from your brothers' mouths . . ." And then he would be collared and run off to the nearest lockup.

During the bitter strike of the coke miners in 1922, Hapgood sent a postcard from the cell he was then occupying, reading:

"Please send me five dollars to pay off the Sheriff. I lost it to him playing poker last night. I have been moved over to the woman's section. It is better over here as there are fewer bugs. Fraternally, Powers."

The rank and file adored this ally from another world. The men took him readily into inner union councils, the women consulted him on all sorts of problems from the raising of children in a tent colony to diets for the relief kitchens. He listened gravely and was listened to as gravely, so that all through the coal regions of Western Pennsylvania the name of Hapgood became as well-known as that of Brophy. Here was a man out of Harvard who had chosen to make his living in the pits and to work for the better organization of the men at his side.

Lewis was puzzled by the reports of Hapgood's activities. He sent for him and asked what he was doing in the fields. "Organizing," said Hapgood simply. "Not writing a book?" asked Lewis skeptically. Hapgood brushed this aside and asked Lewis for more relief from the national office for his evicted diggers.

It was a sore point with the Brophy group—this lack of national backing. They once sent Hapgood to New York at the head of a delegation of evicted miners and their wives. The men were on strike against the mine company that provided coal for the city's subways, and Hapgood used the City Hall and the surprised Mayor Hylan as a sounding board. That day New Yorkers learned about things going on beneath the earth not continents away. In the delegation was Mrs. Harry Armstrong who was pregnant, but had come along anyway, not realizing how close was her time. The day after the hearings, her son was born in a room in the little unionized hotel which housed the delegation. There was a great scurrying around among Hapgood's well-to-do friends to provide clothes for the baby, comforts for the mother. The telephone operators and chambermaids in the hotel went out shopping, and the baggage porter arrived with a great bunch of flowers. "I'm glad," said Mrs. Armstrong, "he was not born in the chicken coop." She meant the coop in which she, her husband and her other children had spent the winter, following their eviction from the company house. It had been lent to them by a neighbor, a Negro farmer. Powers, to the clicking of cameras held by the news photographers, read to the squealing baby the obligation of membership in the United Mine Workers of America. Powers Hapgood Armstrong, as the child was named, was the youngest member of the United Mine Workers. Though John Leary, labor reporter for the old New York *World* and a Gompers crony, said sourly, "This is just a publicity stunt of Hapgood's," the delegation went back to the fields and the picket lines with a good-sized sum for the relief commissary. And more important, perhaps, the sense that they had friends outside the mines in their *Strike for Union,* as Blankenhorn called that struggle in his memorable little book, written after the strike had been lost.

For it was lost, despite all the sacrifices of such good fighters as the Armstrongs. Lewis, in his anxiety to sign up as much tonnage as he could get in the negotiation of the settlement of the national strike, left out the men of the coke fields, a fact which the opposition harped on for years to come.

In the Midwest, opposition of a more orthodox nature was crystallizing around Howat and Farrington. In Kansas, Governor Henry Allen, close friend of William Allen White, elected on a supposedly liberal platform, had pushed through the legislature an antistrike law for the defiance of which Howat was jailed. Lewis refused to intervene. Farrington took up Howat's case, giving it national publicity and underscoring the indifference of Indianapolis.

Oscar Ameringer, editor of the *Illinois Miner,* and a New York newspaperman were watching a group of delegates to an Illinois miners' convention come down the street to the hall. "Sonny," said Ameringer to the reporter, "which do you think is the bull in that herd?" The reporter pointed to the big figure of Farrington, looming with more than six feet of brawn.

The aggressive president of District 12, first elected in 1914, was born in Fairburg, Illinois, in 1873. He went into the mines at Streator with his father when he was nine years old, and he wrote in an autobiographical note that he never attended school. In 1886 he joined the Knights of Labor, but when Gompers came to power, Farrington went along with the cigarmaker, accepting his philosophy of business unionism. Like Lewis, Farrington could shout down his opposition on the floor of a convention, yet be patient and canny and tenacious in negotiations with the operators. Repeatedly Farrington would come back to the rank and file with terms a little bit better than those in Indiana and Ohio and Pennsylvania. Even his enemies, and he had plenty in his membership, admitted that Farrington could bring back the bacon.

Between Lewis and Farrington there had been a feud of long standing, the original cause of which is lost in the mists of labor history. That it was irreconcilable was of no benefit to the union torn by the frequent clashes between these two powerful men. Lewis spoke of Farrington's "surreptitious and nocturnal activities." Farrington wrote to Lewis, on being challenged to a debate: "Dear Sir and Brother [the conventional union salutation]: Debating with you would be like shooting fish in a barrel. Fraternally yours, Frank Farrington."

Up to 1922 Farrington had depended chiefly upon his success as a bargainer and his power of invective, not so colorful perhaps as that of his rival, but certainly as forceful. In this year he took on Oscar Ameringer as editor of his district paper, the *Illinois Miner,* and thereby placed himself and his district, in the public's mind at any rate, on the side of the progressives.

Ameringer was no "outsider." He had come to this country from Germany in 1886, joined the Knights of Labor, worked as organizer for the musicians' union and led picket lines in strikes of the brewery workers' union. He had agitated for socialism and industrial unionism all through the Southwest. He was an editor on Victor Berger's Milwaukee *Leader* in the war days when that paper was denied its mailing privileges by Burleson and now, in Oklahoma City, he was head of a printing plant which was turning out the *Oklahoma Leader* and several other farm and labor papers.

When he took over the editing of the *Illinois Miner,* Ameringer at once espoused Brophy's nationalization program which had been received with thunders of silence on the part of the national organ, the *United Mine Workers Journal,* edited by Ellis Searles, formerly a press agent for the Indianapolis Chamber of Commerce. The *Illinois Miner* ran H. G. Wells's *Outline of History* and the writings of Upton Sinclair and Covington Hall. The paper backed the "Giant Power Plan" for the co-ordination of hydroelectric and coal, first proposed for Pennsylvania by Morris L. Cooke, the industrial engineer who was to be the head of the Rural Electrification Administration years later. In the columns of the *Miner* the interests of women, which most other labor papers ostentatiously neglect, were fed by articles by Mary Heaton Vorse and Agnes Burns Wieck. Ameringer's own column, "Adam Coaldigger," soon became as famous in labor circles as the columns of Heywood Broun and "B.L.T." in commercial journalism.

Farrington, every bit as far to the right as Lewis, scrutinized some copies of the *Miner* at arm's length, but he realized that here was something more potent in his fight against Lewis than the old ad hominem attack and he let Ameringer bring in trained newspapermen—Carl Leathwood, Len De Caux, and others—to edit the paper which every week reached the 60,000 organized diggers in Illinois.

Very soon he had reason to be thankful for his paper, because in Southern Illinois there exploded that dynamite which the Brophy report had seen in the tense situation in coal. On a fateful, sun-drenched June morning in 1922 outside the mining camp of Herrin, nonunion men, strikebreakers and guards were brutally massacred by an armed mob. The press of the nation called for the destruction of the Illinois union. Only the *Illinois Miner* presented the story of the happenings in Egypt before the mob took command. It was a story, grim enough in all conscience, that needed no yellow journalist touch for its embellishment. Yet until it was told in the union's paper and from the *Miner* copied in the labor and liberal press, the public had no reason to suspect that there was another side to Herrin.

XII. BLOOD AT HERRIN

BY THE SPRING OF 1922 THE OPER-
ators in the Central Competitive Field, whose average earnings for
the past year had been around 3 per cent, flatly challenged the Lewis
"No backward step" slogan. Lewis was insistent that the wage scale
of $7.50 for day men, upon which the entire wage structure in soft
coal hung, be written into any new contract. When the operators
refused to bargain with the union on this basis, a strike of the nation's
soft-coal diggers was begun on April 1st.

Illinois, in spite of its reputation for "separatism," was in the
van of the strike. The state's 60,000 miners took out their tools from
the mines, went home, and stayed there. There was no need for them
to throw out picket lines. Or so they thought. Not for twenty years
had any operator attempted to work his mine in this 100 per cent
union territory. The men worked in their gardens, took odd jobs on
the roads, pitched horseshoes in the peaceful sunlight.

In Cleveland, however, William J. Lester, owner of the Southern
Illinois Coal Company, which operated a strip mine halfway between
the towns of Herrin and Marion, the county seat of Williamson, decided to risk the wrath of the union by mining and shipping coal
to Chicago where spot prices of $18 a ton were being paid.

He had a heavy investment in a monster Bucyrus shovel, which
had seen duty at the Panama Canal, and other mining machinery.
He brought in from Kansas as his superintendent C. K. McDowell,
who had a reputation for breaking strikes in the belligerent Howat's
state.

Lester started negotiations with the local Herrin union whereby

Lester would be allowed to strip the overburden from the rich coal bed without interference from the union. There was, however, to be no shipping of the coal until the national strike was settled. The agreement gave Lester an advantage over his near-by competitors inasmuch as he would have the coal for the eager Chicago market on his cars ahead of the rest.

It was soon evident that Lester and his hard-boiled super had other plans than those discussed with the union. McDowell, whose right leg had been shattered in the mine wars in Kansas, limped about the courthouse square in Marion boasting that he had broken strikes called by Howat, and that he would do the same in Egypt. He slapped a gun in a holster on his hip and warned all hands not to come near the strip. The idle diggers looked at him with inscrutable eyes and turned away. They figured "Old Peg," as they called him, was a stupid mouth-shooter who certainly didn't know his Egypt.

But McDowell meant business. Down from Chicago flophouses came nondescript members of that footloose army known as "finks" in the labor movement, derelicts whose profession is that of breaking strikes. These are not, in any sense of the word, workers. Their presence at a struck factory or mine is supposed to create consternation among the strikers, at the same time that it encourages nonunion men, legitimate laborers, to go back to work. The strikebreakers, who were taken to the Lester strip in a covered truck with an armed guard sitting by the driver, spent most of the time hanging around the mess hall of the commissary set up within the mine. Either that or arguing about their pay. The actual work of stripping was done by the crew of the Bucyrus, who were members of a small, independent union charged by labor leaders with being an "outlaw" organization.

Williamson's Sheriff Melvin Thaxton, a former miner elected by union votes, as were the majority of the officials in Egypt, warned the newcomers dropping off trains at the Marion station that there was a strike in progress, that in this thoroughly organized territory they were seeking out trouble if they went to work at the mine. For by now cars loaded with Lester's coal were moving up a spur from the mine to the main line of the railroad. Colonel Samuel Hunter of the state militia and other officials notified McDowell not to continue shipping operations and to stop his importation of strikebreakers.

McDowell, bossing a crew of sixty, twenty-four of them armed guards, laughed at his visitors. When two young strikers in their Ford rode down a public road past the mine they were stopped by a guard armed with a high-powered rifle and marched to the mine office. There in a storeroom behind the office McDowell showed them an arsenal of rifles, sawed-off shotguns and hand grenades and told the two that he was ready for anything. The next day the shovelmen dug up and blocked off this public road, against the protests of the sheriff and of State Senator William J. Sneed, president of the Herrin sub-district of the United Mine Workers.

From then on, for several days, the guards rode around the countryside in the company truck, firing their rifles at farmhouses and farm stock and generally attempting to terrorize the community. What they succeeded in doing was to bring the farmers, who were usually neutral in mine wars, solidly behind the strikers. A letter from a Lester guard, and written to a farm girl and intercepted by the miners, read: "I have been sitting up here on the bank [the high mound of dirt around the mine which made the strip a natural fortification] waiting for a goddam coaldigger to stick his red neck out. They give us all the white mule we can use, a high-powered rifle and ten dollars a day."

On June 13th, the McDowell crew started loading coal into cars on a siding for shipment to Chicago. By now strikers from all parts of Southern Illinois and from adjoining states were milling around in the neighborhood of the mine. They were joined by farmers and other organized workers, roused by the action of the guards.

The lame super had told Sneed that he was working his mine with union men. The state senator questioned Lewis at the national headquarters of the U.M.W. of A. at Indianapolis as to the status of the Steam Shovel Men's Union. Frank Farrington was out of the state and this was Lewis's first intimation that a dangerous situation was developing in Southern Illinois. On June 19th, Lewis wired Sneed as follows:

Your wire of 18. Steam Shovel Men's union was suspended from affiliation with the American Federation of Labor some years ago. It was also ordered suspended from the mining department of the American Federation of Labor at the Atlantic City convention. We now find that this outlaw organization is permitting its members to act as strikebreakers at numerous strip pits in Ohio. This organization is furnishing steam-shovel engineers to work under armed guards with strike-breakers. It is not true that any form of agreement exists by and between this organization and the mining department or any other branch of the A. F. of L. permitting them to work under such circumstances. We have, through representatives, officially taken up this question with the officers of the Steam Shovel Men's Union and have failed to secure any satisfaction. Representatives of our organization are justified in treating this crowd as an outlaw organization and in viewing its members in the same light as they do any other common strike-breakers.

John L. Lewis

To this day Lewis's enemies, chief among them the labor-baiting columnist Westbrook Pegler, charge that this telegram was the immediate cause of the bloody events of three days later. Sneed later testified, and it was the consensus of those on the scene that no incentive from Indianapolis was needed to arouse the Williamson people, farmers and miners alike.

On the afternoon of June 21st, a young striker standing with a group of his friends in the yard of a farmhouse half a mile from the mine was shot through the heart by a bullet fired from a high-powered rifle over the strip bank. Later, members of McDowell's crew said that the super had gone to the bank with the rifle saying that he would shoot a striker and get in the militia to save money paid to the guards. At all events, this shot touched off the whole tense situation. Through Christopher and Zeigler, where strikers had fought in the streets with strikebreakers twenty years before, and Benton and Johnston City, and all the big and little coal camps in Egypt, men drove hard that day knowing that their union was in peril. Into hardware and general stores, and even into American Legion halls and private homes where it was known that weapons were kept, stormed excited men to seize shotguns and revolvers and rifles and drive off in the direction of the Lester strip. By twilight of the 21st a thousand armed men were advancing toward the mine through the cornfields outside the strip, in skirmish waves commanded by ex-service men wearing trench helmets. An airplane, hired at a nearby field, dived over the strip dropping dynamite bombs on the railroad ties put up for shelter by the strikebreakers. Along the bank, clustered for the most part around a machine gun camouflaged by bushes, the guards kept up a steady fire into the corn. All that night the townspeople of Herrin and Marion were kept awake by the sounds of rifle fire deepened by dynamite explosions. And cars from Kansas, Indiana and Ohio arrived, bringing reinforcements for the attackers.

Among those firing into the mine were, of course, many drawn to the strip by love of adventure or animated by mass cruelty and the darker blood thirst of any mob. There were also those who felt that they were fighting for a cause—the preservation of unionism in Southern Illinois. The editor of a local paper wrote: "The whole of Williamson and Franklin Counties was in turmoil until late Tuesday, and on Wednesday afternoon the miners in Zeigler and West Frankfort were canvassing the business district for arms and ammunition, and we doubt whether there was much of either one left in their towns after the cars had left for the scene on Wednesday evening and almost every car was loaded with men, guns, and ammunition . . . no city in the community showed their colors so much as the city of Zeigler which is located in Franklin County. At least 300 strong, men journeyed in cars from Zeigler on Wednesday afternoon, realizing that the future peace of their county was at stake." Thoreau Cronyn, of the New York *Sun,* who was in Williamson shortly after the massacre, wrote: "Nearly every one in the region knew the mine was to be attacked and the scabs cleaned out. . . . One story is that 25 union miners, who were ex-service men and knew the rules of warfare, had been picked to receive the surrender and guard the prisoners." Colonel Samuel Hunter of the State National Guard said: "It was a seemingly well-organized, remarkably sober, determined, resolute aggregation of men and boys fighting, as they put it in their own words, 'to preserve the union.'"

The firing on both sides continued until sunup when a white flag in the shape of a cook's apron was raised above the embankment. The attackers, cheering wildly and holding their rifles above their heads, stood up in the cornfield and started toward the mine. As they did so, they were raked by a burst of fire from the machine gun under the bushes on the bank. Finally, during a lull in the firing, there was a shouted peace parley between McDowell and the leaders of the miners and the super said he was ready to quit.

The unionists came pouring into the mine, lining up the scared scabs, disarming the sullen guards. They dynamited the deck of the big shovel and blew up several loaded coal cars standing on the siding ready for shipment. Then, after a heated discussion, it was decided to march the prisoners to Herrin, four miles distant, and put them on a train to Chicago.

Many of the attackers went home to get some needed sleep. A few picked men marched alongside the prisoners, who were formed in columns of two, until a crossing a half mile from the pit was reached. There McDowell was taken out of the line after a man had made a speech urging the crowd "To end this breed of finks and show the world this ain't West Virginia." Down a lane, dragged by two armed men, limped McDowell. Shots were heard by the crowd at the crossing and then the two came back without the super. Later, McDowell's bullet-riddled body was found in the lane.

Farther down the road, a crowd coming out from Herrin again stopped the marchers. The miners who had been in the fighting handed over their prisoners to this mob, consisting of men and boys armed with shotguns, revolvers and knives. The members of this second group had taken no part in the battle. They were mainly small-town riffraff eager for the kill now that the danger was over. These fell upon the wretched Lester men, backed them against a barbed-wire fence running in front of a wood lot with a small pond in the center of it, and told them they would have a chance to run for their lives—the Herrin version of ley de fuga.

A moment later, two hundred men standing at a distance of a few yards were firing into the defenseless group of prisoners. Many of the latter were killed instantly, many others wounded. Some managed to crawl through the fence and run into the woods. A whooping man hunt followed, with guards and scabs hanged from the trees, their throats cut, their bodies mutilated by the knife-wielding followers of the riflemen.

Six Lester men, who were caught alive in the woods, were taken down one of the principal streets of Herrin, past the schoolhouse where children jeered at them as they were forced to crawl on their hands and knees, and out to the cemetery on the outskirts of the town. There a rope was thrown around the six and they were shot to death into an open trench.

All that bloodstained day, men, women and children trooped

past the improvised morgue at Herrin where seventeen bodies of the slain prisoners were put on display, their bodies stripped and twisted into grotesque shapes.

The entire nation was aroused by the gruesome stories of the massacres. Cronyn's special articles alone gave any hint that there might have been provocation for the original attack on the mine. The Chicago *Tribune* called for the extermination of the Illinois union. The Chicago Chamber of Commerce raised a fund to pay for special prosecutors of the two hundred men, the overwhelming majority union miners, who were indicted for the murders.

The trials, which dragged on from October until the next spring, were mere formalities. Farmer juries acquitted eleven defendants in all. It did not need the eloquence of Angus Kerr, chief counsel for the union, to convince Williamson juries that the slain men were enemy invaders, bent on destroying the union which had become the shield and buckler for all the working people in that community. The jurymen knew of the early struggles for union in Egypt and at heart they agreed with the speaker on the line of march that the breed of strikebreakers had best be wiped out, that Williamson wanted none of West Virginia's antiunion tactics. Justice in the matter of industrial disputes, it seemed, was largely a matter of community sentiment. A strikebreaker had no more chance in a Southern Illinois court than did a union miner with a Colorado jury.

Government investigators for the Bituminous Coal Commission of 1923 summed up the attitude of Southern Illinois toward the union as follows:

When mining began in that country it was upon a ruinously competitive basis. Profit was the sole object; the life and health of the employees were of no moment. Men worked in water half-way to their knees, in gas-filled rooms, in unventilated mines where the air was so foul that no man could work long without seriously impairing his health. There was no workmen's compensation law; accidents were frequent, and there was no common ground upon which employer and employee could meet. They had no interest in common as they regarded each other with hostility and distrust. The average daily wage of the miner was from $1.25 to $2.00. Then came the union. . . . Peace and goodwill and mutual respect have been the general rule since that time. The Workman's Compensation Law was enacted. Earnings advanced to $7 even to $15 a day; improvements in the working conditions was reflected in the appearance of the workmen, their families, their manner of life and their growing cities and public improvements. There are 13,000 miners in Williamson County, 62 per cent of whom own their homes and most of them own automobiles. All occupations are unionized. They believe in the union, for they think it brought them out of the land of bondage into the promised land when their government had been careless of or indifferent to their needs. They hold themselves to be good Americans and proved it during the Great War, but what they have of daily comfort they think comes from the union and not from the government.

The Illinois miners paid for the heavy costs of the defense of their members and the damages to the mine machinery out of a special assessment, estimated in the neighborhood of a million dollars, without seeking aid from the international union or from any other labor body for that matter.

Lewis, seeing a chance to weaken Farrington, charged that the Communists were responsible for the Herrin massacres. He had his editor Searles write a series of articles alleging that the Reds were active in Southern Illinois and were attempting to take over the entire Mine Workers Union. Many newspapers carried these releases in good faith. I showed a clipping from one of them to a union miner who had led in the attack on the mine. His people had come into the state from Kentucky at the time of the Civil War. His father had fought on the side of the North and he himself was a veteran of both the Spanish-American War and World War I. He looked over the Searles charges with vast contempt.

"Bolsheviki!" he exclaimed. "If any of them Bolsheviki came down here we would treat them just like we treated them Lester scabs."

Others than unionists concerned with the root causes of this constant warfare over the nation's coal brought pressure upon the flustered President Harding, first, to end the strike and then to appoint a responsible body to see why our coal should be constantly stained with blood.

On August 15, 1922, the strike was called off with the day rate of $7.50 in the new contract, although by now it was estimated that 64 per cent of all the country's coal was being mined south of the Ohio. It was evident that the settlement was no more than an armistice, covering but a small proportion of the nation's total tonnage. The public's interest centered on what the newly appointed Bituminous Coal Commission could accomplish.

The commission, headed by men of ability and competently staffed, worked diligently at collecting the most impressive body of facts about the actual running of coal ever gathered up to that time. Its findings were incorporated in four fat, statistics-strewn volumes. Its researchers checked the union's charge that the life of the American miner is a drab business at best, the most hazardous of occupations, to be compensated by good pay under contract. The commission also substantiated the charge of the operators that in many instances the United Mine Workers had resorted to violence to obtain contracts and that high labor costs had compelled mine owners in the Central Competitive Field to sell their product at less than cost. Charges of reckless waste of men, machines and an irreplaceable natural resource were fully confirmed in those four volumes, which cost the taxpayers some half million dollars and which for a long time were not accessible to the general public. On the whole, the final report was little more than an underscoring of the obvious. Hamilton and Wright, in *The Case of Bituminous Coal,* summed up the general impression of students of the industry as to the value of the commission's findings as follows:

The four volumes which make up the report consist of a series of reports on various phases of the mining industry. They contain a mass of factual material, honestly and painstakingly collected. The report as a whole constitutes the chief source of information about the coal industry of today. [This was written in 1925.] The serious student will find it indispensable.

The reports, however, are uneven. Some of them are extremely valuable; others, perhaps the majority, are inferior products. Their facts are uninterpreted or misinterpreted; they are badly presented; some are unintelligible, if not quite meaningless.

On the whole, although the report has many gaps in the facts it presents, its most serious weakness is that it fails in adequate analysis and interpretation of its own material.

Even as the commission's investigators went through the fields, a swift change in the entire economic and technical phases of mining was under way. The march of the operators away from the Central

Competitive Field to the highly mechanized, low-cost labor mines in the South went on at the double-quick. Nonunion operators were finding docile diggers satisfied with wages as low as $3 a day in Virginia, (with the exception of the organized Panhandle) and in Kentucky, Tennessee and Alabama.

New and ingenious machines were almost daily arriving at the unionized pits, throwing more and more organized men out of work. The laissez faire recommendation of the commission that the "largest opportunity and the largest responsibility for putting the coal industry in order lie with the industry itself" was accepted by the operators to mean low wages and high mechanization.

Idle union miners watched gondolas clatter past their camps carrying coal for New England and the Great Lakes markets from the southern fields and they wanted to know what their union was doing to stop this disastrous invasion, outside of reiterating the "No backward step" defiance. Lewis went to see Secretary of Commerce Herbert Hoover, who had been unusually caustic in his criticism of the operators and who might be expected to be sympathetic with the union. The two men agreed that the venerable cliché "too many mines and too many miners" was the grim truth of a situation where the industry was capable of producing twice as much coal as the country could normally consume, with twice as many miners as were needed, waiting around in demoralizing, enforced idleness in the vain hope that operations, closed for lack of orders, might be resumed. To be sure, unemployed miners could retain their membership in the United Mine Workers by the system of "exoneration" from dues payment during slack spells, but Lewis was by now willing to forgo the rather empty satisfaction of announcing to his conventions that he had close to half a million organized men—and then have to add how many were exonerated. It seemed more sensible to him and to Hoover also to continue the high wage scale of $7.50 a day which under the conditions of the market would force many operators in the Central Competitive Field to close down their high-cost mines. This of course would drive more miners out of the fields, but Lewis was willing to face that contingency. It was the contention of the miners' leader that higher freight rates for the long hauls from the nonunion territory balanced the higher wages paid in the North.

And that the presence of the union on the borders of the unorganized fields would eventually keep up wages.

This hopeful formula for stabilization without governmental intervention was embodied in the contract made between the union and the Central Competitive operators signed in Jacksonville, Florida, in February, 1923. The Jacksonville Agreement was to last three years. In his annual report, in 1924, the elated secretary of commerce wrote:

The coal industry is now on the road to stabilization. The benefits lie not only in the provision of coal to the consumer at lower prices than have been attained at any time since the beginning of the war. The gradual elimination of high-cost and fly-by-night mines is bringing about a greater degree of concentration of labor upon a smaller number of mines, the increase in days of employment per annum, and thus a larger annual return to the workers. The inherent risks in the industry will be decreased because the efficient and stable operator will no longer be subjected to the type of competition that comes from those mines that exist only to take advantage of profiteering periods. No better example of co-operation to secure the elimination of national waste can be presented. The past year, as compared to 1920, shows a saving to the consumer of about $1,000,000,000, which must be reflected in decreasing cost of production in every avenue of industry and commerce.

Lewis was equally jubilant. He exclaimed shortly after the signing of the agreement: "Exactly as was foreseen by the United Mine Workers, the law of supply and demand is working a cure."

But when the figures were collected for the first period of the working of the agreement they showed that, whereas in 1920, 28.9 per cent of the nation's more important coal had been mined in union fields and but 25 per cent in nonunion, with the balance unaccounted for, in 1924, 24.6 was union coal and 36.1 was nonunion. Machine-cut tonnage had risen 7 per cent above that of '20. Output per man in '24 was close to five tons per day as compared to four in 1920. Mines were closing down but with no assurance that they would not reopen on a nonunion basis. Everywhere there was chiseling on the contract, in some cases open violation of it. Early in 1925 two mines in long unionized Ohio opened on the 1917 wage scale.

XIII. A MIGHTY SICK
INDUSTRY

TUMULTUOUS AS WERE THE EARLY
gatherings of the miners, they could not equal the "sound and fury"
of the conventions of the U.M.W. of A. during the dark decade
following the Jacksonville Agreement when the union was fighting
a losing rear-guard action. Labor reporters covering the conventions
soon looked for a definite pattern. Following the opening prayer and
the address of welcome by the mayor of the city where the convention was held, the first order of business was to have the chairman
instruct the sergeant at arms to eject Powers Hapgood and other
insurgents from the hall. Then amid boos and derisive whoops from
the opposition, Lewis would read his report for the year, throwing the
onus for repeated defeats upon the Reds, the railroads and the operators. With every sign of perturbation William Green, in the first years
of the decade, would read his treasurer's report, skipping hurriedly
over the "miscellaneous" section of the expenses of the national office.
The chair would then refuse official recognition to Alex Howat, who
would come charging down the middle aisle, to scramble over the
press table onto the platform. Whence he would be hurled back by
administration supporters into the milling midst of the rank and file.
Holding fast to the public address amplifier on the platform, Lewis
would boom his defiance of the opposition.

"May the chair state," he thundered at the Indianapolis convention
of 1924, "that you may shout until you meet each other in hell and
he will not change his ruling?"

"For what purpose does the delegate arise?" Lewis would ask an objector.

"I want to go on record . . ."

"If you want to go on record, write it on a slip of paper and hand it to the secretary. Next business."

He would point suddenly at a Communist in the gallery and intone:

"All day there has lurked in that gallery the arch prince of communism in the United States who makes annual visits to Moscow to make his reports and receive his orders."

Thereupon the departing Communist would be waylaid in the lobby of the hall and fists would fly.

Red-mustached John Hindmarsh of Illinois, a lone-wolf oppositionist, hostile to both Lewis and Farrington, would call on the rank and file in a voice fully as organ-toned as Lewis's to get rid of their dictators, elect their own organizers, re-establish the autonomy of the districts. In these demands he was joined by a group of young progressives and one or two Communists in Illinois who, like Hindmarsh, had no more love for Farrington's rigid rule in Springfield than they had for Lewis's in Indianapolis.

When finally the opposition steam was blown off, and wearied delegates, their expense money running low, were thinking about adjournment, the Lewis forces, often defeated in the opening days, would put through quick motions for reconsideration of measures which the opposition had previously passed. With the result that the administration would win the second and final round and somewhat bewildered delegates would go back to the fields to explain to their locals why, having once defeated Lewis, they couldn't make it stick.

No question but that Lewis's way was that of the dictator as charged, but his enemies had no better way out of the problem of holding together an organization of men fighting desperately in the dark against seemingly insuperable odds.

Suspicion, fear and hate were in the wings of every convention platform in those days. Men from Indiana and Ohio accused progressives in Illinois and Pennsylvania of trying to wreck the union by working at less than the Jacksonville scale. There were ugly rumors that the operators were paying to keep organizers out of the nonunion fields. Communists fishing in these muddied waters made hauls among the discontented rank and file.

The miners lashed out fiercely enough but their blows fell only on their brothers. No one of the leaders could come to grips with the elusive economics of the industry. In less than a year after the signing of the contract, Lewis's Jacksonville formula was proving futile. Brophy's long-range nationalization proposals offered no immediate provision for the paying of tomorrow's grocery bill. Farrington still clung to his parochial attitude. If the Communists had anything to offer other than the dictatorship of the proletariat—i.e., the Workers' party—they did not explain it to the miners.

Competitive throat cutting was the order of the day in bituminous; tight-held monopoly in anthracite. The hard coal was dominated by these railroads: Delaware, Lackawanna & Western; Delaware & Hudson; Lehigh Valley; Reading; Erie; New York, Ontario & Western; Lehigh & New England; Central Railroad of New Jersey, and the Pennsylvania. In 1923 the roads and their coal operating companies owned and controlled between 75 and 80 per cent of all anthracite mined and 90 per cent of the future supply. In bituminous, as we have seen, there was no such concentration of control possible, though such large operations as the Consolidation Coal Company, controlled by the Rockefeller interests, with mines in both union and nonunion fields in West Virginia, and the Mellon-owned giant, Pittsburgh Coal Company, furnished psychological if not actual leadership for the other operators.

In July, 1925, Consolidation repudiated the Jacksonville Agreement and cut wages of day men to $6. On August 12th, Pittsburgh Coal, operating in Western Pennsylvania, followed suit. A host of lesser companies in Pennsylvania, Ohio and Northern West Virginia tore up the union contracts.

The spearhead of the struggle for unionism that followed was Pittsburgh Coal, with its 17,000 miners in the heart of Pennsylvania's District 5, U.M.W. of A. headed by Patrick Fagan, who in boom times had 45,000 organized men in his jurisdiction.

While other industrial workers in the Pittsburgh area were on rising payrolls at the outset of the march to prosperity in the Coolidge era, the miners were caught up in the tragic toils of wage cuts, discharges and evictions. The same dramatis personae as trod the stage

in West Virginia appeared around Pittsburgh Coal's struck mines—
the picket lines with as many as 1,500 men and women walking them,
the state troopers and deputies, the strikebreakers coming in to take
over the homes from which the strikers had been evicted. In place
of the tents in West Virginia, there were barracks for the evicted
families, provided by the union; in place of the tough-boy tactics of
Don Chafin, there was the smooth talk of E. S. McCullough, hired by
the Pittsburgh Chamber of Commerce and the operators at $1,000
a month to set up an "independent union," forerunner to the "Johnstown plan" which later was to harass the C.I.O. When McCullough
failed, the coal and iron police took over with their traditional tactics
of terrorism.

Lewis protested loudly but vainly that he had been promised
backing for the Jacksonville Agreement by Washington. When, however, Washington asked how it could force operators to stick to the
contracts, Lewis shied away from any proposal for arbitrary federal
legislation. He still held to the laissez faire philosophy incorporated
in his book, *The Miners' Fight for American Standards*. He could
only protest: "The union miner cannot agree to the acceptance of a
wage principle which will permit his annual earnings and his living
standards to be determined by the hungriest unfortunate whom the
non-union operators here can employ."

Though the props of the miners' union were crashing with repercussions felt throughout the world of labor, the United Mine Workers
of America was still in a strategic political position within the American Federation of Labor. As was evidenced, when on December 5,
1924, Samuel Gompers died and there was a scramble to elect his
successor. Matthew Woll, lawyer, president of the tight, little craft
union, the International Photo-Engravers, fifth vice-president of the
A.F. of L., who moved easily through the two worlds of the National
Civic Federation and the labor movement, was generally assumed to
be Gompers's "crown prince." He was far better known to the public
than was Lewis at that time, and was, and is, a favorite of the conservative press. His sententious statements faithfully reflecting the
cautious philosophy of the A.F. of L. hierarchy were always treated
deferentially and he was in constant demand as window dressing
for any committee in search of a conservative labor representative.
Between him and Lewis no love was lost and the miners' leader made

it plain that so intransigent a craft unionist as Woll would not be acceptable to the United Mine Workers. To avoid a public row, Woll and Lewis finally hit upon a compromise in the chubby person of William Green. The treasurer of the Miners would be colorless enough to suit the Federation's hierarchy, and at the same time amenable enough for Lewis's purposes whatever they might be. His impeccable background—state legislator, Sunday-school superintendent, humble toiler risen from the ranks—would presumably be acceptable to the public.

In Green's place as secretary-treasurer, Lewis appointed the shrewd and capable Thomas Kennedy, who, with Philip Murray and Lewis, was to make the triumvirate of negotiators and policy-makers which dominated the councils of the miners until yesterday.

In the bitter winter of 1926-1927, out-of-work miners were begging for handouts at the doors of steel and coal owners in the suburbs of Pittsburgh. Union officials were in Washington begging the government to do something to reassemble the Central Competitive Field operators and force them to live up to the Jacksonville Agreement. At the same time, Lewis was attacking the Interstate Commerce Commission for its apparent favoritism in the setting of freight rates. Nonunion mines in the South, he claimed, were enjoying lower rates than the organized operations in the North. The very nature of the complaint indicated the competitive shift. There was no realistic basis left for the Central Field. Ohio was competing not with Indiana and Illinois, but with West Virginia and Kentucky and Tennessee. Recognizing this, the union scale committee authorized the miners to make district agreements as best they could. The operators, however, were resolved to press their gains, and few $7.50-a-day contracts were signed.

Overseas, the British general strike in May, 1926, set off by the miners' strike and lockout, had so alarmed the middle classes on both sides of the Atlantic that there was little public support for the despairing strike in the soft-coal fields called on April 1, 1927. Less than 200,000 men responded to the call and their places were soon filled with strikebreakers.

The state of the miners' union was symbolized by the fact that the Brotherhood of Locomotive Engineers, owners of the Coal River Collieries in Kentucky and West Virginia, were persistently refusing to pay their diggers the union scale though Lewis indignantly proclaimed that this was "a disgrace to organized labor."

Though, as Lewis said, striking miners of the Pittsburgh Coal Company had been "evicted from their homes, and a reign of terror and intimidation inaugurated that has excelled for brutality and lawlessness any union-busting endeavor this nation has witnessed in recent years," still the Mellon company showed a deficit for 1926 of $2,175,-000. The Mellons decided to move south, and in the summer of 1927 they bought 27,000 acres of coal fields in West Virginia for their sprawling congeries, the Koppers Company of Massachusetts, a voluntary association beyond the reach of federal regulation. The Massachusetts collaborators had organized the Koppers Gas and Coke Company of Delaware with the Mellon bank, the Union Trust, floating a bond issue of $25 million. Companies that bore the magic name of Koppers or could trace their lineage back to the time when, as alien property custodian, A. Mitchell Palmer sold the invaluable German-inspired processes of ore treatment to the Pittsburgh millionaires, ranged from coal, coke and gas operations to moth balls, dye bases and railroad ties. In the Midwest, the Mellons were allied with the Insull utility empire; in New York, with the Morgan interests. Koppers was soon shipping coal from West Virginia, Kentucky and Western Pennsylvania into New England for highgrade coking and by-product gas, as well as to the Midwest for fueling electric power stations. In 1925 Lewis charged that the Mellons, Charles M. Schwab, the steelmaster, and John D. Rockefeller, Jr., were conspiring to destroy the United Mine Workers. No one paid much attention. The nation had pretty well accepted the Mellon success formula, namely, that through some sort of financial osmosis prosperity would seep through from the tax-free rich to the pliant poor.

Only in rebel Illinois in the fall of 1927 was the union scale still in force through a temporary agreement between Springfield and the state operators. In the following April, however, Illinois joined with the rest of the states in the North in a general soft-coal strike. The strike was no more than a gesture. Early in July, 1928, Illinois, Indiana and Iowa accepted basic day rates of $6.10. The "No backward step" slogan was no more than a phrase which Lewis's opposition was to use for his discomfiture.

At long length, the leaders of the miners turned to their government for relief in the shape of regulation of an industry which was so palpably sick. Into the fields of Pennsylvania, West Virginia and Ohio went a subcommittee of the Senate Committee on Interstate Commerce to collect the facts from which to write legislation. The committee was in the Pittsburgh area in the worst of the bleak winter of 1927-1928. The hearings before this body, headed by Senator James E. Watson of Indiana, and consisting of Senators Gooding, Couzens, Fess, Goff, Pine, Sackett, Metcalf, Bruce, Wheeler and Wagner, fill 3,414 pages. The senators talked to union men living with their families in the rough barracks down the frozen roads from the company houses from which they had been evicted. They talked to U.M.W. of A. organizers and to the embittered women of the evicted strikers. And to state troopers and to coal and iron police and to nonunion workers and strikebreakers. They went back to Washington with two pictures of a war in the industrial heart of America, pictures contradictory and confusing.

Before them came Fannie Hurst, the novelist, who had done some investigating of her own and who said that so serious was the situation that merely ameliorative measures would be "touching iodine to a cancer." And then came J. D. A. Morrow, president of the Pittsburgh Coal Company, to testify that contented workers, with the tonnage men earning $9.32 a day, were living in "the clean, electric-lighted, well-kept villages of the Pittsburgh Coal Company, with their paved streets, their filtered, tested water, their systematic garbage disposal, their approved sanitation and the shacks of temporary strike colonies located elsewhere." But Senator Frank Gooding of Idaho had said after his inspection of the company's camps:

"Conditions which exist in the strike-torn regions of the Pittsburgh district are a blotch upon American civilization. It is inconceivable that such squalor, suffering, misery and distress should be tolerated in the heart of one of the richest industrial centers in the world. The committee found men, women and children living in hovels which are more insanitary than a modern swinepen. They are breeding places of sickness and crime."

In the midst of the hearings E. L. Greever, counsel for the West Virginia operators, suddenly challenged the fundamental right of the committee to do any investigating whatsoever. Coal was a purely state matter, contended the lawyer, and the Senate had no business sending out "fishing" committees. Whereupon T. C. Townsend, attorney for the United Mine Workers, countered:

"If anyone friendly to the union undertakes to enter the wilderness of industrial autocracy existing in the smokeless coal fields of southern West Virginia, he must run the gantlet of injunctions, 'yellow-dog' contracts, house leases and mine guards. If the United States Senate undertakes to enter in quest of information as a basis of contemplated legislation, it must run the gantlet of alleged constitutional barriers. If neither can enter, there is nothing left except to invoke divine providence to roll back the waters of the Red Sea and let 'God's people go.'"

Percy Tetlow, West Virginia union leader, testified that from 1922 to 1925, there were 50,000 union people evicted from their homes in Southern West Virginia.

> The Chairman: Where are those people?
> Mr. Tetlow: God knows.
> The Chairman: Are they still about there?
> Mr. Tetlow: Everywhere.
> Senator Bruce: They are spread all over the country, are they not?
> Mr. Tetlow: Everywhere.
> Senator Bruce: Of course many of them went back as non-union laborers?
> Mr. Tetlow: Yes, they have gone back to work on a non-union basis.
> Senator Wheeler: You mean they had to do that or starve?
> Mr. Tetlow: Yes.[1]

When Richard B. Mellon, Andrew W.'s brother who had been chairman of Pittsburgh Coal's Board of Directors from 1923 to 1925 and who had stayed on as director through the long-drawn struggle with the union, took the stand, the reporters sat up. But Mr. Mellon pleaded ignorance of the details of the corporation's business. He said that his concern had broken the Jacksonville Agreement because they could not make money under it. Asked about the starvation among the discharged union men he said: "I do not go out feeding them or anything. I would not be out there, way out in the mines." He thought private charity would suffice. What about machine guns in the hands of his coal and iron police? "It is necessary," he said: "you

---

[1] Hearings, Interstate Commerce Commission, U. S. Senate, 70th Congress, S. Res. 105, p. 1439.

cannot run the mines without them." Later he qualified this by adding that he had meant the coal and iron police had to be armed like any other police force. But neither from him nor from any other official could the investigators get Pittsburgh Coal's production figures.

Before the Committee passed scores of miners and sympathizers who recounted the details of beatings inflicted on strikers by coal and iron policemen, of their usurpation of the offices of the regularly constituted authorities, of homes invaded without warrants, of automobiles stopped and searched on the public highways, of miners' daughters, fourteen and fifteen years old, taken away to rooms rented by the coal and iron police, where they were kept for days. At Pricedale, the Senators saw ragged children, barefooted in February.[2]

From bootlegging to the gruesome details of the rape of a six-year-old child by a strikebreaker, who was defended by the company, from stories of houses of prostitution run for strikebreakers under the auspices of the coal and iron police to brutal assaults by these same police upon suspected union sympathizers, the testimony dragged its sordid course. And then turned suddenly to the relations between the railroads and the mine operators, to the selling of coal below cost of production, to the general economic symptoms of coal's fundamental sickness. It was only upon this last point that senators, operators and unionists agreed. Coal was a mighty sick industry.

What to do about it? Richard Mellon, John D. Rockefeller, Jr., Charles Schwab, the other witnesses for management, had been uneasily vague about what any legislative body could do. Generally it seemed to be the coalmasters' hope that given what they euphoniously called the "open shop," preferential freight rates, freedom to trustify without running into the Antitrust Act, laissez faire would come to their rescue with controlled prices. But they would make no definite proposals for legislation. Setting precedents for public control of their industry was no part of their program. On the other hand, John L. Lewis had evinced no more love than his opponents for governmental interference. Yet now Lewis, with the Jacksonville Agreement torn to bits, with the union going down to defeat in Pennsylvania, already beaten in West Virginia and seriously threatened in Ohio, had perforce to turn to outside sources for help. The

<hr>

[2] *Mellon's Millions*, p. 220.

cautiously written bill drafted by Henry Warrum of the U.M.W. of A. legal department and K. C. Adams, the union's economist, and introduced by Senator Watson was the result.

The bill provided for the licensing of coal producers engaged in interstate commerce, for the setting up of sales agencies and the forming of mergers, and finally for the recognition of the right of labor to organize and to bargain collectively. Congress adjourned without passing the bill. The collective bargaining clause was not to bother the legislators again until it popped up in the famous 7(a) of the National Industrial Recovery Act.

No sooner had the senators left the fields than an immediate confirmation of the charges of sadistic brutality leveled against the coal and iron police was on hand in the shape of the murder of John Barkoski. He was a union sympathizer who had been taken into custody by the Pittsburgh Company's police. At the police barracks, Lieutenant Walter J. Lyster and Policeman Harold P. Watts, who had been irked by the orders from the company to stay out of sight while the senators were investigating, went to work on Barkoski. Lyster said: "I need a little warming up." While Watts held the miner, the lieutenant heated a poker with which he beat Barkoski so savagely that the man's ribs were stove in. Watts twisted the victim's ears until blood flowed, broke Barkoski's jaw and eventually, between the two police, every bone in the miner's body was crushed. A company doctor who came into the torture room protested feebly. But the police paid no attention.

Of this affair, even the hard-boiled district attorney said: "It was the most brutal murder I have ever investigated." The Mellon company defended their police so successfully that Lyster and Watts were given light sentences for manslaughter. The company paid the widow of the miner $13,500. She said: "The money doesn't mean anything to me now. We'd be all right if John was living."

XIV. DRIFTING TOWARD
REGULATION

I T WAS A WOMAN IN COLORADO,
scene of so many union defeats, who dared stand out in 1928 against
the rush of the nation's operators to tear up their union contracts.
Josephine Roche, president, manager and owner of the majority stock
of the Rocky Mountain Fuel Company operating six soft-coal mines
in the fast-held nonunion state, signed a contract with the United
Mine Workers of America on August 16th to last two years for the
purpose of "stabilizing employment, production and marketing
through co-operative endeavor and the aid of science," as the wording
of this unique document put it.

Another woman whose contribution to the annals of mining has
been notable, Mary Van Kleek, director of industrial studies of the
Russell Sage Foundation, wrote of Miss Roche:

"She is acting from an inner conviction of what constitutes social
justice, reenforced by an intellectual grasp of the larger significance of
the problems for which her solution, in her view, is merely the best
that can be done in a changing world."[1]

The Rocky Mountain Fuel Company's union contract covered
only six hundred workers in mines whose production cut no great
figure in the total tonnage of the State. But nevertheless it shone in
the darkness of strife and insecurity and waste that enveloped all the
industry those years and constituted, as Miss Van Kleek pointed out:

[1] *Miners and Management.* New York, Russell Sage Foundation.

"A challenge to the people of the United States to remove the obstacles which stand in the way of substituting reason for violence." [2]

To the average coal digger the phrase in Miss Roche's contract about "the aid of science" seemed a bit ironic. Science would appear to be on the way to making his labors superfluous. Everywhere engineers and technicians were taking heed of the criticisms heaped upon the coal industry by such authorities as C. G. Gilbert and J. E. Pogue, Hugh Archbald, Walter Polakov, Stuart Chase, even Herbert Hoover in his less lyrical moods. Henry Ford was showing the way to effective utilization of coal by extracting from a ton of bituminous, which cost him $5 at Detroit, $13.56 worth of by-products from gas to grease with 1,500 pounds of coke left over for smokeless fuel. In the vast new cathedrals of industry, the generating stations of the electric utilities, modernized stoking devices were marching toward the goal of producing electrical energy units with 1.25 pounds of coal whereas in 1919 it took 3.2 pounds. Steadily the amount of coal used for coking was declining. Mechanical stokers in large plants and small homes were giving more heat and power from less and less coal. And always there loomed the increasing threat of the oil burner and the hydroelectric plant. "Next to a scab, in my opinion," said a union organizer, "the lowest form of human life is an oilburner salesman, or a big dam builder."

Yet all the leaders of the union could say to economists who came to them with these alarming facts was "We have the skilled men." True that a union miner in Illinois, for example, with two years' experience underground before he could work at the face, was a far better man than a raw recruit from the Kentucky hills; but what price the skills of the Illinois digger in competition with a newly installed Joy loading machine? In 1924, Southern Illinois diggers were getting out 5.3 tons a day, well above the national output. But within the next five years, when mechanization in Egypt really got under way, production increased to 6 tons per man-day. Between 1923 and 1925, in three Southern Illinois counties alone, 9,300 miners were thrown out of work, either by the abandonment of mines on the part of owners who could not meet nonunion competition or by the introduction of laborsaving machines.

More than $7 million of union funds had been spent in vain

[2] *Ibid.*

attempts to make the Jacksonville Agreement stick. As an offensive weapon the strike, as was proved by the 1927 failure, was as obsolete as the crossbow. With such potent pressures as the operators could bring to bear, Congress would listen to no belated pleas from the United Mine Workers. Giving financial difficulties as the reason, the International Board announced that, following a referendum, there would be no convention of the U.M.W. of A. in 1929.

In Illinois, the last remaining stronghold of unionism in the nation, a scandal of the first dimension had given Farrington into Lewis's hands and thrown the former out of his office as president of District 12. Farrington, while still president of the Illinois Miners in 1926, had signed a three years' contract with the Peabody Coal Company, the most influential of the Illinois operators, to serve for $25,000 a year as their "labor representative."

Farrington was on the high seas, a delegate to an international convention of miners, when Lewis called in the reporters and gave them the story. In vain the friends of the large-framed Illinois official protested that Farrington had done nothing more than had other union officials, from the days of the pioneers on, in moving over to the operators' side of the fence. What about Phil Penna or, for that matter, John Mitchell himself, hero and friend of Farrington? Hadn't Penna taken a job with the operators, Mitchell with the Civic Federation? But the argument fell flat when Lewis pointed out that Farrington had signed with the Peabodys, *while still in office*. It might have been true, as his defenders claimed, that he intended to resign within a few months, but there was the fateful signature under the fateful date for all the rank and file to see. Harry Fishwick, who had served as vice-president under Farrington, a verbose little man with a cockney accent, an abounding sense of self-importance, and with none of his predecessor's ability, was hurriedly elected president of the Illinois district.

The downfall of the foremost of his conservative opponents, and the selection of so inept a character as Fishwick, gave Lewis his chance to discipline the Illinois insurgents.

The Farrington affair, combined with widespread unemployment, or at best intermittent work, worked havoc with the morale of the Illinois rank and file. Corruption began to seep through the local unions. There were charges that petty officials were dividing up union burial funds with undertakers, that "bean money" sent for relief to the unemployed by the union was finding its way into the pockets of insiders, that everywhere organizers were padding expense accounts.

In the fall of 1929, Lewis came storming into the demoralized district to announce that he was dismissing the officials from Fishwick down on charges of corruption, and setting up provisional officials of his own appointing. The internecine strife was no longer the clash of two strong personalities as in the Farrington-Lewis feud. Now it was between the parent organization and its lustiest offspring. Statisticians for the Illinois miners stated that at this time out of 522,150 miners digging soft coal, only 84,395 were dues-paying members of the U.M.W. of A., and that of these 53,088 were in Illinois, 10,609 in Indiana, and the rest scattered over the country. Though the Indianapolis headquarters questioned the accuracy of these figures, no statistics were offered by the International for their refutation.

It was one thing for Lewis to appoint his own men to run the district, another to get the rank and file to accept them. When the provisional officers arrived in Springfield, they found the headquarters of District 12 barred to them. They couldn't even get into the lobby of the big office building where Fishwick was consulting with the Illinois union lawyers. The elevator man, a former miner, patted his hip suggestively and the Lewis men withdrew to a near-by hotel, in whose plush lobby there presently followed some lively fist fights that sent alarmed legislators scurrying for cover.

Both sides went to court to the undisguised delight of the labor-baiting papers of the state whose editors lost no chance to emphasize the irony of union men using the long-hated injunctive process against one another.

Oscar Ameringer, saying, "Running a labor paper these days is like feeding melting butter on the end of a hot awl to an infuriated wildcat," went to see Brophy and Hapgood and other progressives. These agreed with the crafty Miners' Ulysees that the time had come for a showdown. Lewis was technically vulnerable, as his failure to call a convention showed. He could and would be charged with striking at Illinois, the stout heart of all that was left of his union. As for his war chest, no one knew exactly how much there was in the International treasury, but the bulk of the money must be coming from the checkoff of union dues in anthracite. Illinois locals were sending no more per capita to Indianapolis. In place of the sniping tactics of the Communists, organizing small groups of malcontents into the National Miners Union in outlying districts, the progressives resolved upon a full-dress attack. They called a convention of the United Mine Workers of America to meet in Springfield on March 10, 1930. They told the newspapermen that this was no dual movement, no communist-led agitation. Rather it was "an official convention of the majority of the membership of the United Mine Workers of America." The Pennsylvania, Indiana and Ohio progressives were sending delegates. John H. Walker, head of the Illinois State Federation of Labor, and long a popular mine leader, was going to be there. Alex Howat was interested.

At once Lewis countered by calling a convention to meet at the same time at Indianapolis. The labor movement was bewildered, the operators edified by the spectacle of two conventions each calling itself the official U.M.W. of A. The bulk of the reporters went to the Springfield convention.

In Springfield, the rank and file took over at the start by shouting down Fishwick, who attempted to preside. When Farrington came on the platform to indulge in a long rambling speech of apology for the Peabody affair, in the course of which he said that he had not accepted nor would he accept one cent of his Peabody contract price, the delegates listened in a stony and skeptical silence and Farrington drifted unhappily out of the convention and the movement to which he had devoted his very real ability. Then the insurgents proceeded to elect Alex Howat president of the United Mine Workers of America at one-half the salary paid John L. Lewis—$12,000 at that time. They chose Adolph Germer, husky veteran of the early mine wars in Illinois, for vice-president and made Walker their secretary-treasurer. With the blessings of Ameringer, who had lost neither his sense of humor nor his union idealism in all this infighting, the rank and file went out prepared to do battle with the still potent Lewis followers.

These last, meeting at Indianapolis, watched Lewis dramatically tear up and stamp on a copy of the *Illinois Miner* in which he was denounced as a "wrecker" and "racketeer." They saw William Green give the imprimatur of the A.F. of L. upon their gathering, and they counted on the hard-coal miners and the still strong Lewis locals in Southern Illinois to put down the rebellion at Springfield.

All that spring there was civil war centering in Southern Illinois. Coming down from Springfield, Germer, who was notably outspoken in his indictments of Lewis's "dictatorial tactics," was brass-knuckled on the streets of a Lewis-held camp. With blood streaming down his face, he went on into the meeting hall and defied Lewis for an hour of invective. At first the weapons of this war were knuckles, blackjacks and pick handles. Soon guns began to pop. Brother shot it out with brother, father with son. Through twisting alleyways of the small towns, out along the new hard roads, union man hunted union man in feudist fury.

In the courts, Acquilla Lewis, chief counsel for the insurgents, obtained orders staving off the provisional government. The rebel movement made headway in Pennsylvania and Ohio. For a space it looked as though the old Lewis-Murray-Kennedy regime was done for. Then money from Indianapolis began pouring into Southern Illinois and Walker could find no funds for counterattack. Many important locals held onto their dues awaiting the outcome of the general battle. In this the insurgents were tooled into the position of advocating seemingly reactionary policies. In attacking Lewis for clinging overlong to his "No backward step" formula, the Howat-Germer-Walker group had perforce to suggest an alternative and the only alternative was the far from militant acceptance of the "best terms to be had" from the operators in the union fields that remained. As a consequence, the fight degenerated into the old Farrington-Lewis ad hominem squabble with little sustenance for a despairing rank and file. In such times of storm and stress, a primitive economics—the "belly urge" of the I.W.W.'s —was a powerful determinant of men's loyalties and better financed Indianapolis was finally able to break the revolt. Within a year the insurgents were back in the fold, with Lewis once more the victor. Victor, however, in a strife that had further torn an already pitifully weak organization, and that had given comfort to every open-shop employer in the country. Lewis had defeated all his opponents, conservatives, progressives, radicals, only to preside, or so it seemed in the first days of the depression, over the obsequies of the United Mine Workers of America.

The mines were being abandoned fast. Whole populations of a

coal camp where the mine was down for good would drift across the field to the next camp where the mine was already crowded. No one said anything about unionism. Men who were known to be active in the United Mine Workers were laid off first, no matter how skilled they were. A blacklisted miner might as well get out of the pits for good.

"The Franklin, Saline and Williamson mine pay roll in 1926 amounted to about 40 million dollars, enough to provide a comfortable livelihood for the entire working population and enough to initiate a boom in the trade and service industries," say the authors of the survey of unemployment in Southern Illinois called *Seven Stranded Coal Towns,* a study made by Malcolm Brown and John N. Webb for the Work Projects Administration. The study continues:

Miners were averaging between $50 and $60 for each 2-weeks' work in 1926, and sometimes "a pay" would run as high as $100. The automobile dealers, the grocers, the clothing merchants, the furniture and music stores all flourished, and the newspapers carried advertisements for grand pianos, Earl Carroll's Vanities and men's $10 shoes, as well as necessities. When someone discovered a destitute family living on a garbage dump near Sesser, the entire community was shocked. Bank deposits in the three counties increased three million dollars in 1926, bringing the aggregate to 32 million dollars and breaking still another prosperity record. "The thing for our people to do," said a local newspaper that year, "is to settle down to a life of enjoyment and contentment."

But there was little time left for either enjoyment or contentment, for the collapse came quickly. Within less than a decade the whole structure of prosperity lay in utter ruin. Where great noisy tipples had stood, one found a few years later only weed-covered railroad sidings, crumbling mine buildings and scrub oaks growing in the silent mine yards. Sesser once had three mines and Benton had four; all were abandoned. Johnston City had eight mines, and they were all abandoned too. Out of the sixteen mines which could once be seen from the Herrin city hall, fifteen were gone forever. Throughout the three counties, 109 mines were abandoned from 1923 through 1938 leaving the countryside dotted with industrial tombstones—burnt-out slack piles, rotting tipples, here and there a smokestack standing alone in the midst of a pasture—to mark the graveyard of almost 20,000 jobs.

Throughout what was once the Central Competitive Field, to a greater or less degree, there were replicas of the drab Egyptian scene.

Veterans of the labor movement, signing up for such work as there was, repudiated their union sympathies, Galileo fashion. Others went south to work nonunion for the first time in their lives. Youngsters who had mechanical proficiency worked on the machines that were nearly doubling the average mine output, without bothering about contracts. As for the thousands who could find no jobs, for whom the Hoover administration had only optimistic press releases, they were in the condition of Percy Tetlow's evicted miners in the South. God only knew what was happening to them.

In the hard-coal fields in 1931 American workers in large numbers made a business of stealing coal from private owners. When production of anthracite was at its peak in 1917, 154,000 men worked on an average of 285 days mining 100,690,000 tons. In 1931 production had dropped to 59,646,000 tons and the number of men employed, all working under union contracts, had dropped to some 50,000. These cold figures convey but small hint of the calamity that had overtaken that part of Pennsylvania whose whole community life was tied in with the fortunes of anthracite.

Unlike their fellow workers in bituminous, the unemployed anthracite miners were not content to watch the closing down of the mines. When an operator announced the last pay, the laid-off men went back to the holes and started working them on their own. Never before in the history of American labor had the property rights of the vested interests been so brazenly flouted. Union officials were fully as alarmed as were the state authorities over this unprecedented action. Here were neighbors, outwardly God-fearing, sober-sided, conventional-minded American miners, going out every day to work together in the abandoned collieries, uncontested title to which still reposed in the hands of the absentee owners. Here was nothing short of revolutionary confiscation—on a small scale, to be sure, but breathtaking nevertheless.

State troopers throughout the anthracite counties rode to the bootleg openings to warn the diggers to leave. "Will Harrisburg give us work?" asked the miners. There was no answer to that, and the men went on digging. Some arrests were made, but it was hard to find judges or juries in the six counties who could see anything fundamentally wrong in the fact that men of otherwise good repute would dig the coal rather than see their families starve. The union representatives pleaded with the bootleggers. "Will John L. Lewis get us work?" was the question, to which again there was no answer. The troopers filled the holes with gas. The bootleggers fanned out the gas and went on digging. Presently they had the help of friendly truckers to take their coal to markets in Pennsylvania, New Jersey, and even farther north. It is estimated that in 1933 one and one-half million tons of stolen coal were going to market, the bulk of it mined by licensed miners out of work. So rapidly did this illegal enterprise grow that by 1937 there were probably 12,000 men engaged in mining and another 6,000 engaged in marketing the stolen goods. In 1937, in a report submitted to the governor of Pennsylvania by Morris Ernst, the New York lawyer and liberal, who made an investigation of the situation for the Anthracite Coal Industry Commission, wrote:

> Sentiment in the anthracite territory respecting bootlegging has altered in recent months. Originally it was condemned by most people. Now it is condoned by an increasing number, including the clergy, court, juries and other sections of respectable opinion. It is said that if the untold riches lying in the soil of Pennsylvania are not so exploited by the operators as to give all a living wage, the miners have a moral right to exploit these riches for themselves. A changed attitude is also noticeable respecting the concept of property as applied to the natural resources of the State. Miners will tell you that the coal does not belong to any group of persons or corporations but to the people at large and therefore may be seized by self-help. In any case, there has begun a subtle process of differentiation between private property and social property, induced by the necessities of making a living and keeping one's family out of the poor house or off the relief rolls.

"Fear and hesitancy," said John Lewis to his 1932 convention, "dominate American thought in industry and finance."

The convention was meeting at the beginning of a presidential campaign year and the ending of as disastrous a year for the mine workers as they had known in their latter-day history. In 1931 soft-coal production was down to 1909 figures—379,744 tons, an ominous part of which was mined by diggers in the South earning around $2.50 for a 9- to 10-hour day underground. Of that period, Glen L. Parker writes in his book, *The Coal Industry:*

> The breakdown of collective bargaining and the wage structure is revealed by the wage rates which were in effect at the time of the adoption

of the Bituminous Coal Code. About 32% of the mines were paying less than $2.50 a day to miners. Eastern Pennsylvania had a better showing than the average with about 81% of the mines paying $3.00 or more but with none paying more than $4.00. . . . In the Northern fields with intermittent employment a greater problem, weekly earnings were from $6.00 to $10.00 and in the Southern fields the monthly earnings were frequently only slightly more.

When outsiders—economists, researchers, liberal sympathizers with labor—went to ask Lewis at Indianapolis what was to become of his union, he put them off with strange language about a "star that guides the destiny of the United Mine Workers of America." They thought him hopelessly reactionary. His record seemed to prove the charge of the Illinois insurgents that he had led the miners through one backward step after another since the day when he said, "I will not fight my government." There was his book to show his complete acceptance of the status quo. There was his Red-baiting. Politically, he was one of the few leaders of organized labor to endorse Coolidge in 1924 when the majority plumped for La Follette. He had publicly collaborated with Hoover on the ill-fated Jacksonville Agreement.

Franklin Roosevelt was an unknown quantity in the mine fields, but, like the rest of labor, the diggers felt that almost anyone would be better than Herbert Hoover. "I don't know about this Roosevelt," said a young mine leader toward the end of the campaign. "His heart seems to be in the right place as far as labor is concerned. But he has two dangerous hobbies—battleships and big dams. Just the same I'm going to vote for him. Anything to get rid of Hoover."

In the late summer of 1931, Philip Murray, at the head of a delegation of mine workers' officials, went to see the Democratic candidate about the sorry state of the miners. Roosevelt listened sympathetically. After that Murray saw the campaigner frequently and finally Roosevelt said in one of his labor speeches that he intended to do something about the mines. The promise was vague, as was the general labor program of the Democrats. But the miners, as Norman Thomas, the Socialist candidate, said, "were voting their fears rather than their hopes," their fears lest the Hoover drift toward complete collapse go on for another four years. Even though southern nonunion operators and their congressmen were bound to have an important say in the event of Roosevelt's election, better from the diggers' standpoint to risk that than another try at letting economic nature take its course. Lewis had scrapped the bottom of the laissez faire philosophy. He sat down with Henry Warrum, his chief counsel, to write out the draft of a bill for governmental regulation of the coal industry.

XV. UNDER THE BLUE EAGLE

SUDDENLY, IN THE SPRING OF 1933, there was a glimpse of that star of the U.M.W. of A. over which the intellectuals had had such fun.

"History will probably record," said Franklin Delano Roosevelt, "the National Industrial Recovery Act as the most important and far-reaching legislation ever enacted by the American Congress. It represents a supreme effort to stabilize for all time the many factors which make for the prosperity of the nation and the preservation of American standards. Its goal is the assurance of a reasonable profit to industry and living wages for labor with the elimination of the piratical methods and practices which have not only harassed honest business but also contributed to the ills of labor."

There was considerable discussion in Washington as to where NIRA had come from. Certainly the chief labor provision had come from the miners. Spokesmen for the National Association of Manufacturers and the National Coal Association of operators seemed to approve the measure as cordially as did the labor leaders. The owners and managers liked the sections which gave them the right to consolidate without governmental interference, provided they subscribed to a code of fair competition. They knew that some sort of governmental regulation was inevitable and they infinitely preferred NIRA to Senator Black's 30-hour-week bill or the bill introduced at the instance of the mine workers' lawyers by Senator Carl Hayden which prescribed quota systems, government licensing of mines, the setting of maximum prices. As for the labor provisions recognizing the right of workers to join unions of their own choosing and bargain collectively, well, that right had been affirmed by the War Labor Board in 1917, reaffirmed by Supreme Court dicta and in countless orations of the most respected statesmen, industrialists, conservative molders of public opinion generally. There were many ways of interpreting the words "collective bargaining."

John L. Lewis, however, saw only one interpretation of the famous Section 7(a) of the NIRA. This was not strange since Henry Warrum had been hammering away at the "right of labor to organize" clause incorporated in Section 7(a) since the measure was first considered. In the minds of the miners' president and his chief counsel that section meant this one thing—the chance to organize the unorganized fields with legal sanction.

That spring, Lewis put himself at the head of an organizing campaign which union men still refer to with awed admiration. Assembling the largest force of organizers the United Mine Workers had ever put into the field, some hundred professionals and volunteers, he set aside for their use the last cent of the International treasury and bade them go forth and say to all nonunion men: "The President wants you to join the union."

Here, of course, was the brashest of assumptions, warranted by nothing in the NIRA nor by any statement from the White House. But it was a compelling summons and it worked. Van A. Bittner went into Southern West Virginia; William Turnblazer, Samuel Pascoe, Edward Morgan and Samuel Caddy tackled Kentucky. In the North, Philip Murray had charge of such veterans as Patrick Fagan, James Mark and Lee Hall. Forgetting all their differences with the Lewis administration, progressives, young and old, flung themselves into the job.

Through territory where, not long before, federal troops and government men had deployed against the marching unionists, into the Rockefeller domains of Consolidation and the Mellon-held strongholds of Western Pennsylvania drove the organizers calling out: "The President wants you to join. Your government says 'Join the United Mine Workers.'"

The instantaneous mass response to the organizers' appeals on the part of men who had never seen the inside of a union hall stunned the nonunion operators and must have come as a surprise to Lewis himself. His emissaries were deluged with applications for membership. They gave the obligation to jammed mass meetings in such supposedly antiunion bastions as Mingo County, West Virginia, and the Connellsville coke regions in Pennsylvania. When hard-working organizers met and compared notes they exclaimed exultantly: "The old union is coming back, by God."

And so it was. Organizers shouted their summonses under the noses of the horses of the coal and iron police. The sullen riders did not dare attack men who seemingly had behind them the support of the federal government. Nonunion operators were loath to order the terrorization of such numbers of their workers who were obviously eager to join the once-outlawed organization. All the elaborate antiunion defenses crumpled that summer with the fall of West Virginia. All save Harlan County in Kentucky, and certain of the captive mines of the U.S. Steel Company. The operators comforted themselves with the thought that the Supreme Court would throw NIRA out the window. But in the meantime the United Mine Workers of America had staged the most dramatic comeback of any trade-union in the history of the American movement. By 1934, Lewis could again stand on the floor of an American Federation of Labor convention and boast that he was head of 400,000 organized miners, still the shock troops of American labor, who had been to all the wars and had turned black defeat into shining victory. If critics of Lewis would discount that victory by pointing out that it was the New Deal philosophy which saved the union at the end, he could show from the record how much of that philosophy, as far as labor was concerned, was formulated by the men on the gob piles.

The next job was to implement the rather misty wording of NIRA with the codes for fair practices as directed in that measure. General Hugh Johnson, the robustious ex-cavalryman, farm implement salesman and as ardent a lover of the mouth-filling phrase as John L. Lewis, was assigned to this monumental task. He and Lewis hit it off all right. It was the operators, stunned by the sudden shift in their labor relations, the overnight return of collective bargaining, and the resurrection of the union, who balked at putting anything on paper. And made the general revert to his cavalry vocabulary during sessions of the conferees at the Shoreham Hotel in Washington.

The miners and those few operators who had long recognized the union had their own code suggestions, the larger operators theirs.

In all, twenty-five bituminous coal codes were submitted, wrangled over, thrown away. Both sides went to the White House where the President warned them that if the soft-coal industry couldn't write its own code it would be written for the industry by the government. Though the die-hard group among the more important operators said that the final code was "paternalistic," a document was finally drawn up with the active intervention of the NRA officials with whom Lewis sat as labor adviser.

Article V of the code, adopted on September 18, 1933, carried over the liberal verbiage of Section 7(a) of the act, still leaving plenty of room for the interpretation of what "representatives of their own choosing" might mean and just what constituted "collective bargaining." Three days after the wearied Johnson had called in the newspapermen to announce that his toughest job had been completed, the operators, Northern and Southern alike, signed a contract with the revivified United Mine Workers of America—the first Appalachian Joint Wage Agreement. A new competitive field had been set up with the miners receiving a basic day wage of $4.60 in the North, $4.20 in the South. Though this was a far cry from the $7.50 of the Jacksonville Agreement, it was better to have the cash of paid-out wages than the credit of a high wage scale. As Lewis once told a senator who had remarked on the fact that the miners were always asking for higher wages, though their wage scale had increased 75 per cent since 1913: "Members of the United Mine Workers of America are gifted with a number of talents but they cannot eat percentages."

Though the Blue Eagle, symbol of the national recovery effort, flapped proudly at the head of parades, though General Johnson and the New Deal propagandists blew their publicity trumpets around the walls of the depression, no serious student of the situation believed that the mere writing of code prescriptions would cure the fundamental sickness of the economy.

"The handwriting is on the wall," exclaimed Lewis at the code hearings; "eighteen million stomachs clash against backbones."

Less dramatically, Dr. Alexander Sachs, an economist for the NRA, put the situation so far as coal was concerned:

The secret, if it is a secret after years of publicity given to the problems of the coal industry, lies in the fact that under the regime of competitive individualism to the limit, no one mine, no one company could alleviate the hardships alone. In fact any forward step made by one mining company, good by itself, brings about conditions that are prejudicial to the industry as a whole, and makes the inherent contradictions only more acute.

And even if by the move of a magic wand the demand for coal should double, and partly idle mines begin to cover the financial charges on their past excessive investments and even show some profit, then the bankrupt mines will be reopened, and new mines will be opened, and the competitive war will go merrily on. Then retrenchment, wage cuts, strikes, unemployment, cutthroat competition, bankruptcies commence all over again. The old, squeaky merry-go-round will again commence to cycle; too many mines, too many miners, too much equipment, too little management, no planning, no profits, no living wages.

The NRA code, though it was the first step on the part of government to regulate the industry on an over-all plan for consolidation of regional operations, collective selling agencies and collective bargaining leading to uniform labor costs, could not, of course, affect the fundamental position of coal at the bottom of a collapsing economic structure. All it could do was to police practices of themselves with a dubious social value. Practices which had grown around the exploitation of a natural resource for private profit with no primary concern either for the conservation of coal or for the need of the consumer. But mild as was the code for coal, the operators saw dangerous precedents being set in its labor sections and they chafed openly under its provisions.

U.S. Steel, operating important mines in Pennsylvania through its subsidiaries, the H. C. Frick Coke Company, the Sharon Coal and Limestone Company and the National Mining Company, refused to go along with the code on the ground that its mines were captive, i.e., producing for the steel mills only, and so were not under the jurisdiction of the code covering commercial coal. The captive mines had been organized in the great drive of the summer of 1933, so the miners, with no union contract, walked out that autumn. When in October, the President agreed to refer the matter to the newly appointed National Labor Board, headed by Senator Wagner of New York, the miners took up their tools again. They succeeded in getting contracts, following NLB supervised elections at the captive mines, in four of the Frick operations and both of the other subsidiaries. The union at long last had a foot in the coke region. But it was not until the fateful December of 1941 that the captive mine dispute was finally settled.

No code was ever written for anthracite where the depression was cutting production in half, creating the American counterpart of Britain's "blighted areas," through the Pennsylvania counties. Hard-coal miners were called "the forgotten people of America." One investigation after another resulted in no more than descriptions of the panic exodus from the region of those who could somehow get away, the drift to demoralization of miners on the relief rolls, the sinister rise of bootlegging. No commission could check the eastern seaboard's conversion from the "luxury" coal to oil and a generation of hard-coal diggers seemed doomed to the exacerbations of part-time work or the degradations of relief.

Jubilant as were the delegates attending the 1934 convention of the U.M.W. of A. over the impressive comeback of the union—"It is a far cry from the decimated industry of 1932," said the report of the International, "with its persecuted and harried workers, to the organized coal industry of 1934"—the men on the convention floor realized well enough the long road ahead of them in their struggle against depression. The road led clearly enough away from the mines into steel and automotives and utilities where unionism was practically unknown. These unorganized key industries, the chief customers of soft coal, lay all around the United Mine Workers of America, an ever-present menace to the progress of industrial unionism. The convention endorsed the leaders' encomiums of the New Deal. "May the prayers of countless thousands in the mining communities of the nation sustain him [President Roosevelt] in his great humanitarian work." Then it sent representatives to the American Federation of Labor convention with the demand that the A.F. of L. issue industrial union charters to such workers as the Executive Committee of the Federation deemed appropriate. At the same time, the miners succeeded in increasing the size of the Federation's Executive Committee from eight to fifteen, with John L. Lewis very much in evidence among those calling for a rejuvenation of the entire philosophy of the A.F. of L. Cautiously the A.F. of L. hierarchy announced that it would encourage "whatever form of organization seemed best suited to meet the situation and requirements of the mass production workers." To a few groups of workers in mass production industries the Federation granted charters making them affiliates as federal unions, with limited organizational powers and always subordinate to the craft unions in jurisdictional matters. The offer of Lewis to appropriate funds from the mine workers' treasury for the organization of the unorganized was ignored.

When delegates to a Federation convention meeting in Detroit were taken around the Ford plant, they looked with amazement at the number and variety of jobs being performed by the workers. "You would have to have a separate union for each man," said one of the veteran craft unionists. This attitude still prevailed even on the enlarged A.F. of L. Council. The majority could not, would not think in terms other than the division of the mass production workers into separate crafts whose only unifying link would be the craft union officials. The entrance into the A.F. of L. of great numbers of mass production workers organized along the industrial union lines of the U.M.W. of A. would instantly jeopardize the comfortable position of the craft placemen. The newcomers would demand votes and a voice in the parent organization's policies. Better fob off Lewis and the other protestants on the Council with the gesture of federal unionism and in the meantime think up reasons why industrial unionism was impossible in the big plants. With no signs of the slackening of the general depression, Lewis and the miners would be fully occupied looking for work in the mines.

Later Lewis said he had been "gullible" and had believed the craft unionists when they told him that they really meant to organize in rubber, steel, automotives, textiles. He had the more immediate problem of putting the thousands of organized coal miners to work and here he was beginning to lean more heavily upon governmental aid. A symbol of this was the move of the headquarters of the United Mine Workers to Washington where before long the union of the mudsill men was ensconced in the impressive building formerly occupied by the exclusive University Club.

Lewis in his hotel room (he had not yet moved his family into the lovely old Fendall house in Alexandria) could look back with justifiable satisfaction on his past two years' performance. No raucous insurgent voices had howled at him at this last convention, not even from the Illinois delegation. In that state the only dissident group was the Progressive Miners of America, later called the Progessive Mine Workers of America. This was frankly a dual movement and had no relation to the Howat-Germer-Walker insurgency of 1930. Organized at a convention in Southern Illinois in 1932, the Progressive Miners called an unsuccessful strike that autumn. Hundreds of its members were blacklisted, others pursued as Reds by officials of the old union and agents of operators as well. Claiming a membership of some 40,000, practically all of it in Illinois, the Progressive Miners sought to be recognized as a bargaining agent by the NRA, on the ground that they already had some impressive contracts signed with Illinois operators. When, however, Washington refused to recognize the organization, its prestige waned, and many of its members went back to District 12 over which the provisional officers appointed by Lewis were now ruling in comparative peace.

With the abatement of internal feuding, the signing of the North-South wage agreement, the increasing political influence of the Mine Workers behind him, Lewis was rapidly becoming an outstanding figure not only in his union world but in the national scene as well. And more and more men were looking, in days of doubt and hesitation, to the tough-fibered structure of the U.M.W. of A. as a pattern for a new sort of industrial democracy.

Still the depression rolled on, with the tipples standing silent alongside the stacks of the mine powerhouses from which no smoke curled. In many a camp the younger men had known no steady work since they left the grade schools. The miners had celebrated the official passing of the 8-hour day in their 1934 contract and the new scale of $5 in the North, $4.60 in the South for the 7-hour day, with parades on April 1st. But these gains were academic when the mines worked two, three days a week or were down entirely. "When I think about the future, I get the blues so bad I can't stand it," said an unemployed Southern Illinois digger to a WPA investigator. "Times are sure bad for everybody, but the young ones—they got it worse." They tried "divided time" with the work rotated so that all worked a little less and that none would lose his job outright. They hoped the shorter workday would help, but the orders were not there and a man working a few hours a week would be ineligible for the relief rolls. Ameringer sought in vain for private or government financing of his plan to move unemployed miners, who knew farming, to the rich delta lands of Louisiana onto which the topsoil of the midwestern states had been sliding. Finally, he did set down some mine families whose new way of life might have made a pattern for authorities interested in "guided migration" and resettlement.

As it was, the depression story of the miners was an old one, in the case of many fields dating back to 1923, and dulled for the public by reiteration in good times and bad alike. The plight of the urban worker was so much easier to dramatize than that of these remote, stubborn diggers who always seemed to have hard times. Even the Joads had the get-up-and-go spirit that the miners apparently lacked. What compulsion held them workless around the abandoned pits?

Spokesmen for the miners were eloquent enough in describing the woes of their people. John Lewis rang the changes on "all the miners ask is a crust of bread" until the operators, meeting with him in wage conferences, cried out for him to stop. Delegates to the Mine Workers' convention at the beginning of 1935 (1,700 as compared to the scant 200 in 1933) brought heartrending stories of wholesale destitution in what were once flourishing coal camps. But to what avail? "We are all dressed up," growled a man from the pits, "we got our union back and our wage scale and nowhere to go but the relief station."

Then the Supreme Court struck down the NRA in its decision handed down on May 27, 1935, in the Schecter sick chicken case. Of that blow to the high hopes of a short two years before, Lewis said:

"We are living in a state of continuous crisis under the negative autocracy of five former corporation lawyers on the Supreme Court bench. Only industrial democracy can save America from a position of permanent social and economic disequilibration."

On some of the operators, rejoicing over what they took to be a body blow to unionism, Lewis served hasty notice there would be a strike of the soft-coal men in June if new contracts were not forthcoming. The head of the miners was rudely shaken, as were other alert-minded labor leaders by this legal show of "negative autocracy." The old contract was extended, pending conferences.

With Senator Joseph Guffey of Pennsylvania, whose wealth ironically enough had flowed from oil, and with Representative J. Buell Snyder, also of Pennsylvania, the mine leaders sat down to write a bill that provided for the regulation of the bituminous industry on much the same lines as the code, incorporating price fixing and the recognition of labor's rights. Coal's "Little NRA" was passed in August.

On October 2, 1935, a new agreement giving the soft-coal men an increase of 50 cents a day was signed. With this proof of the potency of bargaining on the industrial union pattern, Lewis went to Atlantic City, and what was to prove the most momentous convention of the American Federation of Labor in this century.

XVI. THE FOUNDING OF THE C.I.O.

EVERYTHING LEWIS HEARD OR SAW at Atlantic City indicated that things were rotten ripe for a change in the A.F. of L. On the Boardwalk, in the hotel lobbies, at the bars the iron-gray hierarchs talked, as they had always talked, about stocks and bonds, horses and the World Series, swinging their heavy watch chains across their expansive middles. "Mein Gott!" exclaimed the leader of a visiting delegation of German miners, "are these your proletarian leaders?" If these craft unionists knew what time it was in the labor movement or the world beyond the convention hall, they kept it to themselves.

There was, however, other talk, and this time it didn't come from the professional left, talk of the mass organization of mass industries, the "vertical union" idea of taking in everyone from the bottom up under the same organizational ceiling. "The miners have the idea, get 'em all in one union from the trappers to the pickmen."

In his cool, detached manner Sidney Hillman, long head of the Amalgamated Clothing Workers of America, a semi-industrial union, analyzed the situation. David Dubinsky, shrewd president of the International Ladies' Garment Workers, Charles P. Howard, president of the Typographical Union, following his years in a Kansas mine, Thomas F. McMahon, once active in the Knights of Labor, now the conservative president of the United Textile Workers of America, Max Zaritsky, a former Socialist, head of the Cloth, Hat, Cap and Millinery Workers' International Union, Thomas H. Brown of the Mine, Mill and Smelter Workers' Union, and Harvey C. Fremming of the Oil Field, Gas Well and Refinery Workers of America—these consulted with Lewis and decided to get behind a minority report of the Resolutions Committee on the subject of industrial unionism. Howard was to present the report for his group on the committee consisting of Lewis, Dubinsky, John C. Lewis, head of the Iowa Federation of Labor, a former miner, and Frank Powers and A. A. Myrup.

The minority leaders represented a well-balanced section of the progressive labor movement from the Amalgamated, with its "New Unionism" program of banks, co-ops, recreational and educational activities to the highly skilled typos under Howard. The strong nucleus was of course the U.M.W. of A. with a war chest of some $2 million and a membership of half a million men under a contract covering all but four districts in the North-South competitive fields.

Old-timers were mildly astonished at the vehemence with which John L. Lewis denounced the do-nothing policy of the Federation in regard to the organization of the 30,000,000 beyond the A.F. of L. fold. They thought back to the days when Lewis was shouting "Red" at any member of his union who suggested that the conservative policy of the president of the United Mine Workers was destroying the organization. They recalled his studied indifference to the implications of the industrial union setup of the diggers, his deafness to the argument that the coal fields could not have peace so long as they remained half organized, half nonunion. They remembered that for years he had sat in the inner circles of the Federation, making no protest audible beyond the closed doors, against the doldrum dronings of the craft unionists in defense of the labor status quo. This was indeed a new Lewis, talking of industrial democracy, mass organization of the masses, the pressing need for an all-out militant program.

Absorbed with their own depression problems, these other leaders had not realized how deeply recent events in the coal fields had affected Lewis. The newspapers had given little space to the stunning success of the organizing drive of 1933—the operators saw to that. The liberal weeklies were skeptical of anything that bore the conservative stamp of Lewis. Outside of the group around Lewis—Philip Murray, Thomas Kennedy, Henry Warrum, Jett Lauck—most of the unionists figured that Lewis was playing some sort of power politics to strengthen his own position on the Executive Council. They couldn't know how the response of the unorganized diggers of the South to the union's call had convinced Lewis that the industrial formula was outstandingly the most potent to meet the problem not only of the miners but of the steel workers and the assembly-line men in the Detroit plants, and in the rubber pits at Akron as well. They couldn't be expected to know, and certainly Lewis wasn't going to tell them, that heading a union of workers in an industry apparently assigned to a permanently subordinate role in the American scene was not congenial to a man of such ambition and energy. All very well to acclaim the miners as "the shock troops of American labor." For his part, Lewis was wearied of seeing his striking diggers pursued by yellow-legged militiamen, and gun thugs of the operators and state troopers, while unorganized workers in other mass industries stood idly by. The time had come when the miners would welcome a few reserves in the shape of unionized steel puddlers, auto workers, and gum miners.

In his speech to the A.F. of L. convention supporting Howard's minority report in favor of "organizing the unorganized," Lewis put the case for the miners in these words:

The organization I represent has an interest in this question. Our people work in a great base industry, basic in its service to the American people and the economic and commercial processes of the nation. They struggle against great odds and against great influence, and the intensity of their struggle and the weight of their burden is greatly increased by reason of the fact that the American Federation of Labor has not organized the steel industry and a few other industries similarly situated.

We are anxious to have collective bargaining established in the steel industry, and our interest in that is, to that degree, selfish because our people know that if the workers were organized in the steel industry and collective bargaining there was an actuality, it would remove the incentives of the great captains of the steel industry to destroy and punish and harass our people who work in the captive coal mines throughout the country, owned by the steel industry.

As I talk to you now, 21,000 of our members are on strike in the State of Alabama—not on strike, they are locked out, and the operators will not accept wage increases granted in the Appalachian Joint Wage Conference, which they are obligated to do. They are locked out because the Tennessee Coal & Iron Company, owned by the United States Steel Corporation, the Schloss-Sheffield Steel Company and others there are

encouraging the poor, defenseless commercial coal operators of Alabama
to fight the United Mine Workers of America and to refuse to apply
these wage agreements. And the Youngstown Sheet and Tube in Western
Pennsylvania has our people locked out. The steel industry is anxious to
eliminate the United Mine Workers of America from its captive mines,
so that they will constantly have that buffer between the coal-mining
industry and collective bargaining in the steel industry.

I know that to be true, because I have conferred with the officers of
the United States Steel Corporation in relation to our contracts at their
captive properties. and they frankly admit that they oppose making collective bargaining contracts in the coal-mining industry because they do
not want that power to follow and annoy them in the iron and steel
industry—and they have no more fear of the iron and steel workers
annoying them than they have that the League of Nations will come over
and impose a mandate or sanctions upon them.

He detailed the fumbling of the Federation with the problem of
organizing steel, accused the A.F. of L. of "tinkering" in rubber,
called out that the labor movement was being "taunted, taunted,
taunted" with its inadequacy and weakness.

"Whereas today," said Lewis, "the craft unions of this country
may be able to stand upon their own feet and like mighty oaks stand
before the gale, defy the lightning, yet the day may come when this
changed scheme of things—and things are changing rapidly now—
the day may come when these organizations will not be able to
withstand the lightning and the gale. Now, prepare yourselves by making a contribution to your less fortunate brethren, heed this cry from
Macedonia that comes from the hearts of men."

Lewis saw clearly enough, and Hillman and Howard and Dubinsky and the other dissidents saw, the current configuration of the
industrial society with finance capitalism, weakened, yet rescued
from total collapse by the impingements of the New Deal, still strong
enough to check any such flurried sorties as the Federation's craft
unions might attempt. None of these veterans, however, was pleading
for anything more radical than organization. None, despite the Socialist backgrounds of the needle trade leaders, asked for any fundamental change of that configuration. Nor did they urge the Federation to drop its craft philosophy. Over and again, the Lewis-led forces
insisted that industrial and craft unionists could live amicably in the

same Federation house, and they pointed to the miners' union as evidence of that. Wasn't it so that, since 1890, the United Mine Workers of America had furnished funds and fighting men too for many battles of the craft unions?

When Lewis sat down, the progressives looked curiously over at the miners' chief and at one another. Had they heard correctly? Was this John L. Lewis delivering the most scathing indictment of the entire philosophy of the Federation since the days when the Socialists hectored Gompers? He was talking the language of Brophy and Hapgood and Ameringer, and it was not centuries ago that he had denounced these men and all their progressive followers on the floor of the Federation convention, thrown them out of the United Mine Workers, damned them as "Reds."

For their part the craft unionists stirred uneasily. The Macedonian cry fell on the deaf ears of Matthew Woll, John P. Frey, the tired old man who edited the iron moulders' journal and liked to be called "the Federation's brains," William L. Hutcheson, 61-year-old president of the United Brotherhood of Carpenters, whose chief claim to fame was the setting up of a luxurious home for his retired stalwarts.

To these well-padded men whose vested interests lay in sheltering the skilled, the thought of taking in the hordes of factory workers in the great unorganized plants was as repugnant as would be the suggestion that the Union League receive the Young Communist League into its staid halls. For years the elders of the Federation had given the entire American labor movement its bourgeois coloration so puzzling to foreign laborites. Some of its craft unions had gone so far in labor-management "collaboration" as to enter into collusive contracts with the bosses for maintaining high prices to the consumers. Once the contract covering the hours and wages of the skilled men was signed, the rank and file of the unskilled could shift for themselves. High initiation fees would serve to keep out the unwashed masses. When an A.F. of L. union stepped into a left-wing strike at Passaic, New Jersey, and it was a question of receiving some 8,000 new members, most of them foreign-born, the head of the craft organization said to me: "Why, we couldn't take them in. We haven't got the secretarial staff to handle their applications."

With a rush, the craft unionists voted for the majority report, a report which made no definite promise as to organizing the unorganized. Then up came the question of acting on the application of the rubber workers of Akron, threatened with a wage cut, anxious to obtain an industrial union charter from the Federation. William Hutcheson rose to make a point of order. The matter of industrial unionism had been disposed of, he shouted, when the minority report was voted down.

Stung, John Lewis said:

"It is pretty small potatoes to make points of order on such important matters as these."

"That's all right with me, that small potatoes," said Hutcheson, towering six feet three from the floor, "I was raised on small potatoes. That's why I am so small."

Lewis marched over to the carpenters' chief. The two big men put their heads out like fighting cocks. Delegates heard the word "bastard," and then the solid impact of Lewis's first beneath Hutcheson's eye. The two wrestled until the delegates got them apart. Newspapermen ran to the telephones to report the first fist fight on the floor of an A.F. of L. convention for more than fifty years. William Green was deeply distressed. That night in his hotel room Lewis tore open a telegram from a union carpenter.

"Good work," it read, "sock him again."

There was no hint of bitterness in the graceful speech which Lewis made on the last day of the convention renominating Green for the presidency of the A.F. of L. and incidentally paying off a fourteen-year-old debt for Green's unsuccessful nomination of Lewis at the Federation convention in 1921. But there was no doubt that Lewis meant business when he had in John Brophy for a talk. Lewis told his former opponent that he was going ahead with this mass organization program and that he wanted Brophy to be director of the Committee for Industrial Organization which he was organizing. Lewis was chairman, Howard was secretary, and the other members were Hillman, Fremming, Dubinsky, McMahon, Brown and Zaritsky.

Later Brophy said:

"I would be with Lewis in this fight for industrial unionism even if I did not like him; in fact, even if I did not trust him. His mere program is enough for me. But, you know, I am sold on him today. After he put me on the job he asked me, 'Well, John, who timed this thing right, you or I?' And I had to say, 'I guess you did, John.' And that's just it. He is a genius on timing."

On the Boardwalk, Lewis ran into Powers Hapgood and told him about the new movement. Powers agreed to go to work as organizer for the C.I.O., provided he was restored to the U.M.W. of A. with full membership rights. Lewis, who knows a top-rank organizer when he sees one, signed Hapgood up. Then Adolph Germer came along. Overnight the magic formula of the words "industrial unionism" was dissolving ancient grudges.

Next Lewis handed in his resignation from the Executive Council of the A.F. of L. He said scornfully of the hierarchs: "They flit from flower to flower while they sip the golden honey of industry." And, "I have neither the time nor the inclination to follow the peregrinations of the Council from the Jersey beaches in the summer to the golden sands of Florida in the winter."

Still Lewis retained his vice-presidency of the A.F. of L., and still he and his seven associates in the C.I.O. insisted that theirs was no dual union but that the purpose of the Committee was "to encourage and promote organization of the workers in the mass production and unorganized industries of the nation and affiliation with the American Federation of Labor."

The new group set up small headquarters in the Rust Building in Washington and sent an organizer to Detroit to look over the situation in the automobile plants, where three small independent unions were functioning on a limited scale. The C.I.O. man urged the independents to join with the Federation's union.

In January, 1936, Lewis was in Akron talking to a mass meeting of the Goodyear Rubber Company workers. There were 14,000 of them, a few organized into the United Rubber Workers, affiliated with the A.F. of L. There was a company union, The Goodyear Industrial Assembly, which was widely advertised as the ideal type of labor representation. The ads spoke of the "Goodyear Happy Family." The company union setup was being widely copied by other companies in rubber and steel and automotives seeking to give the form rather than the substance of collective bargaining.

Even the company-owned members of the Industrial Assembly stirred uneasily that autumn when a reduction of wages was announced, although Goodyear's net profit in 1935 had been $5½ million. The $81,000-a-year President Litchfield wouldn't meet his workers to talk about the cut. In important departments in November, the men sat down, i.e., they reported for work, took their places at the benches or in the pits, and then did nothing.

The origin of the sit-down strike in this country, first headlined by the Goodyear gum miners, was long a subject of dispute. Coal miners in Terbovlyé, Jugoslavia, and Pecs, Poland, had stayed in the mines for hungry days rather than accept wage reductions. In France, before the Popular Front, millions of workers had sat down. Students of American labor tactics, however, insist that the Goodyear sit-down was an indigenous product.

"The sit-down strike is an American product," wrote Clinton S. Golden and Harold J. Ruttenberg in their book, *The Dynamics of Industrial Democracy,* "invented and perfected by management and later adapted by labor unions to serve their own purposes. Management showed unorganized workers the way to the sit-down strike. The lost outdoor picketing strike, broken by housing strike-breakers inside the plant, is the mother of the sit-down strike."

Wherever it came from, the sit-down was no invention of the C.I.O. leaders. They were as astonished at this rank-and-file tactic as were the flustered foremen, running up and down the lines asking the silent men and women what the trouble was. "What do you know?" exclaimed an Akron C.I.O. organizer just out of the mines of Illinois. "They say they won't go down to the street to get their heads busted. They just stand there doing nothing all day. The straw bosses is nuts and I don't know what to make of it either."

Miners openly stealing coal in Pennsylvania, rubber workers in America announcing that the "right to a job" was as sacred as any other property right and sitting down by their machines to prove it, conservative A.F. of L. leaders talking about industrial democracy and the organization of 30 million unorganized men and women—what was going on downstairs as America swung wearily into the sixth year of the "temporary" depression?

On February 17th, however, the Goodyear workers did come down into the streets, pouring out of the plant buildings that stretched for eleven snow-covered miles outside the startled city of Akron. Behind them they left a few hundred "loyal workers," as the Goodyear advertisements termed them, who were from then on to live unhappily in the plants, hemmed in by the long picket lines.

The company obtained an injunction against mass picketing and called upon the sheriff and the local police to enforce it. The law men looked through whirling snow at the solid ranks of husky young workers, many of them mountaineers brought up from the South on the grounds that they would not be amenable to unionization, and went back to headquarters. Failing in its appeal to the governor to send in troops, the company then started to do business with Pearl Bergoff, the notorious strikebreaker, who sent some of his professional tough boys into Akron to organize the white-collar people into a Law and Order League. Both sides made ready for open warfare. The pickets whittled clubs in their huts set out at every entrance to the far-flung plant. The Law and Order League drilled with guns and called on the people of Akron to run the "Red agitators" of John L. Lewis out of town.

The C.I.O. representatives were Adolph Germer, Powers Hapgood, Leo Krzycki of the Amalgamated Clothing Workers, who had been an alderman and undersheriff in Daniel Hogan's Socialist Milwaukee, and Rose Pesotta of the International Ladies' Garment Workers' Union. These took over the conduct of the strike, carefully excluding from all their councils all representatives of extremist groups who were seeking to capitalize the situation.

At the outset of the fourth week of the strike, the defeated candidate for mayor, who had been picked by the company to head the vigilantes, announced that he would move his forces on the picket lines and would give instructions for the attack over the local radio station. Late on the afternoon when the announcement appeared in the papers, Frank Grillo, secretary of the United Rubber Workers, came into the heavily guarded press room in the hotel where the C.I.O. organizers were living, to announce with a casual air that he had bought the radio station for the night and that he expected me, as publicity man for the union, to keep it going, according to the radio rules, with a program of talks and music from six that evening until eight the next morning.

We went over to the station with union bodyguards marching at our heels, and held the air fort all that night, with talks on unionism, selections from *I Break Strikes,* the book about Bergoff by Edward

Levinson, a play in which I impersonated Fanny Fink, the daughter of a professional strikebreaker, and Grillo took the part of the fink, and endless hillbilly songs nasally sung to the accompaniment of ukeleles by flustered pickets taken from the huts at a moment's notice. "When the Moon Comes Over the Mountain" was sung twelve times during the program, but no instructions were issued to the waiting strikebreakers and no move was made against the hard-held picket line.

Women who a few years before had been feeding their miner-husbands on the picket lines in West Virginia took over the huge commissary job, cooking meals for 1,100 hungry men coming off the lines in shifts. Former miners drove trucks out to the countryside and returned with food from friendly farmers. In place of the tents of the mine strikers there were the board huts, covered with tarpaper, heated with fires in abandoned oil tins, sometimes furnished with radios and armchairs from the homes of the strikers, bearing names scrawled above the doors: "John L. Lewis," "John Mitchell," "Mae West." Hapgood and Germer and Krzycki talked to the company representatives, to the handful of liberals in Akron, to reporters, to convocations of the clergy, or tramped the picket lines, while Rose Pesotta set up classes in unionism for the women and gave a hand at the commissaries.

At the end of six weeks of the worst snowstorms Akron had known in years, Litchfield and his lawyers assented to a verbal agreement containing recognition of the United Rubber Workers as the bargaining agency for Goodyear. The attitude of the erstwhile "happy family," the threat of a boycott of Goodyear tires on the part of the entire auto-riding labor movement, the changed attitude of the public when the newspaper readers saw the C.I.O. men in action—these gave the new industrial organization its first major victory. Lewis and his miners were the heroes of the labor movement. What the C.I.O. did from then on was front-page news.

XVII. "A PLAGUE O' BOTH
YOUR HOUSES"

HE STORY OF THE UNITED MINE
Workers from 1935 to 1939 is the story of the C.I.O. and the aggressive
head of both organizations. No other man, not John Mitchell at the
peak of his career, had made the American people so conscious of
the problems of labor, fearfully conscious for those who saw in Lewis
the embodiment of sinister revolutionary aims, jubilantly so for those
who had long awaited the surging march of the rank and file which
he now led.

"The workers of the nation were tired," said Lewis, "of waiting
for corporate industry to right their economic wrongs, to alleviate
their social agony, and to grant them their political rights. Despairing
of fair treatment, they resolved to do something for themselves. They,
therefore, have organized a new labor movement, conceived within
the principles of the national bill of rights and committed to the
proposition that workers are free to assemble in their own forums,
voice their own grievances, declare their own hopes, and contract on
even terms with modern industry for the sale of their only material
possession—their labor."

Fully as perturbed as the captains of "corporate industry" at this
rush to unionize were the members of the Executive Council of the
A.F. of L. A month before exultant workers paraded the slushy
streets of Akron to celebrate their victory over Goodyear, the council
ordered the C.I.O. "to cease and desist" on the ground that it was a
dual union. The prompt reply of the C.I.O. was: "We wish to emphasize again that the C.I.O. is trying to remove the roots of dualism by

167

making it possible for the millions of mass production workers, now outside A.F. of L. to enter on the only basis they will accept—industrial unionism."

A committee from the council was appointed to confer with Lewis and the other C.I.O. leaders. No conference was held until the spring of 1936 but in the meantime the C.I.O. had performed so effectively that its members could afford to ignore the warnings of the older body. William Green went to the 1936 convention of the mine union to plead with the delegates to return to the Federation's fold. He spoke for more than an hour while Lewis sat staring out across the hall, through inscrutable, gray-green eyes. At the end of the appeal, Lewis asked delegates to stand who thought as Green did that the C.I.O. should quit and all hands go back to the Federation. Two delegates stood, one sat down hurriedly as the seated two thousand hooted. Lewis said:

"There is your answer, Mr. Green."

To call his former secretary-treasurer "mister" instead of addressing Green by the usual union "brother" was a typical Lewis touch. In August, Green announced the suspension of the eight unions which had organized the C.I.O. But the Committee's organizing campaigns in steel and automotives were in full swing that summer and the long-expected verdict of the Federation hierarchs made scarcely a ripple.

Onto the political field from which he had so long held back, Lewis marched his diggers with a contribution from the Mine Workers' treasury of more than $500,000 for the re-election of Franklin Roosevelt, the largest single contribution from any source recorded by the Democratic accountants. Of Alfred Landon, the Republican candidate, Lewis said: "This little man out at Topeka, Kansas, has no more conception of what ails America or what to do about it than a goatherder in the hills of Bulgaria."

By this time labor news had been brought out of its customary obscurity on the back pages and the few competent labor reporters in the country went to work at anything but union hours. Feature writers, newspaper columnists, top men from the "background magazines," researchers, free-lance economists, and photographers and more photographers swarmed into the little offices of the C.I.O. in Washington, stormed the grounds of the spacious Lewis home at Alexandria.

"At once," wrote Dwight MacDonald in the *Nation*, "Lewis found himself the center of a journalistic whirlpool. 'The March of Time' got him to speak and pose for its camera men, the embryonic 'Life's' photographers shot him and his office from every coign of vantage. 'Fortune' descended on him for a full length biography. 'Time' phoned inquiries almost daily. Lewis is reported to have finally inquired whether he was working for the C.I.O. or for 'Time, Inc.'"

Within a hectic six months the bristling brows and jutting jaw of the miners' leader had become almost as familiar to newspaper readers as the smiling features of President Roosevelt. It was of course routine journalistic practice to set the aggressive Lewis off against the hesitant Green, to exploit the personalities of the protagonists in labor's thundering family row. Here was what newspapermen call a "human interest" story—one man turning with expansive vituperation upon another of his own making. All that was lacking was the feminine angle and that was soon provided in the course of the steel campaign by an imaginative reporter who announced that behind the union contract signed at the end of nine months of struggle by Myron C. Taylor of the Board of Directors of U.S. Steel, there moved the attractive figure of Mrs. Taylor. The steel man's wife was supposedly so taken by the charms of Mr. Lewis whom she met once at luncheon at a Pittsburgh hotel that she persuaded her husband to sign up with the Steel Workers' Organizing Committee of the C.I.O. Further research indicated, however, that it was more the danger to Big Steel's British armament orders in the event of a strike, together with the conciliatory efforts of the former coal digger, Thomas Moses, a vice-president of U.S. Steel, than any hypnotic effects of Mr. Lewis upon Mrs. Taylor that led to the signing.

Though the most significant social upheaval of contemporary times was treated in terms of a prize fight, little blame for this attached to hard-pressed reporters, editors, columnists, radio commentators. Their audiences were not prepared for anything less superficial. Only the other day did the bulk of our economists and historians recognize the existence of a labor movement in this country. There were many and formidable barriers to a non-academic presentation of the labor scene. The archives of labor are hidden away in obscure labor halls, or the often faulty memories of the veterans of "battles long ago." For fifty years the attitude of the leaders of the organized movement had been the suspicious one of Samuel Gompers in regard to all "out-siders." When the intellectuals were rebuffed, they turned to writing "proletarian literature" which had no general acceptance save in the cases of Upton Sinclair, John Dos Passos, John Steinbeck and a few others. If the public, hanging onto straps in the New York subways or riding buses across Michigan, gained the impression that the idea of industrial unionism sprang full-armed from the massive head of John L. Lewis it was because of these factors.

Miners looked at pictures of their leader reading Homer or Donne or Welsh folklore before the coal fire in the Virginia home where once Light Horse Harry Lee had 'to 'd his campaigns. They saw him, in the movies, pausing before the door of his Cadillac car with the chauffeur up front or standing at the entrance of his Fifth Avenue hotel, for a last word with the newspapermen. Contrary to the hopes of Lewis's foes, this manner of living caused no perceptible resentment among the rank and file. Diggers making less than $1,000 a year looked upon the $25,000 annual salary of their president as not un-reasonable compensation for a man who was in constant conference with highly paid executives not alone in coal but in steel and rubber and automotives as well. As head of the C.I.O., Lewis received no salary and he was steadily and conspicuously giving status to the United Mine Workers such as that organization had never enjoyed in its history. Were not Philip Murray, Van Bittner, William Mitch, all men from the pits, the leaders of the S.W.O.C. who were organizing the steel plants? In Detroit, U.M.W. of A. men were advising the temperamental Homer Martin, head of the new, lusty United Auto-mobile Workers of America, which had grown in one short year from a membership of 30,000 in the highly skilled trades to 300,000, promis-ing soon to rival the miners' union in its size and militancy. In Washington, Lewis and Murray were running in and out of the White House, and in Pennsylvania Thomas Kennedy was lieutenant governor under Earle. Men living in camps far away from the heart of things enjoyed this vicarious sense of belonging, of being part of an organization that loomed mighty large on the national horizon. John Lewis was bringing home the bacon in a number of ways.

Of all this acclaim of Lewis and the miners, however, the most lyrical arose from the left where but a short time back the name of Lewis was anathema. Heywood Broun, frankly captivated by Lewis's personality, moved his Newspaper Guild over into the C.I.O. He wrote starry-eyed columns about the miners' chief in the *Nation*. The *Daily Worker*, the organ of the Stalinists, abruptly changed from its "mis-leader of labor" characterization of Lewis, which Foster had used so freely, to such adulation as was usually reserved for high-ranking commissars. In general, the leftists wrote of Lewis in terms of a labor Saul smitten by the light of industrial democracy on the Damascan journey. A leftist biography of him in which great stress was laid upon his physiognomy, the bushy eyebrows, the square, pale face, the husky frame, "thewed like an Auroch," suggested that he was of presidential timber.

The Communists came late to the C.I.O. board, but they found a place at the table, though a good distance below the salt. In the old radical tradition of "boring from within" and following the "wooden horse" line laid down by Dimitroff at the Moscow session of the Comintern in 1935, the Communists sought to infiltrate their members into the executive offices of the new unions. Tight-lipped, humorless youngsters, burning with the hard flame of the class struggle, were soon displacing the easygoing, slap-dash run of clerical help at union headquarters and making themselves invaluable by their diligence and willingness to take any job no matter how menial. They were indefatigable meeting-goers, caucusing before every gathering, acting as a group and bewildering the rank and file by their references to *Roberts' Rules of Order*. No such disciplined, religious-minded zealots had appeared in the labor movement since the days of the Socialist Labor party, and while the old-line unionists looked on them with cold distaste, they had to admit that the Communists were "horses for work." When accused of harboring Reds, labor leaders would retort: "The bosses hire them, why shouldn't we organize them?" Presently among the transport workers, important locals in the United Automobile Workers and the steel workers, on the West Coast among the marine workers, among white-collar workers in the East the Communist influence spread. But not among the United Mine Workers. Unhappy experiences with the National Miners Union and other abortive rebel movements pretty well convinced the great majority of the diggers that, as in the case of Howat, there was nothing in communism for them.

For all the demands which his C.I.O. work put upon him, Lewis did not neglect his miners. He made a concession to those of his members who murmured about "one-man control" and increasing centralization in the United Mine Workers by backing the proposal that the vice-president, at a salary of $18,000 a year, be elected by the districts, but he still retained the much-criticized appointive power over organizers and "provisional officers" for the districts. Apologists for this strange and undemocratic device maintain that it is necessary to train labor officials at the national headquarters and then keep close watch on them as they function in the districts. It is doubtful if any progressive labor leader with less prestige than Lewis acquired during the first years of the C.I.O. could have succeeded in taking so much power unto himself.

On April 1, 1937, at a time when a wave of sit-down strikes was causing the liberals to waver in their support of the C.I.O., Lewis announced that another Appalachian Agreement had been signed, this time setting the basic wage rate at $6 for the northern day men and $5.60 in the South. Pay of time and one-half was granted for work over the 7-hour day, 35-hour week. Soon after, a renovated Guffey Bill was passed by Congress setting up the National Bituminous Coal Commission, later functioning in the Department of the Interior as the Bituminous Coal Division. The new Bituminous Coal Act provided for the promulgation of a code dealing with fair trade practices and minimum prices, with a tax of 19.5 per cent of the value of coal at the mine payable by all operators who failed to accept membership in the code. The labor clauses in the original Guffey Bill to which the Supreme Court objected were omitted from this revised version.

By now the C.I.O. was claiming a membership of 3,200,000 in its twenty-eight national and international unions, as compared to the 3,600,000 of the Federation which had finally officially outlawed the new organization. The latter's honeymoon days were definitely over.

"Up to this time," said a statement by the C.I.O., "we had confined our activities to those of an organizing committee. In a vain attempt to preserve the unity which the A.F. of L. Executive would have ruptured, the C.I.O. had refrained from issuing charters or from doing anything else that might give color to the charges of dualism leveled against it. But by the time the C.I.O. met in March, 1937, it had become abundantly clear that the A.F. of L. leaders were determined to continue the split which they had created. Not only had they repeatedly refused to rescind their illegal suspension of the C.I.O. unions—the only action which could have restored unity—but they were also taking steps to split all state federations of labor and city central bodies, as well as the national movement."

At its March meeting in 1937, the new movement took action to issue certificates of affiliation to national, international, state, regional, city central bodies, and local groups. This changed the entire character of the Committee from that of an organizational group within the Federation to a rival of the Federation all along the line. And at the same time it brought the Committee both new friends and enemies.

The Federations' answer was to start an organizing drive of its own, and to announce that the Federation felt that from its inception, in the words of President Green, the C.I.O. "had been steeped in the cesspool of illegality and of irresponsibility."

The publicity drive against the sit-down strike tactic rose to furious heights. Carried to its logical conclusions, said the editorial writers, columnists and radio commentators, it could mean the invasion of private homes by all sorts of workers and their refusal to leave the property unless their demands were met.

The strikes of the employees of General Motors, centering in Cleveland, Ohio, and Flint, Michigan, had provided the second major test for the C.I.O., of which Akron was the first. The General Motors strikes, which ran through January and February, 1937, and resulted in a victory for the workers, as well as a personal triumph for Lewis, had been marked by violence on both sides when attempts were made forcibly to evict the workers sitting down in auto plants. While the sit-down seemed to members of the younger unions a fascinating, ingenious and usually effective weapon, the technique threw the fear of John L. Lewis into the hearts of the middle people who saw nothing short of revolution in such action. Most of the sit-downs were in automotives, rubber and textiles. The miners did not resort to this device nor did the older and more disciplined unions in the garment trades. Nevertheless, it was Lewis and his miners who were the villains in the public opinion.

Over against Lewis a new hero was posed by pronounced anti-unionists and such columnists as David Lawrence, Westbrook Pegler, and Boake Carter, special writers who in the old days were known as "trained seals" by the regular staff of a newspaper but whose syn-

dicated comments had long since outweighed in the public's estimation
the old-fashioned editorials. This hero who was, in the opinion of
some, to save the country from going hell-bent to a labor dictatorship
was Tom L. Girdler, president of the Republic Steel Corporation and
leader of "Little Steel's" fight against organization.

Girdler flatly refused to have anything to do with the Steel
Workers' Organizing Committee of the C.I.O., headed by Phil
Murray and largely staffed by miners lent by the United Mine
Workers. His adamant stand vastly enheartened not only his colleagues
in "Little Steel"—Ernest Weir's National Steel Corporation, Bethlehem,
Inland Steel, and the Youngstown Sheet and Tube Company—but
set in train "back-to-work movements" in all parts of the country.
There appeared the "Johnstown Formula" with its "Law and Order
Leagues," its wide use of newspaper advertising calling on "loyal
workers" to return to the plants, the use of industrial spies and of
small armies of private detectives. All this elaborate preparation for
war served to surround the C.I.O., against which it was aimed, with
an air of terrorism, as though "American institutions," as the advertisements had it, were being threatened by the invasion of hostile
armies.

On Memorial Day of 1937 at a Republic plant outside of Chicago
ten workers were ruthlessly slain by Chicago police, and men and
women in a crowd of unarmed strikers were beaten to bloody pulps.
There was a slight shift in public sentiment when the full details of
the "Memorial Day Massacres," details at first sedulously suppressed
by the authorities, were brought to light, largely through the efforts of
the La Follette Civil Liberties Committee.

All these "alarums and excursions" kept labor news on the front
pages, very much after the manner of war correspondence. Picket-line
fracases were built up into the proportions of major engagements.
Reporters who had never seen a strike were assigned to cover complicated industrial situations and the columnists had field days. Debates
over labor's rights to organize, the right to a job, the right to work
during a strike filled the air of 1937. Anti-Administration forces were
quick to link Lewis's name with that of Roosevelt and predict that
the President's favorable attitude toward union organization would
lead to a labor dictatorship.

In June, soon after the steel strikers had buried their dead, Roosevelt was asked at a press conference as to his attitude toward the strike. Reflecting the nervous tension of the times, as his supporters would have it, or reflecting his wonted indecisiveness when confronted suddenly with a disagreeable decision, as his unfriendly critics insisted, he cried out:

"A plague o' both your houses!"

This Shakespearean quotation, so much in the Lewis vein, stung the big mine leader to the quick. Though a White House secretary attempted to soften the blow by saying that the President was referring only to the "extremists" on both sides of the strike, Lewis brooded long over what he regarded as a raw defection. In his Labor Day speech, after recounting the fact that more than eighteen workers had been killed during the Little Steel strike and hundreds seriously injured, Lewis intoned as his peroration:

"Labor, like Israel, has many sorrows. Its women weep their fallen and they lament for the future of the children of the race. It ill behooves one who has supped at labor's table and who has been sheltered in labor's house to curse with equal fervor and fine impartiality both labor and its adversaries when they become locked in deadly embrace."

Here was the first open break between Lewis and the Administration. Evidently more than that one quotation was involved in the estrangement between two strong personalities which, as it continued, was to rock the labor world. Lewis is said by his intimates to have all along regarded the President as lacking in "follow-through" on fundamentals. In the matter of the NIRA, for example, Lewis is said to become indignant when credit is given to Roosevelt for "saving" the miners' union. "Lewis's answer," according to an article by Dale Kramer in *Harper's Magazine,* August, 1942, "is that he [Lewis] wrote labor's protective 7(a), put it through Congress against the President's wishes, and singlehandedly obtained its enforcement while he conducted the organizational drive which brought back the membership and replenished the treasury. In all subsequent controversies between capital and labor, Lewis declares, the President 'equivocated.' "

Lewis had apparently begun to feel that Roosevelt's advisers were warning him against showing overmuch sympathy for the labor side of the strikes that were stirring up the nation and that the President was too easily persuaded. It was this belief, again according to the mine leader's intimates, as much as any personal pique at not being called as frequently as in the early days of the New Deal to congenial White House conferences, which led Lewis to make his bitter Labor Day speech. He wanted to remind the President of his obligation to the miners and to all progressive labor when he spoke of "supping at labor's table." This was no time for equivocation on the part of any thoroughgoing friend of labor. Men were being killed for attempting to exercise their legal right to join unions of their own choosing. The loss of the Little Steel strike might well endanger the whole forward march of labor with all the implications that march held for the future of our industrial civilization. And to dismiss this with a shrugging quotation delivered in the presence of newspapermen, the overwhelming majority of them representing papers hostile to the C.I.O. and all it stood for . . . There was "fair weather friendship" indeed.

On the other hand, Roosevelt's defenders insisted that Lewis had become too presumptuous if he expected the Chief Executive to take sides in such an outright class struggle as the Little Steel strike. Lewis was dreaming too much, to use one of the mine leader's favorite expressions, if he thought that Roosevelt could be influenced by any campaign contribution, no matter how sizable. The President, despite his repeated manifestations of sympathy for the legitimate objectives of organized labor—and no other occupant of the White House had ever been so friendly to labor—spoke for the majority when he condemned both parties to this dispute which was disturbing the national peace.

That the matter rankled in the breasts of both men was plain enough. Although Lewis, soon after his Labor Day speech, was at the White House again and came out to report that his talk with the President had been "pleasant," there were fewer and fewer of these "pleasant" confabs, until finally they ceased altogether. It was evident that forces in the Administration were bent on dissociating the New Deal from the aggressive mine leader's activities in the mind of the public. It was difficult enough in those days to carry on a program of mild social reform against the powerful opposition of industrialists who were now recovering from the shocks of the depression—a recovery, though few industrialists would admit it, speeded up by the ameliorative agencies of the New Deal—without taking on the added handicap of defending sit-down strikes. Those interested in widening the breach between the vanguard of militant labor and the Administration began the behind the scenes maneuvers which ended with the dramatic down-stage clashings of two contrasting personalities, clashings which had their momentous reverberations for years to follow.

With the drumfire of public disapproval aimed at the C.I.O., William Green and the hierarchy of the A.F. of L. threatened Lewis's flank in the miners' union. The chief weapon against Lewis was the Progressive Miners' Union of Illinois.

Although the Progressive Miners had no connection with the Howat-Walker attempt to reorganize the U.M.W. of A., the latest Illinois insurgency was a rank-and-file movement begun over discontent with a wage agreement in the state and directed at Lewis's "autocracy." Soon, however, the genuine progressives were forced out, and the movement by 1937 was no more than a Lewis-baiting affair. Edward Levinson wrote in *Labor on the March*:

> Its members worked at less than union scales and were forced to pay kick-backs to some of the companies. Its publication, "The Progressive Miner" held an unmatched record for red-baiting and anti-Semitism. It gave warm applause to Huey Long, dubbed Townsend a savior, eulogized Father Coughlin and wound up in 1936 by supporting the Republican party in the Illinois primaries and Lemke for President. The paper declared President Roosevelt a "Jewish agent," and the C.I.O. "an unholy conspiracy of international Jewish bankers to enslave the American people." The Supreme Court, the paper held, was being made the target of "sinister forces which sought to subdue American institutions." Attacks on the Wagner Act and the Guffey Coal Act were given extensive space.

In June, 1937, the A.F. of L. granted a charter to the Progressive Miners, which at that time claimed a membership of 30,000 and pointed to contracts signed with important Illinois operators. Soon after the granting of the charter, thirty-six of the leaders of the Progressive Miners were convicted in federal courts on conspiracy charges. In many parts of the state, miners who had gone on strike at the call of the Progressives were blacklisted. At the time of the convictions it was estimated that more than a score of miners had been killed or wounded in the gun fighting between the Progressive and the old union members.

In this crucial year of 1937, though Little Steel had been temporarily lost and public opinion was seemingly lining up against the trade-unions or, perhaps more specifically, their leaders, the rush of workers to join the C.I.O. reached such a tempo that the membership of the two-year-old movement outnumbered its 56-year-old rival.

Taxi drivers in New York, shoe workers in New England, textile workers in the deep South, auto and rubber workers, electrical and radio workers, shipbuilders on the East Coast, longshoremen and seamen on the Pacific—employees of 30,000 companies by the fall of 1937 were under C.I.O. contracts. It was claimed by C.I.O. leaders that in two years of industrial organization nearly one billion dollars in wage increases had been won for the workers under these favoring agreements and that what amounted to a nation-wide maximum of forty hours a week had been secured through the new setup.

Everywhere members of the United Mine Workers were in the forefront of this march. Murray, Brophy, Hapgood, Van A. Bittner, Germer, Allan Haywood swung from one strategic front to another, soothing the growing pains of such young and obstreperous unions as the United Auto Workers, teaching promising recruits the patterns of industrial unionism, the elements of collective bargaining, and the other practices and disciplines of unionism which they had first learned in the pits. The miners' union filled no small part of the war chest for the new offensive. In all, from the start of the C.I.O. to the end of this eventful year, the miners contributed $1,404,000 to the Committee. There were those who thought that no less a contribution was the driving and relentless energy, the shrewd strategy, and the brilliant organizational performance of the President of the United Mine Workers of America. The prestige of the United Mine Workers of America and its leader among all ranks of labor was never so high as in the year that saw the C.I.O. pass triumphantly through its baptism of fire.

XVIII. FARMING, POLITICS
AND COAL MINING

WHICH OF THESE IS IN MOST NEED
of reform: labor unions, public utilities, stock exchanges, the Supreme Court?"

That was the question which the magazine *Fortune* asked of 5,000 Americans, "distributed with mathematical care according to area, place, age, sex, and economic condition" at the end of 1937. Of those asked this question, 38 per cent felt that the unions were in most need of reform. In July, 1936, nearly 60 per cent of those questioned had declared that "some if not all wage earners should belong to a union."

Said *Fortune:*

"The issue on labor is clear. Labor organizations have made themselves decidedly unpopular with the public at large, and particularly with the working group with which they are mainly concerned. Some of this hostility is certainly intended for union rackets; some may be inspired by a feeling that Lewis has overplayed his cards and brought a useful cause into disrepute."

However dubious may have been *Fortune's* interpretation of the attitude of the working groups toward unionism, it is not to be doubted that the poll did reflect the sentiment of the "respectables" of that time toward unionism.

In the summer of 1938, a neighbor of mine on the little island of Martha's Vineyard, off Cape Cod, was a sweet-faced New England woman. One day we were talking of unions and she looked from her rose garden to the blue-dreaming harbor where the fishing boats were at anchor. Suddenly her lips tightened and she waved her shears toward the boats. Her voice shrilled as she said:

"I'd like to take that old John L. Lewis, and Franklin D. too for that matter, and put them both aboard that boat and take them out to sea—and sink the boat."

She had been reading Boake Carter's profuse lamentations over the sad state of "Johnny Q. Public" caught without an umbrella in the midst of a labor tempest. She had been reading the editorials of Paul Block, the proprietor of a newspaper chain, editorials widely reprinted at Mr. Block's expense, informing a listening world: "America is at a crossroad. Our country must decide, and decide promptly, whether uncurbed defiance of the law on the part of John L. Lewis and his lieutenants is to be stopped or whether we shall calmly permit him to lead us down the road to fascism or dictatorship."

If my neighbor was indeed to be led down any such road by John L. Lewis and such "Red" lieutenants of his as Phil Murray, Van A. Bittner and Percy Tetlow, captain in World War I, she was not going calmly. She was prepared to resist to the last drop of her good *Mayflower* blood any appearance on Martha's Vineyard of what William Green was telling her was "the evil influence which has caused groups of newly organized workers connected with the C.I.O. to follow a destructive policy." She agreed with members of the Dies Committee who found that it was the sinister purpose of John L. Lewis to raise the Red Flag over the White House and she read with approval the resolution of the Philadelphia Board of Trade accusing President Roosevelt and Governor Earle of "political chicanery calculated to excite class hatred," and concluding that the conduct of both officials as far as the C.I.O. went was "clearly seditious." Finally, to show her interest in what she called "our cause," she had sent $5 to the Citizens' Committee of Johnstown, Pennsylvania, in their beleaguered headquarters in the Johnstown Bank and Trust Company. For, as the Committee pointed out in its full-page advertisements in a score of papers, "If this can happen in Johnstown it can happen anywhere else." My lady was not sure just what "this" was, but whatever it was, she knew that "that old John Lewis" was at the bottom of it.

The move for the "reform" of labor unions ranged all the way from the proposal to incorporate trade-unions to straight-out antistrike legislation, breathing the spirit of the "conspiracy acts" of the dawn of unionism in America.

The cards which Lewis was playing ("overplaying," according to *Fortune*) were the following: a tightening of union contracts to include a union shop, with union dues checked off the worker's pay by the companies, a device taken over from the miners; the threat of the formation of a labor party contained in the organization in 1936 of Labor's Non-Partisan League to which the mine union contributed $30,000 in 1937; gestures toward peace with the A.F. of L.; and finally, despite the new coolness between the White House and Lewis, continued reliance upon President Roosevelt's neutrality in labor disputes.

At the U.M.W. of A. convention of 1938, Lewis was cheered to the echo when he said that Roosevelt was "the only President in our lifetime who has tried to give a square deal to the common people of this country." There were many resolutions from the locals urging the miners to back Roosevelt for a third term.

The New Deal relief program was approved, with recommendations that it be extended to agricultural workers. Both the officials and the rank and file of the miners were looking more and more into the conditions of farm workers. In 1936 a catch-all organizational device called District 50 had been added to the other districts of the U.M.W. of A. The formal function of District 50 was to organize the workers on the by-products of coal, an intentionally vague classification which could be used to cover almost any worker from the coke handlers to the makers of fountain pens. While officials of District 50 asserted that they were making no attempts to raid industries where the workers were already organized, C.I.O. spokesmen, after the split with the miners, made frequent charges that the district's organizers were employing terroristic tactics. Soon both sides were talking of "goon squads" and "Gestapo" underground work. When two groups of organizers would arrive at the same time in a town where there was little or no unionism, fighting would break out on the streets or in the headquarters of the rivals. Oft-repeated charges of racketeering leveled against Lewis after he had left the C.I.O. seemed to center around the activities of the catch-all district.

At the outset District 50 was used more as a threat to the Federation of the invasion of craft jurisdiction by the Lewis forces than as an actual organizing body. Apparently, however, Lewis had for a long time in the back of his massive head the idea that District 50 would come in handy when the organization of farmers came to the fore. In all his speeches and interviews, Lewis stressed the plight of the unorganized farmers. He devoted much time to the sharecroppers in his address to the C.I.O. convention of 1937, concluding:

"Economically and politically they [the sharecroppers] are nothing. Yet they are human beings and they are citizens. It is for the labor movement to demand a participation by these people in the bounties and the blessings, material and otherwise, in our country which are ample for the provision and participation of all."

Lewis had Brophy keep a close watch over the development of the C.I.O.'s United Cannery, Agricultural, Packing & Allied Workers of America, formed in Denver in July, 1937, and soon claiming a membership of 100,000. In his radio talk of 1937, the mine leader said of the farmers:

"In this connection let me call attention to the propaganda which some of our industrialists are carrying on among the farmers. By pamphlets in the milk cans or attached to machinery and in countless other ways of direct and indirect approach, the farmers of the nation are being told that the increased price of farm machinery and farm supplies is due to the rising wage level brought about by the Committee for Industrial Organization. And yet it is the industrial millions of this country who constitute the substantial market for all agricultural products."

In his copies of that speech, Lewis had the following put in bold-face:

The interests of the two groups are mutually dependent. It is when the pay roll goes down that the farmer's realization is diminished, so that his loans become overdue at the bank and the arrival of the tax collector is awaited with fear. On the other hand, it is the prosperity of the farmer that quickens the tempo of manufacturing activities and brings buying power to the millions of urban and industrial workers.

At the 1938 miners' convention, the head of the miners made a sardonic peace gesture in the direction of the Federation. He proposed that all the 4 million members of the C.I.O. march over and rejoin the A.F. of L., "horse, foot and artillery," or that the reverse process be undertaken. After all the organized workers, craft and industrial, were under one roof, said Lewis, with his tongue very much in his cheek, matters of differences between the two organizations might be threshed out.

When the newspaper men took it to him, William Green recoiled with horror from this proposition. The worried head of the Federation suggested that David Dubinsky of the International Ladies' Garment Workers' Union might be the man to fix up peace terms. Though the shrewd little Dubinsky had long hesitated in resigning from the Executive Council of the Federation at the time of the C.I.O. split, and though he had constantly advocated peace, he was not going to be part of any such scheme as this.

Characteristically, after making his peace proposal, Lewis went on the platform to call Green "a pusillanimous little man who sees ghosts at night," and to term the Executive Council, "the Lord High Stuffed Shirts of the A.F. of L." The convention voted to try Green for treason to the miners' union for his part in chartering the Progressive Miners. Following his ejection from the U.M.W. of A., Green had obtained a card in the musicians' union. "That is appropriate," said Lewis. "Like Nero, he fiddles while Rome burns."

Evidently such exchanges were not calculated to further the cause of peace. The rank and file of the miners followed Lewis in cutting from their Constitution all reference to the A.F. of L.

It was at this convention that Lewis accepted the salary raise from $12,500 to $25,000 per year, first voted in 1936. Vice-President Murray and Secretary Kennedy were advanced from $9,000 to $18,000. In spite of huge outlays of moneys for preceding years, among them the $554,000 for Roosevelt's 1936 campaign and the $550,000 for the purchase of the University Club in Washington as their new headquarters, the miners still had $2,534,668 in the treasury in December, 1937.

They voted to exclude from membership in the mine union members of the Communist party, the Ku-Klux Klan, the National Civic Federation, the National Chamber of Commerce, the I.W.W., the Working Class Union, and the One Big Union. This was the first time the Communists were included in the banned list. Spokesmen for the Communists said their members would "disregard" the vote against them.

Despite Lewis's praise of Roosevelt, rumors persisted that there was a final break between the two. In March, 1938, Senator Guffey, speaking for Lewis, found it necessary to deny at a press conference that there was any real rupture. And in May, Lewis was again a White House visitor.

The antiunion publicity drive headed by the National Association of Manufacturers, which in 1937 alone spent $793,043 on its "public information service," had reached the point where a pamphlet was being distributed, "Join the C.I.O. and Help Build a Soviet America": "a forgery so blatant," said Herbert Harris in his book, *American Labor*, "that its distributors must be disappointed in it." One of the objectives of the drive was the amendment of the Wagner Act (a measure obviously written to equalize the balance of power between capital and labor) on the ground that it was one-sided and unfair to capital. The N.A.M. wanted to have excluded from the benefits of the act all unions whose members might be guilty of "violence" during strikes, a delightfully vague concept calculated to vitiate the entire act. Though, on the other side of the fence, the La Follette Committee looking into violations of civil liberties was producing a mass of evidence of the use of violence, stool pigeons, agents provocateur, industrial spies and vigilante groups on the part of the employers fighting the C.I.O., Lewis apparently felt that this was no time to break openly with the White House.

In the autumn of 1938, Lewis, who evidently had no idea of making any serious move toward unity with the A.F. of L. until he was leader of a movement as strong, if not stronger than the older body, dropped all pretense of being head of an organizing committee vaguely associated with the Federation. He had the convention of the C.I.O. change the name to Congress of Industrial Unions, indicating to all the world that here was a full-fledged labor movement standing on its own feet. The Congress unanimously elected Lewis its president. Of the original rebels only the I.L.G.W.U. stood aside from this setting up of a permanent body. Dubinsky announced that his powerful union, whose delegates had but recently cheered Lewis to the echo when he came on the platform of their convention, would go it alone for a while. The garment workers, he said, would support "every genuine effort, whether C.I.O. or A.F. of L. in their organizational activities for the improvement of the condition of the workers, and in every effort to achieve peace in the labor movement." Two years later the I.L.G.W.U. went back to the Federation.

There was a growing coolness between Sidney Hillman, since 1914 head of the Amalgamated Clothing Workers, the other progressive needleworkers' union, and the chief of the miners. In their background, their temperaments, their thinking, the two were as far apart as the poles. Hillman came from revolutionary activities, as a youth in Russia, to leadership of a union indoctrinated from top to bottom with Marxist ideology. The original constitution of the Amalgamated Clothing Workers of America inspired by the Socialists, announced that it was the ultimate object of the workers to take over the tools of production. Although Hillman grew more conservative with the years, notably so under the fire of his rank-and-file Communists, he was intellectually at all events, far to the left of Lewis. While at first the two strongest men in the C.I.O. had agreed to disagree, there was an underlying incompatibility between the rather cold, carefully calculating Hillman and the tempestuous Lewis that sooner or later was bound to cause a break. It is one of the ironies of the recent history of labor that it should be Lewis who was accused of conniving with the Reds whereas Hillman, who was once Commissar of his village during the Russian Revolution of 1905, should be held up as the model for patriotic labor leadership.

The Communists, who had no love for either Dubinsky or Hillman, since both had thwarted them in their drive for control of the needleworkers, now decided to ingratiate themselves with Lewis. Just what arrangements were made in the case of the Steel Workers' Organizing Committee, for example, where many Communists were given responsible organizing posts, will never be known. But wherever a Communist appeared in a position of authority, sooner or later, a stalwart from the United Mine Workers of America showed up, with orders to report back to the Washington headquarters of the mine union. Lewis was taking no chances of letting any "jot or whit," as he would put it, of his centralized authority pass into other hands.

In his own union in 1938, the constantly agitated question of autonomy for the districts had been settled temporarily at least by the national convention which granted a hedged and limited autonomy with control still very much in Lewis's hands.

On the political field, the outstanding achievement of the C.I.O.

was the building of the American Labor party in New York under the guidance of the Lewis-dominated Labor's Non-Partisan League. This fledgling organization setting out to be the nucleus of a national farm-labor party surprised veteran politicos by gathering more than 400,000 votes in New York City and state under its own emblem, in 1938 enough to swing the election of Herbert Lehman, the Democratic candidate for re-election as governor, endorsed by the A.L.P. Originally the aims of the party were to keep a balance of power in the state welcoming to its ranks farmers, small businessmen, salaried and professional people, as well as wage earners. Soon it became recognized in New York as the trade union wing of the Democratic party, although it endorsed some progressive Republicans. Faithfully it followed the New Deal line, with few deviations of its own. In 1942, however, it lost its balance of power status in the course of the Republican sweep which put Thomas Dewey into the governor's chair at Albany and while in a Republican year it amassed the handsome total of nearly 400,000 votes in New York for its gubernatorial candidate, Dean Alfange, it succeeded in electing none of its candidates.

Busied as he was with the varied activities of the C.I.O., Lewis kept a close eye on his own industry and its working force. He watched the price of coal go steadily down throughout the slump of 1938, in spite of the efforts of the Bituminous Coal Commission to prop it up by price setting. Slack declined from $1.81 in January, 1938, to $1.50 in March and spot prices followed suit. Nevertheless, in the spring of 1939, Lewis was again pounding the table under the noses of the assembled operators asking for a 6-hour day and a 15 cents a ton advance for his miners and 50 cents raise for the day men, vacations with pay and, in general, improvement in working conditions. The operators brought out figures for 1938 to bolster their claim that they must cut wages if they were to stay in business. Then the Progressive Miners bobbed up with the demand that the operators bargain with their group instead of the U.M.W. of A.

The Scale Committee of the United Mine Workers, realizing the hopelessness of pushing for wage raises at this time, concentrated on the demand that a union mine clause be written into the Appalachian Wage Agreement. Under this provision, loudly damned as a closed-shop subterfuge by the operators, soon after a man goes to work in a mine where there is a union contract he is obligated to join the union. This means the U.M.W. of A., as the Progressive Miners failed to obtain recognition. As no agreement was reached by April 1st, the members of the U.M.W. of A., grounded their tools. The mines were down all through the Appalachian area. On May 9th, President Roosevelt at the White House told both sides that the country must have coal and two days later the operators agreed to the writing of a union mine agreement. It had been a shutdown of six weeks with no violence, no headlines. But with the very substantial gain to the U.M.W. of A. of the union shop agreement.

WHILE THE REST OF THE COUNTRY'S operators were signing U.M.W. of A. contracts, in two strategic fields antiunion forces remained strongly entrenched. In battle-torn Harlan County, Kentucky, and in the captive mines of the steel companies in Pennsylvania and Northern West Virginia, there were no union contracts in May, 1939, when the national strike ended.

Harlan County had long presented the reverse of the Herrin picture. In Southern Illinois the balance of law enforcement was tipped in favor of the union. In Kentucky the belligerently antiunion Harlan County Coal Operators' Association had all the local "lawmen" on its side. So far as justice went, it would seem to the lay observer to be on the side of the heaviest battalions.

When the Communists in charge of the National Miners' Union had succeeded in organizing a committee of sympathetic writers and artists in New York in 1933 and had brought them down to tell the rest of the nation what went on in the nonunion fields of Kentucky, Harlan was very much on the front pages. Theodore Dreiser, the novelist, a member of the delegation, was promptly arrested on a trumped-up "morals charge" and instead of the expected exposé of conditions in the mines newspaper readers were treated to a juicy bit of gossip about the alleged philandering of the aging writer and his young secretary. Other members of the committee were beaten up and shot at, but all that came of the adventure was a book in which members of the N.M.U. set forth their grievances to their "fellow travellers" from New York.

More serious, however, was the testimony of a large number of evidently fearful witnesses who came before the La Follette Committee on Civil Liberties to tell of brutal shootings of miners suspected of union sympathies by "road killers" in the employ of the operators. Gun thugs deputized by the company paid sheriff-guarded approaches to every mine town. Homes were bombed. Miners, union sympathizers and nonunion men were killed from ambush. Senator La Follette had to reassure many of the witnesses to these bloody doings, appearing before him in Washington, that they would be protected from bodily harm.

In 1938, the federal government moved in. Charges of criminal conspiracy to violate the Wagner Act were brought by the Department of Justice against 53 Harlan coal companies, their executives, the majority of them from outside the state, and a number of deputy sheriffs. The conclusion of the case was as foregone as were the dispositions of the trials arising from the Herrin massacres. The jury was hung. Following the announcement that the government would ask for a new trial, the operators had a change of heart. Many of the influential northern executives, finding themselves at the defendants' table alongside notorious gun-toters, had no wish to repeat that experience. In September, 1938, after a number of secret conferences, the bulk of the Harlan operators signed with the U.M.W. of A. a standard agreement recognizing the union and agreeing to rehire workers dismissed for union activities. As the Progressive Miners were left out of the picture, President Green of the A.F. of L. denounced the settlement in an attack described by Lewis as "characteristic of what might be expected from a traitorous renegade." The National Labor Board agreed to drop proceedings against the companies signing the contract.

Now, a year later, as though to prove to the world that they might die but never surrender, the Harlan operators refused to sign the Appalachian Agreement with the rest of the southern operators. National Guardsmen, as had so often been the case in the past, marched into Harlan County. More blood was spilled but by the end of July, 1939, the seemingly intransigent coalmasters once more changed front and signed a contract yielding exclusive bargaining rights to the U.M.W. of A., with the abolition of the strike penalty clause. No longer could "Old Ben" Unthank, the Association's top deputy who, according to testimony before the La Follette Committee received $2,300 monthly expenses in addition to his salary, ride the roads in search of United Mine Workers' organizers. No longer would Lawrence Dyer, top organizer for the mine union, have reason to say: "I bear a charmed life. I've been shot at so often by Ben Unthank's road killers, I've lost count." For the time being, at any rate, there was an end to the gassing of organizers' hotel rooms, the kidnaping of any suspect stranger, the wholesale jailing of "outside" unionists.

Though Harlan, more because of its antiunion fame than its importance in the national coal setup, was an outstanding victory, and though as a whole the miners went forward with the signing of the Appalachian Agreement, the year 1939 was not a propitious one for organized labor in general. The constant interchange of insults between Lewis and Green gave the public the impression that what had begun as a difference between principles was now degenerating into a feud between personalities. True, the C.I.O. had signed contracts with important corporations which had been open-shop and the movement could boast a small gain in membership over 1938, but on the political field it was fighting a defensive battle against an intensive antilabor drive in Congress and the legislatures of the various states.

Florida passed a law requiring registration of all labor organizations in what seemed to be a step toward compulsory incorporation of trade-unions. Michigan's mediation law forbade sit-down strikes and strictly limited picketing. Minnesota, Wisconsin and Pennsylvania legalized the stepping up of the injunctive process against strikers. On the national field, Assistant Attorney General Thurman Arnold started inquiries into monopolistic practices in the building trades with a view to prosecuting unions for violation of the Sherman Act. At the same time, John L. Lewis announced the formation of the United Construction Workers Organizing Committee to invade the long-held A.F. of L. monopoly of the trades, with brother A. "Denny" Lewis at its head, and daughter Kathryn as liaison officer. While the labor lobbyists were able to head off the drive for the emasculation of the Wagner Act, headed by southern poll-tax congressmen with the aid of influential northern newspapers, chief among them the New York *Times,* everything pointed to a renewal in force of the frontal attack on the unions, following the 1940 elections.

To his associates, Lewis fumed over the apparent coolness of the White House. To the press, he denounced Vice-President Garner, who moved behind the antilabor, anti-New Deal forces as a "labor-baiting, whisky-drinking, poker-playing, evil old man."

Repercussions of the international situation rolled through gatherings of the C.I.O. when Stalin, in August of this doldrum year, signed his pact with Hitler. The American Communists changed their line overnight, howling against Churchill and the British imperialists with all the gusto with which they now support the United Nations. With the swastika flying beside the red flag above the heads of the Nazi visitors to the Kremlin, there was a stampede from the American Communists of their leading converts among the intellectuals. The rank and file of the party, however, accepted with religious fatality the bewildering shift. They sang "The Yanks Aren't Coming" and in the unions their representatives adopted strong anti-interventionist tactics. At the 1939 convention of the C.I.O., after hearing a report that the organization had held "its own in the face of the most vicious and concentrated attack of its enemies," the delegates passed an antiwar resolution. "Labor," said the C.I.O., "wants no war nor any part of it, and while countries in Europe are engaged in their barbaric orgies of conquest and aggression as they have been doing for centuries, it must ever be the purpose of the United States to remain out of these wars." At the same time, the convention went on record as pledged "to defend our country and our free institutions against foreign invasion."

At such a time of doubt and hesitation, the miners prepared to celebrate the fiftieth anniversary of the founding of the U.M.W. of A. at Columbus, Ohio, the union's birthplace, in the beginning of 1940. Before he went west, Lewis made another call at the White House. He came out tight-lipped. On January 24th, he startled the delegates, celebrating their Golden Jubilee, by thundering:

"In the last three years labor has not been given representation in the Cabinet, nor in the administrative or policy-making agencies of the government. . . . Labor today has no point of contact with the Democratic Administration in power, except for casual, occasional interviews which are granted its individual leaders. In the Congress the unrestrained baiting and defaming of labor by the Democratic majority has become a pastime never subject to rebuke by the titular or actual leaders of the party." He assured the miners that if Roosevelt ran again he would suffer "ignominious defeat."

Then Lewis brought forward his own presidential candidate, Senator Burton K. Wheeler of Montana, who had run for vice-president with La Follette in 1924, when Lewis was supporting Coolidge, had made exhaustive investigations of both coal and transportation and had but recently emerged on the winning side in the fight against the President's plan for overhauling the Supreme Court. Nominally a Democrat, Wheeler had long been recognized for his independent progressivism, his sympathies with the aims of organized labor. Now he was in the anomalous position of being cheered by the conservative forces opposing a third term for Roosevelt, among them the comparatively unknown head of the Commonwealth and Southern holding company, Wendell Willkie, and at the same time being taken to the collective bosom of the coal diggers, who gave him a big ovation at Columbus. Like Lewis, Wheeler suggested the possibilities of a dictatorship in the event of a third term, though the convention's resolutions committee had before it a mass of documents from the local unions advocating just such a third term.

The day after Lewis's attack on the Administration, someone flung out a huge red flag from the balcony above his head while he was discussing routine affairs at the convention's loud-speaker. Lewis was enraged and lit into the Communists. He reaffirmed his patriotism, reiterated his noninterventionist stand on the war and denied that he was blocking negotiations for unity with the A.F. of L. He repeated his offer to have both organizations meet in the same hall, but to vote separately on the terms of peace. As there were no questions of contracts before the convention, the gathering then devoted itself to recollections of past glories. As the union scribes had it:

The ghosts of Daniel Weaver, John Siney, John Rae and the handful of men who cried out so joyfully in 1890 when they formed the United Mine Workers of America can once again be jubilant. Their dream has been fulfilled. Their union, and the union of the millions who followed them, has wage contracts which give it exclusive bargaining rights and union mine agreements in the anthracite and bituminous industries of the United States and Canada. Almost every coal miner in America is a member. The membership figures are 612,000, an all-time peak record. The treasury is sufficiently strong to withstand any ordinary shock which might come. Complete co-operation exists in a well-balanced executive staff. But what is more important—the coal miners are strongly cohesive and loyal to the principles of the United Mine Workers, its traditions and its objectives.[1]

The convention's preoccupation with political and international issues was reflected throughout the labor movement in that presidential year. William Green, calling Lewis an "ingrate" for the attack upon the Administration, announced that the A.F. of L. would stick to the New Deal. The Federation's returned prodigal, the International Ladies' Garment Workers' Union, was vociferous in its demands that Roosevelt run again. Hillman's Amalgamated, still in the Congress of Industrial Organizations, plumped squarely for a third term, as did Emil Rieve's oncoming Textile Workers.

In its foreign policy the labor movement as a whole was as confused as the wayfaring man everywhere. To become "the arsenal of democracy," giving all aid to England short of a "shooting" war, was a goal of a sort that had no clean-cut outline. Coal diggers and auto workers had been prominent in the organization of the first Keep America Out of War Congress, an amalgam of liberals, laborites and pacifists. Kathryn Lewis was active in the organization of the America First Committee, a fact which to this day the enemies of Lewis never cease to stress. Lewis's personal choice for the Presidency, Burton Wheeler, was ranging the country urging that we keep out of the "European slaughterhouse." His most enthusiastic audiences were in midwestern industrial centers.

In March, Lewis addressed the Youth Conference, a loosely knit organization, with a compact group of young Communists dominating its policies, just after the President had testily chided the sulky youngsters for tackling problems beyond their comprehension. It was a patronizing speech received with muted boos by the delegates standing in the rain on the White House lawn and Lewis was quick to rub it in when he came before the affronted youngsters. He urged them to join with farmers, Negroes and industrial workers in a mass movement which many of his listeners took to mean an independent political party. He repeated his warnings that "labor was not to be taken for granted" and again aired his grievances against the Administration. At the conclusion of his speech Lewis had to pass Mrs. Roosevelt, who had been sitting on the floor with the other enthralled

[1] David J. McDonald and Edward A. Lynch, *Coal and Unionism*. Lynald Books, Md.

delegates at the feet of a man who had, to put it mildly, been raking her husband fore and aft. She smiled, and the two shook hands with every outward sign of friendliness.

By now the columnists were writing of the chances of a dark horse who would outrun Thomas Dewey, Senator Taft and other favorites in the race for the Republican nomination. They were writing about Wendell Willkie, known to the general public as the private utility champion who had fought the T.V.A. with spectacular ferocity. Willkie, early in the spring, had scoffed at the idea that a man branded with the stamp of the House of Morgan, a lawyer who had such fame as was his for his defence of the private monopoly of public resources, could be considered a likely presidential candidate.

Back of the Willkie candidacy, however, was a streamlined promotional campaign, engineered chiefly by the bright young men of *Time, Life* and *Fortune* who boasted of their discovery of the utility man and were now busily engaged in building him up as "a liberal at heart," who would crusade for the restoration of old-fashioned "free enterprise." It was at the Greenwich Village home of a New York liberal lawyer that Lewis first met Mr. Willkie.

The two got along famously from the start. In their common hatred for That Man in the White House they had the beginnings of a beautiful friendship. Both were conservatives who could don a homes-spun liberalism when the "timing" called for it. Willkie had his liberal vocabulary from his parents back in Indiana in the days when wandering rebels used to drop in at Judge Willkie's house to expound their theories from socialism to the single tax. In the course of his five-year leadership of the C.I.O. Lewis learned by heart many of the precious liberal words. Again both were "practical men" (as the first Roosevelt said of himself and Harriman) who looked with scorn upon the often-bewildered gesturings of the amateurs in the New Deal. So far as political party allegiance went, neither had a record of regularity. "I am not a Republican, I am not a Democrat, I am not a Socialist, I am not a Communist. I am for labor," said the miners' head who had successively supported Harding, Coolidge and Hoover. And Willkie had to be introduced at the Republican convention to many a veteran G.O.P. wheel horse. So far as Willkie's struggle against the march of the big dams down the Tennessee Valley went, that had Lewis's wholehearted endorsement. The very word "hydroelectric" is still anathema to the miners' chief who sees in the expansion of waterpower a threat to his industry. The fact that Commonwealth and Southern was an offshoot of J. P. Morgan's superholding company, the United, did not sit so well with Lewis but, on the other hand, Willkie's earnest protestations that he was out to free private enterprise from the dead hand of bureaucracy could not help but persuade the author of *The Miners' Fight for American Standards.*

Lewis stood apart from the confused campaign which followed the nomination of Willkie and Roosevelt's re-renomination. Stood apart until October 25, 1940, when he went to the microphone with a speech that stirred the nation. Millions of listeners from all walks of life, gasped with amazement as the booming voice of the president of the coal diggers' union called for the election of the former president of a Morgan-dominated holding company, the white hope of every corporate interest in the nation.

"I think," rumbled Lewis, "the election of President Roosevelt for a third term would be a national evil of the first magnitude. He no longer hears the cries of the people. I think the election of Mr. Wendell Willkie is imperative in relation to the country's needs. I commend him to the men and women of labor as one worthy of their support and as one who will capably and zealously protect their rights, increase their privileges, and restore their happiness."

"It is obvious," went on the deep voice, "that President Roosevelt will not be re-elected for the third time unless he has the overwhelming support of the men and women of labor. If he is, therefore, re-elected, it will mean that the members of the Congress of Industrial Organizations have rejected my advice and recommendation. I will accept the result as being the equivalent of a vote of no confidence and will retire as president of the Congress of Industrial Organizations at its convention in November."

Pressure was put on the C.I.O. officials to swing the rank-and-file vote for the utility man. Some yielded to it. Others would have no part in it. Eli Oliver, capable head of Labor's Non-Partisan League, came out in favor of Roosevelt. Lewis got his resignation. Powers Hapgood took a plane from Washington to his home in Indiana to vote for Norman Thomas, running for president on the Socialist ticket for the fourth time. A large group of labor sympathizers of a liberal bent who had been working with various C.I.O. groups left the Lewis camp. So far as the chance for any effective organization of the labor vote for Willkie went (if indeed Lewis intended such) the time was much too short between the Lewis speech and election day. In all the industrial centers and in the remote mine camps as well, the workers went to the polls and voted for Roosevelt. They were fed up with Willkie buttons and high-pressure ballyhoo. They would trust John Lewis's judgment in a wage negotiation or a strike situation. They would not follow his political vagaries.

The November convention of the C.I.O. was charged with emotion. Delegations visited Lewis beseeching him to reconsider his decision to resign. Why throw away the heroic labors of five stormy years to pay off an election bet? Admitting that his sense of timing had failed him in this instance, why shouldn't Lewis allow himself to be drafted, after going through the motions of resigning? Lewis, looking stonily at the protesting delegates, went to the platform to make his final accounting of stewardship. He reported that the C.I.O. had 4,000,000 members, 35 national and international unions, and eight general organizing committees. In the cities it had 225 industrial union councils and 419 local units, comparable to the federal unions of the A.F. of L. "On advice of counsel" there was no financial report. The C.I.O. was making progress in bringing the airplane workers on the West Coast into the United Automobile Workers but there were few other notable advances to be recorded.

Then Lewis handed over the gavel and the leadership of the organization which he had founded to his long-time lieutenant Philip Murray, with his blessings. The two were photographed with their arms entwined.

Murray warned that it would be of no use for the Administration to attempt to force "a shotgun marriage" between the A.F. of L. and the C.I.O. He intimated that until the C.I.O. had completed its organizing campaigns in steel, aircraft, shipbuilding and other defense industries there would be no use talking unity between the two organizations. The A.F. of L. now was claiming a paid-up membership of 4,247,443, an all-time high, with 108 national and international unions. Murray was following Lewis's policy of staving off peace with the Federation until the C.I.O. could do more than talk in round numbers and show a paid-up membership equaling if not exceeding the Federation figures.

The labor world turned to speculation as to what manner of leader Philip Murray would make. He had moved so long under the large shadow of Lewis that it was difficult to picture him acting on his own initiative. To be sure, he had shown intelligence, courage and a keen comprehension of the larger problems of industry in his direction of the Steel Workers' Organizing Committee. His reputation, however, was that of the canny negotiator rather than a working-class leader. That he had beneath his gray hair a wealth of knowledge of the increasingly complicated setup of the production and distribution of goods and services, no one doubted. The public outside the labor movement could find his philosophy set forth in the book which he wrote with Morris Cooke, *Organized Labor and Production*. Here he pounded away at his thesis that there could be no genuine democracy in industry except through the process of collective bargaining with labor organizations, on one side, "able to regard the interests of the industry as a whole" and, on the other, organizations of employers "prepared to assume the responsibilities of economic statesmanship." As to the government's part, he and Cooke agreed:

A generation ago only a skeleton file of so-called radicals could see the necessity of a creative role of government in the economic system. Today only a reactionary fragment, gradually dwindling under the scythe of the grim reaper, questions the necessity of government aid to low rent housing, of government intervention in the flow of purchasing power. As younger and better-trained men rise into positions of industrial leadership there is multiplying evidence of the infiltration of social-mindedness into the stubborn tissue of business self-interest. We see great labor unions taking seriously the idea of responsibility for continued production. We see important progress making toward more extended and better administered social security. We see the farmer, always before an economic exile, brought into the scope of national economic policy, and in time we shall form rational ideas as to what to do with him.

The book set forth more the philosophy of the "New Unionism" of the needle trades with its ideas of labor-management collaboration than the old hell-for-leather strategy of conflict of the miners. Murray went so far as to propose that in steel, before technological advances threw men out of work, outside researchers, to be paid for by both labor and management, be called in to see if savings could not be made that would permit the introduction of new processes without the need for wholesale firing. He was all for greater participation on the part of the unions in the field of production policies and in general he showed an alert awareness of what was the economic time of day. "We are just leaving a period," he wrote at the end of the book, "in which collective bargaining was scarcely ever really accepted. Employers dealt with unions only because they had to. If we go back to such conditions now [1940] in view of the present world-wide attacks upon democracy the outcome may well be a weakening of the democratic processes here and the possible setting of the scene for a dictator. If American political democracy is to survive, we must succeed. We must have democracy in industry."

Nothing startlingly new, certainly nothing radical in this collaborationist philosophy of Murray's, but it was a break from his miners' tradition. He was talking more in the quiet voice of Sidney Hillman than the sonorous tones of Lewis. The new president of the C.I.O. had the difficult task of combining militancy with collaboration at the same time that the government was increasingly encroaching upon the domain of organized labor as well as organized business. As Murray took over, Lewis watched grimly from the side lines. Some of the more starry-eyed New Dealers and other foes of the head of the miners were jubilating over what they took to be the elimination of Lewis form the national labor picture. More sophisticated observers warned that Lewis with 600,000 loyal coal diggers behind him was still a power to be reckoned with in any calculation of the future of American labor.

XX. THE CAPTIVE MINE
STRUGGLE

As THE YEAR 1940 CLOSED, IT FOUND
Lewis out of the leadership of the C.I.O., at serious odds with the Administration, and so far as the press and the radio were concerned, a repudiated man, sulking in his isolationist tent. Sidney Hillman, on the other hand, and vicariously the new Murray leadership, was recognized by the Administration through Hillman's appointment to the associate directorship of the Office for Production Management under William S. Knudsen.

It was not, however, in the Lewis scheme of things to stay long on the side lines. There was a final touch to be added to the over-all Appalachian Agreement which would write finis to one of the most contentious phases in American labor's development. Lewis decided that the time had come to wipe out the wage differential between Northern and Southern operators.

When in the nineties the young miners' union had persuaded the operators in the Central Competitive Field that it would be to their advantage as well as to the advantage of the union to concede the checkoff, it was on the understanding that some of the steady flow of funds which this ensured would be diverted to organizing work in the South. We have seen something of the bloody struggles that followed. Though the operators below the Ohio River were now bargaining collectively, a wage differential in favor of the South of around 40 cents still prevailed and Lewis was free to devote his entire energy to its elimination. A number of factors favored the union. The Southern operators were making the most of the defense boom with its ever-increasing demand for industrial fuel. They knew the strength of the U.M.W. of A. and were in no mood for another struggle at this time. The entire price situation was confused by the emergence of new governmental agencies, to deal indirectly with the economics of coal, in addition to the Bituminous Commission. A month's shutdown at the expiration of the Appalachian Agreement in April, 1941, followed by a threat of the union to strike again in July, brought the Southern coalmasters to terms. They signed the agreement which the Northern operators had already signed, raising the basic inside day rate for laborers to $7. This was an increase of $1 in the North, $1.40 in the South. Higher tonnage rates and vacations with pay were written into the agreement which would expire in the spring of 1043.

Over in anthracite, the defense boom also had its effects. Hard-coal miners had won the checkoff throughout the field, the 7-hour day and the 35-hour week, and the union shop. Now, through Lewis, they demanded wage increases of a dollar a day for day men and 20 per cent for contract miners. After one day's stoppage, a new contract was drawn up giving the anthracite day men a raise of 60 cents per diem and the contract miners a 75-cent increase. There was a vacation payment of $20. Anthracite was on its way back, though in many parts of the fields investigators were still calling the hard-coal miners "industry's forgotten men."

These significant gains of the miners were overlooked in the confusions attendant upon the question of intervention, the hurried defense preparations, and the rising storms of antiunion propaganda. In England, Labour Minister Ernest Bevin announced that the British government had decided to register working men and women for drafting into war factories. President Roosevelt's declaration of "an unlimited emergency" gave our labor leaders a foretaste of the possibility of something of the sort over here in case of our active participation in the war. Everywhere labor stirred uneasily. Thirty or more bills curtailing, and in some instances completely destroying, the functions of unions were in the Congressional hopper. These ranged from compulsory registration, to making the calling of a strike in a defense industry a capital crime. A major activity of both A.F. of L. and C.I.O. was lobbying against such measures.

Lewis lost no opportunity to warn American labor that it was taking the humiliating role of the "tame cat" British movement which lent its leaders to the Tory government as a front behind which labor could be regimented. He struck hard at Hillman's acquiescent part in the suppression of the strike at the Inglewood, California, plant of the North American Aviation, Inc., by the President's orders sending federal troops to take over. Lewis had looked with sardonic eyes at the picture of the former revolutionist, ex-Socialist and propagandist for the "New Unionism" standing at the President's shoulder as Roosevelt phoned his order for the troops to break up the picket lines. At a legislative conference of the C.I.O. the miners' head lashed out at Hillman and put through a resolution denouncing the sending of federal ▮▮▮▮▮▮▮▮▮▮▮▮ came to break strikes.

▮▮▮▮▮▮▮▮▮▮▮ between Lewis and the C.I.O. interventionists had now become practically unbridgeable. Murray moved unhappily between the two. He had submitted a memorandum to the congressmen considering the Lease-Lend Act, in opposition to the measure. However, Murray, with William Green, was a member of the Committee on Fair Employment of the War Production Board and his relations with the White House were pleasant. He had the prestige of signing up Henry Ford with a closed-shop clause in the contract and of signing Girdler's Republic Steel Corporation, and Bethlehem Steel as well. His stature as a labor leader was growing, but he was in no wise prepared to risk a head-on collition with his predecessor in the C.I.O., and still his president in the miners' union.

Then, in June, Hitler invaded Russia and once more the American Communists changed their line. First it had been "collective security" with warlike gestures at all "aggressor nations." Then it had been complete isolationism. Now it was intervention. "Defend America," read the official Communist appeal, "by giving full aid to the Soviet Union, Great Britain and all nations who fight against Hitler." Noninterventionists were violently attacked in the columns of the *Daily Worker* as appeasers and pro-Fascists. For Lewis, "the Samson of Labor," as the Communist intelligentsia were calling him but a short time back, the comrades were sharpening the devastating shears.

Lewis watched the Communists make overtures to Sidney Hillman, for whom at one time they could find no epithets strong enough, watched them move on Washington seeking to infiltrate themselves into governmental agencies that would deal with labor relations in the war which they now felt was bound to drag this nation in as an active participant, watched them put away the posters picturing Churchill as an imperialist monster devouring the children of workers. Then he turned to the reorganization of the catch-all District 50 of the miners' union, as though building against the day when it would be necessary for him to have a new, nation-wide organizational weapon that would rival both the A.F. of L. and the C.I.O. He put a dependable wheel horse, Ora Gasaway, at the head of the district, and his daughter Kathryn as secretary in the district office in the United Mine Workers Building at Washington where he could have personal supervision. Soon thirty district officials in the field were demoted in the course of a general shake-up. It was ░░░░░░░░░ that this somewhat mysterious stepchild of the miners' union ░░░░░░ ░░dergo a marked change in status.

In that year, Lewis's was the first and often the only voice to be raised on behalf of labor against the increasing trend toward governmental encroachment. While speaking against the St. Lawrence Waterway project, he took occasion harshly to criticize such agencies as the National Mediation Board and, as the year drew to an end, he girded up his loins for a new organizational struggle at a time when other large unions were quiescent.

Lewis chose for his battleground the captive steel mines, the last important operations to hold out against the union shop. In 1934, following strikes in Western Pennsylvania and Labor Board elections, the H. C. Frick Coal Company, a subsidiary of U.S. Steel, had signed an agreement outlining terms of hiring with the officials of the U.M.W. of A. acting as representatives of the miners. But the union was not named in the contract, although there was a rush on the part of the coal diggers to join the U.M.W. of A. Other steel companies fell in line with this oblique arrangement by "Big Steel" but still the miners in the corporations' controlled pits were not receiving the union benefits or wages of their fellow unionists working under union-shop contracts. The steel men feared that to concede the union shop to the U.M.W. of A. would set a precedent for the organization of the steel mills on such a basis and they insisted that their miners were "different." Lewis thought otherwise and, in the fall, put his union-shop demand before the steelmasters. It was promptly rejected Whereupon Lewis set October 27th as the date for a strike of the miners in the captive pits. Twice the President sent him messages urging that the strike be called off. When the 53,000 miners walked out at the appointed hour, a third letter came to Lewis from the White House warning that the mine shutdown would cut fuel supplies for the steel mills at a time of crisis. Lewis answered this last appeal as follows:

I have no wish to betray those whom I represent. There is yet no question of patriotism or national security involved in this dispute. For four months the steel companies have been whetting their knives and preparing for this struggle. They have increased coal storage and marshalled all their resources. Defense output is not impaired and will not be impaired for an indefinite period. The fight is only between a labor union and a ruthless corporation—the United States Steel Corporation.

On the heels of this came an offer from the National Mediation Board that that agency decide the dispute. U.S. Steel accepted the proposal, and on the morning of October 30th, Lewis called off the strike. On the afternoon of the same day he set November 15 as the deadine for the calling of a new strike in the event that the government mediators got nowhere.

The press and radio did not accept Lewis's version of the struggle as an ordinary labor dispute. They denounced him for blocking the defense effort and called on the President to force the miners to accept arbitration. Even the liberal weeklies joined in this, pointing out that Lewis's adamant stand was making the entire labor movement the more vulnerable to antiunion legislation. Lewis was not impressed.

On November 10th the Mediation Board by a 9-to-2 vote rejected the U.M.W. of A. demands for a union shop. In its decision the fact that 98 per cent of the workers involved were union members anyway, was underscored, and it was made plain that it was not the function of the board to order the retention of the steel companies' employees in the mines on the condition that they become members of the union, after a certain period—the gist of the union-shop contract. The board, it seemed, was bent on continuing its policy of treating each dispute as it arose, rather than laying down any general principles, as Lewis was insisting. In several instances it had found in favor of union membership maintenance clauses in the contracts under which union members must remain in good standing with their organization as a condition of continued employment, though no employee was forced to join a union. The miners' leaders looked upon this as a weak compromise between the union shop and the open shop.

Throughout this dispute Lewis was hewing to the line laid down by the 1941 Labor Day editorial in the *United Mine Workers Journal*, which said in part:

> The United Mine Workers will not accept the defeatist attitude of some weak-kneed union leaders. To follow the accepted course of such leaders would in effect mean that the principles of collective bargaining would either be arbitrated out of existence or shelved during the preparedness period. President Lewis and his co-workers feel, and rightly so, that if there ever was a time in American history when it was imperative for labor to assume the aggressive and complete the job of organizing American working men that time is now. The economic order that lies ahead, the future of American enterprise, the hopes and aspirations of American working men, require and demand alert leadership, if the pitfalls of economic damnation are to be averted when the adjustment period arrives. The United Mine Workers propose to do their part, in fact more than their part, in providing such leadership, in building an impregnable labor force. What's more, President Lewis plans to finish the job of organizing the mine workers employed in the captive mines.

The editorial voiced the traditional militancy of the miners, their distaste for governmental impingements, which, in spite of the aid given to their organization by the NRA and the generally friendly attitude of the White House in Roosevelt's first two terms, was still deeply impregnated in the rank and file.

The two votes against the board's decision had been cast by Philip Murray and Thomas Kennedy. With the announcement of the decision came word of the resignation from the board of both the mine union's members, thereby destroying the effectiveness of the board and drawing down upon Lewis's head the renewed wrath of the press and the Administration. There were demands upon Roosevelt that he take drastic action to end all labor disputes in defense industries. On November 13th the House of Representatives by a vote of 212 to 194 accepted the Senate's amendment to the Neutrality Act permitting the arming of merchant ships and their sailing through war zones. The White House put the strongest pressure upon hesitant congressmen, promising that if the measure were passed, steps would be taken to curb labor. Here was a warning earmarked for Lewis, and in many quarters it was believed that he would reconsider his strike call for the 15th. Over the tense weekend Lewis was once more at the White House. On Monday morning, November 17th, the first shifts failed to report at the captive pits in the Pittsburgh, Youngstown and other steel-dominated fields. The strike was on as scheduled and the nation's press pictured it as a life-or-death struggle between the leader of all the forces opposed to the Administration's policies, domestic as well as foreign, and the pleasant-spoken man in the White House. Some prominent C.I.O. leaders accepted this version, though the majority agreed with Lewis that here was no more than the renewal of the ancient warfare between the U.M.W. of A. and the steelmasters.

At the November convention of the C.I.O., in Detroit, the magic of the Lewis name still held sway. On Philip Murray's motion the delegates voted full support to the strike. Out of the commercial pits in the vicinity of the struck capitive mines in Pennsylvania, Ohio, West Virginia, Maryland and Kentucky came sympathetic diggers in such numbers that within a week it was estimated that some 200,000 miners, including the 53,000 originally affected, were idle. Violence broke out. C.I.O. mass picketing lines clashed with members of a company union attempting to enter the pits at Gary, West Virginia. At a Frick coke plant at Edenborn, Pennsylvania, eleven pickets were shot. There were the usual conflicting reports from the various fronts. Correspondents sent back word that the strikers were being dragooned, that there was no heart for the strike among the rank and file. All that was missing from such stories was the allusion to "Communist agitation." With the Administration liberals, the Communists were standing well apart from the strike, following the line that no stoppage of production was justified now that Soviet Russia was in peril.

When those who read past the headlines intimating that the strike was being apathetically supported found that every important operation in steel's mining domain was closed tight, and that sympathy strikes were actually on the increase, there rose a vast clamor for speedy arbitration. Lewis had been talking with the steel men, but he complained that the negotiators sent to him were only second-stringers. He kept the name of Morgan well up in his press releases, indicating that the grand strategy of the struggle was laid down in the banking house at the corner of Broad and Wall streets.

On November 22nd, Lewis accepted the proposal from the White House that the union-shop issue be arbitrated by a board consisting of Benjamin F. Fairless, president of the U.S. Steel, John R. Steelman, director of the United States Conciliation Service, and Lewis. The miners' chief now had his top man to bargain with in Fairless. His experiences with Steelman had convinced him that the conciliator was sympathetic with the chief objectives of unionism. The miners went back to work, as the three arbitrators gathered for their first sessions.

Looking back on it now, with our knowledge of the vast events that were in train in the Pacific that November, we may wonder how an industrial dispute of a highly technical nature involving but 50,-000 workers could have so perturbed the public. For the second time in his life, Lewis was placed in the position of defying his government. Now, however, he was in no mood to repeat his surrender to Wilson. He stuck to his guns, though anti-Administration papers (which the year before had been uttering dire warnings of dictatorship in the event of a third term for Roosevelt) joined with the Administration press in heated denunciation of the strike and its leader. In Congress, men talked about Benedict Arnold.

Despite the admonitions of the press, the lack of support of many of Lewis's former followers in the C.I.O., and the pressure of the Administration's labor liaison men, on the fateful 7th of December the arbitration board by a vote of 2 to 1 (Lewis and Steelman against Fairless) decided in favor of the union shop for the captive mines. The grim news from Pearl Harbor overshadowed the story of the award, but the trade-union movement knew well enough that the victory signified Lewis's return to power. "Verily," exulted the *United Mine Workers Journal,* "this fight constituted a show of hands in the trade-union movement of America. It was a poll of the daring and strong, the weak and the hesitant."

XXI. THE WAR LABOR BOARD
TAKES OVER

N O SOONER HAD THE ATTACKS ON
Lewis over his captive mine stand died down, than his critics were
once more in full cry over the miners' chief's unexpected move for
unity between the A.F. of L. and the C.I.O. Lewis was still the chairman of the Peace Negotiating Committee of the C.I.O., having been
appointed to that post at the third annual convention. On January
17, 1942, he sent a letter to Murray and Green suggesting the resump-
tion of peace conferences.

This innocent-seeming proposal put Lewis once more in the headlines as plotting to "capture" the labor movement in collusion with the
reactionaries in the A.F. of L., headed by William Hutcheson of the
carpenters, who now, according to the newspapers, had forgiven Lewis
for punching him in the eye in 1935 and was eager to get the movement from under the president's wing. As an adornment to this tale
there was the story of a cocktail party at the home of a prominent
Washington woman pacifist at which Lewis, Norman Thomas and
Senator Wheeler were supposed to have concocted the plot.

Murray was highly incensed at being bypassed by Lewis and
promptly announced that if there were to be any negotiations with
the A.F. of L. they would be initiated through his (Murray's) office.
On the other hand, William Green as promptly accepted the invitation.
Roosevelt's labor advisers urged the President to take speedy action to
head off Lewis. As a result the Labor Victory Board was set up, consisting of three members of the C.I.O. and three of the A.F. of L., the
majority of them anti-Lewis men, with the President dominating their

counsels. Though this new creation was in reality no more than a discussion group meeting at the White House from time to time to talk over labor matters, it gave a semblance of unity which served for the time being to fend off the threatened Lewis comeback.

In the meantime the War Labor Board, successor to the ill-fated National Mediation Board, had been set up, following a conference of labor and industry called by the President, at which labor representatives agreed to forgo strikes in war industries for the duration. The head of the WLB was William H. Davis, the former patent attorney who had been chairman of the Mediation Board. The labor members of the new board were Thomas Kennedy, R. J. Thomas, head of the United Automobile Workers of America—C.I.O., George Meany, secretary-treasurer of the A.F. of L., and Matthew Woll.

The executive order for the board provided that parties to a labor dispute "which might interrupt work which contributes to the effective prosecution of the war . . . shall first resort to direct negotiations or to the procedures provided in a collective bargaining agreement. If not settled in this manner, the Commissioners of Conciliation of the Department of Labor shall be notified if they have not already intervened in the dispute. If not promptly settled, the Secretary of Labor shall certify the dispute to the Board, provided, however, that the Board in its discretion, after consultation with the Secretary, may take jurisdiction of the dispute on its own motion. After it takes jurisdiction, the Board shall finally determine the dispute, and for this purpose may use mediation, voluntary arbitration, or arbitration under rules established by the Board."

From the beginning, Lewis was critical of both the Labor Victory Board and the War Labor Board, despite the fact that on the latter sat his lieutenant Kennedy. He was frankly skeptical of the seemingly harmonious get-together of labor and industry which led to the formation of the WLB. While labor representatives had insisted that their surrender of the strike weapon (a surrender, by the way, not made by labor in World War I) be accompanied by guarantees that labor would be paid a living wage and that such protective labor measures as the Wagner Act, the National Labor Relations Act, the Wages and Hours, etc., be continued unimpaired, Lewis voiced his doubt that labor's gains could be long held under the compulsions of increasing governmental control. He believed that he saw labor leadership usurped by the White House and the entire movement hamstrung by bureaucracy. Though he himself had been in on the labor-industry conference, he felt that its recommendations would have little effect upon congressmen implacably hostile to labor who were attempting to wipe out the New Deal's protective measures. Lewis had insisted that the War Labor Board as a first step adopt certain clear-cut policies which he and Murray had drawn up as a code of principles. These included restrictions of the lengthening of the workday, equal pay for women workers, a living wage, with a minimum for unskilled workers, a 6 per cent limit on profits in war industries, the right of employees to appeal to the board in case of violations of the rules of other federal agencies, an end to jurisdictional disputes, and finally the establishment of industry councils with equal representation of labor and management in all basic industries. The mine leaders' suggestions were ignored by the board, which decided to take up "each dispute purely on its own merits." The only good that Lewis could find in the board was that it was "the only real important board that has actual bona fide representation of labor sitting in its councils with equal voice and vote with industry and the public."

Murray, on the other hand, sorely harassed by the ever-increasing chances of his own union withdrawing from the C.I.O., by the threat of sweeping antilabor legislation and advancing governmental regimentation, decided to go along with the Administration. As a price for this, he insisted on the establishment of industry councils, but he was vague as to the functions of such councils.

Soon after he assumed the presidency of the C.I.O. Murray became ill and underwent a serious operation. His sickness had upset him emotionally. He began to talk with a religious mysticism which astonished those who had known him as a brass-tacks negotiator whose whole concern had been with wages and hours. He was not ready for an open break with his old chief, yet he spoke broodingly of Lewis to C.I.O. intimates as one who had "betrayed" him. In May, however, Murray, addressing the Joint Policy Committee of the U:M.W. of A., said:

"Now as to the constant reference that has been made about Phil Murray calling John L. Lewis a Jap. Nothing could be further from the truth. I don't know how often it should become necessary for me to repeat and repeat and repeat that as a man and as a citizen and as an American, I have always regarded Mr. Lewis as without a peer in the realm of America. I dislike and I resent, no matter whose mouth it flows from, the implication that I made any filthy, insinuating remark concerning President Lewis's Americanism."

Eight days later, speaking before a C.I.O. Executive Board meeting at the Press Club in Washington, Murray said:

"Last fall, Mr. Lewis suggested that I go to the Detroit C.I.O. national convention with him and fight the foreign policy of the President of the United States. I told him that I would not, that to do so would be treasonable to the United States government. Mr. Lewis is hell-bent on creating national confusion and national disunity."

The C.I.O. committee promptly passed a resolution which, among other things, stated:

"In contrast to other affiliates of the C.I.O., officials of the U.M.W. of A. have put forward no plans whatever for increasing production, for an offensive for victory over the Axis, nor have they come forward with any proposals for gearing the nation's economy to the needs of war."

The Executive Committee of the mine workers' union promptly retorted that miners were enlisting in the army and navy, buying war bonds," co-operating completely" in increasing coal production 30 per cent since Pearl Harbor. An apology was demanded from Murray. Ray Edmunson, president of the Illinois Miners, District 12, resigned his job as regional director of the C.I.O. to start a stream of resignations of other mine union officials from the Congress. The miners' officials then sought to collect from the C.I.O. $1,665,000 which the U.M.W. of A. maintained was part of a loan made in the period from 1935 to 1942. In all, the mine workers' union asserted that $7 million had come from their treasury to finance the C.I.O. The rest had been written off but now the miners were demanding immediate payment of close to $2 million. When the C.I.O. refused flatlly to recognize any debt, holding that the officials of the U.M.W. of A. who had advanced the money upon the approval of their union had no authority to collect it, the mine workers withheld their per capita dues of $30,000 a month, a telling blow to the organizational plans which Murray had in mind.

Murray was now anxious to press for unity with the A.F. of L. but Green and the Federation's hierarchy were in a better bargaining position then they had been since 1937. The loss of dues from the miners and the probable complete withdrawal of the mine union from the C.I.O. had put the latter organization in such a shaky position that Green could afford to be a bit highhanded about the way in which he would receive the C.I.O. into the Federation.

The vituperative exchanges between Murray and Lewis, with R. J. Thomas, head of the United Automobile Workers, noisily backing up Murray, and the great majority of the miners' officials supporting their president, led to a rush of resignations on both sides. In June, Van A. Bittner, who time and again had served as Lewis's representative in ticklish interunion situations, threw up his job as president of District 17, the battle-torn West Virginia district, to be succeeded by Percy Tetlow as provisional president appointed by Lewis. And then the Executive Board of the miners by a vote of 17 to 1 declared the office of vice-president of the U.M.W. of A. vacant. This was the office so long held by Murray. Murray on June 1st had taken the presidency of the steel workers' union. Technically he could not hold both jobs and it was on this ground that his resignation was accepted, though everyone in the movement knew that this marked the end of all connection of the veteran Scotchman with the coal diggers.

Thomas Kennedy, the other member of the old "Big Three," watched Murray's departure with sadness, but kept his place at Lewis's side. Said Kennedy:

"I have been associated with John Lewis and Phil Murray now for seventeen years. We have been through some trying times over that period. We have been down in the depths of despair upon many occasions, and we have risen to the heights indicated by the ideals and the great principles of the United Mine Workers of America. Over all this period of years, ever since I joined the United Mine Workers of America, it has been a sort of second religion with me, this organization, its constitution and its great leadership. My friends, it is a very sad moment in my life. I know both these men intimately. I love them, and I would give my life for either of them. But, my friends, sentiment does not take precedent over the constitution and great principles of the United Mine Workers of America. No matter what is said or done, John Lewis is the responsible officer of this organization. . . ."

There was a hint about what the more thoughtful of the rank

and file felt about the feuding among their officials in resolutions prepared for the coming U.M.W. of A. convention by locals in remote fields, resolutions imploring the bickering personalities to patch up a peace before the whole movement suffered irreparable damage. But there was to be no peace.

In the summer of 1942, Lewis's wife was seriously ill and he gave up all his other duties to spend his time at the bedside of the gallant and devoted woman who had gone with him from the days of obscurity back in Iowa through all the stormy journey. Intimates of the Lewises never failed to comment on the way in which the presence of the wife could draw out an unsuspected tenderness in this man seemingly all steel. What John L. Lewis had of education beyond the stern economics of industry he had from this gentle schoolteacher daughter of a country doctor. When she died in the fall, Lewis was sorely stricken. He made one reference to his sorrow when he told the miners' convention of that year that he had been "carrying the cross."

In the meantime Murray was everywhere repeating the story of his "betrayal" by Lewis in the manner of the victim of a persecution mania. Holding his hand on his heart, the burring Scotchman would compare his betrayal with that of Jesus, with references to Gethsemane and Golgotha, and with Lewis in the role of Judas Iscarot.

Communists, now all-out for no strikes or stoppages in the war industries, and, if necessary for the winning of the war, the surrender of the full range of labor's rights, were assuming a prominence in the Murray regime which they had rarely enjoyed under Lewis. When charged with aiding and abetting the Stalinites, Murray's reply was that all of them had first been given jobs by Lewis. Whatever their status, these Communist hereditaments were soon undertaking to lay down the new C.I.O. line of sending representatives, with no powers to the various governmental agencies, to "observe" the industrialists and political appointees making labor policies. The fate of the war conversion plan for the automotive industry hopefully submitted by Walter Reuther of the auto workers' union, only to be kicked around from one agency to another, might have early persuaded Murray of the futility of such tactics, but he could merely repeat his demand for the establishment of industrial councils, with a labor-management setup. In some instances these councils were allowed to function as advisory bodies, whose suggestions might or might not be accepted by the powers that were. On the whole, however, labor, for more than a year at any rate, had no real voice either in the conduct of the war or in the allotment of its own place in the economic scheme of things. Among the important unions the only dissident voice was that of the miners. In the *United Mine Workers Journal,* edited by K. C. Adams, there was caustic criticism of this subordination of the interests of the workers to those of the large industrialists.

Lewis was using District 50 as a weapon for guerrilla warfare, keeping his opponents within the labor movement guessing and scaring conservatives in all walks of life. His announcement that District 50 would conduct a nation-wide organizing campaign to form the 3 million dairy workers into an industrial union was received first with amazement, and then with the charge that Lewis was attempting to control the milk supply of the country on his march to dictatorial power. Kathryn Lewis in March gave out figures to the effect that small dairy farmers in Michigan and New York were affiliating with the U.M.W. of A. to the number of 30,000. Alarmed, the large farm organizations which had devoted most of their energies to lobbying for the Farm Bloc program in Congress joined with the big milk dealers in damning Lewis. Lewis had his picture taken with the leaders of the Michigan and New York dairy farmers who signed a statement reading:

The one hope of all farmers is in a national organization. Supported by the United Mine Workers of America, we will be able to obtain the necessities of life for our families and for the first time in the history of the country the dairy farmer will be independent and self-sustaining. John L. Lewis, great President of the United Mine Workers of America, demonstrated his ability in welding five million people into the C.I.O. Under his leadership the dairy farmers can obtain the same benefits that have been obtained by the industrial workers of this nation.

Gasaway and Miss Lewis conducted this novel campaign on the streamlines of the earlier C.I.O. organizing drives. They set up substantial offices of the field men in the heart of the dairy territory, kept pounding away at the gains made by the younger unions under the Lewis regime, and brought in many converts from among a group traditionally hostile to unionism in all its forms.

While the relations between milk and coal were not obvious to the casual observer, organizers for the catch-all District 50 could more rationally claim jurisdiction over the unorganized workers on coal's by-products. As these by-products ranged from perfumes to medicinals and explosives, coal diggers visiting industrial centers were hailed by some oddly assorted groups of workers as union brothers.

Organization, collective bargaining, and the other functions of unionism, however, were rapidly being displaced by governmental decrees and proscriptions and the activities of such agencies as the War Labor Board, the office of the Fuel Co-ordinator, the War Production Board, the War Manpower Commission, the Bituminous Coal Division and the office of Price Administration. President Roosevelt issued an executive order for price and wage stabilization, freezing wages except where "maladjustments of the wage structure" might be ameliorated. In its findings in the Little Steel wage dispute the War Labor Board granted a 15 per cent raise, estimating that there had been an increase in living costs of that percentage between January, 1941, and May, 1942. Where wage raises had met the increase, according to the board's formula there could be no further raise. Manpower Commissioner Paul McNutt, long before any general labor conscription bill had been seriously considered by Congress, "froze" copper miners and lumberjacks in the Northwest to their jobs, against the most strenuous objections of the progressives in the labor movement. Thus, with the strike tactic or, what is often as important, the threat of a strike in industries essential to the war effort (and this included practically all industries) voluntarily surrendered, it was difficult for organizers to persuade the large army of newcomers to factory work that union membership would be of any benefit to them. Young men and women with a middle-class psychology, many holding their first jobs at what seemed to them fabulous wages, saw no reason for paying dues to unions confined to gestures of protest against regimentation. In many production centers "independent unions" suspiciously similar to the abandoned company unions were set up. In other places the union maintenance of membership clause was written into contracts. This permitted the employer to hire personnel regardless of union membership. After a certain period, usually two weeks, the employee had a choice of joining the union. In the event of his joining it was then obligatory for him to remain a union member in good standing for the duration of his employment. Dues were paid through a checkoff or at the union offices. With great cross sections of the new labor army exercising what the employers called "the escape clause," i.e., refusal to join the union, organizers for the C.I.O. and the A.F. of L. looked wistfully at the clear-cut union-shop arrangement of the U.M.W. of A.

In Pittsburgh steel mills, members of the United Steel Workers, now headed by Philip Murray with Van Bittner as his assistant, were uttering their "stereotyped complaints" to such reporters as Eliot Janeway and Willi Schlamm of *Fortune* magazine, and Harold Ruttenberg, the brilliant research director of the union, to the effect that, as Janeway wrote, "rather than pay overtime, the companies keep production down." "For the first time we've got a break," said a rank-and-filer to a *Fortune* writer "and could make real money. For years I've been hungry for work. Now I want to pay off my debts. But no, they won't give us a chance." Everywhere from Pittsburgh to the Pacific shipyards, the story was the same in the fall of 1942, labor smarting under charges of "slackerism," demanding fuller participation in running the war, an equality of sacrifice that the profits of the big contractors and the salaries of the top industrialists seemed to the rank and file of the workers to negate. "Drafting labor is perfectly O.K. with me, mister," read an interview with a steel worker, "I'll work in the mill as a soldier for board and fifty bucks a month—if the president of Carnegie-Illinois takes a colonel's pay for the duration. Did you ask him?" [1]

The repeated rejections of the plans for fuller labor participation in war production offered by the leaders of the steel workers, the aluminum workers and the automobile makers shook the faith of the rank and file in both the Administration's sincerity and the effectiveness of the C.I.O. Speeches "selling the war to labor," whether emanating from the White House or from Murray's Pittsburgh headquarters, fell flat on the ears of workers as perturbed as were their employers over the way the war was going on the production front. Labor was far more mature than in World War I. Its tragic collective experience during the depression, the "consciousness of kind" which the first surging march of the C.I.O. had liberated, the new philosophy of industrial democracy—all these had worked together to make alert-minded workers impervious to the superficial crudities of most of the

[1] From "What's Itching Labor," *Fortune*, November, 1942.

"morale" propaganda. Labor's itching was further exacerbated by the viciousness of the nation-wide newspaper and radio attacks upon the patriotic integrity of the movement. Newspaper columnists such as Westbrook Pegler, whose information was mainly supplied by corporation press agents, industrial spies and such labor-hating groups as the National Association of Manufacturers, pontificating radio commentators like H. V. Kaltenborn, and a vast array of editorial writers, the majority of whom were hopelessly ignorant of the history or practices of unionism, joined in holding up the American worker as the chief saboteur of the war effort. The middle people, harassed by mounting taxation and ever-stricter rationing, accepted this portrait of labor villainy without much questioning.

It was in such a troubled atmosphere that the coal diggers headed for Cincinnati for the Thirty-seventh Convention of the United Mine Workers of America in October, 1942. Every delegate realized that he was to be participant in one of the most fateful gatherings of the union since its founding.

XXII. ONE MAN'S WILL POWER

THE RECORD OF THE CINCINNATI convention is written in terms of one man's will power. John Llewellyn Lewis stood on the platform at the opening session while delegates cheered him for five hilarious minutes. Then he banged the gavel until there was silence and in his address outlined the exact course which the gathering was to take. There was no opposition for him to shout down. He defended his anti-interventionist position before Pearl Harbor, lashed at his critics in the C.I.O., was caustic about the activities of the War Labor Board, assailed the administration of the Guffey Act. He stated bluntly that at the expiration of their contracts in April, 1943, the miners would ask for a wage raise. With timetable precision he marched the half million members of the United Miners out of the C.I.O. and into what many took to be the start of a new mass labor movement. When the convention was over, Lewis's entire program had been put into effect with practically no opposition and the lines of the whole American labor movement had once more been shifted.

Acting upon the mandate of its president, the convention voted to extend the jurisdiction of the U.M.W. of A. to take in all unorganized workers. The delegates voted to increase the monthly dues of all members of the union from $1 to $1.50 (90 cents to the International Office, 30 cents to the district, 30 cents to the local) and even went so far as to leave it to Mr. Lewis as to whether or not to call another convention for the duration of the war. The moot question of district autonomy was dismissed, although there now remained but one or two districts which had any real control over their affairs.

In all the rest "provisional" officers appointed by Lewis and reporting to him at the Washington headquarters ruled the roosts.

For some time before the convention, the newspapers had been filled with stories about dissatisfaction with the Lewis "dictatorship" on the part of the rank and file. Especially in regard to District 50, from which it was said there were to be wholesale desertions as soon as the split with the C.I.O. was officially confirmed. The convention heard that the catch-all district had doubled the number of locals in 1941, as compared with the number chartered in the first five years of its existence, that it had carried its organizing campaign into 307 cities in 39 states in the past two years. Among the delegates who rose to cheer Lewis when he made his first appearance were representatives of the United Dairy Farmers' Division of the district. Though there were no exact figures made available, the membership of the new dairy group was said to number "thousands." Membership gains were reported by the district officials among chemical and coal by-product workers. Lewis went out of his way to urge an especial effort on the part of miners working near the new large war chemical plants to enroll their fellow workers in District 50. The extension of the district's jurisdiction to cover all unorganized workers was Lewis's grim answer to the stories that he was through.

Not even the fireworks forecast over the convention's ratification of the expulsion of Philip Murray came off. Murray made his exit undramatically. Lewis concentrated his fire not upon his erstwhile lieutenant but upon the financial "debt" which he insisted the C.I.O. owed the miners' union. And when the vote came on changing the Constitution of the U.M.W. of A. to eliminate all reference to the C.I.O. only a few feeble "nays" were heard. Brophy and Hapgood, the veteran leaders of the Lewis opposition, were not at the convention, having elected to stick with Murray and the C.I.O. Nothing had been heard from Howat, who was running a labor paper in Kansas. Farrington was dead. The only articulate opponents of the regime, the Communists, were on the side lines, officially barred from membership in the union and the object of unconcealed derision on Lewis's part.

How did it happen that a group as indigenously democratic as the American miners could so willingly accept the dictates of one man? Lewis had long been out of favor with the Roosevelt Administration. He was the object of contumely on the part of both the

A.F. of L. and the C.I.O. Since 1937 the press as a whole had adopted an increasingly hostile attitude toward the mine leader, and because of his anti-interventionist war stand the liberal and more latterly the Communist journals had held him in dark suspicion. In the minds of millions of the middle people he was the archobstructionist of our war effort, the man who would be dictator. And yet the miners, more than half a million of them, cheerfully gave into his hands the complete management of their affairs.

Perhaps the answer is to be found in a letter quoted by Edward Levinson in, *Labor on the March*. It was written by a worker in Detroit when the C.I.O. first got under way and it went as follows: "Boy, do I hate this man Lewis! We used to get sixty cents an hour. . . . My raise amounted to eighty cents a day, or sixteen dollars a month, and out of that I pay one dollar a month in dues. Do I hate this man John L. Lewis!" [1]

The miners at Cincinnati knew that Lewis had won for them a minimum wage of $35 a week and had, as they put it, "brought home the bacon" in the shape of the Appalachian Agreement of 1941. Further, he promised that he would fight for still higher wages. There were $6,346,852 in the mine union's treasury in 1942, and with the extra assessment of 50 cents a month there would be a "war chest" estimated at $2,400,000 additional annually.

So far as Lewis's stand on the war was concerned, the miners took his word for it when he declared that the union members would make every sacrifice "until the nation has achieved its objective of destroying the dictators of the totalitarian nations who would destroy our liberties and the safety of America." Lewis reported that by the autumn of 1942 more than 61,000 members of the U.M.W. of A. in this country and 7,378 Canadian members were in the armed forces, that the miners had put nearly $40 million into war bonds, and had contributed $1 million to relief agencies. As to production, storage of bituminous stocks had reached a record of 90 million tons by October, 1942, averaging a 61-day supply of fuel for basic industries. At the time of the convention the soft-coal miners were producing 11½ million tons per week as compared with 9 million tons in 1941. Over-all production of bituminous for 1942 was estimated by the miners' statisticians at 580,308,000 tons as compared with 450,864,000 in 1941.

[1] New York, Harper Bros., p. 294.

Anthracite production for the first eleven months of 1942 was estimated by the Pennsylvania Bureau of Mines at 52,206,000 tons, an
increase of 3 million tons over 1941.

"This," said Lewis, "is a record of sincere and enduring support
of the free institutions which flourish under the American and Canadian flags. It is not a casual support," he continued, flinging out at
the Communist change of line, "it is not a whim of circumstances.
It is not a policy of expediency designed to deceive or to delude people
to believe that our members are good citizens."

As to his anti-interventionist stand, Lewis said that it was one
held by millions of other Americans before Pearl Harbor.

"That was my position and I understood it to be the position of
the United Mine Workers of America, until the time came when it
was evident that a war could not be avoided when our nation was
attacked by foreign enemies," explained Lewis. "When that time came,
like millions of other citizens, and like hundreds of thousands of our
members, I abandoned every other consideration and stated publicly
and acted accordingly in support of our government, of our institutions, of our policies, of the integrity of our nation and the well-being
not only of the United Mine Workers of America, but the well-being
of every American.

"There have been individuals abroad in this land," he continued,
"who for reasons of their own have seen fit to question the loyalty
of the president of the United Mine Workers of America to the principles of his government and sometimes have questioned the loyalty
of the United Mine Workers. There can be no greater misrepresenta-
tion and no greater distortion of the truth. But because men may
misrepresent and distort and sometimes seek to defame an individual
or an organization is no reason for that individual or that organization to be influenced in its policies by such consideration, or to abate
one whit of its efforts to hew to the line in proper participation,
proper support, in unyielding determination to carry on to a point
where the armed forces of our nation will triumph, where our free
institutions will be preserved and where the minimum inconvenience
and suffering to the population may be brought about."

By their practically unanimous votes in favor of every Lewis-
sponsored proposal the delegates accepted this first full-dress statement of their president's war stand. There were few who did not go

along with him in his criticism of the War Labor Board's policy in regard to steel wages and the lack of miners' representatives on the Bituminous Coal Commission. When liberals who had opposed Lewis's "isolationist" stand attempted to pass resolutions mildly censuring the mine leader for his backing of Willkie and his anti-Administration attitude in general, the resolution died in committee with no important protest. As an overwhelming majority the miners, outwardly at any rate, agreed with Lewis that the labor movement was in danger of being taken over, horse, foot and artillery into "the bureaucratic camp at Washington." In their turn, union officials were in danger of becoming unofficial representatives of the Administration, disciplining the rank and file, and shifting from militant independence to pliant dependence upon the good will of the government administrators. What would happen to the movement when the war was over? Would the powers that were to be then accept the dictum of William H. Davis, head of the War Labor Board that "the element of compulsion" in the framework of collective bargaining, injected by the WLB and other agencies, would not be continued when the guns were finally silenced? Mr. Lewis thought this compulsory element in all dealings between government and labor would not only continue after the peace, unless it was strenuously opposed during the war, but would grow ominously greater. In speaking against the proposal to "freeze" coal labor, for example, he said:

"The coal industry does not need and does not want, in so far as its men are concerned, those same restrictions upon manpower recently put into effect in the lumber industry and the metalliferous mining industry. The time has not yet come in America to say to the man who earns his bread by the sweat of his brow that he cannot leave his employment, except by the consent of his master, his employer, and his government."

One of the chief arguments used for the 50 cents increase in the monthly dues of the members was that it would be necessary for the mine union to have a sizable treasury to protect its collective bargaining and wage standards after the war. The International Executive Board in the summer of 1941 had voted unanimously for this increase. A letter sent by the board to the membership read:

While the trend of the times indicates wage increases and the rise of commodity prices, every economist is of the opinion that the pendulum

in due time, following the national emergency, will move in the opposite
direction. If we take a page from our own history following the World
War, you will find that the United Mine Workers of America was compelled to fight in every coal district in this country to protect its wage
standards in the face of falling prices and wages. Very costly strikes were
engaged in after the last war and the finances of our organization were
dissipated as a result of these troublesome times. Only in our anthracite
jurisdiction were we able to maintain the wages secured up to 1923. The
lesson learned from our experiences from 1923 to 1933 should not be lost.
We must prepare for any eventuality. We believe the time to start is now.
We must not only build up and maintain a strong numerical organization
but also the strongest financially in order to be able to consolidate our
gains and make it possible to meet any emergency that may arise and
that may threaten our security, our wage and condition standards or our
existence as an organization.

The International ordered a referendum on the dues matter, with
the result that the membership voted 151,857 for the increase as against
87,388. Twenty districts with a membership of 400,000 sustained the
proposition, while seven districts numbering approximately 100,000
turned it down. Among the districts against the raise was District 1
in the Wilkes-Barre hard-coal fields where although the district president was a Lewis man, there had long been rank-and-file opposition
to Lewis. When the question of dues came up on the floor of the
convention, only a handful of delegates spoke against the increase. In
all, 36 out of the 2,490 delegates voted against the measure, with 18
of the dissenting votes coming from District 1. Though both the
referendum and the convention votes seemed conclusive enough, the
whole matter was to arise a short time later to plague Lewis.

What seemed to many the heart of Lewis's dictatorship, the appointment of provisional officials for the various districts, was the subject of prolonged debate at the convention in the course of which
Lewis again brought up the argument that only a centralized and
well-disciplined union government could negotiate satisfactory national
agreements for the entire coal industry. Instead of the plant-by-plant
bargaining of the other big unions, the United Mine Workers came
out of negotiations with over-all contracts setting up a national minimum wage for bituminous workers ($7 daily for a 5-day week at the
time Lewis was speaking). He agreed with the opposition that the

miners were receiving little overtime pay and that there were "malad-justments of the wage structure" which demanded amelioration. But he said that he refused to go back to the "confusion and inefficiency" which he alleged had for many years marked the wage negotiations when the districts had complete autonomy. He had no direct answer as to what new leadership was being developed in the amorphous "provisional" training schools centered at Washington headquarters, but he showed what a strong hold he had upon the rank and file when the report of the Resolutions Committee upholding the centralized form of union government was adopted by the convention by a vote of 20 to 1, with only some 100 delegates in opposition.

Overshadowing these intra-union affairs, however, was specula-tion as to where Lewis would take his miners now that he had them out of the C.I.O. At the outset of the convention he had said: "Had there been no United Mine Workers of America, there would not now be any Congress of Industrial Organizations. Perhaps the child has become greater than the parent. Perhaps the pupil has become wiser than the master. The convention will decide." But the conven-tion's only decision was to accept the Lewis mandate that the parent abandon its child. It was in strict accord with the "leadership prin-ciple" that the miners left their fate entirely in the hands of John L. Lewis and his submissive International Board. Convention reporters devoted a large amount of space wondering as to what were Lewis's intentions. He gave them no clue as to whether or not he would take his powerful organization, with the largest national treasury of any union in the nation, back into the American Federation of Labor or whether, under the auspices of the miners' union, he would build up a third labor front as a challenge to both the Federation and the C.I.O.

Soon after the miners' convention adjourned, the latter course seemed more likely. William Green stated flatly that Lewis would not be invited to any peace talks between the Federation and the C.I.O. The action of the miners had a twofold effect upon the policies of the C.I.O. First, it imposed upon the Congress the tight control of a hierarchy consisting of Philip Murray, Sidney Hillman and Clinton Golden, and other avowed "collaborationists" with the large indus-trialists and the governmental agencies. Second, it convinced the insiders of the need for a speedy patching up of differences with the Federation, lest Lewis, in spite of Green's objections, force his way into the A.F. of L. there to dominate the labor scene. Steps toward unity were taken when it was agreed to arbitrate jurisdictional disputes between the two major organizations.

At the C.I.O. convention in November, 1942, while there was criticism of the proposal to "freeze" manpower and objection to some of the activities of the War Labor Board, the drastic demands of the United Automobile Workers of America for labor representation on all governmental agencies having to do with production were soft-pedaled by the hierarchy. Murray outlined to the convention the promises that he said had been made to him by Donald Nelson, head of the War Production Board, in regard to genuine labor representation on the board. A month later in the December 15th issue of the *United Automobile Worker,* Murray claimed that Nelson had broken faith. No top-ranking labor leader, said the head of the C.I.O., had any real say as to the administration of the board's policies and the joint labor-management production committees were directed by a representative of the employers. The program of the auto workers called for a national council of all labor organizations to handle the problems of the labor movement in relation to government, a program very similar to that suggested for consumer and farmer representation by the Co-operative League of America and the Farmers' Union.

The C.I.O. convention was meeting after the singularly confused Congressional elections of 1942, which indicated a general dissatisfaction among all classes of Americans with the Administration's handling of the war effort and the domestic issues involved. In many labor centers there had been definite swings away from the Democratic party, swings surveyed with no little satisfaction by John Lewis, with dismay by Philip Murray. The latter at a gathering of liberals in New York to do honor to George Norris, called upon the aged ex-senator for "leadership" of a new movement. But Murray was vague as to what he had in mind.

Now, just as newly elected Congressional conservatives in both parties were laying plans for an attack upon the Administration's labor and social welfare programs, there came what seemed to some anti-laborites a heaven-sent opportunity to strike a telling blow at what they called the "coddling" of labor by the Administration and the "dictatorial aspirations of Lewis" as well. This was the strange work stoppage of the anthracite miners in the mountain ridges of North-eastern Pennsylvania. What seemed to be a rank-and-file revolt brought the hard-coal men out on December 30, 1942, when the first checkoff of the 50 cents additional dues came due. Leaders of this "wildcat" strike told newsmen that they were protesting the additional dues on the grounds that the anthracite miners had been outvoted by the bituminous diggers. Their story was that the more than $6 million in the national treasury was enough to meet any postwar emergency and that it was "tyranny" for Lewis to demand the extra 50 cents. However, within a short time, the same leaders were announcing that their followers were striking for an increase in wages of $2 a day, despite the fact that the hard-coal contract of 1941 did not expire until April 30, 1943. Under the contract which prevailed at the time of the wildcat strike, the hard-coal men worked a 7-hour day for a 35-hour week until, acceding to the request of Fuel Administrator Ickes, the week was lengthened by an extra day. The anthracite contract provided for a complete checkoff of dues, whereas in previous agreements the checkoff had been voluntary. The 1941 contract raised the pay of daymen 60 cents with a 75-cent raise for contract miners. On the whole the weekly take-home pay averaged around $30.

As more and more of the hard-coal miners walked out, heedless of the pleas of the union officials or the angry protests of the War Labor Board, the press talked about a fuel famine in the eastern states and the extremists in Congress considered bills repealing the bulk of labor's protective legislation. Although at no time were more than 15,000 of the nation's 90,000 hard-coal miners involved, the public received the impression that the entire anthracite area was on strike, and on strike against not only John L. Lewis but the government as well. As the unauthorized stoppage continued, Secretary Ickes began issuing statements calling the nation's attention to the fact that hundreds of thousands of tons of hard coal were being held back from consumers' bins in the midst of an unusually cold winter and a global war. Indignation of the editors was directed not so much at the rebel miners as at Lewis and the dues checkoff system.

It was in vain that spokesmen for the union pointed out that the checkoff of dues had long been accepted by the bituminous operators and had been in the demands of every anthracite miners' negotiation committee for years before it was finally won in hard coal in 1941. Originally introduced by the operators to check off from the wages of miners such items as coal, rent and light in company houses, charges for powder, safety equipment and blacksmithing and, in some cases, medical services, schools, hospitalization, even ministers' salaries, the system was made to apply to union dues as well, when the U.M.W. of A. grew strong enough. Invariably foes of unionism raise this issue during crises such as the anthracite stoppage, maintaining that the system indicates that "tribute" is being levied by unscrupulous union leaders from unwilling members. Veteran operators, however, make no great fuss about the addition of one more item on their books. There are some who say frankly they would prefer to check off the dues at the pay window rather than have union collectors regularly at the mines. When there was no checkoff in anthracite, union officials at the collieries had at times to pass on the eligibility of every man reporting for work, with consequent confusion and often "button strikes" caused by the refusal of men wearing union buttons to work alongside those who could not show this proof of membership in good standing.

Before the outlaw walkout had lasted a month, the public, or so the press had it, was at an emotional boiling point in New York apartments and New England farmhouses where shivering inmates cursed John L. Lewis and his stiff-necked, if not indeed "traitorous" miners. The fact, as we have seen, that the vast majority of the hard-coal men were at work not five days but six in response to Ickes's plea for a longer workweek, and that there were sufficient anthracite reserves on top to make a serious shortage most unlikely, was ignored by the press, the radio and anti-Administration congressmen denouncing the miners' "unpatriotic" stand. Ignored also was the fact that in the midst of the strike the government started antitrust proceedings against a score or more of the larger anthracite corporations on the ground that they were conspiring to fix prices. Apparently the widely heralded Supreme Court breakup of the concentration of hard-coal ownership in the hands of a few great railroad corporations had not been effective.

The appeals of both Secretary Ickes and the War Labor Board having failed to get the outlaws back, President Roosevelt issued a stern warning to the miners to go to work or else— In this he was joined by Lewis, who told the diggers to "stop this foolishness." By January 21st the majority of the rebels were back at work.

Issues raised by the stoppage were not settled by its ending. Outstanding was the question of the raise of wages of all the miners, anthracite and bituminous alike. It was Lewis's contention that the War Labor Board's policy with its Little Steel formula allowing only 15 per cent raise in wages in any industry over January 1, 1941, levels was "arbitrary and stupid" and a "betrayal" of the workers' agreement not to strike during the war. Soon after the end of the hard-coal stoppage he announced that the bituminous representatives would ask for a $2-a-day increase when their contract expired on April 1st and intimated that the hard-coal miners would make the same demand at the expiration of their agreement a month later. Everything seemed in train for a head-on collision between the mine union and the governmental agencies controlling coal, with the public looking on apprehensively from the side lines. In the meantime, bills, some of which practically abolished all union activity "for the duration" and others of which limited the right to strike, picket or bargain collectively, were thrown into the Congressional hoppers.

Lewis's attitude toward the anthracite stoppage had been contemptuous of "this foolishness." He had let the news photographers take him, in the midst of prodigious yawns at the WLB hearings at Washington. He had been impeccable, from a union standpoint, in his refusal to reopen the anthracite contract during its life, which would have been necessary had the $2-a-day wage issue been officially pressed. But now he was moving into larger combat zones. He was putting to the stern test of battle the resolve of his government not to permit any considerable wage increases until the guns ceased firing overseas. Would he withdraw this time as he had in the other war saying: "I will not fight my government"? Or would he go into action against operators and government agencies alike, the press united against him, the public aroused? It has not happened often in the history of American labor that a solitary leader has had to face such decisions as John L. Lewis faced in the spring of 1943.

From THE MOMENT THAT THE OPER-
ators and unionists held their first sessions on the signing of a new
Appalachian contract for the bituminous mines, in New York on
March 10, 1943, there were rumblings of the enormous storm that was
about to break over the head of John Lewis and his organization.

Back of Lewis were Kennedy, Tetlow, O'Leary, K. C. Adams
and the two hundred members of the United Mine Workers Policy
Committee, representing every bituminous district to be covered by
the contract. Since their split in 1941, the operators had divided into
Northern and Southern groups, meeting separately at first, but joining
in the negotiations that followed to present a common front against
the miners' demands.

As is usual in the case of such collective bargaining, the miners
at the outset asked for far more than what they could hope to receive.
The heart of the demands was in the $2-a-day wage increase "for all
classes of work performed in and around bituminous coal mines." In
addition, Lewis wanted the newly organized union of mine foremen
and other members of the supervisory staffs included in the conference
on the side of the miners. The mere suggestion that the foremen
move to the other side of the bargaining table set the operators mutter-
ing that this was an attempt to "socialize" the mines. Nothing more
was heard of the suggestion.

Lewis also asked that certain outlying districts, among them
Indiana and Illinois of the old Central Competitive Field, be included
in whatever agreement was made. He knew that midwestern operators
through their long dealings with the union would be more inclined

to accept terms favorable to the miners than the Appalachian operators might grant. The operators said that the outlying districts could, as in the past, follow the general agreement reached by the New York conference. From the standpoint of war production the strategic soft coal was now under West Virginia and Western Pennsylvania, with special emphasis on the captive mines of the U.S. Steel around Pittsburgh, and in West Virginia.

Both these demands were soon lost sight of in the uproar over the unexpected insistence by Lewis that his men be paid for the time consumed in traveling in the mine from the portal to their workplaces and back. This portal-to-portal pay demand was taken by the operators to be no more than a device of the union for sidestepping the imperatives of the War Labor Board's Little Steel formula prohibiting any wage increase in excess of 15 per cent subsequent to January, 1941. Of course the miners' $2-a-day demand was far in excess of this, but it was argued that if the WLB refused to consider an out-and-out raise, the agreement to pay travel time might be a solution which would save face for everyone concerned.

Here, then, were the union demands, "nothing more, nothing less," as Lewis bluntly put it to the operators—a $2-a-day increase for a 6-day week with a basic $8 daily wage, with double time for Sunday work; vacation compensation pay; the ending of the checkoff by the operators for safety equipment, tools, and blacksmithing, and, on top of these, portal-to-portal pay.

The sheer audacity of the demands left the operators and the public breathless. John L. Lewis, said the editors of nearly every paper in the country, was deliberately bypassing the War Labor Board, the governmental agency set up for the express purpose of stopping wage raises that might be inflationary in their nature. He was proposing to bargain collectively with the employers of his members as though no global war were raging. If his demands were granted, the price of soft coal, now recognized by everyone as all-essential to both the war and the domestic economy, would be raised, other great unions would follow the lead of the miners in pressing for increases, the farmers would insist that they share with labor in richer rewards, and the dread spiral of inflation would begin rolling skyward.

To this the miners' Policy Committee replied:

"The War Labor Board has been encouraged to freeze the wage

structure. An arbitrary formula has been devised, known as the Little Steel formula, which deprives labor of any wage increases in excess of 15 per cent to the date of January, 1941. This formula is an outrageous breach and violation of the no-strike agreement between labor, industry, and government, made in December, 1941. At this conference, organized labor abandoned the right to strike for the duration, contingent upon the government creating an agency that would judiciously determine labor's complaints against management. No such judicial findings have been made. The War Labor Board violates the government agreement with labor each day that it operates. Under its arbitrary and miserably stupid formula, it chains labor to the wheels of industry without compensation for increased costs, while other agencies of government reward and fatten industry by charging its increased costs to the public purse. Assuredly labor, despite its present weak and vacillating leadership, cannot long tolerate such economically paradoxical and socially unjust treatment."

With the WLB thus summarily dismissed, the union representatives went on to attack the operators' contention that if a $2 wage raise were granted, the total cost of wage increases would impose an annual burden of $750 million on the industry. Said an editorial in the *United Mine Workers Journal*:

The facts are that the total addition to the wholesale price of manufactured products of the miners' increase, if none of it could be absorbed by the operators, would be less than eight-tenths of one percent of the sales dollar. In steel it would amount to less than one-half of one per cent. And as regards railroads, the total cost of coal at $3 a ton, f.o.b. the mines, would amount to less than three per cent of gross revenue. Certainly the prosperity of American railroads which have earned approximately a billion dollars net in 1942, and increased cash dividends $6,300,000 in January 1943 is so secure that they will not suffer bankruptcy as the result of increased coal prices amounting to but a few cents per ton.

As for the inflation danger, it was Lewis's contention, made repeatedly in a four-hour speech at the first session of the joint conference, that "the government is creating inflation in this country by its cost-plus quantitative purchasing policy on the part of the Army, the Navy and Procurement. Its purchase of billions and billions of dollars of supplies annually on a cost-plus basis is an incentive to inflation. For every billion dollars' worth of expenditures by the government—and there are many such billions—industry is given a billion dollars of profit, and profits are inflationary."

But was not the Office of Price Administration set up to control prices, as WLB was controlling wages? Lewis was scornful of "the feeble control of the price fixing instrumentality of the government known as OPA." He read an analysis of the retail prices for food in the Appalachian districts and maintained that "the average medium increase in basic food prices to the miners since August, 1939, was 124.6 per cent." He said that small stores in the mine fields, especially the company stores, were in no way controlled by ceiling prices set by the OPA but were charging what the traffic would bear. Lewis said the mine worker was well aware that his country was at war, "that the nation is in peril, that he has a part to play . . . that he wants to preserve himself as an individual productive unit in American industry . . . to continue to play the part of a man, of a neighbor and of a patriotic citizen. . . . To do that the miner must eat, and he must eat strong meat. He needs strong food. He must have it. The nature and the hazards and the laboriousness and the strain of his industry require it, or his bodily strength disappears, his resistance is lowered, and he becomes a victim of the ills that follow malnutrition and bodily weakness. . . . When the mine workers' children cry for bread, they cannot be satisfied with a Little Steel formula. When illness strikes the mine workers' families, they cannot be cured with an anti-inflation dissertation. The facts of life in the mining homes of America cannot be pushed aside by the flamboyant theories of an idealistic economic philosophy. Neither can these facts be suppressed nor concealed to appease employing coal corporations who smugly hope that the government will chastise the mine worker for daring to make known the miserable facts of his existence."

Many laborites saw back of the formulation of the miner's demands a struggle to preserve the fundamental gains of labor—independent trade-unionism, collective bargaining, the use of the strike, the rejection of arbitrary formulae for settlements of disputes imposed from outside and above the industry. Others saw in it no more than another phase of John Lewis's private vendetta against Franklin Roosevelt. Still others regarded it as a sinister conspiracy against the Republic at a time when it was straining every nerve to defeat the Axis. The last group, to which the bulk of the New Deal liberals attached themselves, was the most articulate both in the press and over the air, and once more Lewis was portrayed as a would-be dictator who would rule or ruin, heedless of the welfare of his country or, for that matter, of the trade-union movement as a whole.

Lewis was not unmindful of the gathering press attack upon him and his organization. He counter-attacked with the accusation that the editors, columnists and commentators, who were bedeviling him before the negotiations had gone into their first stages, were animated not so much by patriotic motives as by the checks of their large corporation advertisers.

"We are seeing lots of things in the newspapers these days," he brooded in his opening speech at the negotiations, "and did you notice or do you happen to remember that this new access to the advertising columns of the newspapers on the part of corporations has recently become an epidemic in this country? Why? All they have to do is to take out a full-page ad in any newspaper proclaiming their own virtues and charge it up to cost of production, and the government allows it. It is legitimate advertising. So every day or two we can pick up any metropolitan newspaper and read a full-page advertisement by General Motors, or by General Electric or by any one of the corporations back of the coal operators here, telling what fine things they are doing to promote the war, singing their own virtues, creating a new admiration society and paying a thousand or fifteen hundred dollars a page, as the case may be, in somebody's newspaper and charging it up to the cost of production. And our coal miners pay for some of it in the 5 per cent Victory tax that is deducted from each one of their pay checks, because the money that goes into that advertising does not reach the coffers of Uncle Sam. It is charged up to the coal miner along with ten thousand other items that the coal miner cannot charge off. He charges off nothing."

When Charles O'Neill, an ex-miner, now spokesman for the Northern operators, rose to answer Lewis it was plain what the tactics of the coalmasters would be. Stating that successive raises had brought the average miner's annual income to above $2,000 and that any further raises could not be borne by the industry, he voiced an emphatic "No" to all the union's demands and then, breaking a precedent, he said the operators would present no counterproposals. It must be for the government to decide on whether or not any wage raise was justified under the Little Steel formula.

So far as the operators went, that would seem to put a stop to bargaining over any major issue. There was desultory talk about such matters as lamp rentals, blacksmithing, car delivery and the hazards involved in working a third shift, but the operators refused to talk wages. Toward the portal-to-portal pay demand they were completely indifferent until word came to the conference that the United States District Court of Appeals for the Fifth District had handed down a decision upholding travel pay for iron-ore workers for the time they were underground. It was Lewis's contention that this decision affected the portal-to-portal pay for the soft-coal men and that the decision of the court made it mandatory for any agreement with the bituminous operators to cover travel pay.

The union took the travel-time pay issue to the public in page advertisements in 58 newspapers. The average coal miner, said the U.M.W. of A. ads, was receiving only 7 hours' pay for the 8½ hours he spent in the mine. Most miners have to walk or ride on man-trips for great distances before they get to the workplaces. "A study of 60 mines in Eastern Kentucky revealed that the miners spend an average of 8 hours and 48 minutes underground daily," stated the advertisement, which concluded:

We American coal-miners are doing our part in the war effort. We don't mind hard work. If we did, we wouldn't be in a coal mine. We know we could go to war plants and get a lot more money for much easier work. We also know somebody has to mine coal—the prime mover of American industry. Because of our years of experience in the coal industry, we know we are serving our country best by remaining there. We are proud of our war-time production record.

We are asking that an injustice be corrected. We are not asking to be paid for the time we spend getting our tools and necessary equipment. We are not asking that the company give us the powder we now pay for, nor to stand other charges which are rightfully theirs. We do ask that we be paid for the most dangerous part of our day's work, the time we spend in travel into the mine in the morning and coming out again at night. This is portal-to-portal pay as now paid to the miners in the country's metal mines and other industries.

To the reading public the demand for travel time seemed as capricious as though office and factory workers were to insist on payment of their transportation to and from work. However, it was true that in the case of drift or slope mines where much of the travel consisted of riding in unprotected empties with sudden changes of temperature from the cold or heat outside to the even temperature of the pit, the miners were exposed to ailments not suffered by other workers, and that the rate of accidents to individuals walking through the semidarkness to their places was high. Many of the older mines extended for miles from the portals. While the operators replied with advertisements of their own, that for years the union had refused to raise the question of travel pay on the ground that the matter was too difficult for negotiation, the demand soon became a major one in the negotiations that followed.

When the expiration date of the contract, midnight of March 31st, drew near, Roosevelt sent telegrams to the opposing parties informing them that he wanted no cessation in the mining of coal and urging them to go on with the collective bargaining under the terms of the old contract until an agreement was reached. At the same time Lewis was subpoenaed to appear before the Senate War Investigating Committee headed by Senator Harry S. Truman of Missouri, on March 26th.

Lewis took the witness chair in a hearing room, packed to suffocation, under the hostile scrutiny of many of the members of the committee. He was in a fighting mood. He was irked by the issuance of a subpoena by the senators, who had served it on him regardless of the fact that he had voluntarily consented to appear. The days of futile wrangling with the intransigent operators and the virulence of the attack upon him in the press and over the radio had roused all his native belligerency. It was evident at once that the Labor Board's "anti-inflationary formula" was uppermost in the minds of the senators, many of whom had never before seen the mine leader in action. Asked about "the inflationary spiral," Lewis said:

"In my opinion we will not be able to restrain inflation to the degree that we would wish as long as the government has two policies with respect to inflation. On the one hand, the government super-induces inflation by the excessive rewards to industry for producing war essentials. On the other hand, the government seeks to fight inflation by saying to fifty million workers in America gainfully employed and largely employed in war industries, 'We cannot do for you what we are doing for industry because that would cause inflation. You must not ask for a wage increase above and beyond a certain formula which we have arbitrarily computed: and, as a patriotic duty, you cannot expect your wages to keep pace with the rising cost of living. As a citizen you must make sacrifices in the interests of the whole nation and the war effort.' There is an implication that the individual worker is unpatriotic if he asks the same consideration as industry from government."

Senator Brewster of Maine interposed that under existing tax legislation the government still hoped "that the rich would not be getting richer out of this war."

Lewis said: "We all hope with you, but 'hope deferred maketh the heart sick.'" Having in mind the Truman Committee's uncovering of exorbitant profits made by many war contractors and the evidence of wholesale fraud on the part of some manufacturers of war materials, Lewis hammered away at the profits made by U.S. Steel, owners of the captive mines and, of course, tremendously influential in the coal negotiations. He pointed out that the cost-plus contracts which yielded such profits as to enable industrialists to wipe out their debts, rebuild their entire plants and still pay dividends from the public funds, had never been renegotiated by the government in spite of the revelations of the various Congressional investigations. In contrast, he held up his miners' situation, insisting that "the hungry workers of this country whom I represent want at least enough to eat out of this situation while United States Steel is running away with these hundreds of millions of dollars."

Senator Ball of Minnesota leaned forward to glare at Lewis.

"Surely," growled the senator, "you are not contending that any worker is not getting enough to eat. If so, that is demagoguery, pure and simple, and you know it."

Lewis shouted back:

"When you call me a demagogue before I can reply, I hurl it back in your face, sir. And I say, sir, when you call me a demagogue, you are less than a proper representative of the people of this country."

When things quieted down, Lewis went on to say that his people "were not getting enough to eat in the sense that it maintains their strength. The coal mine burns a man out pretty fast."

He read off his figures showing rises in food prices throughout the coal regions and then said:

"I still recognize that $1 an hour for a coal miner in a hazardous industry, that requires great expenditure of energy and bodily and nervous strength, as compared to $1.80 an hour for a carpenter in New York is not equity or justice."

To senators asking Lewis to join with them in stopping inflation Lewis responded:

"I am not going to join with you in an attempt to do it after the fact of inflation has arrived, and is affecting the living standards of the workers. . . . I point out that the mine workers won't be able to join with anybody unless you put some food in their stomachs. I will gladly join you, if you don't make the workers of this country the victims of your experimentation."

Senator Burton of Ohio commented:

"We want help to make sure we don't start off inflation from this corner."

Lewis said: "Do you mind first inflating the stomachs of some of my members?"

Though the newspapers featured the flare-up between Lewis and Senator Ball and insisted that Lewis's statement that the miners would not work without a contract was the equivalent of a strike threat, there were many who felt that the miners had a case. Metropolitan newspapermen venturing into the coal camps of Pennsylvania and West Virginia reported that the miners and their wives were restive over the struggle to keep going on weekly wages estimated by union officials as around $30 a week after deductions. The reporters found that the coal diggers were solidly back of Lewis. The so-called anthracite "revolt" of the previous December had not noticeably diminished Lewis's power over his people. "We are patriotic Americans, buddy," the miners told a reporter, "and our boys, a powerful lot of them, are out there fighting for Uncle Sam. Back here we're digging all the coal Washington is asking for, and we're buying War Bonds, subscribing to the Red Cross, paying war taxes and all. But this OPA is doing nothing to hold down the prices and we have to have more money to keep up with those prices. If John says the word, we'll all walk out and, by God, we'll stay out until somebody gets busy."

In the public mind the shocking possibility of a national work stoppage in an industry so essential to the war as coal outweighed all considerations of the rights or wrongs of the miners' case. From every influential quarter came demands that the miners be kept in the mines.

The leaders of the C.I.O. were in a predicament. They knew well enough how large numbers of their membership, especially the older men and women who remembered the antilabor injunctions handed down by the Wilson administration after the last war, were looking on Lewis's fight against governmental coercion with approval. R. J. Thomas, head of the powerful United Automobile Workers of America, whose members, by and large, were earning far more in airplane plants than the highest paid miners, swung indecisively between the group in his union who preached the new doctrine, devoutly subscribed to by the Communists, of the infallibility of Franklin Delano Roosevelt, and the progressives under Walter Reuther critical of both governmental agencies and the war contractors. Philip Murray still kept his hand on his heart when he spoke of his "martyrdom" by Lewis. In Washington, the *C.I.O. News* damned Lewis roundly in every issue. On the Pacific Coast, Harry Bridges deplored Lewis's policy as tending toward disruption. Former aides of Lewis in the building of the C.I.O. went to meetings of workers to call the mine leader a wrecker and at the same time praise the courage of the rank-and-file miner. The tactic of the C.I.O. seemed to be that of the press in general, namely, to differentiate between the labor leader and his membership.

The attitude of the leaders in the organization which Lewis had founded was noted with satisfaction by the National Association of Manufacturers, the chambers of commerce, the U.S. Steel, and the utility and rail interests. Given enough rope, Lewis might well hang himself, his union and the entire trade-union movement as well, through his hatred of the Roosevelt administration and all its agencies. That this hatred was heartily reciprocated was evident to all men. To the foes of Lewis and labor, the end of the long "appeasement" of the trade-unions by the Roosevelt administration now seemed definitely —and gloriously—in sight.

Eddie Rickenbacker, war hero and airplane executive, was going up and down the land stirring the wrath of the middle people against labor. In the farm states, Senator Lee ("Pass-the-Biscuits-Pappy")

O'Daniel of Texas was urging the passing of antistrike legislation similar to that which his own state had passed. Senator Tom Connally of Texas and Representative Howard Smith of Virginia, in consultation with the House Military Affairs Committee, were busy reviving their bill to fine and jail any laborite who would so much as "encourage" a strike in a war industry. Everywhere inveterate foes of unionism were quick to ride the rising tide of public resentment over wartime strikes or threats of strikes, absenteeism of war workers, racketeering, and other major offenses of unionism. A labor movement, hopelessly divided, with no policy-making powers in any important war agency, with no marked skill in presenting its case to the public, and finally with no fundamental philosophy with which to confront the articulate protagonists for unrestrained "free enterprise," could do nothing to stem this tide.

Over all the deliberations of men in these days, the policies formed, the decisions made, hung of course the shadow of war, war on a dimension such as the world had never known. There were those who saw clearly enough that the immediate task was the winning of this war and who felt that the interests of every group in the country must be subordinated to this grim business. Labor must forgo its hard-won gains, capital its profits, the farmers must refrain from charging exorbitant prices for their food. "Equality of sacrifice" was the theme of editorials, mass meetings, sermons. It was when this ideal was brought out into life that the contradictions and confusions inherent in an economy that was half-collectivist, half-individualistic were distressingly revealed. When spokesmen for the miners compared the situation of a stockholder in U.S. Steel with that of a digger in one of Steel's captive mines, undoubtedly they scored a point. But the public was in no mood for debate. All that the "wayfaring man," as Veblen called him, harassed by increasing restrictions, wanted to be sure of was that there would be enough coal to take care of the needs of the war plants, and keep the home fires burning as well. He didn't believe everything he read in the papers about the perfidy of this man Lewis, but he did emphatically oppose any suggestion of a stoppage in the mining of coal. That would be letting down the boys at the front in the shabbiest manner and anyone who encouraged strikes at this time was too close to treason for comfort.

There was no question but that Lewis and the miners in his union understood this attitude. Back in New York, after his appearance before the inquiring senators, Lewis renewed his attacks on the War Labor Board on the ground that it was impeding rather than aiding the war effort, by refusing to grant the miners' demands that would give the mudsill workers a greater measure of security. He dubbed the patient, good-natured and not too brilliant William Hammatt Davis, chairman of the WLB with whom Lewis had so successfully battled during the captive mine controversy, "a rapacious, predatory, Park Avenue patent attorney." He said that Mr. Davis's board had "befouled its own nest and the greatest contribution it could make to economic stability would be for that board to resign and not cast its black shadow in the face of Americans who want to work and live and serve their country." Whereupon Secretary Kennedy, representing the mine workers in the anthracite negotiations, which commenced April 1st and were dragging on awaiting the result of the Appalachian bargaining, resigned from his place on the board, leaving John Brophy and Van Bittner, his former miner associate among the labor members of the board, still functioning. The *United Mine Workers Journal* was caustic about the presence of the latter two on a board to consider the mine workers' demands.

Lewis, searching for a representative of the government other than the WLB, hailed the appearance on the scene of Dr. John R. Steelman of the United States Conciliation Service. Dr. Steelman had decided for the miners in the captive mine case and was generally acquainted with miners' problems. To the conciliator Lewis proposed that the whole soft-coal controversy be settled by a guarantee on the part of the operators of a 6-day work week all year around, together with an annual wage potential according to the existing scale. In return for this he promised to scale down his $2-a-day wage raise demand. Both Steelman and Secretary Perkins were said to be in favor of this plan, but the operators rejected it. Ex-Senator Burke said that the industry could not guarantee any annual employment and he wired President Roosevelt urging that the matter be taken out of Steelman's hands and sent to the WLB.

Domestic issues were dragging the President unwillingly away from his preoccupation with the military phases of the war. Lewis's criticism of Roosevelt as an inept administrator, unwilling to give final power to those whom he gave responsibility, seemed to be justified by the state of affairs on the domestic front, referred to as a "shambles" by some Washington correspondents.

Chester C. Davis was made food administrator, taking over the war duties of the harassed Claude Wickard, secretary of agriculture. The Congressional Farm Bloc was threatening to raise farm prices through the enactment of the Bankhead Bill, denying the government the right to deduct incentive and subsidy payments in computation of parity prices. Though the President vetoed the bill, upon its return to Congress it was referred to the Senate Agricultural Committee to be kept as a "club in the closet" should there be any concession to labor on the part of the Administration in the line of wage raises. Price Administrator Prentiss Brown, successor to the hell-roaring Leon Henderson, was attempting to placate a suspicious Congress and an exasperated public and at the same time keep a ceiling on commodity prices. Black markets were springing up everywhere. Paul McNutt's War Manpower Commission was having its struggles freezing jobs. Economic Stabilization Director Byrnes was bustling vaguely about. The War Labor Board was swamped under ten thousand or more demands for wage raises both by employers seeking to hold their skilled men by granting more pay and by unions seeking raises to enable their members to meet the skyrocketing costs of living. There was a hysterical air about Washington. In some agencies signs were hung on the walls, "You don't have to be crazy to work here—but it helps." Resignations of key men in the various bureaus were announced daily. "The Battle of Washington" was soon getting nearly as much coverage in the papers as the shooting battles overseas.

President Roosevelt on the evening of April 8th issued an order against further inflationary moves. "To hold the line," said the Chief Executive, "we cannot tolerate further increases in prices affecting the cost of living or further increases in general wages or salaries except where clearly necessary to correct substandard living conditions." The hold-the-line order made it clear that Director Byrnes was above the WLB. Lewis announced that he would revise downward his $2-a-day demand.

Soon it was evident that the hold-the-line order was no more than a stressing of the various duties already assigned to the agency heads. It did seem to give more power to Stabilizer Byrnes, a favorite of the

President who now came in and out of the coal picture with no one able to say definitely just what were the functions of the ex-justice.

That hectic April was described by the editor of *United Mine Workers Journal* as "the blackest month of American history for the working people of the United States. A whole set of orders and decrees were issued which practically revoked every freedom that labor has gained in 167 years since the Declaration of Independence."

Contemplating the WLB's insistence on its formula, the hold-the-line order, and the job-freezing activities of the Manpower Commission, the editor exclaimed: ". . . into the hands of political stooges have been given powers that can make the U.S.A. into one big Uncle Tom's cabin." The miners' spokesman, countering the charges of the C.I.O. chieftains that Lewis was endangering the future of the labor movement by his stubborn stand against the WLB, put the blame for the increasing "crackdown on labor" on "bootlicker labor misleaders" who tried "to kid labor with promises of low prices through rationing and the OPA."

In New York, operators and unionists went through the motions of collective bargaining. At the conclusion of a desultory session, Lewis would slap on his hat and stamp from the meeting room. Senator Burke would thereupon take a train to Washington to press his demand that the WLB take over the controversy. The members of the policy committee would drift uncomfortably around the lobbies of the high-priced hotels in which the sessions were being held and then wander off to a blacked-out Broadway. "We're all dressed up to negotiate," complained one of them, "but we've got nobody to negotiate with."

Though there was no news from the New York negotiations, Lewis kept the miners' case on the front pages through press conferences and statements, saying in effect: "The War Labor Board will not give the men who mine your coal enough wages for them to live decently. What are you, the public, going to do about it?" He told assembled newsmen, clamoring for copy outside the closed doors of the conference room, that the Administration was attempting through its hold-the-line order "to make the rich more affluent and the poor more despairing." He issued a statement calling on the embattled farmers to join with the miners in a fight against the large industrialists whose profits he estimated at $6¼ billion in the lush nine months ending in April, 1943. He was employing the appeal for the formation of farm and labor alliances which the left had been repeating since the days of the Knights. Only now, liberals and Communists alike, pinning their faith on Roosevelt's good will toward labor, saw nothing in Lewis's statements but the use of the Huey Long tactic of lining up the underprivileged in preparation for a dictatorial "putsch." The labor editor of the New York *Post,* spokesman for the American Labor party which had long sought alliance with the dirt farmers, voiced the wistful hope that the Administration would make some sort of concession to the miners and thereby retire Lewis to the wings. Both William Green and Phil Murray had come out in favor of the hold-the-line order, and of their attitude Lewis said:

"It is beside the point that other labor organizations such as the C.I.O. and the A.F. of L., through their leaders, have adopted a policy of cringing toadyism to the Administration in power, coupled with a blind worship of the astoundingly unsound economic policies of that Administration."

There was a stirring in every coal camp as the May 1st deadline for the extended wage negotiations drew near. A few "wildcatters" stayed in bed when the dawn whistles blew on the tense days at the end of April and it was plain that at a word from Lewis all of the 450,000 soft-coal miners would quit the pits, if no contract was forthcoming.

There were other factors than wages and hours back of the solidarity among the rank and file of the country's miners—a solidarity astonishing to the metropolitan reporters who went to the fields expecting to find hostility to the mine leaders as a result of the press and radio hate campaign against Lewis. It seemed that such a campaign, when it got any attention at all among the men from the picks, served only to strengthen the miners' loyalty to their union's president. It did no harm at all to Lewis in the mind of the rank-and-file digger to be excoriated in the columns of the capitalist press. In fact, if the editors of the big city papers had been for Lewis, there would have been a revulsion against him among the membership. As it was, from local unions all over the fields telegrams assuring Lewis of unswerving support poured into New York and Washington union headquarters. And from individual members of the C.I.O. and the A.F. of L. there came word congratulating the U.M.W. of A. on its militant stand. The historian of the future who looks over the newspaper files of these bitter days may conclude that Lewis stood alone as the object of the public's hatred. The historian will do well to remember that the mine leader was fortified by the favoring expression of that "public opinion" which counts heaviest with the leader of any organization—the opinion of his own rank and file.

Further, the miners bitterly resented the charge that they were unpatriotic. They pointed to a record year of production, their extended workweek, the number of their young men with the armed forces, a number which they asserted was well above the average of those selected from any other heavy industry, and the fact that all across the fields young miners were fighting against being deferred as essential, rather than seeking to dodge the draft. The mine women were in despair over the complications of ration books and the other restrictions which they felt were aimed with deadly precision at "the poor folks of the country." It was all very well to limit city workers to two and one-half pounds of meat a week, but how could anyone expect a coal digger's family to exist on such a pawky feed? Western Pennsylvania union officials showed James Wechsler, labor reporter for the newspaper *PM*, this table of comparative prices which the paper published alongside of editorial denunciations of Lewis:

	January, 1941			*February, 1943*
Shoulder of lamb	22	cents a pound		39 cents
Bacon	18	" "		39 "
Leg of pork	25	" "		39 "
Butter	35	" "		57 "
Oranges	25	" a dozen		59 "
Spinach	5	" a pound		10 "
Knee and rubber boots			$4.50	$5.25
Work shoes			$2.95	$4.95

No government officials had been in the camps with any explanation for this rise. OPA inspectors to enforce ceiling prices in the company stores were nonexistent. Some of the chain stores in the larger centers did post ceiling prices but they were chiefly for food not found on the counters. The miners' vegetable gardens, which usually tided them over the summer months, were not yet coming in.

At this time I received a letter from a miner's wife living in a Pennsylvania district where, in the old days, opposition to Lewis had been most bitter. She wrote:

You know how we used to feel about John L. Well, now I figure he's right and we will go out for him one hundred per cent. How does it happen that the two classes of people in this country who do the hardest work always get the dirty end of the stick? I mean the farmers and the miners. I hear the editors of the big city papers are bawling us out for asking for more money and now we turn off the radio except for band music because there is always someone on the air hollering for John L's scalp. As for the editors and the radio people, not one of those fat loafers could last an hour in a pit. As for this War Labor Board, where did they get that formula from? You would think God gave it to them straight from the mountain. I wish some of the fancy wives of these big shots would try feeding a family of coal-diggers on a formula. My man takes home thirty-five dollars a week after working five days underground. Our mine isn't working the sixth day. The operator got a rise in the price of his coal on the ground that his expenses would be more working six days, but he only works five days and saves paying the overtime and gets his extra price f.o.b. the mine as well. I hear that is going on all over.

Now a man who works underground seven or eight hours—eight if you count his travel time—can not do that on canary seed. What meat we get goes to my man but I got a boy thirteen and two growing girls who like to eat as well. When you spread that thirty-five dollars around our supper table for a week it gets pretty peaked. They say the soldier boys are sore at us for asking for more and threatening to go out on strike. I don't know what boys are writing those letters and giving out those stories but I know they are not ours. Our boys know what it is like on these patches and they do not think to win the war by breaking the union. I thought it was for democracy and equal bargaining and free unions and all they were out there fighting. But it looks now judging from the papers that I was mistaken.

Eight days before the deadline, the operators had their way. Secretary Perkins certified the wage dispute to the War Labor Board for final settlement, after the President had sent telegrams to both sides stating that any agreement made must conform to his hold-the-line order. The northern operators went immediately before the WLB, which held a preliminary hearing on the situation on April 24th. The miners pointedly ignored the board's order for their appearance.

As the board had no power of subpoena, there was no way to force Lewis or any other officials of the union to show up. The board then appointed a three-man fact-finding panel "to define the issues and to collect and state the relevant facts and make its report to the Board." The three were Walter White, of the United States Chamber of Commerce, representing the employers, Morris Llewellyn Cooke, representing the public, and David B. Robertson, of the Brotherhood of Locomotive Firemen, representing labor.

The board ordered both sides to continue negotiations, with the understanding that if any wage adjustments were included in the new contract they would be subject to the approval of the WLB and applied retroactively to March 31, 1943. The operators accepted the order. The union's policy committee rejected it out of hand. By April 27th it was estimated that 26,000 miners in the Appalachian region had quit work. On that day Lewis said to reporters that the northern operators had "wantonly disrupted the wage conference by appearing before the War Labor Board." The Southern coalmasters appointed alternates to carry on the negotiations with the miners and at the same time pressed their demands that all final adjudication of the dispute must rest with the WLB.

By the next day it was estimated that 60,000 miners had left the pits. The three-man fact-finding commission called further hearings off so long as the diggers were walking out. The full membership of the WLB met and after a heated session voted to turn the whole dispute over to the President. In the announcement of their decision, the board said:

The National War Labor Board unanimously and deeply believes that the people on the home front in the United States are filled with a calm but grim determination to exert their very utmost efforts for maximum production of those war materials which are necessary to conserve the lives and to crown with success the war efforts of their sons and brothers who are at the fighting front. For the peaceful determination of labor disputes without interruption of production, a procedure has been established by the lawfully constituted agencies of the government under the executive orders of the President of the United States and Commander-in-Chief.

The Board firmly believes that to maintain these procedures against attack from any source is essential to the winning of the war; that this particular dispute can and must be handled like any other dispute under these established procedures. It is the unanimous conviction of the Board that any departure from these procedures in this particular case would destroy the entire plan for the peaceful settlement of labor disputes during the war.

Therefore the Board, following the precedent set in other cases where either employees or employers had defied its orders, threw the matter into the President's lap.

On Saturday morning, May 1st, the whistles brought out no miners. They were staying home in defiance of the order of the War Labor Board and in the absence of any word from Lewis or the Policy Committee.

When the public read the headlines, the storm that had been mounting since early spring burst in full fury upon the miners and their leaders. Men used passionate words to express their wrath over this stoppage of the industry in such crucial days. Lewis was compared with every traitor in history from Judas Iscariot to Benedict Arnold. So violent was the abuse leveled at him by the New York newspapers that his worried lieutenants urged him to hire a bodyguard to accompany him through the streets of the city when he went to the three hotels where the negotiations with the operators were being held. Every variation of the theme that the miners were stabbing the nation in the back, while our fighting men on far-flung battlefronts were fighting for survival, was played by editorial, cartoon, radio. J. N. Darling, a widely syndicated cartoonist, pictured Lewis as twisting the fetters on one of our servicemen, while the Japanese harried the soldier from the front. In the usually liberal St. Louis *Post-Dispatch,* Cartoonist Fitzpatrick pictured Lewis as a successor to Huey Long.

Men who had never seen a coal miner in all their sedentary lives matched invectives against Lewis and the miners on commuters' buses, on Pullmans rolling through the Pennsylvania countryside where the tipples stood lifeless, on New York subway trains running beneath the hotel where Lewis was conferring with the operators.

New Deal liberals, southern Democrats, Old Guard Republicans, Willkieites, Communists, the hierarchy of the C.I.O.—all joined in this mass condemnation of the work stoppage. The Socialist party press supported the miners, as did the liberal weekly, the *Progressive,* and there was a silence, hardly noticed at the time, among certain leaders of the American Federation of Labor. But to all intents and purposes, Lewis stood alone, the object of the bitter hatred of millions of Americans.

Through it all, the mine leader moved seemingly unperturbed. As was his wont when under the heaviest fire, Lewis dropped his table-pounding role and became the quiet-spoken gentleman from Alexandria, fresh from his books in the colonial living room. He went up to a newspaperman who asked him if he would change his mind and go before the WLB. Lewis, pointing in the general direction of Central Park, said softly:

"Have you noticed that the scenery in the park has changed any?"

Nobody paid any attention to the operators who sat on the side lines with cat-that-swallowed-the-canary smiles. Though there was some uneasiness among them as to what was going to happen to their mines, they all rejoiced over what they took to be the impending rout of Lewis and his fellow unionists.

Then things happened fast. During Saturday, May 1st, President Roosevelt ordered Secretary of the Interior Harold Ickes, who was also fuel administrator and in whose department the Bureau of Mines and the Bituminous Coal Commission were located, "to take possession of and operate coal mines for the United States Government."

Asserting that an investigation of the cost of living in the coal fields was at that time being made by the government and that, if the miners would submit their case to the War Labor Board, it would "be determined promptly, fairly and in accordance with the procedure and law applicable to all labor disputes," the Commander in Chief called on the miners to return to the mines, "and work for their government."

Ickes was to be "custodian" of the seized mines. The President authorized him "to take immediate possession" and "to do all things necessary for or incidental to the production, sale and distribution of coal." Ickes was to "permit the management to continue its managerial functions to the maximum degree possible consistent with the aims of this order." He was to furnish protection to any miner wishing to return to work, invoking the aid of the secretary of war if necessary. He was to "maintain customary working conditions in the mines and customary procedure for the adjustment of workers' grievances. He [Ickes] shall recognize the right of the workers to continue their membership in any labor organization, to bargain collectively through representatives of their own choosing, and to engage in concerted activities for the purpose of collective bargaining or other mutual aid or protection, provided that such concerted activities do not interfere with the operations of the mines."

In handing down his order to Ickes, the President had announced that he would talk to the miners of the nation over the radio on Sunday, May 2nd, at 10:00 P.M. All day Sunday the air was filled—literally in the case of the radio commentators—with maledictions upon Lewis and the miners. Lewis was closeted with his war cabinet and was not accessible to newsmen during the day. On that momentous evening, however, sixteen minutes before the President was to go to the microphone at the White House, Lewis, in New York, called in the reporters and informed them that he had telegraphed to the fields ordering the miners back to the pits on Tuesday morning, May 4th. He was not ending the 46-hour stoppage unconditionally. Lewis said that the union wanted to negotiate with the government for a new contract. To this end he was calling a 15-day truce. When the President went to the radio with his appeal to the miners, he knew of Lewis's order, but he made no changes in his scheduled speech. "Not as President, not as Commander in Chief," said Mr. Roosevelt, "but as the friend of the men who work in the mines, I appeal to them to resume work." He insisted that the miners' union must negotiate with the operators under supervision of the WLB. His plea, was, of course, an anticlimax in view of Lewis's somewhat malevolent timing of the order to his members.

It was in no happy mood that the miners returned to work for their new employer, the government of the United States, on May 4th. Flags flew from the mine buildings; red, white and blue posters announced here was "United States Property." The announcements, signed by Ickes, and still wet from the Government Printing Office presses, declared:

All of the officers and employers of this company are now serving the Government of the United States and shall proceed forthwith to perform their usual functions and duties in connection with the operation of the mine and distribution and sale of the product thereof, and shall conduct themselves with full regard for their obligation to the Government of the United States . . . no person shall interfere with the operation of the mine by the United States Government, or the sale or distribution of the product thereof in accordance with this order.

So far as the miners could judge the course of events from their distant listening posts, the Administration had done nothing about what were to the miners the all-important questions of wages and conditions. There had been flag waving, radioed admonitions, executive orders, but beyond the talk of investigating the cost of living in the mine fields, nothing tangible seemed coming out of all this fanfare.

On the other side, practically every newspaper in the country applauded the action of the President. Typical was an editorial in the rock-ribbed Republican New York *Herald Tribune,* intransigently anti-New Deal, and, of course, antigovernment-ownership, the day after the President seized the mines. Said the editorial writer in an exceptionally generous mood:

The President deserves credit for reducing the issue to basic terms which permit no equivocation. He has seized the mines in the name of the government; he has offered protection to the men who are willing to work; he has assured the mine workers that the legal road for redress of grievances is still open; he has appealed to their patriotism. He moved swiftly and accompanied his action by a clear and forceful presentation of the case of the people of the United States against the leadership of the United Mine Workers. Whatever governmental errors lie behind the present crisis—and they are many—the fact remains that now the President is right and John L. Lewis and all who support him are wrong. . . . The flag that will fly over the mines is the same that was raised in the dawn at Midway when the whole Pacific battlefront hung in the balance and Americans died for the things that flag represented. If the miners are worthy of the sacrifices which fighting men have made and are making for them, they will find in the flag the strongest argument against their irresponsible leadership. It places the United States in one camp; John L. Lewis in another. He is not alone in his camp: he has company there that any American with a shred of patriotism would shun as he shuns the most virulent plague. The miners of America can no longer have any illusions about the significance of their choice.

But it seemed that either few miners took in the New York *Herald Tribune* or that the overwhelming majority were impervious to plagues. At all events the telegrams in support of Lewis's position continued to pour in from individuals and local unions. Nor were the miners alone in their discontents. All through the labor movement ran sporadic revolts against what the workers felt were the unconscionably long-drawn-out deliberations of the WLB on the wage demands piling up before it. Workers on the railroads, in rubber and airplanes, and in shipping watched the frightening flight of food prices, apparently well out of reach of the Office of Price Administration, and like the miners resented the disposition of the papers to put all the blame for the confusions along the domestic front upon labor, at the same time that the big industrialists were enjoying the rich rewards of cost-plus contracts. That the spokesmen for these industrialists were overwhelmingly in control of the key positions in the various governmental agencies having to do with production and labor shortened the temper of the rank and file, and of alert-minded leaders as well. If labor was called on to accept with due docility job-freezing orders and wage-raise limitations, how did it come, asked the labor press, that so seemingly a simple matter as limiting the incomes of individuals to $25,000 a year for the duration, after the deduction of taxes, presented such apparently insuperable obstacles? The virulence with which Lewis was attacked for following this primitive but mighty effective line of reasoning revived the admiration for his fighting qualities among members of unions who had not forgotten what genuine contributions John Lewis had made to the building of their organizations. Lewis was by no means as anathema as the editorial writers would have him, not among the rank and file at any rate.

As it turned out, nothing had really been settled by the dramatic seizure of the mines. This was no more "nationalization" than was the gesture of the British ruling classes when in the midst of war at their very front door, the miners of England came out of the pits demanding wage raises. There was nothing in the British technique of "taking over" the mines to upset the status quo of ownership, and over here the seizure was regarded as a temporary expedient for heading off Lewis and keeping up production. While no believer in genuine nationalization of coal was satisfied with the new arrangement, in view of the fact that no titles to the mine properties had changed hands and that Ickes was only a "custodian" pro tem, there was considerable perturbation over the President's action on the part of the coalmasters and the big financial and industrial interests back of them. Here was this fellow Ickes, a "curmudgeon," as he had described himself in his autobiography, with a questionable political background of Bull Mooseism and advocacy of government ownership, now custodian of all the important coal mines of the country. The horrid suspicion grew that the mines were not going to revert to the free, enterprising owners as quickly as might be desired. The secretary of the interior had looked sourly on some of the lobbying activities of the operators. He didn't like a lot of things he had heard about, among them the business of handling the 6-day week. Further, he was willing to sit down and talk to Lewis, and did so soon after the seizures. These closed sessions of the two outspoken men started rumors that there was some sort of deal made between the secretary and Lewis, an unlikely story in view of the fact that Ickes had no power to negotiate any question of wages or hours.

The fact-finding panel of the WLB resumed its researches now that the miners were back at work. Since Lewis ostentatiously stayed away from its deliberations, the panel adopted the strange device of appointing a stand-in for the labor leader. This was Nathan Feinsinger, associate general counsel for the WLB. The lawyer was ordered to study the case for the miners as developed in the course of the wage negotiations in New York and tell the fact finders what Mr. Lewis might have said had he been present. Charles O'Neill was present to give the operators' side. He informed the panel that the miners in the Northern Appalachian field were receiving an average annual wage of $2,357.71. The panel asked Mr. Feinsinger to speak up for his side, but he tactfully refrained from telling the panel what Mr. Lewis might have said about Mr. O'Neill's figures. The lawyer explained that he had not had time to digest everything the mine leader had said to the operators since March 10th. When word of this reached Lewis, he smiled grimly and then denounced "the whole farcical procedure of trying the mine workers in absentia."

Lewis was more concerned right now with the activities of Congress than with those of the WLB. The Senate passed the Smith-Connally "antistrike" bill which was aimed obviously and squarely at the miners' leader. In the event of another strike, should the bill become law, Lewis might be facing imprisonment if he so much as "encouraged" a work stoppage in a government-seized mine. Foes of Lewis took pains to point out that this drastic bill was framed by Congressional reactionaries whom Lewis by his attitude of blind opposition to the Roosevelt administration was, consciously or unconsciously aiding and abetting. The hostile critics said that Lewis was now being "hoist by his own petard," a petard compounded of thwarted personal ambition and revenge.

Against this charge, spokesmen for the miners contended that the New Deal had been long dead, that in handing over to the large industrialists the conduct of the war production, at the same time labor was denied any real voice in policies, Roosevelt, once more as in the instance of the "plague o' both your houses," had sadly let all labor down.

Pressure on the Administration to take more vigorous steps toward price control was continued both by the C.I.O. and the A.F. of L. The auto workers were outspoken in their criticism of the OPA, as was George Meany, secretary-treasurer of the A.F. of L., who regarded the government plans to hold down prices by use of subsidies as "peanuts."

Stabilizer Byrnes came once more into the coal situation by issuing a directive which reaffirmed the power of the WLB to raise wages, "to aid in the prosecution of the war or correct gross inequalities." At the same time, he reaffirmed the correctness of the Little Steel formula. And then went on to inform the bewildered War Labor Board that any pay adjustments made by them must not increase prices or production costs and must be approved by his office. This was taken by some to be a "great victory" for labor. Others thought that the stabilizer was salving the sensitivities of the board (whose members resented the former justice's authority over them) while he was taking unto himself the solution of the coal controversy. It was all very confusing to the wayfaring man whose only concern seemed to be "to stop that so-and-so Lewis before he calls another strike."

At the expiration of the 15-day truce, Lewis, responding to Ickes's request, extended the truce to May 31st. "It was very decent of Lewis," said a WLB member, and Ickes said he would not ask for another extension. The new government mines boss made some caustic remarks about the "activities of a few powerful operators who from the beginning have deliberately opposed any compromise that might lead to a reasonable settlement."

The papers were full of speculation as to the "mysterious trips" which Lewis was making from New York to Washington. It was generally taken for granted that these trips had to do with the settlement of the coal dispute and the story of an arrangement with Ickes was revived. Apparently, Lewis had told no one among his confidants in the United Mine Workers the reason for his absences from the negotiations. On May 20th, the reason was revealed. The headlines announced that Lewis had asked the American Federation of Labor to readmit the United Mine Workers of America into full membership.

"ISN'T IT WONDERFUL!"

Thus exclaimed the ecstatic William Green as he told the assembled reporters in the Federation headquarters in Washington of Lewis's lightning move. Green's plump cheeks were red with excitement and his hands trembled a little as he read the announcement of Lewis's application. He said that the A.F. of L. "welcomed" the projected return of the miners and would give the application consideration in "an orderly and sympathetic way." He said that he had appointed a committee of three from his organization to work out questions of jurisdiction in the event of the readmission of the U.M.W. of A. The addition of nearly 600,000 disciplined unionists to the membership of the A.F. of L., a union with a treasury estimated at $6 million and a check from the mine workers for $60,000 for their first year's dues, were not to be treated lightly. The fact that with the addition of the miners, the Federation, now claiming 6 million members, would unquestionably dominate the labor world, with the C.I.O. a poor second, made the new situation even more wonderful in Green's dazzled eyes.

Two barriers lay across the way of the miners' immediate rejoining the Federation—the first, the strenuous objection on the part of the Progressive Miners, the second, the bitterness between District 50 and the C.I.O. The Illinois group maintained that when the A.F. of L. granted them a charter they were assured protection against any rivals entering the Federation. Though tacitly their spokesmen admitted that the younger organization had only about half the number of these in Illinois under the banner of the U.M.W. of A., nevertheless they were noisily determined that Green and the Executive Council of the Federation should stick to their promises made when granting the charter. Irritation was shown over Lewis's stubborn refusal to disclose the figures on membership of District 50. Lewis would say nothing more than that the U.M.W. of A. was a "going concern" and that the entire miners' union should first be readmitted, after which jurisdictional disputes could be ironed out. One disgusted Federation chief said that Lewis was already showing his "arrogance" even before he was taken back, and the matter reached the point where the Executive Council decided to lay the whole question before the October, 1943, convention of the A.F. of L.

Lewis's action coming so dramatically in the midst of his struggle with the Administration was as much a surprise to other labor leaders as to the general public. Though there had been talk about the possibilities of Lewis's return to "his father's house," as Green had put it, there had been nothing to indicate that this return was contemplated at this time. On the contrary, the last issue of the *United Mine Workers Journal* had referred editorially to "the toadyism" of the Federation's "misleaders." Similarly, the organ of District 50 under the guidance of Kathryn Lewis had recently attacked the Federation. Apparently Lewis had not told his own daughter about his plans. If there was anything in the way of cutting invective, culled from Homer, Shakespeare and the classic satirists, which since 1935 Lewis had not applied to the hierarchy of the Federation, students of invective were at a loss to name it. Yet now the application for the readmission of the miners was being handled by none other than that William Hutcheson, big-framed leader of the conservative carpenters' union whose fist fight with Lewis on the floor of the Federation's convention in 1935 had preluded Lewis's formation of the C.I.O. What was the meaning of all this?

Overnight came confusing opinions. David Dubinsky, of the I.L.G.W.U., who had consistently fought for unity in the labor movement, said that the return of the miners would be "a forward step in the direction of a united labor movement and as such is constructive and hopeful." But Dubinsky was generally regarded as the key labor man in the American Labor party which was at this time seeking to expand from the confines of New York City, where it had a following of close to 500,000 voters, to Pennsylvania and New Jersey.

The A.L.P. was passionately pro-Roosevelt. Even when its candidate for the mayorality in New York in 1942 had been snubbed by the President, the party had clung to its belief in the infallibility of Roosevelt. The A.L.P. vigorously denounced all those who, prior to Pearl Harbor, had opposed our entrance into the war, chief among them John L. Lewis. The Communists were articulate in A.L.P. councils and their hatred for Lewis had now developed into a fixation. They did not feel that his return to the A.F. of L. was "hopeful."

Over in the C.I.O. camp, Murray said he too had been taken by surprise. He pointed out that "John's paper" had just attacked the Federation, but gave no indication of what the C.I.O. would do in the face of this new challenge. Murray's lieutenants claimed to see no more than another evidence of crass demagoguery in Lewis's latest move. It was his sinister purpose, they said, to line up all the disaffected elements in the country—Negroes, dirt farmers, workers in low-pay industries—behind whatever candidate the Republican party might nominate for the Presidency in 1944. Lewis was climbing into the same political bed as Hutcheson and Matthew Woll. He would attempt to deliver the labor vote to the reactionaries, said these critics, and the death blow to the liberals, by taking the reins of the Federation from the aged hands of Green and riding roughshod over labor's no-strike pledge and other Federation commitments to an all-out war program.

Apparently the Administration had similar forebodings as to Lewis's future course. Stories came out of Washington, sponsored by old stand-bys, the seemingly omniscient informants—"those in a position to know"—to the effect that the "Palace Guard," such familiars of the President's as Harry Hopkins, Ben Cohen and James Byrnes, were putting pressure on Federation leaders to keep Lewis out of their organization. Daniel Tobin, head of the important teamsters' union, chairman of the three-man committee of the Federation to consider the application of the miners, and a favorite of the White House, was supposed to be won over to barring Lewis. Tobin tried to scotch that rumor by saying that he was opposed to "outside influences" intervening in what was a trade-union matter. He said he favored "speedy and favorable decision on the miners' reapplication for reaffiliation with the American Federation of Labor. Such reaffiliation would be a big step forward to that all-inclusive unity of labor which all its true friends desire. The question is not one of that or this labor leader, but of the interests of all labor." The strange spectacle of those at the seats of power seeking to prevent an individual labor leader from affiliating with the organization of his choice was a left-handed tribute to Lewis's supposed power. It was also a naïve gesture, since events had proved that even his own miners would not follow Lewis's political leadership. "When John says to strike, we strike," said a miner, "because we put him in there to know when to strike. But when John tells us who to vote for, we vote as we please. That's not his business."

There is no doubt but that Lewis was taking a quiet satisfaction over the furor raised by his reaffiliation move. "John L. Lewis," wrote Louis Stark in the New York *Times* of May 9, 1943, "is never so happy as when he is in a fight. His life has been a series of dangerous conflicts. Not many men enjoy teetering on the edge of a precipice. He does. The more formidable his opponents, the keener his delight in matching wits with them."

More realistic labor advisers than the Hopkins group were urging the Administration to do something quickly to quiet not only the complaints of the miners over rising prices (and thereby blunting Lewis's chief weapon) but also the rising clamor of all other labor organizations. OPA investigators came back from the distant coal camps to admit grudgingly that prices in company stores were "somewhat higher" than those in the larger stores in adjacent towns. On the day of the announcement of Lewis's application for re-entry to the Federation, the United Auto Workers—C.I.O. used full-page advertisements in newspapers all across the country demanding that the cost of living be "rolled back" by administrative fiat to May 15, 1942, when wages were frozen by the WLB's Little Steel formula. Ceiling prices, said the advertisement, "must be vigorously enforced." Then the most militant of the C.I.O. unions continued, in gentler tones, to be sure, than those used by Lewis, but in the same vein:

"To enable wages to keep abreast of living costs the War Labor Board must have authority to make all necessary adjustments; the WLB should abandon its piecemeal patchwork methods of handling wage cases and should institute without delay, industry-wide stabilization conferences to apply the sound and fair economic principle of equal pay for equal work."

Now the miners' representatives were sitting around hotel lobbies, still "looking for somebody to negotiate with." And the next strike deadline was perilously close. Would the mine leader and his policy committee dare endorse by tacit consent, if not by official order, a strike against the government? The answer was soon forthcoming. It shrieked from the eight-column headlines of the papers of June 1st:

Miners Strike Against U.S. Government

The second national work stoppage within a month had begun. And the war-frayed, strike-frayed nerves of the public snapped again.

At a conference just before the midnight deadline, the operators had turned down Lewis's compromise offer of $1.50 for portal-to-portal pay. With no contract anywhere in sight, the miners followed the U.M.W. of A. traditional "no contract, no work," and though now the whistles were blowing from mine buildings from which the flag was flying, no miners were at the cages.

This was nineteen-nineteen in reverse. Then Lewis in the face of an injunction had said: "I will not fight my government." Now he was challenging his government while it was embroiled in the greatest war of our history. To judge from the fury with which the press assailed the new walkout, the government had the overwhelming support of that intangible called "public opinion" in its insistence that the miners go back to the pits. While the diggers pitched horseshoes, puttered in their gardens, or sat around union headquarters playing cards and listening to radio denunciations of themselves, the nation's wrath roared against them and their leader.

Whatever the verdict as to the justice of the miners' case, the labor historian will record that this June walkout was an egregious example of union solidarity. In every important coal-bearing center in the nation, half a million stiff-necked miners, bound by their traditional "sense of kind," quit work together because of the lack of signatures on a paper captioned: "Appalachian Joint Wage Agreement Effective—1943." There were no picket lines at the struck mines, no agitational meetings, there was none of the accepted ritual of a national strike. With full consciousness of the grave consequences of their collective action, the mine workers of America in hard coal and soft from greasers, trappers and switch throwers to the skilled veterans of the picks, united as never before, quit work.

Washington raged. Apoplectic persons who write letters to the editor imagined a vain thing. Which was that coal can be mined with bayonets. The demand that servicemen from the camps be sent to the fields to practice on the miners their newly learned Commando tactics was a frequent theme of the more extremely worded communications. And that there would have been volunteers in large numbers was evident from the comments of servicemen here, and overseas as well. The great majority of sympathizers with labor looked with consternation on the sorry scene. What collective madness had seized upon the miners that they should thus cripple their government girding for what might be the decisive combat with the enemies of free workers the world over? What sort of leadership was this, recklessly to sacrifice all the hard-won gains of labor, and the good opinion of millions outside the movement, especially the opinion of a whole generation of youth bearing arms who would not be allowed to forget what the miners were doing while the boys were in the foxholes? Still there were a few, a handful perhaps, who wondered audibly as to what alternative other than the harsh one of a strike Lewis might have? Were he now to go as a penitent before the War Labor Board after all the bitter words, what respect could he retain for himself and what would be his repute among his rank and file? In this minority opinion, things had gone too far for honorable retreat on either side. Irrespective of the merits of the Little Steel formula, the WLB had to stick to it or pass into merited oblivion. And the government, "the new employer," must needs back its own agency. The showdown had come.

It was the time for which every enemy of organized labor had been waiting. With the mines still in the hands of the private operators, there was some question as to how much public support could be rallied to such a drastic bill as the Connally-Smith antistrike measure. But now that the miners were on strike against their own government, Congress prepared to pass the bill and hurry it to conference with the Senate.

Both President Roosevelt and Secretary Ickes ordered the miners back to work. This time the President said nothing about his "friendship for the men who mine coal."

"As President and Commander in Chief," he wrote, "I order and direct the miners to return to their work on Monday, June 7, 1943. I must remind the miners that they are working for the government on important war work. It is their duty no less than their sons' and daughters' in the armed forces to fulfill their war duties."

The President ordered that the mines continue to be operated by the government according to the terms of the old contract, "plus those new terms and conditions which have been approved by the War Labor Board." This last had reference to the WLB's concession to the miners on their demands for minor readjustments in the checkoffs for blacksmithing, cap rental, etc. The raise granted came to about 18 cents a day.

At the time the President issued his blunt order, Lewis and the operators had resumed negotiations. Lewis told the mine owners that Ickes had proposed a formula for ending the portal-to-portal pay question that was satisfactory to the union. Under the proposed arrangement, the operators and miners would agree to a temporary travel pay of $1.50 per day effective from April 1, 1943, until a commission of miners and operators could study the whole matter and report back within a month.

In rejecting this, O'Neill for the operators said:

"When we pay a sum during an agreement it should be all the money we owe. We want a stabilizing agreement, a contingent liability might endanger the financial structure of many coal companies."

"We want stabilization of the mine workers' stomachs," growled Lewis.

With such give-and-take, the negotiations proceeded, with the operators insisting that 48 minutes was a generous estimate for average travel time as against the miners' figure of 90 minutes. For a space both sides seemed about to come to some agreement on this question when Nathan Feinsinger, of the War Labor Board, Lewis's stand-in before the fact-finding panel, got on the long-distance telephone to order all negotiations off. The board, he said, could not permit negotiations to proceed while the miners were out on strike.

"A malicious, interfering, illegal action" was what Lewis had to say of this move. And he added that the board's action was in conflict with the National Labor Relations Act, inasmuch as it interfered with collective bargaining. Whereupon Senator Wagner, the author of that law, rose in his place in the Senate and exclaimed:

"I say that the statement of this labor leader is a cruel blasphemy of the most sacred rights of free labor guaranteed under the labor relations act." He added, however: "It would be a tragic mistake to pass hasty legislation as an expression of justified resentment over the irresponsible course of one leader in one controversy."

On June 3rd, Lewis sent word to Secretary Ickes, who had made another urgent demand that the mine leader "direct" his men to return to the pits:

"I have no power to direct. I shall, however, recommend to the policy committee of the United Mine Workers of America that it direct the miners to return to work on Monday, June 7th."

Though he had ignored orders from both the President and the War Labor Board orders, Lewis could not let the opportunity go by to renew his compliments to the WLB.

"These little strutting men," he exclaimed, "have sought to place upon the miners the responsibility for this work stoppage which rests actually upon their smug shoulders. Fearful lest a solution be reached under auspices not compatible with the self-importance of the War Labor Board, that body maliciously commanded that these negotiations cease."

The operators, reversing their attitude, now joined with Lewis in criticism of the board's action though, of course, they worded their criticism more politely. Above all things, they wanted their properties back and they evidently preferred the old way of bargaining to this new method of receiving orders from Washington. They were a most unhappy group.

To the consternation of the newspapers, which had published the assurance that this time there was no deadline set for the new mine truce, it was discovered that in fact Lewis and the policy committee had set a deadline of June 20th.

Telegrams sent to the locals by the policy committee had set the new deadline for the fourth extension of the old contract and Lewis said: "The miners and their leaders as patriotic Americans placed the law and the national interest above their own ungranted and long-deferred claims for justice and equity." Although the stoppages had been timed to fall on weekends when normally little coal is mined, and on each occasion the Bureau of Mines had reported that there was enough coal on top to fill the needs of industry for a month or more, lack of immediately available coal forced the management of some steel works to close down their coke ovens—a fact given prominent display in the newspapers. On the whole, it was estimated that the June 1st stoppage had cost the country 11 million tons of soft coal "which could never be replaced," as Ickes pointed out, though faulty distribution and the failure of many managements to provide for reserves had something to do with this loss.

For the next twenty days the long dispute dragged out. National politics and the politics of the labor movement were as much a part of the dispute—at times the chief factors in the dispute—as the economics of the situation. The prides and prejudices of men had to be accounted for in the deadlock between the government agencies and the miners' union, the coolness between Ickes and the War Labor Board, the hurt attitude of the operators who complained that having made their contribution to the price stabilization program they had been "punished" by an ungrateful government. There was a great deal of face-saving, there were oblique maneuverings, what might seem to be brilliant publicity strategy on the part of the White House were not graver issues than the winning of a debate in the newspapers at stake.

Soon after the miners had gone back to work the secretary of the interior (who was now in his capacity of "custodian" collecting dues for the United Mine Workers of America through the checkoff) announced that he was fining all the miners who participated in the June 1st walkout, $1 a day for every day they were out, the money to go to some charity. This display of bad temper nearly precipitated another walkout. The secretary, realizing with what high explosives he was playing, hastily rescinded his order when he heard the roar from the pits. O'Neill, of the operators, as representative of his own group of Pennsylvania mine owners, announced that he and Lewis had come to an agreement over portal-to-portal pay and that his group would dissociate themselves from the rest. Two days later, he backed out of the agreement over a technicality, rejoining his fellows. "Can't anyone in this mess act their age?" wailed a miners' spokesman.

On June 12th the Smith-Connally Wage Disputes Bill came before the Senate for final action. The Senate passed the bill by a vote of 55 to 22. Two days earlier the House by a large majority (219 to 130) had approved the measure and it now went to the President's desk for his action.

No question but that this drastic measure stemmed directly from the coal controversy. Supporters of the bill in both Houses contented themselves with denunciations of Lewis, the appeal to patriotism, the stressing of the need for backing up "the boys on Guadalcanal." Senator Elbert Thomas of Utah, in opposition to the measure, warned:

"We cannot win a war in a halfhearted way. We cannot win a battle with unhappy troops. We cannot bring about great production with unhappy labor. We cannot bring about co-operation in industry with unhappy and coerced labor leaders. When we turn from the ordinary processes of voluntary action to forced action, we are asking men to assume an unnatural attitude."

Senator Robert La Follette said that the bill was a product of hysterical public opinion and fundamental ignorance of the real facts in the labor situation.

"I say," said La Follette, "that we are asked to enter into this dangerous and delicate field of labor relations in such a way as to throw the weight and power of government on the side of the private employer and against his employees in plants which have not been taken over by the government. I say there is nothing in the production record of employees which will justify the action we are about to take." He warned of adopting totalitarian tactics and continued: "Once you have adopted the Axis course, once you have drafted all the people and forced them to work, what will be your answer if then they do not produce? The answer will be more force. For my part I do not believe that forced labor is as efficient as free and voluntary labor." Other senators contended that the bill would wipe out the voluntary code of labor relations based on fifty years of experience and would tend to increase rather than check the growing discontent of the workers.

The Smith-Connally Bill, if signed by the President, would provide the statutory strength that the War Labor Board had lacked. Hitherto depending upon acceptance of its findings under the executive order creating it, the board's recourse had been reference of disputes to the President. Now the bill made it the law of the land that the board should "freeze" labor relations during its deliberations, should have the right of subpoenaing any witnesses, which, of course, would force Lewis's appearance, and generally should exercise compulsory arbitration of wage disputes in war industries. The long knife which the framers of the bill had been whetting especially for Lewis was the penalty of $5,000 or a year in jail for anyone inciting, instigating or encouraging a strike in plants seized by the government. In the case of war plants not seized by the government, no strike action would be possible until after a 30-day "cooling off" period and a secret ballot in which a majority of the workers would vote to walk out. During this period the plant might be seized by the government. Seized plants, however, must be returned within 60 days after resuming normal production. Labor lobbyists descending upon Washington to urge a presidential veto pointed out that there was a dubious clause in the bill which might be interpreted as forbidding the War Labor Board from approving any maintenance of membership or other union security clause. They wanted to know what the section of the bill prohibiting the contributions of the unions to political parties during a national campaign had to do with a "Wage Disputes" measure, and how it happened that the bill, in effect, set up machinery for calling strikes in war plants, despite the fact that labor with the exception of the miners, was supposedly keeping its no-strike-for-the-duration pledge.

Enheartened by Congressional support, the War Labor Board on June 18th issued its decision on the soft-coal dispute. Stating that the negotiations between the miners and operators had broken down, the board announced that it would now make its own adjudication. The lengthy document boiled down to a flat rejection of the U.M.W. of A. demand for the $2 increase and portal-to-portal pay as well. The miners were ordered to sign the old Appalachian Agreement with a clause inserted by the WLB stipulating that there would be no strike for the duration of the war.

The four public members of the board and the four representatives of industry presented the majority report. The four labor members dissented, saying that travel pay should have been decided on a temporary basis of 80 cents with a commission to look into the whole perplexing matter.

The only concession that the directive made to the miners, outside of the few cents involved in the checkoff adjustments, was the granting of the right of the union to take the travel pay dispute to the courts for determination of the legal rights of the miners for additional compensation under the Fair Labor Standards Act. This recognized the court's action in the case of the iron-ore workers, but, added the directive, any agreement must embody a "genuine settlement of the law-suit compatible with the stabilization program." Evidently negotiation of some sort was authorized by the board.

The WLB said that it could not grant a general increase to the miners because the stabilization policy forbade it. Using the operators' figures, the board estimated that the miners were receiving a minimum wage of 85.7 cents an hour.

That hourly rate [said the board] is certainly above anything that could be thought of as insufficient to maintain a decent standard of living.

When the increased demand for coal to meet war requirements and the arrangements for operating the mines on a 6-day week are taken into account, the hourly, weekly and annual wages of the bituminous coal miners make a very favorable showing with similar earnings reported for industrial workers in other industries . . . the mine workers have already received an average increase in straight-time hourly earnings of 18.2 per cent since January 1, 1941. With the provision for a six day week and the war-time demand for bituminous coal, the mine workers, in March, 1943, were able to secure an average weekly take-home pay of $42.97 for a work week of 38.3 hours, which is 65.3 per cent greater than their average weekly take-home in January 1941, when they averaged 29.7 hours per week.

The board commented on the fact that since 1932—the depression low point—when the union miners were making but $14, wages have risen to approximately $43 a week, "which puts the mine worker," said the board, "up among the higher paid workers in the war industries."

The directive took a fling at Lewis:

"In this dispute the United Mine Workers under the leadership of Mr. Lewis, have repudiated the no-strike agreement and insisted on coming to the bargaining table with their demands in one hand and in the other the threat of a strike in an industry which affects the war production more vitally, perhaps, than any other industry."

The labor members of the board made this statement to the press:

"The labor members of the WLB, representing the overwhelming majority of organized labor in America are just as firmly convinced that the no-strike pledge we made to the American people through the President of the United States must be carried out today as on the day we made it." The names of John Brophy and Van A. Bittner stood out among the signatures to this statement. Only the other day both men had been trouble-shooting for Lewis on far-flung C.I.O. strike fronts, and in intra-union disputes as well. Now the two former mine workers were signatories to a directive ordering the making of an agreement which the mine leader and his policy committee promptly denounced as a "yellow-dog contract."

So the dispute came to another deadline amidst threats, exhortations, patriotic outcries, the voicing of old union slogans. No still, small voice was audible in this whirlwind confusion.

There was no question this time as to the course the miners would take. The flat rejection of their demands by the War Labor Board and, in turn, the flat rejection on the part of Lewis of the order of the board to sign a dictated contract led straight to another walkout, on June 20th.

The policy committee's statement, couched in the vigorous language of their leader, proclaimed: "This contract would place political and economic manacles and leg irons on each of the members of the union affected for a two year period." It asserted the "willingness of the mine workers to work and continue the production of coal for the government itself under the direction of the custodian of mines. The mine workers have no favor to grant the coal operators nor the members of the War Labor Board who have dishonored their trust, but will make any sacrifice for the government, the well-being of its citizens, the upholding of our flag and for the triumph of our war effort. Accordingly the executive officers of the United Mine Workers of America are hereby instructed to hold themselves in readiness to confer with the Secretary of the Interior, who by Presidential Executive Order of May 1, 1943, is instructed and empowered to do all things necessary for or incidental to the production, sale and distribution of coal."

With the miners out of the pits again, Ickes and Lewis conferred behind closed doors. Outside, the War Labor Board indignantly insisted that the only issue at stake was whether Lewis and his union "would abide by the same rules and the same laws which are applicable to other groups," i.e., the rules of the WLB.

Before President Roosevelt received the dispute, Lewis called off the latest walkout on June 22nd. In ordering the miners back to work,

Lewis, through the policy committee, served notice that the members of the U.M.W. of A. would dig coal until October 31, 1943, a new deadline, if the custodianship of Ickes was expanded to full governmental operation of the mines. "This arrangement is predicated," concluded the committee's announcement, "upon operation of the mines and their collateral production units by the United States Government and will automatically terminate if governmental control is vacated prior to the above-mentioned date."

No one took this to be a demonstration of any newfound love of the miners for nationalization of the mines. It was obviously Lewis's choice between two governmental agencies, the War Labor Board and the custodianship of Ickes, with one or the other of which he was forced under the circumstances to do business. Of course his position all along had been that he wanted an agreement with the private operators, without any outside interference. The mandate of the WLB that he sign an agreement written in the board's office he had now ignored with Olympian scorn, setting forth his own terms for continuation of mining soft coal and even fixing the date for the next deadline, a date about which there was much speculation. Did he choose October 31st because that day would come at the climax of the political campaign of 1943? No one seemed to know, and there was no enlightenment from Lewis.

As on the other occasions, there was an outburst of public wrath when the miners walked out for the third time. Letters from servicemen were widely circulated. Chester Morrison, Columbia Broadcasting System correspondent at Cairo, read over the air the following editorial from the Army newspaper *Stars and Stripes*:

A soldier in the Middle East, who once was a successful artist, drew a cartoon for "Stars and Stripes." We didn't print the cartoon, because soldiers are not supposed to get involved in matters that would be termed political: but we'll tell you what the cartoon portrayed. John Lewis, in miner's dress, was throwing dirt with a coal shovel upon the freshly marked grave of some kid in Africa. It's a grim, bitter piece of work and God knows it expressed the attitude of the overwhelming majority of the soldiers in this and any other theater. We are telling you what that cartoon was about because we believe that the activities of John Lewis have transcended the realm of politics and legitimate unionism and have entered the realm of treason.

Nor is John L. Lewis a traitor to his government alone. He has betrayed by his excesses the cause of union labor with which he has so long been identified. He has betrayed the spirit of the democracy which gives him the right to move against the welfare and will of America's millions. He has betrayed the belief of the American soldier that this would be a war in which the individual's gain and the individual's interest would be sublimated to the common purpose. Speaking for the American soldier, John Lewis, damn your coal-black soul!

Mr. Morrison said that he was not sure that "the editor really can speak for the American soldier or for God either." A number of labor leaders were not so sure either. They pointed out that the Office of War Information, through its foreign division, had given the right of way through the censorship to these supposedly "spontaneous" expressions of rage. The International Longshoremen's Union at its annual convention passed a resolution urging the OWI to send men with a labor background when labor news was to be interpreted to the troops. Many of the soldiers' letters indicated that their authors believed that the miners were striking for shorter hours and exorbitant pay and that the brief stoppages had held up all production of essential war materials. It was not until Secretary Ickes was on the air with a discussion of the coal situation on June 30th that any letter from a soldier favoring the miners' stand was given national publicity.

At all events there was an impressive preponderance of opinion hostile to the miners and their leaders in every cross section of American life sufficient to justify the President's statement, made after the men had gone back to the mines, that the action of the mine leaders "has greatly stirred up the anger and disapproval of the overwhelming mass of the American people." "Intolerable" was the President's adjective for the action and he went on to say:

"The mines for the time being, of course, will continue to be operated by the secretary of the interior under the executive order of May 1st. The terms and conditions of employment will be those announced by the National War Labor Board in its directive of June 18th. There has been no promise or commitment by the government to change those terms or conditions in any way.

"Before the leaders of the United Mine Workers decided to direct the miners to return to work," continued the President, "the government had taken steps to set up the machinery for inducting into the armed services all miners subject to the Selective Service Act who absented themselves without just cause from work in the mines under government operation.

"As the Selective Service Act does not authorize the induction of men above 45 years into the armed services, I intend to request the Congress to raise the age limit for non-combat military service to 65 years. I shall make that request of the Congress so that if at any time in the future there should be a threat of interruption of work in plants, mines or establishments owned by the government or taken possession of by the government, the machinery will be available for prompt action."

This was the Administration's grim alternative to the Connally-Smith Bill still awaiting action by the President. It received little general support even by those who were most bitterly opposed to the mine workers' union policies. Senator Truman voiced a widely held opinion when he said: "I am neither for a military dictatorship nor for drafting labor." The draft as a form of punishment, rather than as what Roosevelt once called "the muster of a peoples' army" was a repugnant idea to most Americans. The President's spokesmen indicated that Lewis had tried the Executive's temper beyond endurance. The President, thoroughly alarmed by now at the state of affairs on the home front, was evidently resolved to act the part of the "Strong Man" and aim a body blow at the one labor leader and his organization that dared openly to defy the Administration's edicts, directives and orders. But that "the friend of the men who work in the mines" should go to the extreme of advocating the drafting of miners dismayed the labor and liberal elements in the Administration. This was far more than a repetition of the "plague o' both your houses" remark. Indeed the President made no mention of the other house. On the contrary, he assured the operators, according to the New York *Times* of June 24th, that "their financial investments and legal rights in their properties would be protected."

The first electrically charged days of this second summer of the war saw such a swift crumbling of important sectors along the domestic front as to lead men to wonder whether or not our civilian population was cracking up under the strains and stresses of the war effort. Petulance and an odd hysterical shrillness marked the public utterances of ordinarily sobersided officials. The sort of infantile bellicosity that had been assumed by both sides to the coal dispute seemed to spread to almost every department of government connected with the domestic economy. Agency heads indulged in temper tantrums in the presence of grinning newspapermen only too glad to report how the New Deal "bureaucracy" was behaving.

None of this bickering was lost upon the miners. The editor of the *United Mine Workers Journal* saw to that. In every issue he dwelt upon the more obvious shortcomings of the "burrocrats," "the male milliners," as he called the members of the WLB and other agencies having to do with labor. The miners felt that Lewis was fully justified in his characterization of the agency personnel as "little, strutting men."

On the Pacific Coast what had seemed to be no more than a fantastic outbreak of adolescent exhibitionism developed into a sinister manifestation of deep-seated unrest. Teen-age wearers of "zoot suits" fought with enraged servicemen in Los Angeles. In Detroit, white men and Negroes were coming to death grips. There was race rioting at the shipyards at Mobile, Alabama, and in Beaumont, Texas.

All across the country, minority groups, resentful at being excluded from any genuine participation in the war effort and apprehensive over the increasing centralization of authority in Washington, were struggling for recognition in a hundred other places than the mine fields of the nation.

The discrimination against Negroes and "aliens," the spread of "blighted areas"—in rural slums, in distressingly overcrowded working-class districts around every major production center, as well as in the desolation of the coal camps—was being paid for by blood on the streets of Detroit, by stirrings in St. Louis, disturbances in the South, and up and down the Pacific Coast.

Such evidences of grave discontents on the part of the underlying population might be expected of a nation on the verge of a serious military defeat. But here was a nation whose armed forces were for the first time since Pearl Harbor undertaking an offensive whose outcome promised impressive success. The news from the far-flung battlefronts was as encouraging as the news from the domestic front was disheartening.

At such a time of doubt and hesitation, the Congress came to the fore with a program dictated in the main by the inveterate foes of the social philosophy of the New Deal. Though spokesmen for the New Deal—what was left of it—protested that there had been no intention of remolding the nation's economy in the midst of a global war, Congress proceeded on the assumption that such had been the case with many of the key agencies. Government by appropriation was substituted for government by agency. By the simple expedient of withholding funds from suspect agencies, Congress signed the death warrants for the Office of War Information's domestic news service, the National Resources Planning Board, the National Youth Administration, and cut other agency appropriations to the bone. Turning to labor, Congress made it clear that no quarter was to be granted to trade-unions, kicking against the economic pricks.

At 3:30 o'clock on the afternoon of Friday, June 25th, a message from the President vetoing the Connally-Smith War Labor Disputes Bill was read to the Senate. Fifteen minutes later, the Senate voted 56 to 25 to override the veto. Seventy minutes later, over in the House, after the reading of the message, representatives by a vote of 244 to 108 overrode the veto. The bill became law by 5:38 o'clock.

"Someone has been feeding Congress on loco weed," said a disgusted miners' representative, and a C.I.O. spokesman called the day "Labor's Black Friday."

The anti-Administration press hailed the overriding of the veto as a body blow to Lewis, the ending of all thought of labor "appeasement" on the part of the Administration, and a "vindication" of Congress. The New Deal papers were at pains to point out that the President had followed the urgent pleas of the labor lobbyists to veto the measure, but they said little about the alternative of drafting labor which the President had so vigorously urged.

If it was the Administration's intention to place upon Congress the onus of the writing of a law so hateful to labor, the veto message was a failure so far as the more progressive of the labor leaders were concerned. In that message, the President had merely stressed the vagueness of certain sections of the bill. He had not condemned it as a whole nor repudiated its general purpose. There was evidence that Administration whips had not bestirred themselves to line up votes for the veto. In the House, the New York and Pennsylvania delegations, usually prolabor, had not voted in any numbers. On the other hand, many Administration wheel horses had sided with the two-thirds overriding.

Learning of the passage of the bill, many miners on their way to the pits turned back in disgust. They agreed with the general labor opinion, expressed by the C.I.O. spokesmen, that the bill was "born of malice and greed, the very essence of fascism, destroying the philosophy of voluntarism upon which free trade unionism is founded."

Upon the passage of the law, the WLB, flexing its statutory muscles strengthened by the measure, struck again at the miners. The board urged President Roosevelt to cancel the governmental checkoff of union dues, seize the $6 million in the U.M.W. of A. treasury, and take civil and criminal action against Lewis unless the latter signed the old Appalachian Agreement as amended by the board. The announcement of this action did nothing to hasten the return of the miners to work.

In the meanwhile Secretary Ickes was going on with extension of his plans for governmental operation of the mines. He appointed Carl Elbridge Newton, president of the Chesapeake and Ohio Railroad, director of mine operations, in charge of production of coal in the more than 4,000 mines which had been taken over. Regional directors appointed by the secretary were in direct charge of operations. Neither Ickes nor Newton was concerned with wage disputes, wages paid and hours worked being those of the amended Appalachian Agreement. Although Ickes had stated that he had made no agreement with the miners' leaders and that he had no intention of "snatching" the property of the operators, the mine owners still expressed lively apprehensions about getting back their mines.

Ickes had written to the New York *Times:* "If the *Times* believes that the operators were a bunch of little Rollos during the dubious proceedings that have been carried on with respect to the coal strike, then the *Times* is too innocent to be allowed out alone at night." Now the *Times* was asking gloomily whether or not the mines were to be "nationalized" at Lewis's behest and the operators, who, according to Secretary Ickes, had "deliberately opposed any compromise which might lead to a reasonable settlement," were in Washington protesting that they might as well have signed an agreement with Lewis at the outset, in view of what was happening to their properties. At the same time the War Labor Board was pressing upon the President its contention that unless he forced Lewis to sign the amended agreement the board would be left high and dry.

At a press conference, the President expressed doubts as to whether he could compel the mine leader to sign any agreement. He asked the newsmen if he should send a polite, little note on pink paper and say: "Dear Mr. Lewis, I hope you will sign the contract"? Later he said that the new Wage Disputes law made it obligatory for the government to return the mines to their owners sixty days after the mines had "attained productive efficiency." As to the meaning of "productive efficiency" there was of course much difference of opinion. Mr. Ickes and the operators might not see eye to eye on that. If, however, the mines were returned before the October deadline set by the union and there were further walkouts which could be traced to any union official, the fines and jail sentences contained in the penalty clause of the new law might be imposed upon any or all of the mine union officials.

Lewis called in his policy committee to consider a new strategy. From the conference, he emerged with a fresh challenge. This was an agreement signed on the dotted line by operators and unionists, arrived at after collective bargaining, conducted on a 50-year-old pattern. The Illinois operators had signed a two-year, no-strike contract with Ray Edmundson, president of District 12, U.M.W. of A., whereby the Illinois Coal Operators Association agreed to pay the 30,500 miners in the union for their portal-to-portal travel time in the amount of $1.25 a day, divided so as to be retroactive at the rate of 50 per cent from October 24, 1938, when the Fair Labor Standards Act became law to April 1, 1943, when the rate became 100 per cent. The agreement expanded the 7-hour day to eight hours with time and a half ($1.50) for the eighth hour of actual work at the face. Thus, while there was no change in the basic day pay, the miner, by working extra time and under other conditions of the contract, could add as much as $3 a day to his pay check. These other conditions were the pay of 25 cents a day allowed by the War Labor Board for vacation time, plus minor benefits.

So now Lewis, having begun negotiations with a demand for a $2-a-day raise, had in his hand a contract calling for what amounted to a $3 raise. It was a contract signed in the state where the techniques of collective bargaining in mining had been in operation to an

extent not approached by any other district. From the heart of the
old Central Competitive Field the miners came with this document
which the policy committee set up as a standard for all other U.M.W.
of A. districts, throwing over the existing Appalachian Agreement.
Once more Lewis had split his opposition, so far as the operators
went. He was plumping before the War Labor Board the accomplished
fact of an agreement made in the traditional manner, signed by
operators who said they wanted to get ahead with the peaceful mining
of coal, and to this end and to avoid threatened suits over the moot
question of portal-to-portal pay had put their names on the paper.

The Appalachian operators, ignoring the Illinois contract, called
desperately on the War Labor Board to enforce its directives against
portal-to-portal pay. "The time for action on your part is long past
due," wrote the operators. While the President was conferring with
his advisers on new plans for cutting the cost of living, plans urged
on the Administration by leaders of both the C.I.O. and A.F. of L.
who had served notice that, unless something was done quickly, the
no-strike pledge would be abandoned, Lewis, for the first time, officially
recognized the existence of the War Labor Board. He asked the board
to hear him and other witnesses on the matter of the Illinois contract.
The Board set August 3rd for the momentous hearing.

When Lewis came at long last before the Board to press for
acceptance of his signed and sealed Illinois contract,[1] there was no
talk of "little, strutting men" or "predatory patent attorneys." On the
contrary, Lewis was as near self-effacing as that "powerful man" (as
he was described at the hearing by one of the lawyers) could possibly
be. He let an attorney who had argued the case of portal-to-portal
pay for the ore workers do most of the talking, contenting himself
with telling the board that in every "civilized" nation save the United
States travel pay was accepted as a matter of course. On the legal
side is was argued that the Illinois agreement did not provide a direct
increase in hourly wages. The board could, if it would, recognize the
supplemental agreement as a compromise on back pay for overtime
due the miners under the provisions of the 40-hour week of the Wage
and Hour Act. The Illinois operators told the board that they had
arrived at an average of 54 minutes' travel time each way from the
portal to the face. Work time of the Illinois diggers from October 1,

[1] See Appendix B.

1938, when the Fair Labor Standards Act became effective, to April 1, 1945, when the contract will expire, was set as 1,300 days, or 200 workdays a year. The compromise portal-to-portal pay to which the operators agreed was $1.25. A no-strike clause was inserted and it was agreed that the 6-day clause in the contract would become inoperative if the demand for coal slackened before 1945.

Though the Appalachian operators insisted that, if the WLB approved the Illinois contract, it would be granting the miners a $3 a day raise instead of the $2 demanded at the outset of the negotiations, the spokesmen for Lewis warned that, as the *United Mine Workers Journal* put it, "A disapproval of the Illinois wage agreement will create widespread dissatisfaction, turmoil and strife in the coal fields." With this the Illinois coalmasters agreed, saying that they had signed the contract to avoid threatened union lawsuits over back pay and to settle the portal-to-portal controversy as expeditiously as possible. D. W. Buchanan of the Old Ben Coal Corporation of Illinois said: "If the government doesn't accept this agreement, I don't see how we are going to get the coal supply this country needs."

The WLB turned down the Illinois agreement, intimating that it was no more than a hidden wage raise and the government commenced returning mines to their owners. Whereupon there was such a slackening of production as to lead to ominous speculation as to the chances of a serious coal shortage. The miners were playing ca' canny, in the manner of their English cousins.

While the board seemed to have won a victory, there was some quiet recapitulation of the surging march of the mine controversy since the spring. Now that the "shouting and the tumult" over the personality of John L. Lewis had died a little, it was possible to hear certain voices urging an evaluation of the man and his program in the larger light of national and labor policies. A writer for *Fortune,* refusing to accept Lewis either as a saint or as a devil, had this to say:

There is no doubt but that Lewis is a supreme opportunist who delights in gathering power unto himself. But it has never been proved that his power has consciously been wielded at the expense of those among the rank and file who trust him. . . . If John L's union Caesarism didn't pay off in the miner's "take home" envelope, it would long since have ceased to exist. The paradoxical fact about Lewis is that the closer you get to those who deal with him, the more respect for him you will encounter.

Coming back from a trip to Washington at this time, John Chamberlain in the *Progressive* quoted a government official, an opponent of Lewis's, as saying: "Lewis keeps his word, even in little things. That's a rare thing in Washington."

In the middle of August, the President, through Director Byrnes and Secretary Ickes, ordered an increase of working hours for the miners from seven hours a day to eight hours and an increase in the work week from forty-two to forty-eight hours. This contemplated time and a half pay for the extra eight hours, just as the miners were receiving overtime pay for the increase from thirty-five hours in the original Appalachian Agreement to forty-two earlier in the year. It was the hope that the extra money would quiet Lewis's demands, but in case the mine leader was persistent in demanding a flat raise, with the strike threat as an alternative, the President, acting in accordance with the Smith-Connally Act, authorized the WLB to order the withholding of union checkoff monies in case of non-compliance with the Board's orders in the seized plants. He also served notice that draft deferments of strikers in such plants would be canceled by the Selective Service System.

Perhaps, after all, the stand of the mine leader for collective bargaining, with the end in view of raising his miners to the status of workers in the other heavy industries, might not have been so calamitous to the cause of all labor, the mine workers included, as Lewis's enemies would have it appear. To be sure, there was the Smith-Connally Act most certainly sired by Lewis's intransigeance. But the act was proving to be as vague as its critics dubbed it during the debates in Congress, and already, within a month of its passage, even veteran antiunionists were considering testing its constitutionality. Apparently, under the interpretation given it by the attorney general, who ruled that a minority of workers in a plant could obtain a strike vote, it would encourage rather than discourage wartime strikes. Lewis was seen by some to have been fighting the cause of the little man in labor, whereas the Administration in its concentration upon the military aspects of the war was moving steadily to the right. The President's brusque repudiation of Vice-President Henry Wallace, generally accepted as an eloquent spokesman for the little men in all cross sections of our economy, the persistent playing of power politics with a fourth-term candidacy in view, the footling with price control, rationing and other phases of the domestic economy—these were leading many ·liberals to doubt their earlier estimate of Lewis as the hornéd leader of the Forces of Darkness moving behind the scenes to destroy the Legions of Sweetness and Light. There was even some dissent from the liberal doctrine of the Infallibility of the President in the matter of the coal strikes. Certainly those brief walkouts had created such shifts in the domestic scene as had never been planned in the White House. Said John Chamberlain in *Fortune:*

Even the strikes of last spring which so many people regard as "traitorous" may have broad-scale beneficial results. For Lewis permitted his three strikes as one who regarded the roll-back of prices as a grisly barbershop joke. Someone had to bell the Roosevelt cat, to jolt the Washington home-front war administration wide awake. And if Roosevelt and Jimmy Byrnes and Director of Economic Stabilization Fred Vinson ever manage to halt the spiral of inflation, and if OPA ever manages to live up to its promises, it will be largely because of Lewis's stubborn and perhaps wrongheaded, (if not wronghearted) action. Lewis is once more having far-reaching effects on the U.S. social structure.

On one estimate friends and foes of the mine leader agreed. John L. Lewis was by all odds the most powerful labor leader this country had ever known. Not Sam Gompers in his organizing prime, not John Mitchell bringing all labor to the surface at the beginning of the century—no other man in our history had so shaken the structure of the Republic from below. At one time or another a disciple of the drab philosophy of business unionism and Adam Smith economics, a passionate propagandist for industrial unionism with all its revolutionary implications, an ardent exponent of "voluntarism" and a Jeffersonian suspicion of centralized government, a potent Hamiltonian lobbyist for increasing governmental controls over the industrial civilization—the man's philosophy could be summed up only with the colorless word "opportunist," though he could say with Napoleon: "Circumstances! I make circumstances." Described by Chamberlain as the possessor of the "finest mind in the labor movement," making "men around him seem like dull, creeping· clodhoppers," Lewis himself, when he takes time off for self-analysis, seems puzzled. Half-jestingly he asks his friends, as Dale Kramer has noted: "What makes me tick? Is it power I'm after, am I a St. Francis in disguise, or what?"

Power, whether used in dictatorial manner in the affairs of his own union or used democratically as the lever to close the gap between the men from the picks and their productive fellows—this was of the essence of the contradictory, contentious man who at a critical time in the Republic's affairs succeeded in diverting public attention from the clashings of a global war to the state of half a million coal miners, far removed from the common concern before Lewis pointed to the upthrusting, clenched fist.

XXV. LIFE AND DEATH IN A COAL CAMP

A TOWHEADED MINER'S YOUNGSTER runs across the cinder patch back of his home, playing soldier. He points his wooden "tommy gun" in the direction of the mine, shouting "rat-tat-tat." Suddenly he stops in amazement as a cloud of dust billows out from the mouth of the hoisting slope. He wheels in his tracks and runs to the little frame house in whose kitchen the mother is cooking dinner. "The mine! the mine!" he shouts.

The woman comes to the door in her house dress and apron, casts one stricken look at that dust cloud, and starts rushing toward the mine where her husband and brother had gone to work some hours earlier. Women and children from the other houses join in the rush to the entrance to the main slope. Ropes are quickly stretched to hold back the tragic little group. Volunteers come forward in response to the white-faced super's call. The rescue party goes down the slope from which the dust is clearing now, and for five dreadful hours the tight-lipped women with their children clinging to them wait, hoping against hope that the stretcher-bearers will not bring out their men. There isn't much weeping among these mine women. Many of them have been through just such agonies before. When the cars finally come up with their burden of blackened bodies, the mothers and sisters of those who have come through unscathed try to comfort the bereaved. There is a quiet heroism in the way in which a mine camp faces its collective grief after a mine disaster that is far more moving than the imaginary mass hysteria in the fictional version of such a scene.

All across the fields, year in and year out, since men went down under the earth to wrest a living from the most hazardous of all our major industries, this dreadful scene has been repeated.

In 1942 there were 1,480 miners killed and 70,500 injured. As soon as Secretary Ickes was given governmental custodianship of the mines in May, 1943, he issued an order directing full compliance with all safety requirements by the federal mine operating managers. Said the secretary:

"Federal operation of the coal mines places the responsibility upon the United States government that the mines are kept safe. Both as a humane measure and as a means of helping to achieve the maximum production of coal to win the war, the Federal Coal Mines Administration will act vigorously to bring safety and health conditions fully up to the legal standards.

"Since Pearl Harbor, more men have been killed and injured in the coal mines of the United States than have been reported killed, wounded and missing in action by all branches of the armed forces.

"Last year 1,480 men were killed in the coal mines and 70,500 were injured. Although this terrible loss of life and limb in the coal mines during the last year is less than that of previous years and better than the record made prior to the establishment of the federal coal mine inspection system, it, nevertheless, is a commentary on the hazards in the industry.

"With the growing pressure upon the mines to increase production, and as the result of other influences of the war upon the operation of the mines, deaths due to mine accidents appear to be increasing. At the rate experienced during the first four months of this year we may expect that 1,500 men will be killed in 1943 unless we can do something to prevent it.

"Every man we lose on account of death or injury by accident means not only grief and loss to his family, but also loss of production. The heavy damage to mining properties and precious equipment also means loss of production. For the most part, accidents are preventable and we must act vigorously to prevent them."

In referring to the accident record in 1940, when 1,400 miners were killed, the Bureau of Mines said:

". . . the situation is so grave that serious thought and relatively quick action are demanded if the coal-mining industry of this country is to avoid stigma of a national, even a world-wide scandal because of the callousness with which the lives of its workers are being sacrificed."

Edward Wieck, himself a veteran coal miner, has made a study for the Russell Sage Foundation of New York, called "Preventing Fatal Explosions in Coal Mines," in which he analyzes six disastrous explosions in the mines in 1940. "It is abundantly clear," he concludes, "that coal-mine management has failed in its responsibility to prevent needless accidents."

Wieck urges the community as a whole to give support to state and federal agencies for the enforcement of mining laws and their more efficient administration. He calls for fuller participation by the workers in accident prevention and suggests that even as unionism was finally accepted by the industry, there is hope that "collective action will become the practice also in matters relating to safer operation."

As the mines became more and more mechanized, there were many who thought that the new machines would bring a greater degree of safety. This has not proved to be the case. Conscientious investigators, such as Mr. Wieck, and writers for the *United Mine Workers' Journal* and *Coal Age* alike, point out that the danger is that the machines are bringing new and more dreadful risks to an already hazardous calling. Miners and operators are both aware that this new menace looms daily larger and at all their gatherings there is discussion of new safety measures and their administration.

A long step toward greater safety in mining was taken in 1941 by the enactment of the Federal Mine Inspection Act. Under this law, whose passage had long been pressed by the United Mine Workers of America, the Bureau of Mines has authority to make annual or "necessary" inspections of coal mines and to make the findings of qualified investigators available to the public. Up to that time the bureau's employees had to obtain the permission of the owners before entering any mine. Now, too, reports on all mine disasters are to be made available to the public. Operators, naturally sensitive to such publicity, long fought this ruling which was enacted by the bureau following a fatal explosion in a mine at Bartley, West Virginia, in 1940.

Stations of the bureau are set up in various strategic places throughout the fields. Instructions in first aid and mine rescue work, as well as safety programs, are given at these stations. From them rescue crews are rushed, at the word of a disaster, with the latest equipment, and from the experiences of these thoroughly trained and courageous men the bureau has accumulated a wealth of data as to the causes of explosions and ways to prevent them.

Not that there is any great mystery about the chief cause of most explosions. It is gas. Methane gas, often called firedamp and marsh gas, is a product of the decomposition of organic matter in the mines. It is a hydrocarbon, inflammable, odorless and tasteless—and deadly. Electrical ignitions of this lethal stuff have, according to Wieck, been the greatest single cause of explosions in mines. With the great increase in electrical equipment and power-driven machines, in recent years, there has been no notable corresponding increase in care in the use and maintenance of the equipment. The machines themselves, working at top speed, often advance the "face" into gas-filled danger spots where there has been no opportunity for inspection. Sparks from overhead trolleys or overheated cutting bars may set off a gas explosion which has comparatively trivial effects at the point of inception but which spreads fantastically throughout the mine, blowing into charred bits the bodies of men at work in distant places.

A forward-looking leader of the operators' group, writing for *Coal Age* of April, 1941, drew up the most severe indictment of management's neglect in safety measures. This was Eugene McAuliffe, president of the Union Pacific Coal Company, whose Wyoming mines have a splendid record for safety. Mr. McAuliffe wrote:

Coal, more than any other industry, is still following the trail blazed by the pioneers of northern England 250 years ago. Woeful waste of a rapidly exhausting natural resource, archaic hand-mining methods, poor ventilation responsible for frequent mine explosions and a too general acceptance of the theory that accidents must happen constitute the sins of omission and commission that, to a large extent still attach to the industry. . . . Time after time the industry gets a fresh black eye out of a mine explosion, with all the gruesome details played up in the newspapers. Do these tragedies bring about better ventilation, rock-dusting, water on cutter bars, sprinkling dust at the source and on roadways, and the other proved preventives we know about? Such unfortunately is not the case; we clean up the mine, pay the workmen's compensation, and get back on production. Why should our accident rate be four times that of Great Britain? Will it take the British theory of more rigid laws and law enforcement to lift us out of the condition we are in? Why, as an industry, have we not made the same ratio of accident reduction achieved by the railroads, the steel industry and manufacturing in general? Again, are the United Mine Workers, through legislation, to further become our pacemakers? It is important that owners and management make a more serious effort towards accident prevention. . . .

Mr. McAuliffe, the operator, and Mr. Wieck, the former miner, agree with the men from the Bureau of Mines that the methods of prevention are well enough known. In general these consist of adequate lighting and ventilation, rock-dusting and redusting to drive the combustible matter from the dust raised by the machines or hand picks, the cooling of cutting bars, the use only of "permissible" materials and explosives, i.e., those permitted by the Bureau of Mines, and above all, constant inspection and frequent meetings of safety committees in the separate mines, with participation by the workers.

It was in 1870 that the first legislation for mine safety was enacted by the state governments following several major disasters, in one of which 179 miners were killed. It was not, however, until after one of the most disastrous periods in the history of our mining, that of 1900-1909, that the miners' union succeeded in establishing the Federal Bureau of Mines. Still our coal is splattered with blood.

Disease, too, stalks through the coal fields. Walter Polakov, director of engineering of the United Mine Workers, told the National Health Conference meeting at Washington in 1938:

"Coal mining is notoriously hazardous and unhealthy but it need not be either. The mortality rate of the miners is appalling, 1,300 per 100,000 in comparison with 900 for all gainfully employed. The mechanization of the mines has been going on at a fast rate and claims an increasing toll of dead, maimed and sick.

"Such enormous intensification of work brings not only physical but nervous strain. Among the prevalent diseases which are breeding under these circumstances we find tuberculosis ranks first. It claims each year 120 per 100,000 for miners against 87 for all workers. Nephritis claims 71 against 57 for all workers. The medical care around mining camps is peculiar to itself. We have had group service for many decades. It is a bastard type, one under which the companies

appoint the physicians, largely without consent of the patients. The
services rendered is largely confined to diseases and injuries incurred
at work. There are no services in venereal cases; it does not include
dental services; it does not include neural pathology; it does not include examination or even X rays for compensation cases; it does
not include maternity cases and care of babies. Yet up to $36 a year
is automatically subtracted from the miner's pay. The system, of course,
covers only those miners that are still employed five or more days per
month. Those who are displaced by mechanization, by economic depression, or by declining demand have to shift for themselves and are
at the mercy of the rugged individualism of the private practi-
tioners."

Hard roads, electricity, sewerage systems—the mechanical fundamentals of civilized living are coming gradually to the communities.
But the fundamental drabness and monotony of the miner's life has
changed but little. To be sure, there are operators who are striving to
bring into the camps some brighter colors than the prevalent blacks
and grays. In scattered places, playgrounds and swimming pools,
recreational halls and movie houses set up by the mine owners are
within reach of miners' homes with their small gardens and curtained
windows, gallant challenges to the all-pervading soot. Few women
visitors from the outside fail to catch the touching significance of those
gardens and curtains. Or the care with which the miners' wives watch
over the manners of their children. The men can eat with a sprawling
gusto, but the youngsters are expected to preserve decorum. To keep
them well-mannered, to give them the best of such schooling as the
neighborhood affords, to give them a sense of individual integrity in
the midst of a none too favoring community life is the concern of
most every miner's wife for her children. The little ones will be growing
up all too soon, the boys to follow their fathers into the mine, the
girls to go through high school if possible and then marry or take a
job in a factory near the fields. In the meantime they are to enjoy
such security as this most insecure of all industries allows.

Though life in these camps today is, at its best, darkened by the
struggle for elementary decencies, it is enhearteningly better than it
was a generation ago when the union was disintegrating after the
failure of the Jacksonville Agreement, and feudal-minded owners
and operators were dictating the terms of their workers' existence. In

the closed "company towns" in Pennsylvania, West Virginia, Kentucky and Tennessee, infrequent visitors found a veritable state of siege in the dark days from 1922 on. Mounted and heavily armed coal and iron police were on hand to inspect the credentials of every stranger. Public roads were blocked off, even post offices made difficult of access. It was a favorite device for battlers for civil liberties to send letters addressed to themselves prior to their arrival in town, only to be refused admission to the post office on the ground that to get to it one had to cross a company-owned road. Huge searchlights, mounted on top of mine buildings, cast their groping beams at night across the shacks of the miners. Frequently machine guns were hidden beneath the lights and often the entire camp was surrounded by barbed wire beyond which no miner could go.

At the company stores in the nonunion fields, only company-stamped "scrip" was recognized as payment. Prices, as a rule, were higher than in "open" towns in the neighborhood. After paying his rent and paying for his powder and lamps and the rest of the long list of the company checkoff, the nonunion miner was usually in debt to the company. At one time it was said: "There is more money in mining the miners at the company store than in digging coal out of the ground."

After Arthur Garfield Hays, counsel for the American Civil Liberties Union, was assaulted by coal and iron police and forcibly ejected from a "closed town" in Pennsylvania, he remarked to the operator of the mine that a number of the miners' wives were going about in bare feet in bitterly cold weather. "Oh," said the operator, "they are Polacks. They are used to that." In this particular town the women had to go long distances to fetch water in buckets as there was no running water in the company houses. Hays's crime was that he attempted to read the Bill of Rights of the Constitution of the United States aloud to a group of miners. Though the miners had signed "yellow-dog" contracts wherein they agreed not to join any union, there was always the fear on the part of the operators that some union organizer might persuade them to the contrary.

In the union fields, though there were few infringements on civil liberties, the life of the miner was and is a pretty meager business. Everything centers on the job. When the mine is "down," i.e., closed (and in spite of war's demand for coal, many of the 6,000 odd bituminous mines were still closed long after Pearl Harbor), the camp goes dead. The men pitch horseshoes or "chew the fat." The women have their children and their housework to attend to, but they go through their tasks with a lackadaisical air in the face of the "No Work Tomorrow" signs.

No such chapter as Joel Seidman wrote about the educational and recreational activities of the garment workers' unions in his book *The Needle Trades* can be written of the U.M.W. of A. The miners' union has been surprisingly neglectful of its cultural opportunities for making the life of the individual in the average coal camp more endurable. The description of that life in *The Case of Bituminous Coal,* written in 1926, holds good in 1943: ". . . life in most mining villages offers to the men little outside of their work, offers to the children less than most cities, and offers to the women almost nothing that is stimulating or developing."

The authors were writing of a coal camp, i.e., a self-contained community of from 500 to 1,000 inhabitants with a mine or mines at its center. Of course, miners living in larger towns or on the outskirts of cities such as Scranton, Wilkes-Barre, Belleville, etc., are in no different state from those of other working people so far as access to educational and recreational facilities goes.

From time to time sporadic attempts have been made to bring the camps into closer contact with American amenities, but the International union has offered little encouragement to the pioneers who for the most part have been with the opposition against union officialdom.

One of the most promising of these attempts was that inaugurated by Tom Tippett, a working miner and leader of a group of alert-minded youngsters in Illinois. Tippett's father, a minister who cast in his lot with the miners, bequeathed to his son a ranging curiosity and a love of knowledge. For a space, Tom left the pits to go into labor journalism in Chicago with the Federated Press, that hopeful organization set up after World War I to supply labor papers with news of the movement which the commercial dailies omitted. Tom came back to institute a circuit-riding series of informal talks in the various camps on social and economic problems which the diggers and their families faced. Speakers were brought in to break through the barriers which kept the miners from the sense of participation in the labor movement as a whole and on Sunday afternoons the union halls in the little camps would be filled with diggers and their families come to hear the men from St. Louis or Chicago or New York. Oscar Ameringer would come down from Springfield, Illinois, with a lump of coal wrapped up in his pocket. He would deposit this solemnly on the podium while the children in the front rows watched closely and for half an hour talk delightfully about the nature of the stuff on which the fortunes of the community hung, telling the story of the rocks and of evolution and of fundamental economics and bringing it down to the 1930's with the statement: "Folks, it's all here in your one hand. Hold out your hand like this." Small fists and big would come up all over the hall. Then Ameringer would hold out his hand with the little finger and thumb thrust out. The thumb, he would say, stood for the owners, the little finger for the miners. The thumb was trying to get higher and higher and so was the little finger. But what of the gap between, represented by the clenched three fingers? There must be some sort of lever under the "pinkie." That lever was union, its upward thrust through organization and education, and he would push the index finger of his left hand against the little finger of the right so that slowly the gap was filled. And all that next week when he walked the streets of the camp small boys would follow the rotund editor holding out their grimy thumbs and "pinkies" as a sign that they had understood.

It was a different story with some of the "wise men from the East," as Ameringer called them, who came to indoctrinate the miners. Soon headquarters at Springfield was alarmed over some strange philosophies that were being taught in the fields. The plans of Tippett and Ameringer for miners' Chautauquas in the summer months when the mines were down, with speakers who knew their audiences and would not attempt to talk down to the diggers, with entertainment for the children and as Ameringer put it, "lovely music, Beethoven, Bach, none of that goddam hillbilly stuff"—these were frowned on by the keepers of the treasury at Springfield.

Union officials, busied with organizational work, knowing themselves since childhood only the life of the mine, looked askance at such programs as those carried on under the auspices of the "New Unionism"—the Amalgamated Clothing Workers, the International Ladies'

Garment Workers, and more lately the United Automobile Workers of America. The heads of the miners figured that these gave the rank and file "radical" ideas. Long-winded speeches by officials on "Mitchell Day" and Fourth of July barbecues would suffice, or so they believed. Had not the miners' co-operative stores in Illinois with an educational program on the side gone bankrupt before the first World War? Wasn't Brookwood impregnated with "Communist doctrine"? Even when the miners touched off the C.I.O. split from the Federation, there was no enthusiasm among the leaders of the U.M.W. of A. for genuine labor education.

Life in a mine camp under such circumstances is essentially drab, monotonous, bleak. The other day the *United Mine Workers Journal* printed on its cover a picture of an Ohio coal town. In the foreground were trees covered with snow. The mine buildings were in the background. The caption read. "This winter scene, showing the Willow Grove Mine of the Hanna Coal Company at St. Clairsville, Ohio, is typical of the appearance of many American coal communities during the season when snow covers the operation and softens the harsh outlines of mine surroundings."

"The harsh outlines of mine surroundings" are in no way softened for any time by nature or man. Such recreation as the young people of a mine community enjoy is supplied by juke boxes, pool tables, baseball fields, or, in some cases, fly-by-night brothels. The older people have their churches, Catholic among the great masses of Southern European immigrants who went to work in the mines in the early days of this century, Fundamentalist among the American-born.

And always at the center of the picture is the union hall where the men gather to discuss in a jargon unintelligible to an outsider the gossip of the mine.

The question remains as to why more than half a million men should chose to earn their living in so perilous an industry amid such desolate surroundings, physical, mental and spiritual. As a matter of fact, few miners actually "choose" their calling. The biographies of the older leaders show that as mere children they were introduced into the pits by their fathers. Foreign-born miners were taken from the "labor markets" of the big cities and sent to remote fields from which they have rarely emigrated. Even in the depths of the depression years they stayed around the abandoned mine works, as the WPA survey of conditions in Southern Illinois showed. Attempts to shift them to other industries and to resettle them on the land which they worked in the old countries as peasant farmers have met with no notable success. True, with the coming of spring, in normal times, and the shutting down of the mines for the summer, younger, single men with itching feet have gone on journeyings all across the continent. But miners marry young and have large families. The necessity for bringing in money when the mines are down sends the older men into road work or small-time farming from which they return when the whistles blow again, with evident relief. Mining is what they know best and while they may curse the mine as though it were a natural enemy, they are forever being drawn back to its dark embrace.

Such, at any rate, has been the case of the men who lead mine labor today. There are few newcomers on the platforms of the conventions of the United Mine Workers. The sons of union officials who grew to manhood while their fathers were at desk jobs or on the road organizing rarely go down to the pits. If possible, they go on through high school into college and then take jobs in business or the professions. The nearest they may come to mining is as a powder or machinery salesman. The son of John L. Lewis is a Princeton graduate, now a medical student at Johns Hopkins Hospital in Baltimore.

It might well be, though that does not seem to be the case, a cause of concern among the leaders of mine labor that there are so few youngsters being groomed to take the place of their elders who have been in office from ten to twenty years. One of the chief arguments for the centralization of authority in the Washington office of the United Mine Workers was that it should become a training school for just this purpose. But the provisional officials who go out to the different districts are for the most part veterans of the movement. Lewis, Kennedy, Tetlow, Gasaway, Mark, Hefferly, Edmundson—these are names familiar to those who have been about the mines for the past twenty years. And these are not passing on the benefits of their wisdom, born of long experience, to younger leaders. It may turn out, as has been suggested, that the extension of mechanization will create a new type of leadership. This would be a healthy thing for the labor force. The small group of insiders, capable as most of them are, tend to become a hierarchy. Traditional principles of leadership will not presumably suffice to meet the new problems—technical, economic, political—revolving around the future of coal.

XXVI. THE FUTURE OF COAL

SINCE THE TURN OF THE CENTURY, the conception of coal as a natural resource has changed as radically as have the methods of mining it. Coal in the bunkers of a modern electric light and power plant is vested with a new significance, technological, economic, even political. Coal in the yards of a chemical works is not a fuel but rather the rich source of a hundred thousand compounds. Industrialists think more of the electric power which coal liberates than of the heat it gives off when burned in a raw state. While the civilian population, in times of war, may have a pressing concern with coal in the grate or the "converted" home furnace, it is the mineral's place in the total machine process around which the productive system is built that is of chief concern to the planners of tomorrow's world.

H. G. Wells, in *The Work Wealth and Happiness of Mankind,* remarks:

The capacity to employ power seems to be illimitable. Oil can never satisfy more than a fifth of the world's present dependence upon coal. And the coal "in sight" will last at the present rate of consumption for twenty generations or so. Twenty generations back in our own history takes us to the Hundred Years' War, the Black Death, the First Statute of Labourers, the Peasants' Revolt, and the first Navigation Act. The changes since then have been many and, in a sense, revolutionary. But the changes in the next period especially as they affect human life and work, will appear more numerous and still more revolutionary to those who will look backwards as we do today, but over twice the length of time. As it nears exhaustion, coal may become more valuable as a source of raw material for the chemical industry than as a means of obtaining mechanical power.

Wells's prophetic mind ranges over the possibilities of harnessing winds and water to a degree which even the sponsors of the ill-fated Passamaquoddy project did not envisage. But for some time to come men will accept the dictum of Charles P. Steinmetz [1] that if all the water power in the country were harnessed it would not suffice alone to turn the wheels of industry.

There was brave talk at the World Power Conference in Washington in 1936 about the possibility of trapping solar energy by means of elaborate arrangements of mirrors. Delegates went out to a yard behind the Smithsonian Institution where a scientist from the West Coast exhibited such an arrangement which he used for cooking, heating and lighting in his own home. And today "popularizers" of science for the newspaper readers throw out tantalizing hints from the fronts where the atomsmashers are at work. For our generation, however, and our immediate descendants, the better conservation, utilization and by-producting of coal will be of more importance to our planning than the use of substitutes.

It is the electric power industry that leads the field in the better utilization of coal. John Bauer and Nathaniel Gold in their book *The Electric Power Industry* [2] made an exhaustive study of the progress in steam-plant economy in the industry. They find that "advancing economy in over-all coal consumption alone has produced complete obsolescence of the most efficient earlier plant within short cycles." They figure that the consumption of coal in pounds for producing a kilowatt hour of electricity decreased from 7.00 in 1900 to 1.44 in 1936 and that a plant with all modern units could further reduce this to 0.80. The authors stress the increased economy of the 1936 turbine over the 1930 and earlier units, with consequent improvements in high-pressure boilers. Automatic control of forced draft in the new boilers, pulverization and feed regulation, and new types of boiler designs which conserve fuel, work together to get the maximum heat content out of every pound of coal in an up-to-date plant. In several of these operations the boiler unit is mercury whose vapor

[1] Charles P. Steinmetz, *America's Energy Supply*. Quoted by Hamilton and Wright in *The Case of Bituminous Coal*.
[2] New York, Harper & Bros., 1939.

attains a higher temperature than steam, at a moderate pressure, with a maximum percentage of the heat content of the coal going directly to electrical generation. It is the fact that the savings effected by such technological advances are not passed on to the consumer which agitates the advocates of lower electrical rates and gives coal in the electric plant yard its political aspect.

Even the railroads, which have been notoriously spendthrift in their use of coal, are reforming to the point where 110 pounds of coal will move 1,000 gross tons of freight a car-mile, whereas in 1919 it took 170 pounds. A reduction to 70 pounds is around the corner in some of the new engines. In steel in 1919, it took 3,777 pounds of coking coal for the manufacture of one gross ton of pig iron. Today, the job is done with 2,800 pounds.

Improvements in stokers, both domestic and industrial, according to United Mine Worker statisticians, have effected coal savings throughout the nation of from 15 to 50 per cent. The march of mechanical stokers at coal's terminal points eliminates much of the backbreaking, brutalizing toil which Eugene O'Neill dramatized in *The Hairy Ape,* even as the new mining machinery cuts away at the size of the labor force at the face of the coal underground. On the other hand, more efficient utilization of coal by large and small consumers leads to better preparation of the product at the mine. In anthracite, hard-pressed by oil's competition, the preparation of the product for specialized markets has long been a subject for the devout study of both engineers and salesmen. An increasingly large proportion of the workers around a modern colliery in the hard-coal fields labor on top of the ground at processing operations. In bituminous, up to a few years ago, no great attention was paid to the quality of the coal beyond its superficial "cleanness." Successive screenings, in some districts more than 100, now give a range of sizings from large to small usually as follows: lump, egg, stove, nut, pea, run of mine, and slack. Increasing interest on the part of buyers for the utilities and other large consumers in the quality of the fuel has the soft-coal people talking about ash content and Btu's. The British thermal unit represents the amount of heat required to raise one pound of water one degree in temperature. A pound of bituminous coal may contain as few as 7,600 Btu's or as high as 15,000, depending on the quality of the vein of the mine where it is dug. Some coal leaves

60 pounds of ash per ton, other coal as much as 400 pounds. While present war demands create a seller's market, which make quality considerations more or less academic, the new interest in the heat content may be counted on to grow after the war, with resultant improvements in processing coal at the pits.

The narrowing of the market in normal times by more efficient utilization of coal by large consumers, together with the constant encroachments of competing fuels, natural gas and oil, has led the more far-visioned of the coalmasters to set up research projects for new uses for the black stuff.

A bill passed by Congress in 1942 provides for the construction of a $450,000 research laboratory in the anthracite regions. This is a minuscule beginning, to be sure, but it is a beginning of what may someday be a large-scale attempt of modern science to lift these regions out of the long depression which has from time to time laid them desolate. The project will strive to "determine how anthracite markets may be regained, maintained and expanded, and to advance the health and safety of the workers in anthracite mining." "Results of the study," according to the sponsors of the project, "are expected to give economic relief to the greatly depressed industry and to furnish employment for the 100,000 miners who worked in the anthracite processes before the present lag in production." The laboratory will be under the supervision of a six-man commission, appointed by the secretary of the interior and representing operators, workers and the public.

Bituminous Coal Research, Inc., an enterprise subsidized by the coal operators, the railroads, and large industrialists, has done valuable work in new utilization of soft coal. Coal research goes on in normal times at the State College of Pennsylvania and the University of Pittsburgh. Interesting experiments which may give us a better knowledge of the basic structure of coal are under way at the Carnegie Institute of Technology whose coal research laboratory is supported in part by coal carriers, producers, and steel and chemical companies. From time to time, glimpses of coal's future have come from the laboratories of the Mellon Institute, the Gulf Research and Development Company, and the Koppers Company.

Since its organization in 1910, the Bureau of Mines in the Department of the Interior has conducted extensive and continuous studies of the properties, mining, preparation and utilization of coal which may well serve as a background for postwar planning. At the present time it is Great Britain that is pioneering in such planning. Coal problems are being studied by a parliamentary and scientific committee which has concluded that "coal must be the basis of the industries on which Britain's postwar prosperity depends." British planners were confronted in 1943 with the immediate prospect of supplying huge quantities of export coal to Italy and other Axis satellites which might be knocked out of the war. Major Gwilym Lloyd George, Britain's minister of fuel, was tackling much the same human problems as those confronting Secretary Ickes at the time of a full-dress House of Commons debate on June 23, 1943, on stepping up coal production. Absenteeism on the part of British miners was estimated to have cost the country 8 million tons of coal yearly. There were 308 work stoppages in British coal mines from November, 1942, to May, 1943, most of them in Scotland and few of them lasting for more than a day. The complaint of the British hewers, like those of their American underground cousins, was over the cost of living and insufficient food. Further, the overseas miners complained that their weekly wages of £6 did not put them on a parity with workers in other essential industries. One of the main objects of Major George's planners was to make life in the coal fields "more attractive," so that the alarming exodus of younger people from the areas might be checked. There seemed to be a realization, in Britain at any rate, of the interrelation of the human with the economic and scientific problems of coal. The dramatic visit of the present Duke of Windsor to the coal fields where the between-the-wars depression had hit hardest of all, earned him, to be sure, the disfavor of powerful forces, but also served to bring forcefully to public attention the plight of those in the "blighted areas." As a result, the wayfaring man in Britain is not so much concerned with "keeping the miners in their place," passing punitive laws aimed at the hewers' organizations, or excoriating their leaders, as he is with putting science to work for the stabilization of the industry and giving some greater measure of security to the workers.

In wartimes in all countries, coke with its capabilities of intense heat for steel's blast furnaces is of the essence of munitions production. Before we entered the war, our chemists were at work on low-temperature coke which they hoped would prove to be the smokeless, easily ignited fuel that would put an end to the smoke palls still over many of our industrial centers. Then coke went to war and this search was temporarily shelved. But coal, carbonized at the mines to produce gas, oil and coke, is in the preview of Dr. Gustav Egloff, director of research for the Universal Oil Products.

Spectacular progress may be expected in the coke fields not only in the production of steel but in the by-products of the modern coke ovens as well. After the passing of charcoal for the smelting of iron ore, the on-coming steel people shoveled bituminous coal into cone-shaped ovens of brick, the old-fashioned and terribly wasteful "beehive ovens" from whose open tops flames and clouds of black smoke vomited toward Pennsylvania's skies. The coke, the result of expelling by extreme heat the volatile elements of soft coal, is a brittle, porous solid, practically smokeless, and consisting chiefly of carbon mixed with sulphur and phosphorus. It is ideal for the making of steel and for other metallurgical purposes, harder than charcoal and quicker in its combustion than anthracite, which is really a natural coke. Until as late as 1893 the "behive ovens," some 44,000 of them, were all that were used in this country's coking operations. Then word came back from Europe that ingenious retort ovens were salvaging the invaluable by-products of burning coke, the gases, light oils and coal tar, wasted by American processes, and soon there appeared in our coke regions ovens that saved these ingredients, ovens bearing the name of Otto-Hoffman and Schniewind, Semet-Solvay, Rothberg and Koppers. In 1908, the first plant of Koppers's regenerative ovens with retorts heated by vertical flues was erected by the Illinois Steel Company at Joliet, and soon United States Steel had 500 Koppers in use at Gary, Indiana.

The modern retort oven consists of the coking chamber, the heating chamber and the regenerative chamber, all made of firebrick and laid out in batteries of from 10 to 90 units. Coal, especially selected, is charged into the ovens through the tops and then subject to extreme heat. The oven is sealed with lined doors and the volatile matter is drawn off by pipe lines to near-by by-producing plants where the gases are separated and purified.

In general, for every ton of coal coked in a modern oven there will be 0.7 ton of coke; 0.06 ton of screenings; 10,500 to 11,500 cubic feet of gas; 26 pounds of sulphate of ammonia; 1.75 gallons of benzol; 0.55 gallon of toluol; 0.24 gallon of xylol; 0.5 pounds of crude naptha-lene and 12 gallons of coal tar.

When the gases and tars have been extracted, power-driven rams force the coke from the furnaces whence the porous stuff is taken to the consumers' bins to be used for fuel. In July of 1942, by-product coke production totaled 5,312,197 net tons, or a daily average of 171,-367 tons, the highest monthly and daily average in the history of the industry. The men of the coke fields of Connellsville, the Warrior Basin of Alabama, and the Tug River district of West Virginia had been loading their turns.

When in 1821 in Baltimore gas produced by the distillation of bituminous coal was used for the first time in this country for illu-minating purposes, scientists noticed that during the process of manu-facture a thick, black liquid collected in the mains and condensers of the primitive gas works. This evil-smelling, oily coal tar is the source of innumerable compounds when it is distilled into groups of substances, chiefly hydrocarbons, phenols and bases, which are further distilled.

From the by-producting and distillation of bituminous coal comes a wide range of medicinals, dyes and plastics, the nuclei for indus-trial enterprises which may be counted on to play an increasingly important part in civilized life. Every woman who wears Nylon stockings can thank or curse a coal digger for supplying the prime source of her hosiery. Coal is used in the making of many plastics—automobile dashboards, radio cases, lighting fixtures, hardware, con-tainers, even complete airplane bodies.

Organic chemists are interested chiefly in the four all-important elements, carbon, hydrogen, oxygen and nitrogen, and the myriad arrangements and rearrangements which can be made from them. Researchers give us a picture of six-sided "benzene rings," each one of which is an arrangement of six atoms of hydrogen and six of car-bon. By a slight change of the relationship among these rings a varity of synthetic medicinals is produced, from acetanilide to zinc sulfanilate. In the coal-tar group of medicinals in 1940 there was a national output of 18,214,000 pounds, an increase of 20 per cent over 1939, according to figures of the United States Tariff Commission.[3]

[3] Report No. 148, second series.

Aspirin and salicylic acid accounted for 63 per cent of the total production in terms of quantity. The 1940 sales figures for these synthetic drugs came to $17,773,743. In this group belong the much discussed vitamins and hormones and the miracle-working sulfa drugs.

Before the entrance of this country into World War I, two German submarines made the hazardous transatlantic trip through the British blockade to bring to our shores cargoes of drugs and dyes distilled from coal tar. Our wasteful coking processes had left us largely dependent upon the enterprise of foreign chemists, chief among them the Germans. Today we are self-sufficient, chemically at all events, with exports of coal-tar products valued at $28,449,000 in 1940, an all-time high. Our imports were the lowest in history in that same year—$9,034,000. In the second half of 1940, there was a tremendous increase in the production of synthetic organic chemicals for military use, an increase which of course has continued with the development of the war effort.

From coal tar comes the annual production of 122,677,000 pounds of dye stuffs with a sales value of $25,000,000. These dyes run through the full spectrum and no longer is it necessary for our dyemakers to look abroad for leadership.

Coal's chief by-product contribution to the immediate waging of war is in the explosives field. There is a steady increase in the production of toluol, with by-product ovens and the coal-tar distillers working overtime. TNT is made from coal tar, petroleum, and nitrogen. The artificial fixation of nitrogen from the air is a vital chemical process which makes modern warfare a thing of unprecedented violence. Blasts of air and steam are shot into coke-filled furnaces with the oxygen content of both blasts going into combustion, leaving nitrogen and hydrogen to be held together by pressure and heat.

From coal-tar crudes we have benzol, motor benzol and xylol, napthalene, creosote oil, and several kinds of distillate and residue tars. These light oils and their derivatives are coming from the distillers in ever-increasing quantities. In Chapter Two we discussed the Bergius process of hydrogenation now being studied with care by our own chemists.

Men had been mining coal for centuries before William Perkin, working in Professor A. W. Hoffman's laboratory in the Royal College of Chemistry, in London, in 1856 discovered aniline purple and thereby started the coal-tar industry. For years to come, it was the Germans who capitalized on Perkin's discovery. With the rise of the Nazis, however, the owners of some of the best chemical brains in the Reich were exiled. Though the name of I. G. Farben, the sprawling chemical cartel, was still something to conjure with, both at home and abroad, German chemistry, dragged at the wheels of the Nazi war chariots, no longer maintained its old position of pre-eminence. Our own chemists, who used to listen respectfully for the last word from overseas, have won a new independence. Further, there is a fresh interest in conservation of our resources which is reflected both in mining methods and in by-producting. Fundamental research, improved methods of engineering, and better utilization of coal and coke—more and more the thoughtful men of the industry are turning, and will turn, to the scientists to help them with their problems.

Twenty years ago visitors to the coal fields were invariably astonished at what, from an engineering viewpoint, seemed frivolous methods of running so basic an industry. They were told that good engineers had little interest in coal mining. Graduates from our engineering schools who went down to the fields soon came back with stories of the ineffable boredom of the life around the pits, the lack of interest on the part of the operators in anything except quick profits, the patronizing attitude with which old coal men looked upon the "college kids." Even the technical schools in the neighborhood of such coal centers as Pittsburgh sent their graduates into steel rather than coal. Coal is today, as it was then, one of the hardest of taskmasters and the life of a coal camp is still no bed of roses. Now, however, new hard roads joining the camps with the larger towns and cities, electrification of the homes, and most of all perhaps, the technological revolution in mining itself, which calls for more intelligence in the handling of both men and machines, are factors making for a better life in the fields. Whenever coal operators gather today there is constant, often wistful discussion of the need for higher engineering skills in the mines. Out of it will come perhaps a better over-all planning.

"The tragedy of waste" in coal, underscored by Stuart Chase, Isador Lubin, Walter Polakov and other economists, is due in part to our conception of the coal resources of the United States as practically inexhaustible. Whereas the British people have long since been warned that the coal measures beneath their island are being mined to the point of exhaustion within a hundred-odd years, America's coal abundance and the fact that in normal times production lags far behind the capacity of our 6,000 or so mines, has led to a complacency which ignores conservation.

Veteran conservationists have lived to see the triumph of their ideas. An essential to the prosecution of a global war is the war on waste at home. In parts of the Appalachian fields shortages in high-grade coking coal are in sight and about 25 per cent of our anthracite has already been mined. These figures are not startling but they do indicate the need for the greatest possible use of our underground resources.

It is doubtful if in our times we will come to the rigid conservation controls exercised by other nations but there are features in the organization of foreign coal policies which cannot be ignored by those with an eye to our own future. In Germany, as far back as 1893, the government became an active party to a national coal monopoly, the Rheinisch-Westfalisches Kohlensyndikat. The syndicate controlled prices and production and was stabilized by an allocation of national requirements of workers, consumers and producers under control of the German Coal Council. With the advent of the Nazis, this setup, which had worked with remarkable success, was abandoned and the powers of the council taken over by the Reichs minister of Economy. Nazi bureaucrats promptly collided with industrialists in an attempt to bring all coal within the orbit of the totalitarian state. There was a confusion of orders and counterorders, with the large coal operators of the Saar mines, the steel magnates and the Krupps resisting sullenly.

Paul Hagen in *Will Germany Crack?* [4] quotes from the German *Year Book for Economy and Statistics* for 1941, as follows:

When the war broke out the coal situation in Germany was already under serious strain. The most important factor was the inadequacy of coal reserves for industrial and home consumption. Even coal distributors did not have especially large stocks. . . . It is simply not possible for coal production to keep up with the tempo of the rapidly growing needs.

[4] New York, Harper & Bros., 1942.

Steadily as the war progressed, despite the fact that by adding the mines of the conquered countries, Hitler controlled an estimated one-fifth of the world's immediately available coal supply, the fuel situation in the Reich grew worse. So that in 1942, Hagen figures there was an over-all coal deficit of some 20 per cent in conquered Europe, with France the hardest hit, and even the favored Reich suffering severely. Persistent sabotage on the part of the slave miners, always an easy matter in the darkness of the mine, the drafting of skilled men into the army, the overtaxing of transport, and the need for supplying "have-not" Italy and other noncoal-producing satellites—these led to constantly changing Nazi policies in regard to coal.

Writing in the New York *Times* of January 18, 1943, Hanson Baldwin estimated that the Reich's production of 4 million tons per year of synthetic oil required about 30 million tons of coal through the hydrogenation process and took the labor of some 50,000 miners in addition to 100,000 workers in the synthetic plants. In the summer of 1943, Dr. Egloff estimated that in the European countries controlled by the Axis more than 600,000 vehicles were being propelled by synthetic fuels produced from wood, wood charcoal, anthracite coal and lignite. The Germans were placing great reliance on the Fischer-Tropsch process of hydrogenation of coal. Our own and Britain's constant bombing of the Reich's industrial centers during the spring and summer of 1943 took a large force away from productive to repair work and upset the nice co-ordination of transport and coal essential to the mass use of synthetics. When the "Now It Can Be Told" books are written about wartime coal in Germany, the Nazis' worry over synthetics will unquestionably prove to have been a major factor in the breakup of her domestic morale.

Japan had been using coal in the synthetic chemical industry and experimenting in hydrogenation long before the first Japanese troops set forth on the Manchurian adventure. Her shortage in strategic minerals was a source of deep concern for both her military clique and the big industrialists. At Fushun, in conquered Manchuria, Japan set up extensive coal operations and built a plant to extract oil from the shales which form a capping to the coal seams. Japan's unexploited coal resources, estimated at 18 billion metric tons in Japan proper at the outset of the war, came under the control of the Coal Mining Union, a production cartel, the Showa Coal Company, a sales organization, and an association of smaller coal owners. This trio gave stability to the nation's entire fuel enterprise. The Mitsubishi Mining Company, which has set up records for manufacturing liquid fuels by low-temperature carbonization at its Naihoro plant, the Mitsui and other smaller holding companies were still functioning at last reports but functioning, of course, with the consent and under the control of the military which invokes the mobilization act of 1938 for the domination of all the economic resources of the islands.

China's coal wealth is in its unexploited reserves estimated as adequate for the country's needs for years to come even with rapid industrial expansion. With China and the United States, Soviet Russia is at the top in regard to sufficiency of coal in the future. Ninety per cent of the Soviet's coal reserves are said to be in Siberia, safe from invasion, and there is a constant and intensive search for new coal measures. The Soviets claim that as a result of past discoveries conducted by their prospectors the coal reserves have been greatly increased in the past twenty-five years. Just before the war, the annual production of coal in the Soviet Union was estimated at 146,800,000 tons.

In Soviet Russia before the war, more than 54 per cent of all Ukrainian coal was mined in the Donetz Basin of the Ukraine. Many American coal diggers, sympathetic to the regime, inspected these mines and returned with the usual conflicting stories told by all visitors to the Soviet Union. Our miners had very little regard for the productive capacity of the average Russian miner. On the other hand, they were impressed by the possibilities for the co-ordination of coal with the chemical and dye industries situated in the Basin and particularly with the largest hydroelectric development in Europe, the Lening Hydroelectric Station at Dnieprostroi, on the Dnieper River. This $110 million enterprise, erected under the supervision of American engineers, was an important part of Lenin's plan for "socialism as the Soviet power, plus electrification." In 1941 before the advancing German invaders, the Red Army dynamited parts of the great dam, but there are stories of similar projects where coal is being co-ordinated, behind the Urals today. This tie-up of "white" coal and black together with the chemical industries in planned industrial areas excites the imagination of the "men who make the future," as Bruce Bliven calls our researchers.

On the democratic side of the fence, Great Britain has blazed many trials toward increasing social controls of the industry. The sickness of Britain's coal was dramatized by the hearings of the Sankey Commission after World War I. In the Robing Room men from the pits, angry, despairing men, ill-housed, ill-fed, ill-clad, faced the coalmasters of England with demands for nationalization of the mines. Listening to both sides were public representatives, among them some of the leading intellectuals of Britain. The miners were bitter over the manner in which they felt that the politicians had let them down. British trade-unionists had been promised that if they would forgo insistence upon standards during the war, at the conclusion of hostilities the government would embark upon a genuine program of economic reconstruction. Then Lloyd George's snap election of 1918, which caught the British Labour party napping, apparently cancelled this promise. Obdurate British coalmasters would deal with the union only under threats of strike. Coal reparations wrested from Germany by the Peace Treaty made matters worse.

The majority of the Coal Commission found in favor of the miners. Advocates of nationalization were jubilant, but there was to be no action on the commission's findings. All that those findings accomplished was to focus attention upon the tragic state of the miners and at the same time set the Conservatives planning against the increasing demand for outright nationalization of England's pits. Ramsay MacDonald's Labour government never got to the first steps toward nationalization. By 1926 the miners revolted against what were almost literally starvation wages. The struggle, starting in the remote fields, developed into the historic General Strike with railwaymen and transport workers and members of a hundred miscellaneous trades walking out in sympathy with the exploited miners. In the next year, the badly scared middle classes supported the Tories in passing the Trade Disputes Act which outlawed sympathy strikes on the scale of 1926, but which in no way affected the long-established methods of collective bargaining in British industry. The Coal Mines Act of 1930 set up a national industrial board for the settlement of disputes which could not be decided by the lower tribunals of pit committees, joint board and conciliation bodies.

A gesture toward nationalization was made not by any left-winger but by that stolid, pipe-smoking squire, the leader of the Tories, Prime

Minister Stanley Baldwin, when it was announced that the government would pay the British coalmasters £66,450,000 in return for the extinction of all future royalties. This amount was less than half of what the royalty takers were asking. Today half the British coal production is from operations whose leases do not expire until 1950, but measures advocated by Conservatives made it possible for the government increasingly to exercise controls without the raising of the dread cry of "socialism."

Coming back from a necessarily hasty survey of the manner in which other nations have tackled their coal problem, we find that in our own country the approaches to the matter of a cheap and abundant supply of the essential fuel have taken many forms from reliance on Providence to guide us by the light of free enterprise to the proposals for cartelization made at a crucial time in 1931 by hard-pressed operators and on to nationalization made repeatedly by the despairing workers in the industry.

Many commentators agree that the most ingenious device for stabilization was that of the Central Competitive Field. In this industry, where the payroll is the major item of cost of production and the breaking out of industrial disputes a constant menace to continuity of operation, it would seem the part of reason to make long-term contracts with the organized workers, granting a common wage level throughout competing territories.

At one time it was thought that through the union agreement it would be possible to plan production for a two-year period, at any rate, in a way that would give cheap fuel to the consumer and fair rewards to both employers and employees. With elaborated techniques of collective bargaining for the entire industry and effective machinery for the settling of disputes, there was reason for this optimism.

In Illinois, for example, at the heart of the old Central Competitive Field, the structure for the settlement of controversies between management and the working force was held up as a standard by those interested in the peaceful development of the industry. The grievances of the individual miner or miners were referred to a pit committee, usually consisting of three workers, sometimes only one, elected by the entire work force of the mine. The committee took up grievances with the mine foreman. If no settlement could be reached on the spot, the president of the Illinois subdistrict of the union brought the dispute before the mine superintendent. From there, if there was still no agreement, the grievance went before the Executive Board member of the Illinois District of the U.M.W. of A. and the operators' commissioner. Thence it might go to a joint board of operators and union representatives, and finally to arbitration by three neutral commission members whose decision was supposedly final.

"Independent action, however, did not disappear," as Waldo E. Fisher sadly comments in *How Collective Bargaining Works.* Mr. Fisher puts the blame for this "independent action"—i.e., strikes or lockouts—on both parties. "The cooperation of the operators," he writes, "has been characterized by reluctance. . . . The union leaders have frequently been uncompromising and at times unduly arrogant in dealing with union operators." Nevertheless, it is significant that in 1943 when the Central Competitive Fields had become "outlying districts" and attention was focused on the Appalachian Agreement, it was the Illinois operators who were first to come forward with a proposed contract with the United Mine Workers saying that in their experience union agreements signed over a number of years had proved a satisfactory stabilizing force.

As we have seen, the extension of the principles underlying the formation of the Central Competitive Field was put to a sudden end when unionization south of the Ohio River proved for a time to be impossible.

When it was evident that voluntary measures within the industry would not bring about the stabilization sought, while the nonunion fields of the South were taking the cream of the business from the organized competitive fields, the workers turned to their national government. The controls exercised by the second Guffey Act,[5] while they moved in the realms of markets and prices rather than wages and hours, went further than anything hitherto attempted in the line of administration from above. The Bituminous Coal Division, operating in the Department of the Interior, set prices and generally supervised production until the coming of the war. Although the division was originally a concept of the union, its activities, or rather lack of them, were caustically criticized by the union officials at the 1942 convention of the U.M.W. of A. The *United Mine Workers*

[5] See Appendix C.

Journal of December 1, 1942, summed up the union's criticism to the effect that:

> The Coal Division meekly surrendered its authority to fix prices and control the industry, permitting such control to pass to the Office of Price Administration without protest. With the passing of price fixing authority to the O.P.A. many mines closed down. In many instances maximum prices were fixed below minimum prices. The Coal Division which was expected to assert its authority and protect the industry against the burrocrats' strong-arm grab . . . failed to measure up to the industry's expectations.

In June, 1943, the Guffey Act died of the neglect of Congress to act on its extension or to consider the amended act put forward by the U.M.W. of A. This new measure would have the act administered by a permanent commission of three to be appointed by the President with the advice and consent of the Senate. On the commission would be a representative of the operators, a representative of the employees, and one from the consuming public. Both management and labor want sales prices fixed so as to allow for planning, and labor wants its own representative on the price-fixing body.

When the mines were taken over by the government on May 1, 1943, there was a great deal of confusion over the controls which the secretary of the interior, as custodian of the mines, would or could impose. The fighting word "nationalization" continually bobbed up in the course of the discussion to the obvious irritation of Secretary Ickes, who denied that he ever had any intention of "nationalizing the mines." As he proceeded, however, to set up what had every appearance of a permanent administration with regional directors of the department's own choosing and the operators relegated to the positions of salaried advisers, the conviction grew that Ickes, while compelled by law to return the mines, which had reached "productive levels," to the private owners at the expiration of three months after seizure, might be drawing up some blueprints for future reference.

The pained outcries of coal operators, utility and railroad executives and the editors of the New York *Times* at the mere mention of the forbidden word "nationalization" might suggest to the wayfaring man the advisability of looking into the entire subject. He is not likely to be frightened by the name of something that might bring peace to a most contentious industry and a low-cost, continuous and sufficient supply of the product of that industry to the bins of the consumers. Though no influential groups are now pressing for the nationalization of the mines and though the present Administration (Secretary Ickes excepted) in its eagerness to circumvent John L. Lewis could not get the mines back to their owners fast enough, the prospects for ultimate government ownership and operation are not to be casually dismissed in our calculations of coal's future. It may well be that even the most conservative postwar government (note the British experience) may have to undertake some sort of modified nationalization as an alternative to the continuation of the economic anarchy that has too long been the order of the day in coal. It will be recalled that Harding and Hoover, as well as the two Roosevelts, were compelled to intervene during crises in coal. The inevitable recurrence of these crises under the present policy of treating coal as the stepchild of industry may well lead to public acceptance of measures which now seem drastic indeed.

For the immediate future, however, nothing more drastic than a revival and possible expansion of the Guffey Act seems to be on the books. Both operators and miners are agreed that the industry must come under some sort of discipline if it is to meet successfully the stresses of postwar economics.

When the bitterness of the present controversies in coal abate, it is permissible to hope that there may be found in the industry and among the public those who will make arrangements for a national handling of the coal problem more advantageous to all concerned than the current ineptitudes. To be sure, this is a hope long deferred and the cause of great sickness of the heart. Yet the democratic spirit which has met such stern tests in the international field need not flinch when faced with a basic problem in an essential industry at home. Whatever the sum total of these arrangements may be called, it must comprehend a long-view, engineering attempt to end the physical wastes involved in the mining and distribution of coal. There must be elimination of antiquated methods of "robbing the coal" which result in robbing all of us of the full enjoyment of a precious natural resource. There must be closer co-ordination of coal, electrical power and transportation. Research on a far larger scale than anything yet attempted in this country is needed to bring coal to its full scientific and social stature. Above all, there must be a concerted attack upon the human problems involved. Planning for a good society in which coal can freely make its enormous contribution takes all the common sense, intelligence and adventuring imagination of which our democracy is capable. Men of good will may understand the significance of the challenge presented by the most frequently forgotten of all our industrial workers—the American coal miners.

APPENDICES

APPENDIX A

Coal Production in the U.S. 1900-1942

(Figures in thousands of net tons from U.S. Geological Survey and U.S. Bureau of Mines.)

Year	Bituminous	Anthracite	Year	Bituminous	Anthracite
1900	212,316	57.4	1921	415,921	90.5
1901	225,828	67.5	1922	422,268	54.7
1902	260,217	41.4	1923	564,564	93.3
1903	282,749	74.6	1924	483,686	87.9
1904	278,660	73.2	1925	520,052	61.8
1905	315,063	77.7	1926	573,366	84.4
1906	342,875	71.3	1927	517,763	80.1
1907	395,759	85.6	1928	500,744	75.3
1908	332,574	83.3	1929	534,988	73.8
1909	379,744	81.1	1930	467,526	69.4
1910	417,111	84.5	1931	382,089	59.6
1911	405,907	90.5	1932	309,709	49.9
1912	450,105	84.4	1933	338,630	49.5
1913	478,435	91.5	1934	359,368	57.2
1914	422,704	90.8	1935	372,373	52.2
1915	442,624	89.0	1936	439,087	54.6
1916	502,520	87.6	1937	445,531	51.9
1917	551,791	99.6	1938	348,544	46.1
1918	579,386	98.8	1939	393,065	51.5
1919	465,860	88.1	1940	453,245	51.5
1920	568,666	89.6	1941	450,864	56.4
			1942 (est.) 580,308	60.0

NOTE: The estimated value of the total tonnage of 1939 was $732,-534,000. Figures for competing fuels show an increase from 1900, when 63.5 million barrels of crude petroleum were produced, to more than 1 billion in 1941. Natural gas production has increased from 225 billion cubic feet in 1900 to 2,770 billion in 1941.

APPALACHIAN JOINT WAGE AGREEMENT

EFFECTIVE APRIL 1, 1941, TO MARCH 31, 1943
EXECUTED IN THE CITY OF WASHINGTON, D. C., JUNE 19, 1941

APPALACHIAN AGREEMENT

Washington, D. C.

THIS AGREEMENT, made the 19th day of June, 1941, between the Central Pennsylvania Coal Producers' Association, Georges Creek and Upper Potomac Coal Association, Somerset County Coal Operators' Association, Western Pennsylvania Coal Operators' Association, Ohio Coal Association, Michigan Coal Operators' Association, Northern Panhandle of West Virginia Coal Operators' Association, Northern West Virginia Coal Association, Operators' Association of Williamson Field, Big Sandy-Elkhorn Coal Operators' Association, Hazard Coal Operators' Association, Kanawha Coal Operators' Association, Logan Coal Operators' Association, Southern Appalachian Coal Operators' Association, New River Coal Operators' Association, Pocahontas Operators' Association, Winding Gulf Operators' Association, Greenbrier Coal Operators' Association, Upper Buchanan Smokeless Coal Operators' Association, Harlan County Coal Operators' Association, and Virginia Coal Operators' Association, voluntary associations on behalf of each member thereof, hereinafter referred to as the Operators, party of the first part, and the International Union, United Mine Workers of America, and Districts 2, 3, 4, 5, 6, 16, 17, 19, 24, 28, 30 and 31, hereinafter referred to as the Mine Workers and on behalf of each member thereof, party of the second part. (New Districts of the United Mine Workers of America may be established in this territory.)

WITNESSETH: It is agreed that this contract is for the exclusive joint use and benefit of the contracting parties as heretofore defined and set forth in this Agreement. It is agreed that the United Mine Workers of America is recognized herein as the exclusive bargaining agency representing the employes of the parties of the first part. It is agreed that as a condition of employment, all employes shall be members of the United Mine Workers of America, except in those exempted classifications of employment as provided in this contract. (See Note.) It is the intent and purpose of the parties hereto that this Agreement will promote an improved industrial and economic relationship in the bituminous coal industry, and to set forth herein the basic agreements covering rates of pay, hours of work, and conditions of employment to be observed between the parties in the following Districts constituting the Appalachian territory:

NOTE: The amendments to the enabling clause of the Basic Agreement, covering recognition of the United Mine Workers of America, do not change the rules or practices of the industry pertaining to management. The Mine Workers intend no intrusion upon the rights of management as heretofore practiced and understood.

Appalachian Territory—Pennsylvania, Michigan, Ohio, Maryland, West Virginia, Virginia, Northern Tennessee, and that part of Kentucky lying east of a line drawn north and south through the City of Louisville.

Maximum Hours and Working Time

Seven hours of labor shall constitute a day's work. The seven-hour day means seven hours' work in the mines at the usual working places for all classes of labor, exclusive of the lunch period, whether they be paid by the day or be paid on the tonnage basis; except in cases of accident which temporarily necessitates longer hours for those Mine Workers required on account thereof; and also excepting that number of Mine Workers in each mine whose daily work includes the handling of man-trips and those who are required to remain on duty while men are entering and leaving the mine.

OVERTIME: Work by Mine Workers paid by hour or day in excess of seven (7) hours in one day or thirty-five (35) hours in any one week, shall be paid for at the rate of time and one-half with the following exceptions:

Employes engaged at power houses, substations, and pumps operating continuously for twenty-four (24) hours daily are especially exempted from the seven (7) hour day and the time and one-half provisions. Special exemptions for individual employes other than those named above when twenty-four (24) hours continuous operation daily is required are subject to arrangement between the mine management and District officers without time and one-half for overtime. Employes so especially exempted are limited to eight (8) hours per day and forty (40) hours per week and time and one-half for time worked in excess thereof.

The seven (7) hour day, five (5) day week (35 hours per week) as provided in this Agreement, shall prevail.

The following classes of Mine Workers are excepted from the foregoing provisions as to the maximum hours of work.

All Mine Workers engaged in the transportation of men and coal shall work the additional time necessary to handle man-trips and all coal in transit and shall be paid the regular hourly rate for the first seven (7) hours and time and one-half for all overtime.

Outside employes engaged in the dumping, handling and preparation of coal, and the manufacture of coke, shall work the additional time necessary, not to exceed thirty (30) minutes, to dump and prepare the coal delivered to the tipple each shift, and complete the usual duties incidental to the operation of coke ovens, and shall be paid the regular hourly rates for the first seven (7) hours and time and one-half for overtime not to exceed the thirty (30) minutes hereinbefore stated.

When day men go into the mine in the morning, they shall be entitled to two hours' pay whether or not the mine works the full two hours, but after the first two hours, the men shall be paid for every hour thereafter by the hour, for each hour's work or fractional part thereof. If, for any reason, the regular routine work cannot be furnished inside day men, the employer may furnish other than the regular work.

Drivers shall take their mules to and from stables, and the time required in so doing shall not include any part of the day's labor, their work beginning when they reach the change at which they receive empty cars, but in no case shall the driver's time be docked while he is waiting for such cars at the point named. The method at present existing covering the harnessing and unharnessing of mules shall be continued throughout the life of this Agreement.

Motormen and trip riders shall be at the passway where they receive the cars at starting time. The time required to take motors to the passway at starting time and departing from the same at quitting time shall not be regarded as a part of the day's labor, their time beginning when they reach the change or parting at which they receive cars, but in no case shall their time be docked while waiting for cars at the point named.

Holidays

Holidays now recognized in various District Agreements shall be effective during the period of this Agreement.

Basic Tonnage Rates

Pick mining is the removal by the miner of coal that has not been undercut, centercut or overcut by a machine. The basic rate for pick mining and hand loading of coal shall include the work required to drill, shoot and clean and load the coal properly, timber the working place, and all other work and customs incidental thereto.

A maximum shortwall machine differential of eleven cents (11c) per net ton between pick and machine mining rates shall be maintained. The minimum rate for pick mining shall not be less than the aggregate of shortwall machine cutting and loading rates.

Any change in mining methods or installation of equipment that relieves the Mine Worker of any of the above duties and increases his productive capacity shall be recognized and a piecework rate agreed to therefor properly related to the basic rate.

The standard for basic tonnage rates shall be 2,000 pounds per ton; where the gross ton of 2,240 pounds is the measure, the equivalent rate shall be paid.

The basic tonnage, hourly and day wage rates for the various producing Districts represented in this conference are shown in the attached schedules which are parts hereof.

Yardage and deadwork rates in all Districts shall be increased fifteen per cent (15%).

Checkweighmen

The Mine Workers shall have the right to a checkweighman, of their own choosing, to inspect the weighing of coal; provided that in any case where on account of physical conditions and mutual agreement, wages are based on measure or other method than on actual weights, the Mine Workers shall have the right to check the accuracy and fairness of such method, by a representative of their own choosing.

Cars shall be tared at reasonable intervals and without inconvenience to the operation of the mine. Tare shall be taken of the cars in their usual running condition.

At mines not employing a sufficient number of men to maintain a checkweighman, the weight credited to the Mine Worker shall be checked against the billing weights furnished by railroads to the Operators, and on coal trucked from such mines a practical method to check the weights shall be agreed upon. Such weights shall be checked once a month.

The wages of checkweighmen will be collected through the pay office semi-monthly, upon a statement of time made by the checkweighmen, and approved by the Mine Committee. The amount so collected shall be deducted on a percentage basis, agreed upon by the checkweighman and clerk, from the earnings of the Mine Workers engaged in mining coal and shall be sufficient only to pay the wages and legitimate expenses incident to the office.

If a suitable person to act as checkweighman is not available among the Mine Workers at the mine, a man not employed at the mine may be selected upon mutual agreement.

The checkweighman, or checkmeasurer, as the case may require, shall be permitted at all times to be present at the weighing or measuring of coal, also have power to checkweigh or checkmeasure the same, and during the regular working hours to have the privilege to balance and examine the scales or measure the cars, providing that all such balancing and examination of scales shall only be done in such a way and at such time as in no way to interfere with the regular working of the mine. It shall be the further duty of checkweighman or checkmeasurer to credit each Mine Worker with all merchantable coal mined by him on a proper sheet or book kept by him for that purpose. Checkweighmen or checkmeasurers shall in no way interfere with the operation of the mine.

Boys

No person under seventeen (17) years of age shall be employed inside any mine nor in hazardous occupations outside any mine; provided, however, that where a state law provides a higher minimum age, the state law shall govern.

Exemptions Under This Contract

The term Mine Worker as used in this Agreement shall not include mine foremen, assistant mine foremen, fire bosses, or bosses in charge of any classes of labor inside or outside of the mine, or coal inspectors or weighbosses, watchmen, clerks, or members of the executive, supervisory, sales and technical forces of the Operators.

Management of Mines

The management of the mine, the direction of the working force, and the right to hire and discharge are vested exclusively in the Operator, and the United Mine Workers of America shall not abridge these rights. It is not the intention of this provision to encourage the discharge of Mine Workers, or the refusal of employment to applicants because of personal prejudice or activity in matters affecting the United Mine Workers of America.

Mine Committee

A committee of three (3) Mine Workers, who shall be able to speak and understand the English language, shall be elected at each mine by the Mine Workers employed at such mine. Each member of the Mine Committee shall be an employe of the mine at which he is a committee member, and shall be eligible to serve as a committee member only so long as he continues to be an employe of said mine. The duties of the Mine Committee shall be confined to the adjustment of disputes arising out of this Agreement that the mine management and the Mine Worker, or Mine Workers, have failed to adjust. The Mine Committee shall have no other authority or exercise any other control, nor in any way interfere with the operation of the mine; for violation of this clause any or all members of the Committee may be removed from the Committee.

Settlement of Disputes

Should differences arise between the Mine Workers and the Operator as to the meaning and application of the provisions of this Agreement, or should differences arise about matters not specifically mentioned in this Agreement, or should any local trouble of any kind arise at any mine, there shall be no suspension of work on account of such differences, but an earnest effort shall be made to settle such differences immediately:

First: Between the aggrieved party and the mine management;

Second: Through the management of the mine and the Mine Committee;

Third: By a Board consisting of four members, two of whom shall be designated by the Mine Workers and two by the Operators.

Should the Board fail to agree, the matter shall be referred to an umpire selected by said Board. Should the Board be unable to agree on the selection of an umpire, he shall be designated by the International President of the United Mine Workers of America and the President of the Operators' Association affected. The decision of the umpire in any event shall be final.

District Conferences may establish an intermediate board consisting of two (2) commissioners, one representing the Operators and one representing the Mine Workers with such powers as said Conference may delegate.

Pending the hearing of disputes, the Mine Workers shall not cease work because of any dispute; and a decision reached at any stage of the proceeding shall be binding on both parties hereto, and shall not be subject to reopening by any other party or branch of either association except by mutual agreement.

Expense and salary incident to the services of an umpire shall be paid jointly by the Operators and Mine Workers in each District.

Discharge Cases

When a Mine Worker has been discharged from his employment and he believes he has been unjustly dealt with, it shall be a case arising under the method of settling disputes herein provided. In all discharge cases should it be decided under the rules of this Agreement that an injustice has been dealt the Mine Worker, the Operator shall reinstate and compensate him at the rate based on the earning of said Mine Worker prior to such discharge; provided, however, that such case shall be taken up and disposed of within five (5) days from the date of discharge.

Illegal Suspension of Work

A strike or stoppage of work on the part of the Mine Workers shall be a violation of this Agreement. Under no circumstances shall the Operator discuss the matter under dispute with the Mine Committee or any representative of the United Mine Workers of America during suspension of work in violation of this Agreement.

Irregular Work

When any Mine Worker absents himself from his work for a period of two days without the consent of the Operator, other than because of proven sickness, he may be discharged.

Preparation of Coal and Mining Practice

Each District agreement shall provide for the preparation and proper cleaning of coal. Proper disciplinary rules and penalties shall also be incorporated in such agreements.

Reject clauses providing as follows shall be eliminated from all District agreements:

"At mines, where, in order to maintain and improve the earnings of both the loaders and the cutters, and where it is impracticable to maintain loader earnings if all the impurities were removed underground, certain portions of those impurities are loaded and rejected either by hand or mechanical methods at the tipple.

"The question of rejects shall be referred to the local Mine Committee who shall, with the mine management, determine the amount and quantity of rejects that reach the coal producers' tipples and cleaning plants and an adjustment shall be made in the tare weight of the mine car sufficient to cover this amount and quantity. Should a disagreement ensue, it shall be handled as any dispute arising under this contract. Operators accepting this plan agree to eliminate the practice of docking for impurities as applying to individual workers."

All reject clauses of a similar character shall be eliminated from District agreements.

Vacations With Pay

An annual vacation period shall be the rule of the industry. From Saturday, June 28, 1941, to Monday, July 7, inclusive, shall be a vacation period, during which coal production shall cease. Day men required to work during this period at coke plants and other necessary continuous operations or on emergency or repair work shall have vacations at other agreed periods.

Employes whose employment record is less than one year in duration shall not be entitled to pay during the aforesaid vacation period. All employes with a record of more than one year's standing shall receive as compensation for the vacation period the sum of twenty dollars ($20.00).

In 1942, the same arrangement shall prevail; the vacation beginning on Saturday, June 27, and continuing until Monday, July 6, inclusive.

Proper rules and regulations to give effect to this stipulation are referred to the District Conferences.

Safety Practices

Reasonable rules and regulations of the Operator for the protection of the persons of the Mine Workers and the preservation of property shall be complied with.

At each mine there shall be a Safety Committee. This Committee shall be designated by the District President of the United Mine Workers of America, who shall also have authority to change its personnel. Its membership shall consist of a maximum of six Mine Workers, not less than 40 years of age and not less than 15 years' experience. No member of the Mine Committee shall be a member of the Safety Committee. The Safety Committee shall serve without compensation.

This Committee shall have the right to inspect any mine development or equipment used in producing coal, for the purpose of observing its safe or unsafe condition when such questions are brought to its attention. If the Committee believe conditions found are dangerous to life, it shall report its findings to management.

The International Union, United Mine Workers of America, may designate Memorial periods provided it shall give proper notice to each District.

Engineer and Pumpers' Duties

When required by the management, engineers, pumpers, firemen, power plant and substation attendants shall under no conditions suspend work but shall at all times protect all the company's property under their care, and operate fans and pumps and lower and hoist men or supplies as may be required to protect the company's coal plant.

Shifts

The Operator shall have the right during the entire period of this Agreement to work all the mines, or any one or more of them, extra shifts with different crews.

When the mine works only one shift it shall be in the day time, but this shall not prevent cutting and loading at night in addition to the day shift cutting and loading.

Seniority

Seniority, in principle and practice as it has been recognized in the industry, is not modified or changed by this Agreement.

Seniority affecting return to employment of idle employes on a basis of length of service and qualification for the respective positions brought about by different mining methods or installation of mechanical equipment is recognized. Men displaced by new mining methods or installation of new mechanical equipment so long as they remain unemployed shall constitute a panel from which new employes shall be selected.

District Conferences shall arrange to incorporate in the several District agreements such rules and formulae as may be necessary to implement and effectuate this provision.

Pay Day

Pay shall be made semi-monthly and at least twice each month. Payment shall be made in cash or par check, with recognition for legitimate deductions. This is designed only to prohibit the discounting of earnings through the use of scrip or tokens.

Coke and Cleaning Plants

Proper rules may be negotiated in District Conferences to provide for continuous operation of coking and cleaning plants.

Medical and Hospitalization Services

All medical and hospitalization questions where Mine Workers make contributions are referred to District Conferences to make satisfactory mutual arrangement.

Physical Examination

Physical examination, required as a condition of or in employment, shall not be used other than to determine the physical condition or to contribute to the health and well-being of the employe or employes. The retention or displacement of employes because of physical conditions shall not be used for the purpose of effecting discrimination.

House Rents

Equitable adjustment of house rents shall be made in District Conferences.

Miscellaneous Provisions

Matters affecting cost of explosives, blacksmithing, electric cap lamps, and house coal are referred to the District Conferences.

To the extent it has been the custom in each District, all bottom coal shall be taken up and loaded by the Mine Workers.

The cutter shall cut the coal as directed by the Operator.

District Conferences

District agreements shall be made dealing with local or District conditions, and it is agreed that such District agreements shall embody the basic rates of pay, hours of work and conditions of employment herein set forth, and all specific rights and obligations of Operators and Mine Workers herein recognized.

This Agreement shall supersede all existing and previous contracts; and all local rules, regulations and customs heretofore established in conflict with this Agreement are hereby abolished. Prior practice and custom not in conflict with this agreement may be continued.

All internal differences are hereby referred to the various Districts for settlement, with the understanding that only by mutual consent shall anything be done in District Conferences that will increase the cost of production or decrease the earning capacity of the men.

Proper arrangements for collections for the United Mine Workers of America shall be made in District Conferences.

Protective Wage Clause

If the United Mine Workers of America make a wage agreement during said period covering wages or working conditions with any person, association, or District within the Appalachian Area, on a basis more favorable than above, then this Agreement shall be modified so that all parties to the Appalachian Agreement shall receive all the benefits of such more favorable wage agreement. The International Union, United Mine Workers of America, reserve the right to call and maintain strikes throughout the entire Appalachian Area when necessary to preserve and maintain the integrity and competitive parity of this Agreement. Such strikes shall not be deemed a violation of this Agreement. The International Union will give reasonable notice to all parties of any such action.

Appalachian Joint Conference

A Joint Conference of representatives of the Central Pennsylvania Coal Producers' Association, Georges Creek and Upper Potomac Association, Somerset County Coal Operators' Association, Western Pennsylvania Coal Operators' Association, Ohio Coal Association, Michigan Coal Operators' Association, Northern Panhandle of West Virginia Coal Operators' Association, Northern West Virginia Coal Association, Operators' Association of the Williamson Field, Big Sandy-Elkhorn Coal Operators' Association, Hazard Coal Operators' Association, Kanawha Coal Operators' Association, Logan Coal Operators' Association, Southern Appalachian Coal Operators' Association, New River Coal Operators' Association, Pocahontas Operators' Association, Winding Gulf Operators' Association, Greenbrier Coal Operators' Association, Upper Buchanan Smokeless Coal Operators' Association, Harlan County Coal Operators' Association, Virginia Coal Operators' Association, and the International Union, United Mine Workers of America, and Districts 2, 3, 4, 5, 6, 16, 17, 19, 24, 28, 30 and 31, shall be held in The Biltmore Hotel, City of New York, New York, March 14, 1943, to consider what revisions, if any, shall be made in this Agreement as to hours, wages and conditions of employment.

This Agreement shall become effective April 1, 1941, and shall continue in effect to March 31, 1943.

IN WITNESS WHEREOF, each of the parties hereto, pursuant to proper authority, has caused this agreement to be signed by its proper officers.

United Mine Workers of America	Operators
By JOHN L. LEWIS, President	EZRA VAN HORN, Joint Chairman,
PHILIP MURRAY, Vice President	Appalachian Joint Conference
THOMAS KENNEDY, Sec.-Treas.	Central Pennsylvania Coal Producers' Association
District No. 2	
By JAMES MARK	

District No. 3
By FRANK HUGHES
District No. 4
By WILLIAM HYNES
District No. 5
By P. T. FAGAN
District No. 6
By JOHN OWENS
District No. 16
By JOHN T. JONES
District No. 17
By VAN A. BITTNER
District No. 19
By WILLIAM TURNBLAZER
District No. 24
By JOHN HATTON
District No. 28
By JOHN SAXTON
District No. 30
By SAM CADDY
District No. 31
By C. F. DAVIS

By CHARLES O'NEIL, President
WALTER A. JONES, Sec.-Treas.
Georges Creek & Upper Potomac
Coal Association
By
Somerset County Coal Operators'
Association
By E. A. SEEMON, Vice President
MARTIN L. MARKEL, Secretary
Western Pennsylvania Coal Operators' Association
By RALPH E. JAMISON, President
BYRON H. CANON, Secretary
Ohio Coal Association
By R. L. IRELAND, JR., President
E. H. MILLER, Secretary
Michigan Coal Operators' Association
By JOHN A. CORYELL, President
Per H. W. BEAN
Northern Panhandle of West Virginia Coal Operators' Association
By O. B. PRYOR, President and
Secretary
Northern West Virginia Coal Association
By WILLIAM FINDLAY, President
T. E. JOHNSON, Secretary-
Treasurer
Operators' Association of Williamson Field
By
Big Sandy-Elkhorn Coal Operators'
Association
By
Hazard Coal Operators' Association
By
Kanawha Coal Operators' Association
By
Logan Coal Operators' Association
By

Southern Appalachian Coal Operators' Association
By

New River Coal Operators' Association
By

Pocahontas Operators' Association
By

Winding Gulf Operators' Association
By

Greenbrier Coal Operators' Association
By

Upper Buchanan Smokeless Coal Operators' Association
By

Harlan County Coal Operators' Association
By

Virginia Coal Operators' Association
By

SCHEDULE A

Basic Tonnage Rates established in the following named Districts:

WESTERN PENNSYLVANIA

Tonnage Rates
Per 2,000 Lbs.
Run of Mine Coal

Pick Mining, Thin Vein	$1.10
Pick Mining, Thick Vein	1.05
Machine Loading, Thin Vein	.87
Machine Loading, Thick Vein	.83
Cutting Shortwall Machine, Thin Vein	.12
Cutting Shortwall Machine, Thick Vein	.11

CENTRAL PENNSYLVANIA

Pick Mining	1.10
Machine Loading	.87
Cutting, Shortwall Machine	.12

SOUTHERN SOMERSET COUNTY, PENNSYLVANIA

Tonnage Rates
Per 2,000 Lbs.
Run of Mine Coal

Pick Mining	$1.10
Machine Loading	.87
Cutting, Shortwall Machine	.12

CONNELLSVILLE, PENNSYLVANIA

Pick Mining	.96
Machine Loading	.75
Cutting, Shortwall Machine	.10

WESTMORELAND-GREENSBURG, PENNSYLVANIA

Pick Mining	1.05
Machine Loading	.83
Cutting, Shortwall Machine	.11

THICK VEIN FREEPORT, PENNSYLVANIA

Pick Mining	1.05
Machine Loading	.83
Cutting, Shortwall Machine	.11

NORTHERN WEST VIRGINIA

Pick Mining	.96
Machine Loading	.775
Cutting, Shortwall Machine	.105

OHIO AND PANHANDLE DISTRICT OF NORTHERN WEST VIRGINIA

Pick Mining	1.10
Machine Loading	.87
Cutting, Shortwall Machine	.12

MICHIGAN

Pick Mining	1.312
Machine Loading	1.041
Cutting, Shortwall Machine	.171

MARYLAND AND UPPER POTOMAC DISTRICT, INCLUDING GRANT, MINERAL AND TUCKER COUNTIES OF WEST VIRGINIA

All Seams Except Bakerstown and Waynesburg

Machine Loading	.80
Cutting, Shortwall Machine	.12

BAKERSTOWN SEAM

Tonnage Rates
Per 2,000 Lbs.
Run of Mine Coal

Pick Mining $1.08
Machine Loading .... .92
Cutting, Shortwall Machine .... .12

WAYNESBURG SEAM

Pick Mining 1.08
Machine Loading .... .87
Cutting, Shortwall Machine .... .12

KANAWHA

Machine Loading .... .772
Cutting, Shortwall Machine .... .11

LOGAN

Machine Loading .... .682
Cutting, Shortwall Machine .... .092

WILLIAMSON

Machine Loading .... .708
Cutting, Shortwall Machine .... .096

BIG SANDY-ELKHORN

Machine Loading .... .815
Cutting, Shortwall Machine .... .12

HAZARD

Machine Loading .... .752
Cutting, Shortwall Machine .... .12

HARLAN

Machine Loading .... .76
Cutting, Shortwall Machine .... .11

VIRGINIA

Machine Loading .... .758
Cutting, Shortwall Machine .... .107

SOUTHERN APPALACHIAN

Machine Loading .... .78
Cutting, Shortwall Machine .... .12

NEW RIVER

Tonnage Rates
Per 2,000 Lbs.
Run of Mine Coal

Machine Loading .... $ .792
Cutting, Shortwall Machine .... .115

POCAHONTAS-TUG RIVER

Machine Loading .... .707
Cutting, Shortwall Machine .... .085

WINDING GULF

Machine Loading .... .734
Cutting, Shortwall Machine .... .11

GREENBRIER

Machine Loading .... .742
Cutting, Shortwall Machine .... .095

UPPER BUCHANAN

Machine Loading .... .708
Cutting, Shortwall Machine .... .096

Cutting rates on track mounted machines shall be increased seventy per cent (70%) of the shortwall cutting machine rate increase in each District, or seven-tenths cents (.007) per ton.

Where tonnage, footage or yardage rates are paid on conveyors or other mechanical loading devices, the percentage of increase to be added to such rates shall be the same percentage of increase as is applied to the basic shortwall loading and cutting rates.

SCHEDULE B

The following classifications and rates of pay shall prevail at all mines in the Appalachian Area:

(1) GENERAL DAY LABOR CLASSIFICATIONS

INSIDE

	Hourly Rate	Day Rate
Motormen, Rock Driller, Rubber Tired Shuttle Car Operator	$1.023	$7.16
Drivers, Brakemen, Spraggers, Snappers, Coal Drillers, Trackmen, Wiremen Bonders, Timbermen, Bottom Cagers	1.00	7.00
Pumpers, Trackmen Helpers, Wiremen Helpers, Timbermen Helpers, and Other Inside Labor not classified	.966	6.76
Greasers, Trappers, Flaggers, Switch Throwers	.736	5.15

OUTSIDE

Bit Sharpener, Car Dropper, Trimmer, Car Repairmen, Dumpers	.891	6.24
Sand Dryers, Car Cleaners, Other Able-bodied Labor	.857	6.00
Slate Pickers	.736	5.15

Skilled labor not classified to be paid in accordance with the custom at the mine.

(2) CLASSIFICATION OF MOBILE LOADING MACHINE RATES

Loading Machine Operators	1.286	9.00
Loading Machine Operator's Helpers	1.137	7.96
Cutting and Shearing Machine Operators	1.286	9.00
Cutting and Shearing Machine Operator's Helpers	1.286	9.00

All other Mine Workers employed on a day or hourly rate in mobile loading machine operations shall be paid according to the rates set forth in the General Day Labor Classifications.

(3) DAY RATES OF PAY ON CONVEYORS

Leader or Cutting Machine Operator and All Other Face men	1.114	7.80
Unloading Operator or Boom Man	1.00	7.00
The rates of pay for moving conveyor from one place to a new setup shall be at the rate of	1.00	7.00

(4) DAY RATES FOR ROCK LOADING EQUIPMENT

Rates of pay for Mine Workers on rock loading equipment shall be the same as those prescribed for men employed on conveyors loading coal by the day.

All other Mine Workers employed on a day or hourly rate on coal conveyors or rock loading equipment as set forth in Subsections (3) and (4) shall be paid according to the rates set forth in the General Day Labor classifications.

(5) STRIP MINE WAGES

Mine Workers employed in strip mines or pits shall receive increases on day, hourly and monthly rates in conformity with the application of the $1.40 per day or $1.00 per day as it was applied to Mine Workers in deep mines. The adjustment of these rates is referred to the respective District Conferences.

Explanatory Memorandum

Explanatory memorandum in re the Appalachian wage Agreement dated May 12, 1939, made by John L. Lewis, President of the United Mine Workers of America, to the Appalachian Joint Conference, is also appended to this Agreement:

The United Mine Workers of America agree that any expulsion or suspension from membership of an individual under the changed terms of the enabling clause of this Agreement shall be reviewed by the Executive Board of the International Union, United Mine Workers of America, before any individual employed is deprived of his employment.

With reference to the sentence in the enabling clause stating that all employes shall "be" members of the United Mine Workers of America, the word "be" is used in its future tense, and the clause so noted becomes effective and operative after an individual has been employed and starts to work.

Memorandum of Understanding Affecting Vacation Clause of Appalachian Joint Agreement, Executed in Washington, D. C. on June 19, 1941

In consideration of denuded domestic coal reserves and as a contribution to the success of the National Defense Program, it is agreed that the vacation period shall be curtailed as follows, as affecting the year, 1941, and without prejudice or modification of the existing vacation clause of the agreement:

The mines shall continue in operation on Saturday, June 28, and continue in operation Monday, June 30, Tuesday, July 1, and

Wednesday, July 2. The curtailed vacation period shall be effective as of Thursday, July 3rd, July 4, July 5, July 6 and July 7th, inclusive. This arrangement shall in no wise affect the token payment of $20.00 to be made by all coal companies to each individual, in conformity with the terms of the Appalachian Agreement.

The above payment to individual Mine Workers, entitled to vacation, shall be made at the option of the employing coal company, except that in all cases, full payment of the amount prescribed shall be made not later than the last pay day occurring in the month of July, 1941.

The vacation payment for the 1942 period shall be made on the last pay day occurring in the month of June of that year.

Negotiating Committee Appalachian Joint Conference

Operators	United Mine Workers of America
CHARLES O'NEILL	JOHN L. LEWIS
J. B. MORROW	PHILIP MURRAY
EZRA VAN HORN, Chairman	THOMAS KENNEDY
	JAMES MARK
	FRANK HUGHES
	WILLIAM HYNES
	P. T. FAGAN
	JOHN OWENS
	JOHN HATTON
	C. F. DAVIS
	JOHN T. JONES

[SEAL]

SUPPLEMENTARY WAGE AGREEMENT BETWEEN ILLINOIS COAL OPERATORS ASSOCIATION, DISTRICT 12 AND THE INTERNATIONAL UNION, UNITED MINE WORKERS OF AMERICA—RETROACTIVE TO APRIL 1, 1943, AND CONTINUING UNTIL MARCH 31, 1945

It is hereby agreed by and between the Illinois Coal Operators Association, the International Union, United Mine Workers of America, and District 12, United Mine Workers of America, that the Wage Agreement between the above-named parties, made and entered into as of April 1, 1941, and effective to and including March 31, 1943, as heretofore amended and supplemented by Supplemental Agreement, dated February 11, 1943, be and it hereby is extended from April 1, 1943 to and including March 31,

1945, upon the same terms and conditions therein contained, as heretofore so amended and supplemented, except as follows:

1. By reason of the emergency of war and as a contribution to the public welfare it is agreed that an additional one hour per day work time shall be added to the present basic seven-hour workday making an eight-hour operating shift for each mine unit, except when lack of market demand, breakdown of equipment, accidents, shortage of transportation, acts of God, or other causes beyond the control of the operator or operators prevent; *Provided,* however, that lack of market demand shall not permit the operators to operate on less than an eight-hour shift. The established rates of pay shall be continued for the first seven hours of each operating day except the sixth operating day of each week, and time and one-half and rate and one-half shall be paid for the eighth hour of each workday except the sixth operating day of each week; and for all hours worked on the sixth operating day of each week time and one-half and rate and one-half shall be paid. This paragraph shall not be construed to require payment of time and one-half or rate and one-half on Saturday if the individual mine worker has voluntarily laid off on Monday, Tuesday, Wednesday, Thursday or Friday of such week.

All employes at mines working six days per week shall be given a fair and equal opportunity to work on each of such six days. Laying off individual mine workers during the week for the purpose of denying them six days' work is prohibited during the term of this Supplemental Agreement.

2. The tonnage, yardage and dead work rates shall be the existing tonnage, yardage and dead work rates for seven-eighths of the tonnage, yardage and dead work for each day plus rate and one-half for the remaining one-eighth of the tonnage, yardage and dead work.

3. The Inside Day Wage Scale for able-bodied trappers, flaggers and switch-throwers (to answer telephone when required) (based on the seven-hour workday) shall be not less than $6.00.

The Inside Day Wage Scale for able-bodied greasers (based on the seven-hour workday) shall be not less than $6.75.

4. The Outside Day Wage Scale for able-bodied slate-pickers (based on the seven-hour workday) shall be not less than $6.00.

5. The provisions relating to vacations with pay are hereby amended to substitute, at the appropriate places therein, fifty ($50.00) dollars for twenty ($20.00) dollars.

In the interest of the National war effort, it is agreed that the vacation period shall be eliminated for the year 1943 without prejudice to or modification of the existing vacation clause of the Agreement. This arrangement shall in no wise affect the payment of fifty ($50.00) dollars to be paid by all operators to each individual in conformity with the terms of the Agreement.

The above payment to individual mine workers, entitled to vacation, shall be made at the option of the employing operator, except that in all cases full payment of the amount prescribed shall be made not later than the last pay day occurring in the month of June, 1943.

The vacation payment for the 1944 period shall be made on the last pay day occurring in the month of June of that year.

6. After the effective date of this Supplemental Agreement the operators shall furnish all mine workers' tools at the operators' cost. At the option of each tonnage mine worker the operator shall purchase and the mine worker shall sell the tools the tonnage mine worker now owns at a price which is equal to one per cent per ton for all coal mined by each tonnage mine worker between April 1, 1943, and the effective date of this Supplemental Agreement, with a minimum payment of $3.00.

Safety equipment and devices, including electric cap lamps, and also carbide lamps, shall be furnished by the operators without charge. This shall not include, however, personal wearing apparel such as hats, clothing, shoes and goggles. In lieu of furnishing carbide lamps and carbide the operator may at his option pay to the mine workers who use carbide lamps at their work 6 cents per day, and the mine workers shall continue to furnish their own carbide lamps and carbide.

No charge shall be made for blacksmithing.

7. In the event of a dispute as to the starting time between any operator and the local union at any mine, either party may make a case of such dispute and thereafter such case shall be handled in accordance with the provisions of the Agreement governing disputes.

8. If the United Mine Workers make a wage agreement during the period of this Supplemental Agreement, covering wages or working conditions with any person, corporation, association or district, more favorable to the operators than as contained herein, then this Supplemental Agreement shall be modified so that the operators who are parties hereto shall receive all of the benefits of such more favorable agreement.

For the duration of this Supplemental Agreement no strikes shall be either called or maintained hereunder.

9. The operators agree that they will not lease any operating mines subject to this Supplemental Agreement as a subterfuge for the purpose of avoiding the provisions of this Supplemental Agreement.

10. It is agreed that the operators who are parties hereto shall be parties to and participate in the conferences to negotiate the basic wage agreement to be effective after March 31, 1945.

11. In full settlement and discharge of and release from claims for all "portal to portal" compensation accruing prior to April 1, 1945, and in settlement and discharge of the impending litigation by the mine workers against the operators for such "portal to portal" compensation, each mine worker shall be paid in addition to the sums provided for in said Wage Agreement and this Supplemental Agreement, the amount of $1.25 for each day worked, retroactive to April 1, 1943, and hereafter to April 1, 1945; *Provided,* that such retroactive payments shall be paid in equal installments during the six months commencing on the first day of the calendar month following the effective date of this Supplemental Agreement, and *Provided,* further, that this paragraph shall be without prejudice to any right of any party signatory to this Supplemental Agreement after April 1, 1945.

12. This Supplemental Agreement, as to general wage rates, may, on thirty (30) days' notice from either party, be reopened for negotiation at the end of the first contract year. The foregoing sentence shall not preclude the parties from mutually agreeing at any time during the term of this Supplemental Agreement on changes in general wage rates, subject to such approval to the appropriate governmental agencies as may be required by an Act of Congress of October 2, 1942, and the Executive Orders and Regulations issued thereunder. Furthermore, if at any time during the term of this Supplemental Agreement a significant change occurs in government wage policy, either party shall have the right to request negotiations on general wage rates.

13. This Supplemental Agreement is an integrated instrument and its respective provisions are interdependent, and shall be in effect only after the approval hereof by the appropriate governmental agencies and after the granting by the Office of Price Administration of advances in maximum prices sufficient to cover the increased costs occasioned hereby.

Executed in triplicate in the City of Washington, D. C., the 20th day of July, 1943.

ILLINOIS COAL OPERATORS ASSOCIATION,

By George F. Campbell, President; D. W. Buchanan, Hubert E. Howard, George F. Campbell, Sub-Scale Committee.

DISTRICT No. 12, UNITED MINE WORKERS OF AMERICA,

By Ray Edmundson, President; Hugh White, Vice-President; Walter J. James, Secretary-Treasurer; John H. Jones, Charles Brosch, Walter C. Jenkins, Sub-Scale Committee.

UNITED MINE WORKERS OF AMERICA, INTERNATIONAL UNION,

By John L. Lewis, President; John O'Leary, Vice President; Thomas Kennedy, Secretary-Treasurer.

APPENDIX C

(The following description of the functions of the Bituminous Coal Division, administrators of the so-called Second Guffey Act, is from *The United States Government Manual,* published by the Office of Government Reports in 1942. The failure of the Congress to extend the act from August 24, 1943, has abolished the division, but it is generally expected that controls functioning along these lines will be again imposed in the near future. *Author's note.*)

Established July 1, 1939, by the secretary of the interior's Order No. 1394, dated June 16, 1939, pursuant to the Reorganization Act of 1939, the Bituminous Coal Division administers, under the supervision and direction of the secretary of the interior, the functions vested in the National Bituminous Coal Commission by the Bituminous Coal Act of 1937. Under these orders the functions formerly vested in the commission are performed by and through the director of the Bituminous Coal Division (except that the power to appoint and fix the compensation of personnel and to make contracts for personal service is exercised by the office of the secretary of the interior).

The purposes of the act are to conserve the bituminous coal resources of the United States; to stabilize the bituminous coal-mining industry; to promote interstate commerce in bituminous coal; to promulgate a bituminous coal code; to study and report upon the problems confronting the bituminous coal industry; and to initiate, promote and conduct research designed to improve standards and methods used in the mining, preparation, conservation, distribution and utilization of coal, and to discover additional uses for coal.

The act provides for the promulgation of a bituminous coal code which was promulgated on June 21, 1937, and contains provisions dealing with fair trade practices in the industry and also empowers the division to establish minimum prices for all bituminous coals moving in commerce subject to the act. Provision is made under Section 4(a) for application of the code, upon the specific orders of the division, to such intrastate commerce in bituminous coal as directly affects interstate commerce. The act provides for the imposition of a tax of 19.5 per cent of the value of coal at the mine, which tax is payable by all producers whose commerce in coal is subject to the act but who fail to accept membership in the code.

Under the bituminous code, coal-producing areas of the United States are divided into 23 districts, in each of which is to be established a district board composed of not less than 3 and not more than 17 members, all but one of whom are to be representative of code member producers of the district, the remaining member to be representative of the mine employees of the district. District boards are required to perform certain administrative and advisory duties, including particularly the proposal of minimum prices and marketing rules and regulations.

The Bituminous Coal Division is empowered and directed to establish minimum prices f.o.b. transportation facilities at the mines, for all kinds, grades and sizes of bituminous coal moving in commerce subject to its jurisdiction; and, where deemed necessary in the public interest, the division is empowered to establish maximum prices.

The division is given jurisdiction over marketing agencies, laying down standards for such agencies. It is vested with authority to file complaints with the Interstate Commerce Commission with respect to rates, charges, tariffs and practices relating to the transportation of coal, to prosecute same, and to intervene in any proceeding before the I.C.C. affecting the interests of the industry.

Section 9(a) of the act sets forth the public policy of the United States on employer-employee relations in the industry, and the division is authorized to hold hearings on complaints for the purpose of determining whether coal producers are complying with the provisions of the section and upon finding noncompliance on the part of the producers, the division is directed to cancel contracts made with the United States by the offending owners.

BIBLIOGRAPHY

Labor on the March, by Edward Levinson. Harper's, New York, 1938.

Organized Labor and Production, by Morris Llewellyn Cooke and Philip Murray. Harper's, New York, 1940.

The Dynamics of Industrial Democracy, by Clinton S. Golden and Harold J. Ruttenberg. Harper's, New York, 1942.

How Collective Bargaining Works. Twentieth Century Fund, New York, 1942.

Seven Stranded Coal Towns. U.S. Government Printing Office, Washington, D.C., 1941.

The Next Ten Years in British Social and Economic Policy, by G. D. H. Cole. Macmillan, New York, 1929.

Clarence Darrow, by Irving Stone. Doubleday, Doran, New York, 1941.

The Electric Power Industry, by John Bauer and Nathaniel Gold. Harper's, New York, 1939.

Thirty Years of Labor, by T. V. Powderly. Excelsior Publishing House, Columbus, Ohio, 1889.

The Labor Spy Racket, by Leo Huberman. Modern Age Books, New York, 1937.

Men Who Lead Labor, by Bruce Minton and John Stuart. Modern Age Books, New York, 1937.

The Case of Bituminous Coal, by Walton Hamilton and Helen Wright. Macmillan, New York, 1926.

The Labor Movement in America, by Richard T. Ely. Crowell, New York, 1886.

Concentration in American Industry, by Harry Laidler. Crowell, New York, 1931.

The Coal Industry, by Glen L. Parker. American Council on Public Affairs, Washington, D.C., 1940.

The American Labor Who's Who. Hanford Press, New York, 1925.

Coal and Unionism, by David J. McDonald and Edward A. Lynch. Lynald Books, Silver Springs, Md., 1939.

History of Labor in the United States, by John R. Commons and Associates. Macmillan, New York, 1918.

U.S. Government Manual. U.S. Government Printing Office, Washington, D.C., 1942.

Minerals Yearbooks. U.S. Bureau of Mines, Washington, D.C.

Eugene V. Debs, by McAlister Coleman. Greenberg, New York, 1930.

Preventing Fatal Explosions in Coal Mines, by Edward A. Wieck. Russell Sage Foundation, New York, 1942.

Will Germany Crack? by Paul Hagen. Harper's, New York, 1942.

Convention Proceedings, United Mine Workers of America. Washington, D.C.

History of the Coal Miners of the United States, by Andrew Roy. Columbus, Ohio.

History of the United Mine Workers of America, by Chris Evans. Columbus, Ohio.

Anthracite, by John Kimberly Mumford. Industries Publishing Co., New York, 1925.

If You Don't Weaken, by Oscar Ameringer. Henry Holt, New York, 1939.

Man and Metals, by T. A. Rickard. Whittlesey House, New York, 1932.

Out of the Test Tube, by Harry N. Holmes. Emerson Books, New York, 1935.

The American Miners' Association, by Edward A. Wieck. Russell Sage Foundation, New York, 1940.

U.S. Bituminous Commission Report, Washington, D.C., 1920-1923.

Investment and Profit in Soft Coal Mining, U.S. Federal Trade Commission, Washington, D.C., 1922.

The Miner's Freedom, by Carter Goodrich. Marshall Jones Co., Boston, 1925.

John Mitchell, by Elsie Glück. John Day, New York, 1929.

A Theory of the Labor Movement, by Selig Perlman. Macmillan, New York, 1928.

The Rise of American Civilization, by Charles and Mary Beard. Macmillan, New York, 1930.

The Working of Coal, by Harrison Francis Bulman. John Wiley, New York, 1927.

Men and Machines, by Stuart Chase. Macmillan, New York, 1929.

The Armies of Labor, by Samuel P. Orth. Yale University Press, New Haven, Conn., 1921.

The Modern Corporation, by A. A. Berle and Gardiner Means. Macmillan, New York, 1934.

The Coming of Coal, by Robert Bruere. Federal Council of Churches, 1922.

The Work, Wealth and Happiness of Mankind, by H. G. Wells. Doubleday, Doran, New York, 1931.

America's Power Resources, by C. G. Gilbert and J. E. Pogue. D. Appleton-Century, New York, 1921.

Miners and Management, by Mary Van Kleek. Russell Sage Foundation, New York, 1935.

Conservation of Natural Resources, Loomis Havemeyer (editor). Macmillan, New York, 1930.

Coal, by E. T. Devine. American Review Press Service, Bloomington, Ill., 1925.

The Miners Fight for American Standards, by John L. Lewis. Bell Publishing Co., Indianapolis, 1925.

Miners' Wages and the Cost of Living, by Isador Lubin. Institute of Economics, 1924.

Sit Down with John L. Lewis, by C. L. Sulzberger. Random House, New York, 1938.

John L. Lewis, by Cecil Carnes. Robert Speller Corp., New York, 1936.

Henry Demarest Lloyd, by Caro Lloyd. Putnam's, New York, 1912.

Coal and the Coal Mines, by Homer Greene, Houghton Mifflin, Boston, 1889.

Conservation of Natural Resources. A Symposium. Macmillan, New York, 1930.

Machine Age in the Hills, by Malcolm Ross. Macmillan, New York, 1933.

Report of Committee for Mineral Policy. National Resources Board, Washington, D.C., 1934. Also *Energy Resources and National Policy* (H. Doc. 160, 70th Congress). Washington, D.C.

World Minerals and World Peace, by C. K. Leith, J. W. Furness and Cleona Lewis. Brookings Institution, Washington, D.C., 1943.

Pamphlets, C.I.O. Washington, D.C.

The Minerals Year Book, published annually by the Bureau of Mines. For sale by Superintendent of Documents, Washington, D.C.

Coal Age, the magazine of the industry, published by McGraw-Hill, New York.

United Mine Workers Journal, published by U.M.W. of A., Washington, D.C.

INDEX

A

Absentee owners, 19, 41, 82, 143
Absenteeism, 90, 295
Accidents, 8, 279-284
"Adam Coaldigger," 114
Adams, K. C., 18, 21, 135, 213, 228
Alabama, 70, 81, 124, 159, 297
Alfange, Dean, 186
Allen, Governor Henry, 112
Allen, Nicholas, 31
Altgeld, John P., 56, 57
Amalgamated Clothing Workers of America, 157, 185, 193
American Civil Liberties Union, 285
American Federation of Labor, 22, 51, 52, 56, 82-84, 94, 97, 109, 117, 118, 129, 247: and C.I.O., arbitration, 224; split with C.I.O., 46-50, 55, 56; membership, 56, 196
America First Committee, 193
American Labor Party, 183, 242, 255, 256
American Legion, 95, 118
American Miners' Association, 39
American Mining Congress, 19
American Railway Union, 56
Ameringer, Oscar, 112-114, 139, 154, 155, 161, 287
Anderson, Judge, 97, 98
Anthracite, *see* Coal
Anthracite Coal Industry Commission, 144
Antilabor legislation, 181, 190, 203, 209, 251, 270, 271
Antilabor propaganda, 200, 216, 237, 238
Appalachian Joint Wage Agreement, 150, 159, 186, 187, 189, 190, 200; 1941-1943, 172, 219, 258, 264, 272, 274, 276, 312-333
Appalachian Mountains, 5, 99
Apprentices, 9
Arbitration, 49, 50, 72, 223, 224, 304, 305
Archibald, George ("Jock Pittbreeks"), 41
Armistice, 92
Armstrong, Mrs. Harry, 111, 112
Arnold, Thurman, 190
Axis, 13

B

Baer, George F., 70-74
Baldwin, Hanson, 301
Baldwin, Stanley, 303, 304
Baldwin-Felts operatives, 86, 99, 100
Ball, Senator, 235
Baltimore and Ohio Railroad, 45
Bandholtz, General, 103, 104
Bankhead Bill, 240
Barkoski, John, murder of, 135
Bates, John, 36
Bauer, John, 292
Beaumont, Master, 26
Belleville, Illinois, 37-39
Belleville *Democrat,* 37-40
Belmont, August, 78
Berger, Victor, 77
Bergius, Friedrich, 20
Bergoff, Pearl, 165
Best, Gideon, 65
Bethlehem Steel, 201
Bevin, Ernest, 200
"Big Steel," 169, 202
Bittner, Van A., 178, 180, 211, 215, 239, 266
Bituminous Coal Code, 22, 145
Bituminous Coal Commission (1923), 21, 22, 121, 122, 186, 200, 221, 247
Bituminous Coal Division, Department of the Interior, 22, 172, 214, 305, 334, 335
Bituminous Coal Research, Inc., 294
Black, Senator, 147
Blankenhorn, Heber, 106, 112
Bliven, Bruce, 302
Blizzard, William, 104
Block, Paul, 180
Bolsheviki, 122
Bootleggers, coal, 143, 144, 164
Bourne, Randolph, 15
Boy Scouts, 82
Bradley, "General" Alexander, 60-62
Breakers, 65-67
Bridges, Harry, 237
British general strike (1926), 130
British Labour Party, 108, 303